ISBN 978-1-331-60903-2
PIBN 10212387

1 MONTH OF
FREE
READING

at

www.ForgottenBooks.com

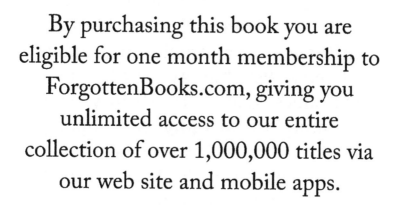

By purchasing this book you are eligible for one month membership to ForgottenBooks.com, giving you unlimited access to our entire collection of over 1,000,000 titles via our web site and mobile apps.

To claim your free month visit:

www.forgottenbooks.com/free212387

English
Français
Deutsche
Italiano
Español
Português

www.forgottenbooks.com

Mythology Photography **Fiction**
Fishing Christianity **Art** Cooking
Essays Buddhism Freemasonry
Medicine **Biology** Music **Ancient
Egypt** Evolution Carpentry Physics
Dance Geology **Mathematics** Fitness
Shakespeare **Folklore** Yoga Marketing
Confidence Immortality Biographies
Poetry **Psychology** Witchcraft
Electronics Chemistry History **Law**
Accounting **Philosophy** Anthropology
Alchemy Drama Quantum Mechanics
Atheism Sexual Health **Ancient History**
Entrepreneurship Languages Sport
Paleontology Needlework Islam
Metaphysics Investment Archaeology
Parenting Statistics Criminology
Motivational

ARVARD HISTORICAL STUDIES

PUBLISHED UNDER THE DIRECTION OF
THE DEPARTMENT OF HISTORY

FROM THE INCOME OF

THE HENRY WARREN TORREY FUND

VOLUME XXV

HARVARD HISTORICAL STUDIES

I. The Suppression of the African Slave-Trade to the United States of America, 1638-1870. By W. E. B. DuBois, Ph.D., Editor of " The Crisis." 8vo. $2.00 net.

II. The Contest over the Ratification of the Federal Constitution in Massachusetts. By S. B. Harding, Ph.D., sometime Professor of European History in Indiana University. 8vo. $1.75 net.

III. A Critical Study of Nullification in South Carolina. By D. F. Houston, A.M., LL.B., Secretary of the Treasury. 8vo. $1.75 net.

IV. Nominations for Elective Office in the United States. By Frederick W. Dallinger, A.M., LL.B., Member of Congress from Massachusetts. 8vo. $2.00 net.

V. A Bibliography of British Municipal History, including Gilds and Parliamentary Representation. By Charles Gross, Ph.D., LL.D., late Gurney Professor of History and Political Science in Harvard University. 8vo. $3.00 net.

VI. The Liberty and Free Soil Parties in the Northwest. By Theodore Clarke Smith, Ph.D., Professor of History in Williams College. 8vo. $2.25 net.

VII. The Provincial Governor in the English Colonies of North America. By Evarts Boutell Greene, Ph.D., Professor of History in the University of Illinois. 8vo. $2.00 net.

VIII. The County Palatine of Durham. A Study in Constitutional History. By G. T. Lapsley, Ph.D., Fellow of Trinity College, Cambridge. 8vo. $2.50 net.

IX. The Anglican Episcopate and the American Colonies. By Arthur Lyon Cross, Ph.D., Professor of English History in the University of Michigan. 8vo. $3.00 net.

X. The Administration of the American Revolutionary Army. By Louis Clinton Hatch, Ph.D. 8vo. $2.00 net.

XI. The Civil Service and the Patronage. By Carl Russell Fish, Ph.D., Professor of History in the University of Wisconsin. 8vo. $2.50 net.

XII. The Development of Freedom of the Press in Massachusetts. By C. A. Duniway, Ph.D., President of Colorado College. 8vo. $2.00 net.

XIII. The Seigniorial System in Canada. By W. B. Munro, Ph.D., LL.D., Professor of Municipal Government in Harvard University. 8vo. $2.50 net.

XIV. The Frankpledge System. By William Alfred Morris, Ph.D., Associate Professor of English History in the University of California. 8vo. $2.00 net.

XV. The Public Life of Joseph Dudley. By Everett Kimball, Ph.D., Professor of Government in Smith College. 8vo. $2.50 net.

XVI. Mémoire de Marie Caroline, Reine de Naples. Edited by Robert Matteson Johnston, A.M., late Professor of Modern History in Harvard University. 8vo. $2.50 net.

XVII. The Barrington-Bernard Correspondence. Edited by Edward Channing, Ph.D., McLean Professor of Ancient and Modern History in Harvard University. 8vo. $2.50 net.

XVIII. The Government of the Ottoman Empire in the Time of Suleiman the Magnificent. By Albert Howe Lybyer, Ph.D., Professor of History in the University of Illinois. 8vo. $2.50 net.

XIX. The Granger Movement. By S. J. Buck, Ph.D., Associate Professor of History in the University of Minnesota. 8vo. $2.50 net.

XX. Burgage Tenure in Mediaeval England. By Morley de Wolf Hemmeon, Ph.D. 8vo. $2.50 net.

XXI. An Abridgment of the Indian Affairs transacted in the colony of New York from 1678 to 1751. By Peter Wraxall. Edited with an introduction by Charles Howard McIlwain, Ph.D., Professor of History and Government in Harvard University. 8vo. $2.50 net.

XXII. English Field Systems. By Howard Levi Gray, Ph.D., Professor of History in Bryn Mawr College. 8vo. $3.25 net.

XXIII. The Second Partition of Poland. By Robert Howard Lord, Ph.D., Assistant Professor of History in Harvard University. 8vo. $2.75 net.

XXIV. Norman Institutions. By Charles Homer Haskins, Ph.D., Litt.D., LL.D., Gurney Professor of History and Political Science in Harvard University. 8vo. $3.50 net.

XXV. Robert Curthose, Duke of Normandy. By Charles Wendell David, Ph.D., Associate Professor of European History in Bryn Mawr College. 8vo.

HARVARD UNIVERSITY PRESS
CAMBRIDGE, MASS., U. S. A.

ROBERTUS DUX NORMANNORUM PARTUM PROSTERNIT

Robert Curthose in the act of unhorsing a pagan warrior, the oldest graphic representation of the duke now extant. From an eighteenth century engraving of a medallion in a stained-glass window at Saint-Denis, which was executed at the order of Abbot Suger. The church was dedicated 11 June 1144, and the window must date from about that period.

ROBERT CURTHOSE

DUKE OF NORMANDY

BY

CHARLES WENDELL DAVID

ASSOCIATE PROFESSOR OF EUROPEAN HISTORY
IN BRYN MAWR COLLEGE

CAMBRIDGE
HARVARD UNIVERSITY PRESS
LONDON: HUMPHREY MILFORD
OXFORD UNIVERSITY PRESS
1920

TO
MY WIFE

PREFACE

ROBERT CURTHOSE, eldest son of William the Conqueror, had been dead but a few years when Abbot Suger set about rebuilding the great abbey church of Saint-Denis, which was dedicated with such pomp and ceremony in 1144. Among the scenes from the First Crusade which filled one of its famous stained-glass windows, there was one which portrayed Robert, mounted upon his charger, in the act of overthrowing a pagan warrior — " Robertus dux Normannorum Partum prosternit," ran the inscription beneath it.[1] It was thus, as a hero of the Crusade, that the great Abbot Suger chose to recall him, and it was as such that his fame survived in after times. Robert was not a masterful character, and it cannot be said that as a ruler he made a deep impression upon his generation. Overshadowed by his great father, cheated of a kingdom by his more aggressive brothers, and finally defeated in battle, deprived of his duchy, and condemned to perpetual imprisonment, his misdirected life offers a melancholy contrast to the more brilliant careers of the abler members of his family. Yet, if he was himself lacking in greatness, he was closely associated with great names and great events; and his unmeasured generosity and irrepressible bonhomie gained him many friends in his lifetime, and made him a personality which is not without its attractions to the modern. It is hoped that a study of his career which attempts to set him in his true relation to the history of Normandy and England and of the Crusade may be of interest not only to the specialist but to the general reader.

It is now more than a generation since Gaston Le Hardy published *Le dernier des ducs normands: étude de critique historique sur Robert Courte-Heuse* (1882), the only monograph upon Robert which has hitherto appeared. In spite of its age, if this were the critical study which its title implies, the present essay need hardly

---

[1] See Frontispiece and Appendix *G*.

have been undertaken. But it makes no use of documentary materials, and is unfortunately a work of violent *parti pris*, quite lacking in criticism according to modern standards. " J' ai entrepris," says the author in his preface, " à l'aide de quelques autres chroniqueurs, une lutte contre notre vieil Orderic Vital, essayant de lui arracher par lambeaux la vérité vraie sur un personnage dont il ne nous a donné que la caricature." It may be granted that Ordericus Vitalis was a hostile critic, who sometimes did Robert scanty justice; but assuredly there is no occasion for polemics or for an *apologia* such as Le Hardy has given us, and I have no intention of following in his footsteps. My purpose is a more modest one, namely to set forth a full and true account of the life and character of Robert Curthose upon the basis of an independent and critical examination of all the sources. To any one acquainted with the state of the materials on which the investigator must perforce depend for any study of the late eleventh and early twelfth centuries, it will not be surprising that there are many gaps in our information concerning Robert's life and many problems which must remain unsolved. I have tried at all times to make my own researches and to draw my own conclusions directly from the sources when the evidence permitted, and to refrain from drawing conclusions when it seemed inadequate. But my indebtedness to the secondary writers who have preceded me in the field is abundantly apparent in the index and in the footnotes, where full acknowledgments are made. The works of E. A. Freeman upon the Norman Conquest and upon the reign of William Rufus have proved especially helpful for Robert's life as a whole, as have also various more recent monographs which bear upon his career at certain points. Among these are the works of Louis Halphen upon the county of Anjou, of Robert Latouche upon Maine, and of Augustin Fliche upon the reign of Philip I of France. For the chapter on the Crusade much use has been made of the detailed chronology of Heinrich Hagenmeyer and of the exhaustive notes in his well known editions of the sources for the First Crusade, as well as of the admirable monograph by Ferdinand Chalandon upon the reign of the Emperor Alexius I. The appendix *De Iniusta Vexatione Willelmi Episcopi Primi* has already been published in the *English Historical Review*, and is here reproduced by the kind permission of the editor.

It is more than a pleasure to acknowledge my obligations to those whose counsel and assistance have been constantly at my disposal in the preparation of this volume. By the librarians and their staffs in the libraries of Harvard University, the University of California, the University of Pennsylvania, and Bryn Mawr College I have been treated with a courtesy and helpfulness which are beyond praise. Mr. George W. Robinson, Secretary of the Graduate School of Arts and Sciences of Harvard University, has given me much valuable assistance in preparing the manuscript for the press and in the correction of the proof. Finally, I have to acknowledge a debt of gratitude which is deeper than can well be expressed in writing, that which I owe to my teachers. It was Professor Dana C. Munro, now of Princeton University, who first taught me to care greatly for the Middle Ages and awakened my interest in the Crusades. He has followed this volume with kindly interest while it has been in the making, and has given me much helpful criticism upon that part which relates to the First Crusade. But above all I am indebted to Professor Charles H. Haskins of Harvard University, at whose suggestion this work was first undertaken and without whose help and counsel it could hardly have been brought to completion. While the author must accept full responsibility for the statements and conclusions herein contained, it is proper to say that the documentary materials which Professor Haskins had collected, as well as the results of his own researches, were placed at my disposal in manuscript before their publication in his recent volume entitled *Norman Institutions*, that separate chapters as they have been prepared have passed through his hands for detailed criticism, and that his unfailing patience has extended even to the reading of the proof sheets.

CHARLES WENDELL DAVID.

BRYN MAWR, PENNSYLVANIA,
September, 1919.

CONTENTS

CHAPTER I

CHAPTER II

CHAPTER III

CHAPTER IV

LIST OF ABBREVIATIONS

Actus Pontificum . . . *Actus Pontificum Cenomannis in Urbe degentium*, ed. G. Busson and A. Ledru. Le Mans, 1902.

A.-S.C. . . . . *The Anglo-Saxon Chronicle*, ed. Charles Plummer, under the title *Two of the Saxon Chronicles Parallel*. 2 vols. Oxford, 1892–99.

Davis, *Regesta* . . . . . H. W. C. Davis, *Regesta Regum Anglo-Normannorum*, i (1066–1100). Oxford, 1913.

E. H. R. . . . . *English Historical Review*. London, 1886– .

G. F. . . . . *Anonymi Gesta Francorum et Aliorum Hierosolymitanorum*, ed. Heinrich Hagenmeyer. Heidelberg, 1890.

Hagenmeyer,   Heinrich Hagenmeyer, *Chronologie de la première croisade*
  Chronologie . . . . . . *(1094–1100)*. Paris, 1902. Also in *Revue de l'Orient latin*, vi–viii (1898–1901).

Haskins. . . . . Charles H. Haskins, *Norman Institutions*. Cambridge, Massachusetts, 1918. *Harvard Historical Studies*, xxiv.

H. C. A. . . . . *Recueil des historiens des croisades*. Publié pas les soins de l'Académie des Inscriptions et Belles-Lettres. *Documents arméniens*. 2 vols. Paris, 1869–1906.

H. C. G. . . . . *The same. Historiens grecs*. 2 vols. Paris, 1875–81.

H. C. Oc. . . . . *The same. Historiens occidentaux*. 5 vols. Paris, 1841–95.

H. C. Or. . . . . *The same. Historiens orientaux*. 5 vols. Paris, 1872–1906.

H. F. . . . . *Recueil des historiens des Gaules et de la France*, ed. Martin Bouquet and others. 24 vols. Paris, 1738–1904.

Kreuzzugsbriefe . . . . *Die Kreuzzugsbriefe aus den Jahren 1088–1100: Eine Quellensammlung zur Geschichte des ersten Kreuzzuges*, ed. Heinrich Hagenmeyer. Innsbruck, 1901.

Le Hardy. . . . . Gaston Le Hardy, *Le dernier des ducs normands: Étude de critique historique sur Robert Courte-Heuse*, in *Bulletin de la Société des Antiquaires de Normandie*, x (Caen, 1882), pp. 3–184.

M. G. H. . . . . *Monumenta Germaniae Historica*. Hanover, etc., 1826– .

Migne . . . . *Patrologiae Cursus Completus*, ed. J. P. Migne. Series Latina. 221 vols. Paris, 1844–64.

Ordericus. . . . . Ordericus Vitalis, *Historiae Ecclesiasticae Libri Tredecim*, ed. Auguste Le Prévost. 5 vols. Paris, 1838–55.

Round, *C. D. F.* . . . . . J. H. Round, *Calendar of Documents preserved in France illustrative of the History of Great Britain and Ireland*, i (918–1206). London, 1899 *(Calendars of State Papers)*.

Simeon, *H. D. E.* . . . . Simeon of Durham, *Historia Dunelmensis Ecclesiae*, in his *Opera Omnia*, ed. Thomas Arnold, i. London, 1882.

Simeon, *H. R.* . . . . . Idem, *Historia Regum, ibid.*, ii. London, 1885.

William of   William of Jumièges, *Gesta Normannorum Ducum*, ed. Jean
  Jumièges . . . . Marx. Paris, 1914.

William of Mal-   William of Malmesbury, *De Gestis Pontificum Anglorum Libri*
  mesbury, *G. P.* . . . *Quinque*, ed. N. E. S. A. Hamilton. London, 1870.

William of Mal-   Idem, *De Gestis Regum Anglorum Libri Quinque*, ed. William
  mesbury, *G. R.* . . . Stubbs. 2 vols. London, 1887–89.

Northwestern France
and southern England
with principal places
referred to in text

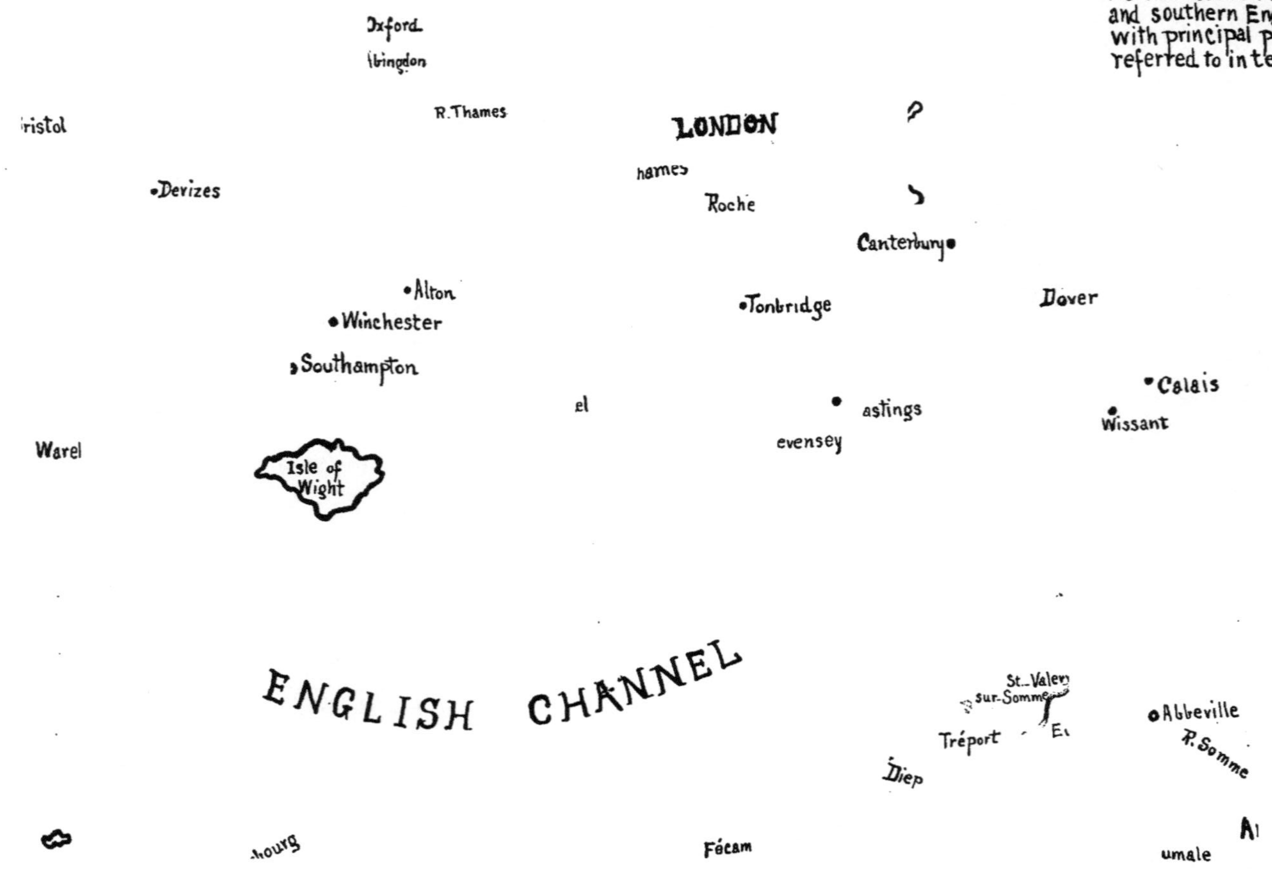

Calais

Wissant

Dover

Canterbury

LONDON

Roche

hames

Tonbridge

astings

evensey

el

R.Thames

Oxford

Ibingdon

Alton

Winchester

Southampton

Isle of Wight

Devizes

ristol

Warel

ENGLISH CHANNEL

Abbeville

R.Somme

umale

A

St..Valery
sur.Somme

Tréport

E

Diep

Fécam

mour

ROBERT CURTHOSE

ROBERT CURTHOSE

CHAPTER I

YOUTH

WILLIAM OF MALMESBURY, in his well known sketch of the life
and character of Robert Curthose,[1] relates an interesting episode.
He tells us that Robert, in the heat of youth, and spurred on by
the fatuous counsels of his companions, went to his father, William the Conqueror, and demanded that the rule of Normandy be
forthwith given over into his hands. William not only refused the
rash request, but drove the lad away with the thunders of his
terrific voice; whereupon Robert withdrew in a rage and began to
pillage the countryside. At first the Conqueror was only con-
vulsed with laughter at these youthful escapades, and said, em-
phasizing his words with a favorite oath: " By the resurrection
of God! This little Robert Curthose will be a brave fellow." [2]

Robert Curthose or ' Short-Boots ' (*Curta Ocrea*), this was the
curious nickname which his father had given him on account of
his diminutive stature.[3] The name seemed appropriate and was
taken up by the people. In time, however, William of Malmesbury goes on to explain, Robert's acts of insubordination became
far more serious, and ended by provoking the Conqueror to a
truly Norman burst of wrath, a curse, and disinheritance.[4] But
all this is a matter which must be deferred for later consideration.

---

[1] *G. R.*, ii, pp. 459-463.

[2] " Per resurrectionem Dei! probus erit Robelinus Curta Ocrea." *Ibid.*, pp. 459-
460.

[3] *Ibid.*, p. 460; Ordericus, iii, p. 262: " corpore autem brevis et grossus, ideoque
Brevis Ocrea a patre est cognominatus "; *ibid.*, iv, p. 16: " Curta Ocrea iocose
cognominatus est." In another passage (ii, p. 295) Ordericus mentions *Gambaron*
(from *jambes* or *gambes rondes*) as another popular nickname: " corpore pingui,
brevique statura, unde vulgo Gambaron cognominatus est, et Brevis Ocrea." In
still another place he calls him ' Robertus Ignavus.' *Interpolations d'Orderic Vital*,
in William of Jumièges, p. 193.

[4] *G. R.*, ii, p. 460.

Whether the episode just recounted be fact or legend,[5] the chronicler in his hurried sketch has, in any event, drawn the picture of an undutiful, graceless son, often harassing his father with wild acts of insubordination. This, too, is the impression which is to be gathered from a cursory reading of Ordericus Vitalis, by far the most voluminous contemporary writer upon the life and character of Robert Curthose, and it is the impression which has been preserved in the histories of later times.[6] A more careful reading of the sources may, however, lead to a somewhat different view of the character of the Norman duke who forms the subject of the present essay. It must be owned at the outset, however, that the sources, especially for Robert's youth, are exceedingly meagre and fragmentary, and only a few details can be pieced together.

The date of Robert's birth is nowhere stated by contemporary writers. We know that he was the firstborn child of William the Bastard, duke of Normandy, and of his wife Matilda, daughter of Count Baldwin V of Flanders.[7] But the date of the marriage of William and Matilda is also a matter of much uncertainty. It has been generally assigned by modern writers, but without any early authority, to the year 1053.[8] It certainly took place after October 1049, for in that year we find Pope Leo IX and the coun-

---

[5] It seems to be a sort of an epitome, moved forward somewhat in Robert's career, of his rebellious course between 1078 and the death of the Conqueror.

[6] Cf. Auguste Le Prévost, in Ordericus, ii, p. 377, n. 1; E. A. Freeman, *History of the Norman Conquest* (2d ed., Oxford, 1870-76), iv, pp. 638-646 *et passim*. The defence of Robert by Le Hardy is rather zealous than critical, and has not achieved its purpose.

[7] Ordericus, ii, p. 294: " Robertum primogenitam sobolem suam." In the numerous lists of William and Matilda's children Robert always appears first: see, e.g., Ordericus, ii, pp. 93, 188; iii, p. 159; *Interpolations de Robert de Torigny*, in William of Jumièges, p. 251.

[8] E.g., Thomas Stapleton, in *The Archaeological Journal*, iii (1846), pp. 20-21; Le Prévost, in Ordericus, v, p. 18, n. 1; Freeman, in *E. H. R.*, iii (1888), pp. 680-681, and *Norman Conquest*, iii, pp. 660-661. Stapleton, Le Prévost, and Freeman all cite the Tours chronicle (*H. F.*, xi, p. 348) as authority for the date. But in point of fact the Tours chronicle gives no such date; and so far as it may be said to give any date at all, it seems to assign the marriage to 1056. Stapleton suggests in favor of 1053 that the imprisonment of Leo IX by the Normans in that year may have emboldened the interested parties to a defiance of the ecclesiastical prohibition.

cil of Rheims forbidding it as an act then in contemplation.[9] It
certainly had been performed in defiance of ecclesiastical authority by 1053, the year in which Countess Matilda first appears
beside her husband among the witnesses of extant legal documents.[10] So, too, Robert's birth has been assigned by modern
writers to *circa* 1054,[11] but this again is conjectural and rests upon
no early authority. Our knowledge of Robert's later career makes
it seem improbable that he was born later than 1054 and suggests
the possibility that he may have been born a little earlier.[12]

[9] " Interdixit et Balduino comiti Flandrensi, ne filiam suam Wilielmo Nort-
manno nuptui daret; et illi, ne eam acciperet." *Sacrorum Conciliorum Nova et
Amplissima Collectio*, ed. G. D. Mansi and others (Venice, etc., 1759–), xix, col. 742.

[10] *Cartulaire de l'abbaye de la Sainte-Trinité du Mont de Rouen*, ed. Achille Deville,
no. 37, in *Collection de cartulaires de France* (Paris, 1840: *Documents Inédits*), iii, p.
441; *Chartes de Saint-Julien de Tours*, ed. J.-L. Denis (Le Mans, 1912), no. 24. Both
these charters are dated 1053, and the attestations of Matilda seem incontestably
contemporary. The Tours charter in addition to the incarnation has " regnante
Henrico rege anno xxviii." This is unusual and might raise a doubt, but it pretty
clearly refers to the year 1053. No. 26 of the same collection similarly gives 1059
as the thirty-fourth year of King Henry. Both evidently reckon the reign as beginning from 1026, when Henry was probably designated heir to the throne a year
before his actual coronation in 1027. Christian Pfister, *Études sur le règne de Robert
le Pieux* (Paris, 1885), pp. 76–77. This conclusion seems to be confirmed by a charter
of 26 May in the thirtieth year of Robert the Pious (1026?) which Henry attests
as king, according to Pfister, 'by anticipation.' *Ibid.*, p. lxxxii, no. 78. But Frédéric
Soehnée does not accept Pfister's conclusion. *Catalogue des actes d'Henri I*[er], *roi de
France, 1031–1060* (Paris, 1907), no. 10. The original is not extant.

Ferdinand Lot has published two charters — both from originals — dated 1051,
which bear attestations of Countess Matilda and of Robert ' iuvenis comitis.' The
attestation of Robert Curthose will save one from any temptation to carry the
marriage of William and Matilda back to 1051 on the evidence of these documents,
for even though the marriage had taken place as early as 1049, it would clearly be
impossible for Robert to attest a document in 1051. Lot explains, " Les souscrip-
tions de Matilde . . . et de son fils aîné Robert ont été apposées après coup, et
semblent autographes." *Études critiques sur l'abbaye de Saint-Wandrille* (Paris,
1913), nos. 30, 31, pp. 74–77.

[11] Le Prévost, in Ordericus, v, p. 18, n. 1; Le Hardy, p. 9; Freeman, *Norman
Conquest*, iv, p. 123, n. 3.

[12] William of Malmesbury says of him in 1066 that " spectatae iam virtutis
habebatur adolescens." *G. R.*, ii, p. 459. In a charter of confirmation by Robert
dated 1066 he is described as old enough to give a voluntary confirmation: " quia
scilicet maioris iam ille aetatis ad praebendum spontaneum auctoramentum idoneus
esset." *Cartulaire de Laval et de Vitré*, no. 30, in Arthur Bertrand de Broussillon,
La maison de Laval (Paris, 1895–1903), i, p. 45; cf. Davis, *Regesta*, no. 2.

Though the evidence is meagre and fragmentary, it is clear that William and Matilda were by no means careless about the education of their eldest son and prospective heir. In an early charter we meet with a certain " Raherius consiliarius infantis " and a " Tetboldus gramaticus." [13] And among the witnesses of a charter by the youthful Robert himself — the earliest that we have of his — dated at Rouen in 1066, appears one " Hilgerius pedagogus Roberti filii comitis." [14] Not improbably this is the same Ilger who, in April of the following year, attested a charter by William the Conqueror at Vaudreuil.[15] Robert, therefore, had tutors, or ' counsellors,' who were charged with his education, and who formed part of the ducal entourage and made their way into the documents of the period.

That these educational efforts were not wholly vain, there is some reason to believe. Robert has not, like his youngest brother, Henry, received the flattering title of Beauclerc, and there is no direct evidence that he knew Latin. Yet some notable accomplishments he did have. Not to mention his affable manners, he was famed for his fluency of speech, or ' eloquence,' especially in his native tongue.[16] And if towards the close of his unfortunate life he became the author, as has been supposed, of an extant poem in the Welsh language,[17] it may perhaps be allowed that in his youth he had acquired at least a taste and capacity for things literary.[18]

[13] *Cartulaire de la Trinité du Mont*, no. 60. According to Le Prévost it is of about the year 1060. Ordericus, v, p. 18, n. 1.

[14] Round, *C. D. F.*, no. 1173; Davis, *Regesta*, no. 2. Le Prévost (Ordericus, v, p. 18, n. 1) refers to an early charter by Duke William in favor of Saint-Ouen of Rouen, in which appears " Hilgerius magister pueri." This is probably Cartulary of Saint-Ouen (28 *bis*), MS., p. 280, no. 345, and p. 233, no. 278, a charter of doubtful authenticity.

[15] Davis, *Regesta*, no. 6a.

[16] William of Malmesbury, *G. R.*, ii, p. 460: " nec infaceti eloquii . . . nec enervis erat consilii "; *ibid.*, p. 463: " patria lingua facundus, ut sit iocundior nullus "; Ordericus Vitalis, who is less flattering, calls him ' loquax,' but he adds, " voce clara et libera, lingua diserta." Ordericus, ii, p. 295. Cf. Ralph of Caen, in *H. C. Oc.*, iii, p. 666.

[17] *Infra*, pp. 187–188.

[18] If we could attach any importance to a speech which Ordericus puts into the mouth of Robert apropos of his quarrel with his father, the young prince would

The hopes of William and Matilda were early centred upon their oldest son, and his initiation into the politics of his ambitious father was not long delayed. As the result of a revolution at Le Mans, the youthful Count Herbert II with his mother and his sister Margaret had been driven into exile, and the direct rule of Geoffrey Martel, count of Anjou, had been established in Maine.[19] William of Normandy, ever jealous of Angevin expansion, was not slow to realize what his policy should be in the light of these events. By giving support to the exiles he might hope to curb the ambition of Geoffrey Martel and to extend Norman influence, conceivably Norman domination, over Maine. Accordingly, at an undetermined date between 1055 and 1060 — probably between 1058 and 1060 [20] — he entered into a treaty of far-reaching significance with the exiled count. Herbert formally became Duke William's vassal for the county of Maine, and agreed that, if he should die childless, the duke should succeed him in all his rights and possessions. And further, a double marriage alliance was arranged, according to which William promised the count one of his infant daughters, and Robert Curthose was affianced to Herbert's sister, Margaret of Maine.[21] Thus Robert,

seem to have shared the opinion of many another headstrong youth about grammarians: " Huc, domine mi rex, non accessi pro sermonibus audiendis, quorum copia frequenter usque ad nauseam imbutus sum a grammaticis." Ordericus, ii, p. 379.

[19] On these events and their sequel see Robert Latouche, *Histoire du comté du Maine pendant le Xe et le XIe siècle* (Paris, 1910), pp. 29 ff.; Louis Halphen, *Le comté d'Anjou au XIe siècle* (Paris, 1906), pp. 74–80, 178 ff.

[20] Latouche shows that the treaty must be later than the election of Vougrin, bishop of Le Mans, 31 August 1055, and earlier than the death of Geoffrey Martel, 1060. He thinks it probably later than the battle of Varaville, 1058. *Maine*, p. 32, n. 5.

[21] William of Poitiers, in *H. F.*, xi, pp. 85, 86; Ordericus, ii, pp. 102, 252. The two sources are not in complete accord. Except at one point I have preferred the former as being the more strictly contemporary. William of Poitiers represents the betrothal of William and Margaret not as a part of the original treaty, but as a later arrangement made by Duke William after Herbert's death in order to forestall a possible controversy as to Norman rights in Maine. But this marriage alliance looms so large in the narrative of Ordericus Vitalis that it seems hardly likely that it was a mere afterthought on Duke William's part. Ordericus represents it as the fundamental provision of the treaty. According to his view it was through Margaret that Norman rights in Maine arose. He does not seem to realize that upon such

while still a mere child, was made a pawn in the ambitious game which his father was playing for the possession of a coveted county. Margaret, too, was young; but the duke brought her to Normandy, and, placing her in the ward of Stigand de Mézidon, made due provision for her honorable rearing until the children should arrive at an age suitable for marriage.[22]

Meanwhile, fortune set strongly in Duke William's favor in Maine. Charters indicate that Herbert had made at least a partial recovery of his authority in the county [23] — through the assistance, it may be presumed, of his powerful Norman overlord. On 9 March 1062 [24] Count Herbert died childless, and under the terms of the recent treaty the county should have passed immediately into the hands of Duke William. But the Manceaux, or at least an Angevin or anti-Norman party among them, had no disposition to submit themselves to the 'Norman yoke'; and within a year after Count Herbert's death they rose in revolt.[25] They chose as Count Herbert's successor Walter of Mantes, count of the Vexin, a bitter enemy of the Normans, who had a claim upon Maine through his wife Biota, a daughter of Herbert Éveille-Chien.[26] They also obtained the aid of Geoffrey le Barbu, who

reasoning they would also terminate with her death. For William of Poitiers, on the other hand, the fundamental provision of the treaty was the agreement that Duke William should be Count Herbert's heir. This would give the duke permanent rights after Herbert's death. It seems not unlikely that both provisions were included in the treaty and that Duke William regarded them both as important. At times he dealt with Maine as if of his own absolute right; at other times he put forward his son as bearer of the Norman rights.

[22] Ordericus, ii, p. 104; William of Poitiers, in *H. F.*, xi, p. 86.

[23] Latouche, *Maine*, p. 146, nos. 32, 33.

[24] *Ibid.*, p. 33.

[25] Latouche has shown that the date of the revolt falls between 9 March 1062 and 14 March 1063. *Maine*, p. 33, n. 4. The account of Ordericus Vitalis is confused, and the date (1064) which he gives is impossible. Ordericus, ii, pp. 101-103. The suit held before the ducal *curia* at Domfront, " cum Guillelmus, Normanniae comes, Cenomannicam urbem haberet adquisitam," should probably be assigned to 1063 rather than to 1064. Bertrand de Broussillon, *Maison de Laval*, i, p. 41, no. 28.

[26] Herbert Éveille-Chien was grandfather of Herbert II. Biota, therefore, was aunt of Margaret, Robert Curthose's fiancée. The genealogy of the counts of Maine in the eleventh century has at last been disentangled by Latouche. *Maine*, pp. 113-115, appendix iii. F. M. Stenton, *William the Conqueror* (New York, 1908), pp. 129 ff., and appendix, table d, is inaccurate.

had succeeded to the county of Anjou upon the death of Geoffrey Martel in 1060.[27] Thus they were able to offer formidable opposition to Norman aggression. But Duke William was determined not to let slip so good an opportunity of extending his dominion over Maine, and he took up the challenge with his accustomed vigor. A single campaign sufficed to accomplish his purpose. Walter of the Vexin and Biota, his wife, were taken and imprisoned at Falaise; and soon after they died — it is reported, as the result of poisoning.[28] The Manceaux were quickly defeated and reduced to submission, and Duke William entered Le Mans in triumph.[29]

With Geoffrey le Barbu, however, William decided to make terms. The provisions of the treaty which was concluded between them have not been preserved; but, in any case, it is clear that Duke William recognized the Angevin suzerainty over Maine.[30] Doubtless this seemed to him the most effective way of consolidating his conquest and throwing over it the mantle of legality by which he always set such great store.[31] At a formal ceremony in the duke's presence at Alençon, Robert Curthose and Margaret of Maine, his fiancée, were made to do homage and swear fealty to Geoffrey le Barbu for the inheritance of Count Herbert.[32]

[27] Halphen, *Anjou*, pp. 137, 293–294, no. 171. Cf. Latouche, *Maine*, pp. 33–34.

[28] Ordericus, ii, pp. 103, 259. William of Poitiers makes no mention of the poisoning. Halphen (*Anjou*, p. 179) and Latouche (*Maine*, p. 34, and n. 6) accept the account of Ordericus as true, the latter explaining that William of Poitiers, as a panegyrist, naturally passes over such an act in silence. Freeman, on the other hand, holds the story to be an unsubstantiated rumor, inconsistent with the character of William the Conqueror. *Norman Conquest*, iii, p. 208.

[29] Cf. Latouche, *Maine*, pp. 34–35. The primary authorities are William of Poitiers, in *H. F.*, xi, pp. 85–86, and Ordericus, ii, pp. 101–104.

[30] It is the thesis of Latouche that " pendant tout le cours du XI° [siècle] le comte du Maine s'était trouvé vis-à-vis de celui d'Anjou dans un état de vassalité," and he points out that it was the policy of William the Conqueror and Robert Curthose to respect " le principe de la suzeraineté angevine." *Maine*, pp. 54–56.

[31] *Ibid.*, p. 35.

[32] Ordericus, ii, p. 253: " Guillelmus autem Normannorum princeps post mortem Herberti iuvenis haereditatem eius obtinuit, et Goisfredus comes Rodberto iuveni cum filia Herberti totum honorem concessit, et hominium debitamque fidelitatem ab illo in praesentia patris apud Alencionem recepit." Ordericus is the sole authority for this homage; and his account of it is incidental to a brief resumé of the lives

This feudal ceremony at Alençon gave formal legal sanction to
Robert's position as count of Maine. Yet he was still a mere
child, and Duke William clearly had no intention of actually
setting him to rule the newly acquired territory. He could have
had no hand in the warfare by which it had been won, and to impose a foreign yoke upon the Manceaux in the face of the ardent
spirit of local patriotism was a task for stronger hands than his.
Robert's countship, for the time being at any rate, remained a
purely formal one, and Duke William with the assistance of Norman administrators and a Norman garrison kept the government
of the county in his own hands.[33] Nevertheless, the new legal
status to which the young prince had been raised found at least
occasional recognition in the documents of the period. In several
early charters we meet with his attestation as count of Maine,[34]
and one document of the year 1076 indicates that at that time he
was regarded as an independent ruler of the county.[35]

Meanwhile, if he had grown to feel any affection for his prospective bride, the beautiful Countess Margaret,[36] his hopes were

of the counts of Maine, and forms no part of his general narrative of William's conquest of the county in 1063. The date of the homage, therefore, is conjectural.
The revolt of the Manceaux took place soon after the death of Count Herbert;
and since Geoffrey le Barbu supported the revolt, it seems natural to regard the
homage as a final act in the general pacification, and to assign it to 1063. This is
the view taken by Latouche (*Maine*, p. 35) as against Kate Norgate (*England
under the Angevin Kings*, London, 1887, i, p. 217), who places the homage before
the revolt.

[33] Latouche, *Maine*, p. 34.

[34] E.g., [before 1066] charter by Duke William establishing collegiate canons at
Cherbourg (*Revue catholique de Normandie*, x, pp. 46–50); [before 1066] charter by
Duke William in favor of Coutances cathedral (Round, *C. D. F.*, no. 957); 1068
(indiction xiii by error for vi), confirmation by King William and by Robert of a
charter in favor of La Couture, Le Mans (*Cartulaier des abbayes de Saint-Pierre de
la Couture et de Saint-Pierre de Solesmes*, ed. the Benedictines of Solesmes, Le Mans,
1881, no. 15; cf. Latouche, *Maine*, p. 147, no. 35); 1074, charter by King William
in favor of Bayeux cathedral (Davis, *Regesta*, no. 76).

[35] A donation by Gradulf, a canon of Saint-Vincent of Le Mans, is dated as follows: " Igitur hec omnia facta sunt in Bellimensi castro viii° kal. Septembris, cur-
rente xiv° indictione, et Philippo rege Francorum regnante, Robertoque, Willelmi
regis Anglorum filio, Cenomannicam urbem gubernante." *Cartulaire de l'abbaye
de Saint-Vincent du Mans*, ed. R. Charles and S. Menjot d'Elbenne (Le Mans, 1886),
i, no. 589.

[36] Ordericus Vitalis (ii, p. 104) describes her as " speciosam virginem "; Wil-

doomed to early disappointment; for, before either of the children had reached a marriageable age, Margaret died at Fécamp, and was buried there in the monastery of La Trinité.[37] This, however, did not mean that the Norman plans with regard to Maine had seriously miscarried. Duke William continued to maintain his hold upon the county; and Robert continued to be called count[38] and to be designated as his father's heir and successor in the government.

Indeed, the assigning of the countship of Maine to Robert was but part of a general plan which embraced all of Duke William's dominions, and under which Robert was early marked out as his successor designate for the whole. In a charter of 29 June 1063 — contemporary, therefore, with the Norman conquest of Maine[39] — the young prince appears after his parents with the following significant designation: " Roberti, eorum filii, quem elegerant ad gubernandum regnum post suum obitum." [40] Clearly at this early date Robert had already been definitely chosen as the successor to his father's rule.

With Duke William still in the prime vigor of manhood, and menaced by no particular dangers, such a provision seemed to

liam of Poitiers (*H. F.*, xi, p. 86) is more lavish of praise: " Haec generosa virgo, nomine Margarita, insigni specie decentior fuit omni margarita."

[37] *Interpolations de Robert de Torigny*, in William of Jumièges, p. 268; William of Poitiers, in *H. F.*, xi, p. 86; Ordericus, ii, p. 104. According to *Gallia Christiana* (ed. the Benedictines of Saint-Maur and others, Paris, 1715–75, xi, col. 205) Margaret died 13 December 1060; but this is clearly an error, since after the death of Count Herbert II (9 March 1062) she joined with Robert Curthose in doing homage to Geoffrey le Barbu, and this act took place apparently in the year 1063. Ordericus, ii, p. 253; and cf. *supra*, n. 32. Latouche suggests that the editors of *Gallia Christiana* have probably taken the day and the month from some obituary and are in error, therefore, only as to the year. *Maine*, p. 32, n. 6. It is probably only a desire for literary effect which leads William of Poitiers to say that Margaret was snatched away by death shortly before her proposed marriage: " Sed ipsam non longe ante diem quo mortali sponso iungeretur hominibus abstulit Virginis Filius." Apparently at the time of her death Margaret had become a nun. Robert of Torigny states that she died a ' virgo Christo devota ', and William of Poitiers says that she died practising great austerities and wearing a hair shirt.

[38] *Supra*, n. 34.   [39] *Supra*, n. 25.

[40] Charter of Stigand de Mézidon, the same to whom Duke William had committed the wardship of Margaret of Maine, in favor of Saint-Ouen of Rouen. *Mémoires et notes de M. Auguste Le Prévost pour servir à l'histoire du département de l'Eure*, ed. Léopold Delisle and Louis Passy (Évreux, 1862–69), i, p. 562.

have no great immediate importance. But with the death of
Edward the Confessor and the inception of the ambitious plan for
the Norman conquest of England, Duke William's future took on
a far more uncertain aspect. Great and careful though the preparations were, almost anything might happen in such an enterprise. It was a grave moment for men with Norman interests as
the duke stood upon the threshold of his great adventure. The
prudent abbot of Marmoutier hastened to obtain from the youthful Robert a confirmation of all the gifts which his father had
made to the abbey.[41] Duke William, too, felt the uncertainties of
the hour and made careful provision against all eventualities.
Summoning the great nobles around him, he solemnly proclaimed
Robert his heir and successor, and had the barons do homage and
swear fealty to him as their lord.[42] Unless the sources are misleading, King Philip of France, Duke William's overlord, was
present and gave his consent to the action.[43]

Robert, however, was evidently still too young and inexperienced to be entrusted with the actual administration of the
duchy at such a critical moment; and the government during the

[41] Round, *C. D. F.*, no. 1173; Davis, *Regesta*, no. 2. The charter is dated at
Rouen, 1066.

[42] The date of the ceremony is uncertain. It can hardly have been as early as
the charter of 1063 which is cited in n. 40 *supra*. It seems more likely to have been
a measure taken in 1066 when the attack upon England was in contemplation.
Thus Ordericus Vitalis (ii, p. 294) speaks of it somewhat vaguely as a measure
taken " ante Senlacium," and in another place (ii, p. 378) he makes Robert say to
his father: " Normanniam . . . quam dudum, antequam contra Heraldum in
Angliam transfretares, mihi concessisti"; and again (iii, p. 242) he makes the Conqueror on his deathbed use language of similar import: " Ducatum Normanniae,
antequam in epitumo Senlac contra Heraldum certassem, Roberto filio meo concessi,
quia primogenitus est. Hominium pene omnium huius patriae baronum iam
recepit." Florence of Worcester, *Chronicon ex Chronicis*, ed. Benjamin Thorpe
(London, 1848–49), ii, p. 12: " Normanniam quam sibi ante adventum ipsius in
Angliam, coram Philippo rege Francorum dederat." Cf. *A.–S. C., a.* 1079; *Interpolations de Robert de Torigny*, in William of Jumièges, p. 268.

[43] The question as to the period and manner of this homage is complicated by
the fact that the ceremony was repeated at an undetermined date after the Norman
Conquest on the occasion of the king's serious illness at Bonneville. The *Anglo-
Saxon Chronicle* (*a.* 1079) and Florence of Worcester (ii, p. 12) are the only sources
which mention the assent of King Philip. From Florence it seems to be clear that
this assent was given on the earlier occasion.

duke's absence on the Conquest was placed in the hands of Countess Matilda and a council of regents.[44] But when in December 1067, after the successful launching of his great enterprise, the Conqueror found it necessary to go a second time to England, Robert was called to higher honors and responsibilities, and was definitely associated with his mother in the regency.[45] From this same year he begins to appear in occasional charters as ' count of the Normans ';[46] and when in the following year Matilda was called to England for her coronation, there is some reason to believe that he was charged with full responsibility for. the administration of Normandy.[47]

Whether this implied a like responsibility for the government of Maine is not clear. If it did, Robert certainly proved unequal to the task of maintaining Norman dominion in that turbulent county. Norman rule had from the beginning been unpopular in

[44] William of Poitiers, in *H. F.*, xi, p. 103; Ordericus, ii, p. 178. According to the former the council was headed by Roger of Beaumont, according to the latter by Roger of Montgomery.

[45] Ordericus, ii, pp. 177, 178. William of Jumièges (p. 139) makes no mention of Matilda or of the council of regents, but says that the duchy was committed to Robert: " Rodberto filio suo iuvenili flore vernanti Normannici ducatus dominium tradidit."

[46] E.g., 1067, April, Vaudreuil, charter by William I in favor of the monks of Saint-Benoît-sur-Loire (Davis, *Regesta*, no. 6a); 1082, June 24, Oissel, two confirmations by William I of grants in favor of Saint-Martin of Marmoutier (*ibid.*, nos. 145, 146); [1079–82], confirmation by William I of a grant in favor of the abbey of Troarn (*ibid.*, no. 172). Lot publishes two charters of 1051, in which Robert's attestation as the ' young count ' has been interpolated at some later date. See *supra*, n. 10. He also publishes a charter, " vers 1071," in which appears " presente Rotberto comite." *Saint-Wandrille*, no. 43, pp. 99–100. Lot supposes that this is Count Robert of Eu, but it is more probably Robert Curthose. See Haskins, p. 66, n. 18.

There is no regular practice with regard to Robert's title in documents during the Conqueror's lifetime. Occasionally, as above noted, he is called ' count of the Normans '; occasionally, as has been pointed out in an earlier note (*supra*, n. 34), he bears the title ' count of Maine.' Often he appears without title as ' Robert the king's son ' (Davis, *Regesta*, nos. 73, 92a, 126, 140, 165, 168, 171, 255); but generally he is called count (*ibid.*, nos. 2, 30, 74, 75, 76, 96, 105, 114, 125, 127, 135, 145, 146, 147, 149, 150, 158, 169, 170, 172, 173, 175, 182, 183a, 199); and very frequently his designation is ' Count Robert the king's son ' (*ibid.*, nos. 30, 74, 75, 105, 114, 125, 147, 149, 150, 158, 169, 170).

[47] This appears to be the implication of Ordericus, ii, p. 188.

Maine. The citizens of Le Mans were alert and rebellious, and Duke William's preoccupation with the conquest of England offered them a unique opportunity to strike a blow for independence. Accordingly, in 1069, they rose in revolt [48] and overthrew the Norman domination more quickly even than it had been established by Duke William in 1063. During the following three years Maine passed through a turbulent era, which — interesting as it is for both local and general history — hardly concerns the life of Robert Curthose; since, so far as can be discovered, no effort was made during that period to reëstablish Norman authority in the county. The collapse of the Norman rule had been as complete as it was sudden.

By the spring of 1073, however, King William had returned to the Continent and was in a position to turn his attention to the reconquest of Maine. Assembling a great army composed of both Normans and English, he marched into the county, reduced Fresnay, Beaumont, and Sillé in quick succession, and arrived before Le Mans, which surrendered without a siege. [49] The authority of the Conqueror, perhaps we may even say the authority of Robert Curthose, [50] was fully reëstablished. The sources are silent as to the part which Robert played in these events or in the struggles of the succeeding years by which the Conqueror maintained the Norman domination in the face of the

[48] On the date see Latouche, *Maine*, p. 36, n. 1. On the revolt generally and its sequel see *ibid.*, pp. 35–38; Halphen, *Anjou*, pp. 180–181; *Actus Pontificum*, pp. 376–381; Ordericus, ii, pp. 253–254.

[49] *Actus Pontificum*, pp. 380–381; Ordericus, ii, pp. 254–255; Latouche, *Maine*, p. 38; Halphen, *Anjou*, p. 181. The campaign took place in 1073 (*A.-S. C., a.* 1073) before 30 March, as is shown by a confirmation by King William in favor of the monks of La Couture: " Anno Domini millesimo septuagesimo tercio iii kalendas Aprilis, roboratum est hoc preceptum a rege Anglorum Guillelmo apud Bonam Villam." *Cartulaire de la Couture*, no. 9. Cf. Latouche, *Maine*, p. 38, n. 7, and p. 147, no. 38.

[50] In a charter by Arnold, bishop of Le Mans, we read: " Acta autem fuit hec auctorizatio in urbe Cenomannica, in capitulo beati Iuliani, iiiº kalendas Aprilis . . . eo videlicet anno quo Robertus, Willelmi regis Anglorum filius, comitatum Cenomannensem recuperavit." *Cartulaire de Saint-Vincent*, no. 175. This charter cannot be certainly dated more closely than 1066–81. But it seems not unlikely that it belongs to the spring of 1073, when, as we know, Norman authority had just been reëstablished at Le Mans by force of arms.

jealous opposition of Fulk le Réchin, count of Anjou.[51] Robert
certainly continued to enjoy the formal dignity of count of
Maine.[52] Indeed, a charter of 25 August 1076 seems to indicate
that he was at that time regarded as an independent ruler at Le
Mans.[53]

Meanwhile, the Conqueror took occasion to reaffirm his inten-
tions regarding the succession to his dominions. At some time
after the conquest of England but before the outbreak of his unfortunate quarrels with his eldest son, he fell dangerously sick at
Bonneville; and, fearing for his life, he summoned the barons
around him, as he had done previously upon the eve of the Norman Conquest, and had them renew their homage and pledge of
fealty to Robert as their lord.[54] Again Robert Curthose was
formally designated as the heir of all his father's dominions.

If, therefore, one looks back upon Robert's life from about the
year 1077, far from feeling surprise at the slowness of his development or at the lateness of his initiation into political and government affairs, one must rather wonder at the early age at which he
became a pawn in the great game of politics, war, and diplomacy
which his father was playing so shrewdly, and at the rapidity with
which at least minor responsibilities were thrust upon him. Affianced to the prospective heiress of the county of Maine when
little more than an infant, he was designated as his father's heir
and successor while still a mere child, and began to give his formal
attestation to legal documents at about the same period. At the
age of twelve, or thereabouts, he received the homage of the Norman barons as their lord and prospective ruler, and soon after
was associated with his mother in the regency during the king's
absence from the duchy.

[51] On these events see Augustin Fliche, *Le règne de Philippe Ier, roi de France*
(Paris, 1912), pp. 270–274; Halphen, *Anjou*, p. 182.

[52] He is so styled in 1074 in his attestation of a charter by King William in
favor of Bayeux cathedral. Davis, *Regesta*, no. 76.

[53] "Roberto . . . Cenomannicam urbem gubernante." *Supra*, n. 35.

[54] Ordericus, ii, pp. 294, 390; cf. *A.-S. C.*, *a.* 1079; Florence of Worcester, ii,
p. 12. That this ceremony took place twice, once before and once after the Conquest, seems to be made certain by the specific phrase of Ordericus, " ante Senlacium bellum et post in quadam sua aegritudine." Cf. *supra*, n. 43.

Down to the year 1077, there is no evidence of quarrels or disagreement between the Conqueror and his eldest son.[55] Indeed, the proof seems almost conclusive that there were no such quarrels until a relatively late date. Not only do the narrative sources upon careful analysis yield no evidence of disobedience or rebellion upon Robert's part, but positive documentary evidence points strongly in the opposite direction. A series of charters scattered from 1063 to 1077 reveals Robert on repeated occasions in close association with his parents and his brothers, occupying an honored position, and attesting legal acts [56] almost as frequently as the queen, more frequently than his brothers. That the family harmony was not disturbed by domestic discord as late as the autumn of 1077 there is good reason to believe. For, in that year, Robert joined with his parents and his younger brother William in the imposing dedication ceremonies of Bishop Odo's great cathedral church at Bayeux, [57] and again, 13 September, in the dedication of the abbey church of the Conqueror's foundation in honor of St. Stephen at Caen.[58]

[55] Unless one so regard a speech which Ordericus (ii, p. 259) puts into the mouths of the rebel earls Roger of Hereford and Ralph of Norfolk in 1074: " Transmarinis conflictibus undique circumdatur, et non solum ab externis, sed etiam a sua prole impugnatur, et a propriis alumnis inter discrimina deseritur." But this speech is probably a work of imagination on the part of Ordericus, and he seems here to have fallen into an anachronism. Cf. Le Prévost, in Ordericus, ii, p. 377, n. 1.

[56] Davis, *Regesta*, nos. 2, 4, 6a, 30, 73, 75, 76, 92a, 96, 105, 114; Round, *C. D. F.*, nos. 713, 957, 1165; Le Prévost, *Eure*, i, p. 562; *Antiquus Cartularius Ecclesiae Baiocensis (Livre noir)*, ed. l'abbé V. Bourrienne (Paris, 1902), no. 5: *Revue catholique de Normandie*, x, pp. 46–50; *Cartulaire de la Couture*, no. 15; Lot, *Saint-Wandrille*, nos. 30, 31, 38; Bertrand de Broussillon, *Maison de Laval*, i, p. 37, no. 20. Though the authenticity of this last document has been questioned, Broussillon regards it as "parfaitement authentique." The attestation "Rotberti comiti regis Anglorum filii " is inconsistent with the evident date of the charter (1055), and must be, in part at least, a later interpolation.

[57] Ordericus, ii, pp. 304–305.

[58] Davis, *Regesta*, no. 96; Round, *C. D. F.*, no. 449.

CHAPTER II

REBELLION AND EXILE

Down to the year 1077 the conduct of Robert Curthose towards the king had, so far as we can see, been exemplary. Even William of Malmesbury, while criticising his later insubordination, still pays tribute to his obedient youth.[1] But difficulties were now at hand. Robert was rapidly growing to manhood, and his character was unfolding. Reared among his father's men-at-arms, residing much about the court, enjoying the privileged position and the social freedom of the king's heir and successor designate, he had developed into a warrior of distinguished valor,[2] and into a chivalrous knight and courtier considerably in advance of the rude society of the eleventh century.[3] Short and thick-set, though probably the coarse full face and enormous paunch[4] of later years had not yet developed; fluent of speech, affable in bearing, and of a jovial disposition; generous to the point of prodigality, giving to all who asked with unstinting hand, and lavish of promises when more substantial rewards were lacking;[5] he had

[1] " Inter bellicas patris alas excrevit primaevo tirocinio, parenti morem in omnibus gerens." *G. R.*, ii, p. 459.

[2] Practically all the sources bear witness to Robert's courage and special prowess in arms. E.g., Ordericus, ii, p. 295; iii, p. 262; William of Malmesbury, *G. R.*, ii, pp. 459–460, 463; *Interpolations de Robert de Torigny*, in William of Jumièges, pp. 267, 284; Guibert of Nogent, in *H. C. Oc.*, iv, p. 149. For the exaggerations to which this was carried in later tradition see *infra*, pp. 190–197.

[3] These qualities will become more evident in the sequel. Stenton characterizes Robert as " a gross anticipation of the chivalrous knight of later times." *William the Conqueror*, p. 349.

[4] William of Malmesbury, *G. R.*, ii, p. 459; Ordericus, ii, p. 295; iii, p. 262.

[5] The inimitable characterization of Ordericus Vitalis is worthy of reproduction in full. " Omnes ducem Rodbertum mollem esse desidemque cognoscebant. . . . Erat quippe idem dux audax et validus, multaque laude dignus; eloquio facundus, sed in regimine sui suorumque inconsideratus, in erogando prodigus, in promittendo diffusus, ad mentiendum levis et incautus, misericors supplicibus, ad iustitiam super iniquo faciendam mollis et mansuetus, in definitione mutabilis, in conversatione omnibus nimis blandus et tractabilis, ideoque perversis et insipientibus despicabilis;

become the centre of interest and attraction for the younger set about the Norman court, and from some points of view a serious rival of his father. His position was not unlike that of Henry Fitz Henry, the 'Young King,' who nearly a century later created such grave problems for Henry II. He had long borne the title of count and had enjoyed an official, or semi-official, position about the court. He had long since been formally recognized as his father's heir and successor. The barons had twice done him homage and sworn fealty to him as their lord and future master. He was titular ruler of Maine. And if, as two charters seem to indicate, he was in some way formally invested with the Norman duchy in 1077 or 1078,[6] the resemblance between his position and that of the Young King after his coronation in 1170 is even more striking.

Yet, with all these honors, Robert enjoyed no real power and exercised no active part in affairs of government. It was not the way of the Conqueror to part with any of his prerogatives prematurely; and if, for reasons of state, he bestowed formal honors upon his son, it was still his firm intention to remain sole master until the last within his own dominions. But for the young prince to continue thus in idleness, surrounded by a crowd of restless hangers-on of the younger nobility, was both costly and dangerous. Robert not unnaturally wished for an independent establishment and an income of his own;[7] but these the king was

corpore autem brevis et grossus, ideoque Brevis Ocrea a patre est cognominatus. Ipse cunctis placere studebat, cunctisque quod petebant aut dabat, aut promittebat, vel concedebat. Prodigus, dominium patrum suorum quotidie imminuebat, insipienter tribuens unicuique quod petebat, et ipse pauperescebat, unde alios contra se roborabat." *Ibid.*, iii, pp. 262–263. Cf. Ralph of Caen in *H. C. Oc.*, iii, pp. 616, 642; William of Malmesbury, *G. R.*, ii, pp. 459–463.

[6] Two charters dated 24 May 1096 at Bayeux, 'xviiii. anno principatus domni Roberti Willelmi regis Anglorum filii ducis Normannie,' the one by Robert himself and the other by Odo of Bayeux and attested by Robert. Haskins, pp. 66–67, nos. 3, 4, and n. 19. The style here employed of dating the reign from 1077–78 is unusual. It is ordinarily dated from Robert's actual accession to the duchy upon the death of the Conqueror in 1087. Cf., e.g., Davis, *Regesta*, nos. 308, 310.

[7] Ordericus Vitalis makes Robert say: " Quid ergo faciam, vel quid meis clientibus tribuam ? . . . Mercenarius tuus semper esse nolo. Aliquando rem familiarem volo habere, ut mihi famulantibus digna possim stipendia retribuere." Ordericus, ii, p. 378. Cf. Achille Luchaire, *La société française au temps de Philippe-Auguste*

unwilling to provide. Robert, therefore, became dissatisfied; and the ambitious companions by whom he was surrounded were not slow to fan the embers of his growing discontent.[8] Apparently it was in the year 1078, or late in 1077,[9] that the unfortunate quarrel broke out which culminated in the siege of Gerberoy and a personal encounter between father and son upon the field of battle.

Upon the cause of the disagreement we are fortunate in having abundant testimony,[10] and it is possible to define the issue with some exactness. Prompted by the rash counsels of his time-serving companions, Robert went to the king and demanded that immediate charge of the government of Normandy and of Maine be committed forthwith into his hands. To Maine he based his claim upon his rights through Margaret, his deceased fiancée, to Normandy upon the twice repeated grant which his father had made to him, once before the Conquest, and afterwards at Bonne-ville, when the assembled barons had done him homage and pledged their fealty to him as their lord.[11]

If reliance may be placed upon the account of Ordericus Vitalis,[12] the Conqueror took some time to reflect upon his son's

(Paris, 1909), pp. 280–282, where it is pointed out that such demands and the quarrels and the open warfare which frequently resulted from them were perfectly characteristic of the feudal age.

[8] Ordericus, ii, pp. 294, 377 ff.; William of Malmesbury, *G. R.*, ii, p. 459; Registers of Gregory VII, bk. vii, no. 27, in *Bibliotheca Rerum Germanicarum*, ed. Philipp Jaffé (Berlin, 1864–73), ii, pp. 420–421.

[9] The date at which the quarrel began is uncertain. It must have been after 13 September 1077, when Robert was present with his parents and William Rufus at the dedication of Saint-Étienne at Caen. *Supra*, p. 16. The siege of Gerberoy, which marks its termination, took place in December and January 1078–79. *Infra*, n. 38.

[10] William of Malmesbury, *G. R.*, ii, pp. 316–317, 459–460; *A.-S.C.*, a. 1079; Florence of Worcester, ii, p. 12; *Chronicon Monasterii de Hyda*, in *Liber Monasterii de Hyda*, ed. Edward Edwards (London, 1866), p. 297; Ordericus, ii, pp. 294–295, 377 ff.; *Interpolations de Robert de Torigny*, in William of Jumièges, p. 268; Registers of Gregory VII, bk. vii, no. 27, in Jaffé, *Bibliotheca*, ii, pp. 420–421.

[11] *Interpolations de Robert de Torigny*, in William of Jumièges, p. 268; cf. Ordericus, ii, pp. 294–295, 389.

[12] Ordericus Vitalis is the only early writer who treats in detail of the quarrels between Robert and the Conqueror. He discusses them at length in two places (ii, pp. 294–298, 377–390), but unfortunately his accounts are confused and very

demands and endeavored to reason with him about them.[13] He
urged Robert to put away the rash young men who had prompted
him to such imprudence and to give ear to wiser counsels. He
explained that his demands were improper. He, the king, held
Normandy by hereditary right, and England by right of conquest; and it would be preposterous to expect him to give them
up to another. If Robert would only be patient and show himself
worthy, he would receive all in due course, with the willing assent
of the people and with the blessing of God. Let him remember
Absalom and what happened to him, and beware lest he follow in
the path of Rehoboam! But to all these weighty arguments
Robert turned a deaf ear, replying that he had not come to hear
sermons: he had heard such " ad nauseam " from the grammarians. His determination was immovably fixed. He would no
longer do service to anyone in Normandy in the mean condition
of a dependent. The king's resolution, however, was equally
firm. Normandy, he declared, was his native land, and he wished
all to understand that so long as he lived he would never let it slip
from his grasp.[14] The argument thus came to a deadlock; yet,
apparently, there was no immediate break.[15] Relations doubtless

difficult to disentangle. There clearly were two quarrels and two periods during
which Robert was in exile. Ordericus himself (ii, p. 390) is specific with regard to
this; and we know independently that the first quarrel — followed by a relatively
short period of exile — ended in the reconciliation after the siege of Gerberoy (1079)
and that Robert was again in exile at the time of the Conqueror's death (1087).
Pretty clearly the second exile was for a longer period than the first. But the two
accounts of Ordericus do not deal each with one of these quarrels. Rather they both
purport to relate to the earlier quarrel and to the banishment which followed it.
Yet it is obvious that Ordericus, lacking contemporary knowledge of the events, has
confused the two episodes and has related incidents of the latter as if they belonged to
the former. For example (ii, p. 381), he represents Robert as wandering in exile for
a period of five years. Clearly this was not after the first quarrel, to which he relates
it, since that could have been followed by no such extended banishment. In the
narrative detail which follows I have attempted to disentangle the accounts of Ordericus Vitalis conjecturally, striving to preserve something of the vivacity of
style of the original, without supposing that I have been able to arrive at rigorous
historical accuracy. Ordericus's own narrative is obviously in a high degree a work
of imagination.

[13] Ordericus, ii, pp. 294–295.

[14] *Ibid.*, pp. 378–380.

[15] *Ibid.*, pp. 294–295.

continued strained, but Robert bided his time, perhaps seeking a more favorable opportunity for pressing his demands. At times he may even have appeared reconciled; yet no lasting settlement was possible so long as the cause of the discord remained.

The actual outbreak of open rebellion followed, it seems, directly upon a family broil among the king's sons; and Ordericus Vitalis, with characteristic fondness for gossip, has not failed to relate the incident in great detail.[16] The Conqueror, so the story runs, was preparing an expedition against the Corbonnais and had stopped at Laigle in the house of a certain Gontier, while Robert Curthose had found lodgings nearby in the house of Roger of Caux. Meanwhile, Robert's younger brothers, William and Henry, had taken umbrage at his pretensions and at the rash demands which he had made upon their father, and they were strongly supporting the king against him. While in this frame of mind they paid Robert a visit at his lodgings. Going into an upper room, they began dicing ' as soldiers will '; and presently — doubtless after there had been drinking — they started a row and threw down water upon their host and his companions who were on the floor below. Robert was not unnaturally enraged at this insult, and with the support of his comrades [17] he rushed in upon the offenders, and a wild scuffle ensued, which was only terminated by the timely arrival of the king, who, upon hearing the clamor, came in haste from his lodgings and put a stop to the quarrel by his royal presence.[18]

Robert, however, remained sullen and offended; and that night, accompanied by his intimates, he withdrew secretly from the royal forces and departed. Riding straight for Rouen, he made the rash venture of attempting to seize the castle by a surprise attack, an action which seems almost incredible, except on the hypothesis that a conspiracy with wide ramifications was already under way. However this may be, the attack upon Rouen failed. Roger of Ivry, the king's butler, who was guarding the castle, got word of the impending stroke, set the defences in order,

[16] Ordericus, ii, pp. 295-296.
[17] Ivo and Alberic of Grandmesnil are mentioned by name.
[18] Ordericus, ii, pp. 295-296.

and sent messengers in hot haste to warn the king of the danger. William was furious at his son's treason, and ordered a wholesale arrest of the malcontents, thus spreading consternation among them and breaking up their plans. Some were captured, but others escaped across the frontier.[19]

The rising now spread rapidly among the king's enemies on both sides of the border. Hugh of Châteauneuf-en-Thymerais promptly opened the gates of his castles at Châteauneuf, Sorel, and Rémalard to the fugitives, and so furnished them with a secure base beyond the frontier from which to make incursions into Normandy. Robert of Bellême also joined the rebel cause. Perhaps, indeed, it was through his influence that Hugh of Châteauneuf was persuaded to give succor to the rebels; for Hugh was his brother-in-law, having married his sister Mabel. Ralph de Toeny, lord of Conches, also joined the rebellion, and many others, among them doubtless being Ivo and Alberic of Grand-mesnil and Aimeric de Villeray.[20] The border war which followed did not long remain a local matter. It was an event fit to bring joy to all King William's enemies; and it caused a great commotion, we are told, not only in the immediate neighborhood of the revolt, but also in distant parts among the French and Bretons and the men of Maine and Anjou.[21]

The king, however, met the rebellion with his accustomed vigor and decision. He confiscated the lands of the rebels and turned their rents to the employment of mercenaries to be used against them. Apparently he had been on his way to make war upon Rotrou of Mortagne in the Corbonnais when his plans had been interrupted by the disgraceful brawl among his sons at Laigle.[22] He now abandoned that enterprise, and, making peace

---

[19] Ordericus, ii, p. 296.

[20] *Ibid.*, pp. 296–298. Elsewhere Ordericus gives another list as follows: Robert of Bellême, William of Breteuil, Roger de Bienfaite, Robert Mowbray, William de Moulins, and William de Rupierre. *Ibid.*, pp. 380–381. Robert of Bellême is the only one appearing in both lists, and it would be rash to assume that all the foregoing supported Robert Curthose against the king in his first rebellion. But if Ordericus Vitalis is to be trusted, they were all at one time or another associated in Robert's treason.

[21] *Ibid.*, p. 297.

[22] *Ibid.*, p. 295; cf. p. 297: "cum Rotrone Mauritaniensi comite pacem fecit."

with Rotrou, took him and his troops into his own service. And thus raising a considerable army, he laid siege to the rebels in their stronghold at Rémalard.[23] But of the outcome of these operations we have no certain knowledge. One of the insurgents at least, Aimeric de Villeray, was slain, and his son Gulfer was so terrified by his father's tragic fate that he made peace with the king and remained thereafter unshakably loyal.

We hear, too, vaguely of a 'dapifer' of the king of France who was passing from castle to castle among the rebels.[24] What his business was we know not; but it seems not unlikely that King Philip was already negotiating with the insurgent leaders with a view to aiding and abetting their enterprise against his too powerful Norman vassal.[25] Philip had made peace with the Conqueror after the latter's unsuccessful siege of Dol in 1076,[26] but the friendship of the two kings had not been lasting. Sound policy demanded that Philip spare no effort to curb the overweening power of his great Norman feudatory; and William had, therefore, to count upon his constant, if veiled, hostility.[27] The rebellion of Robert Curthose and his followers was Philip's opportunity; and it seems not improbable that he looked upon the movement with favor and gave it encouragement from its inception. Clearly he made no effort to suppress it, though the fighting was going on within his own borders. And, in any case, before the end of 1078 he had definitely taken Robert Curthose under his protection and had assigned him the castle of Gerberoy in the

[23] Ordericus, ii, pp. 297–298.

[24] *Ibid.*, p. 298. Freeman's interpretation of this passage regarding Aimeric de Villeray and the dapifer of the king of France, which differs greatly from that which I have given, appears to be based upon a careless and absolutely wrong reading of the Latin text. *Norman Conquest*, iv, pp. 639–640.

[25] This hypothesis would help to explain the vague statement of Ordericus Vitalis: " Galli et Britones, Cenomanni et Andegavenses, aliique populi fluctuabant, et quem merito sequi deberent ignorabant." Ordericus, ii, p. 297.

[26] *A.–S. C.*, a. 1077: "This year a peace was made between the king of France and William king of England, but it lasted only a little while." Henry of Huntingdon, *Historia Anglorum*, ed. Thomas Arnold (London, 1879), p. 206; cf. Fliche, *Philippe Iᵉʳ*, p. 274.

[27] " Philippum . . . semper infidum habuit, quod scilicet ille tantam gloriam viro invideret quem et patris sui et suum hominem esse constaret." William of Malmesbury, *G. R.*, ii, p. 316.

Beauvaisis, close to the Norman frontier.[28]   There Robert was received with his followers by royal castellans and promised every possible aid and support.

But this evidently was some months, at least, after the outbreak of Robert's rebellion.   As to his movements in the meantime, we hear little more than uncertain rumors.   The sources are silent concerning the part which he played in the border warfare which centred around the castles of Hugh of Châteauneuf.   We have it on the express statement of the *Anglo-Saxon Chronicle* that Robert fled to his uncle, Robert the Frisian, count of Flanders; [29] and in this the *Chronicle* is confirmed by Ordericus Vitalis, who adds that he also visited Odo, bishop of Treves.[30]   Other writers indicate simply that he withdrew into France.[31]   Ordericus indeed, represents him as wandering much farther, and visiting noble kinsmen, " dukes, counts, and powerful townsmen (*oppidani*) in Lorraine, Germany, Aquitaine, and Gascony," wasting his substance in dissolute living and reduced to poverty and beggary, and to borrowing of foreign usurers.[32]   But such wanderings, if they actually occurred, it seems more natural to assign — since we are reduced to conjecture — to Robert's second exile.[33]   One incident, however, which concerns his mother, the queen, who died in 1083, must be assigned to this period.

The singularly happy relations which existed between William and Matilda, their mutual love, devotion, and confidence, are of course famous.   Once only during their long union were these happy relations seriously disturbed.[34]   For Matilda's heart was touched by the distresses of her son, and she did not sympathize

---

[28] Ordericus, ii, p. 386.

[29] *A*. 1079.

[30] Ordericus, ii, p. 381.   Bishop Odo died 11 November 1078.   Ordericus is in error in saying that he was the brother of Robert the Frisian.

[31] Florence of Worcester, ii, p. 12: " Franciam adiit, et auxilio Philippi regis in Normannia magnam frequenter praedam agebat, villas comburebat, homines perimebat "; *Chronicon*, in *Liber de Hyda*, p. 297.

[32] Ordericus, ii, pp. 381–382.

[33] *Supra*, n. 12.

[34] William of Malmesbury, *G. R.*, ii, p. 331: " aliquantula simultas inter eos innata extremis annis fuerit pro Roberto filio, cui mater militarem manum ex fisci redditibus sufficere dicebatur "; Ordericus (ii, pp. 382–383) is much more detailed.

with the stern justice of the Conqueror in this domestic matter. Secretly she undertook to provide Robert out of her own revenues with funds for the maintenance of a military force. But the king soon detected her and interfered, declaring, in his wrath, that he had learned the truth of the adage, " A faithless woman is her husband's bane." He had loved her as his own soul and had intrusted her with his treasures and with jurisdiction throughout all his dominions, only to find her giving succor to enemies who were plotting against his life. But undaunted by this outburst, the queen sought to justify herself upon the ground of her great love for her eldest son. Though Robert were dead and buried seven feet under the earth, she declared, she would gladly die, if by so doing she could restore him to life. Respecting the spirit of his proud consort, the king turned to vent his rage upon Samson le Breton, the queen's messenger, proposing to seize him and have him blinded. But Samson received timely warning and managed to escape to Saint-Évroul; and, at the queen's request, Abbot Mainer received him into the monastery. There he dwelt in security and led an exemplary life for twenty-six years, no doubt well known to the chronicler of the house who records his tale.[35]

Whatever be the truth about Robert's wanderings and the vicissitudes of his exile, in the end he returned to France and, as already noted, gained the support of King Philip, and was established with his followers in the castle of Gerberoy in the Beauvaisis. There a military force of considerable proportions began to gather around him in response to his lavish promises. Adventurers came from France; but in greater numbers came the malcontents from Normandy. Many who hitherto had kept the peace and had remained loyal to the king now deserted the royal cause and went over to swell the ranks of the rebels.[36] King William was now obliged to turn his attention to this hornet's nest that was spreading terror among the peaceful and defenceless population on his northeastern frontier. Quartering troops in his strongholds opposite Gerberoy, he endeavored to forestall the destructive raids which the insurgents were making into his

---

[35] Ordericus, ii, pp. 382–383.
[36] *Ibid.*, pp. 386–387.

territory.[37] But, vexed that his enemies should seem to dwell in security at a point so little removed from the borders of Normandy, he determined to carry the war beyond the frontier; and, though it was the inclement season, he assembled his forces and laid siege to Gerberoy itself for some three weeks soon after Christmas (1078–79).[38]

The operations which followed were enlivened in the fashion of the day by the frequent interchange of challenges and by numerous encounters between selected bodies of knights from each side,[39] until finally the besieged garrison brought the contest to an issue by a successful sortie and a pitched battle in the open before the castle.[40] In the general mêlée which ensued the Conqueror and Robert met in single combat, and the elderly king proved no match for his vigorous and skilful antagonist. He was wounded in the hand or arm, and his horse was shot from under him.[41] According to one, and perhaps the better, account, Tokig son of Wigod, a faithful Englishman, hurried to the king with another mount, only to be himself slain a moment later by a shaft from a crossbow.[42] According to another account, however, at the

---

[37] Ordericus, ii, pp. 386–387; cf. Florence of Worcester, ii, pp. 12–13.

[38] The *Anglo-Saxon Chronicle* seems to place the siege at the end of 1079, but this is an error. *A.-S. C.*, a. 1079. The siege took place after Christmas 1078 and in the early weeks of 1079. Ordericus, ii, p. 387. This is made certain by a charter of Philip I in favor of Saint-Quentin of Beauvais, dated " in obsidione . . . circa Gerborredum, anno . . . millesimo septuagesimo viiii^{no} anno vero regni Philippi regis Francorum ix^{no} x^{mo}." *Recueil des actes de Philippe Ier, roi de France*, ed. Maurice Prou (Paris, 1908), no. 94. Freeman, though having this charter in hand, still dates the siege in 1079–80. *Norman Conquest*, iv, pp. 642–643. But Prou has shown conclusively that Freeman is in error and that the correct date is unquestionably January 1079. *Op. cit.*, p. 242, n. 1.

[39] Ordericus, ii, pp. 387–388.

[40] *A.-S. C.*, a. 1079; Florence of Worcester, ii, p. 13.

[41] *A.-S. C.*, a. 1079; Florence of Worcester, ii, p. 13; William of Malmesbury, *G. R.*, ii, p. 317; Henry of Huntingdon, p. 206. According to the *Chronicle* the king was wounded in the hand, according to Florence in the arm. The *Chronicon* in *Liber de Hyda*, p. 279, is still different, stating that the king was wounded in the foot by an arrow.

[42] *A.-S. C.*, a. 1079. Freeman with patriotic pride makes much of this exploit of Tokig the Englishman; but there appears to be no valid reason for accepting, as Freeman does, this version from the *Chronicle* and rejecting the different version of Florence of Worcester. *Norman Conquest*, iv, pp. 643–644; cf. pp. 850–852.

supreme moment of his antagonist's distress, Robert recognized his father's voice — armor had hitherto disguised the king — and, leaping down from his own horse, he directed him to mount and allowed him to ride away.[43] Many of the king's men were slain, others were captured, and many more were wounded, among them being Robert's younger brother, William Rufus.[44] The discomfiture of the royal forces was complete, and they fled from the field.[45]

This unexpected defeat before the walls of Gerberoy was a deep humiliation to the Conqueror. William of Malmesbury speaks of it as the one outstanding misfortune of his long and brilliant career.[46] In the bitterness of his shame and of his indignation against the son who had not only rebelled against him, but had actually met him on the field of battle and wounded and unhorsed him, William is said to have laid on Robert a terrible curse, vowing to disinherit him forever.[47] Though the curse was soon lifted and grudging forgiveness granted, one might easily believe from the misfortunes of Robert's later years that the baneful influence of this paternal malediction followed him to his grave more than half a century later beneath the pavement stones of Gloucester abbey.

The part played by the king of France in the border war around Gerberoy is puzzling. The narrative sources state specifically that King Philip had given his support to Robert and the Norman rebels and had deliberately established them at Gerberoy in order that they might harry the Norman border. Yet we have a charter of unquestioned validity by King Philip in favor of the church of Saint-Quentin of Beauvais, which bears the signatures of both William and Philip and a dating clause which

[43] Florence of Worcester, ii, p. 13.
[44] William of Malmesbury, *G. R.*, ii, p. 317; *A.-S. C.*, a. 1079; Florence of Worcester, ii, p. 13; Henry of Huntingdon, pp. 206–207.
[45] Florence of Worcester, ii, p. 13.
[46] *G. R.*, ii, p. 317.
[47] Henry of Huntingdon, p. 207: "Maledixit autem rex Roberto filio suo"; *Chronicon*, in *Liber de Hyda*, p. 297: "Cumque sanguinem defluere cerneret, terribiliter imprecatus est ne unquam Robertus filius suus haereditatis suae iura perciperet"; *Annales de Wintonia*, in *Annales Monastici*, ii, p. 32; cf. William of Malmesbury, *G. R.*, ii, p. 460.

reveals the fact that it was drawn up at the siege which the two kings were conducting about Gerberoy in 1079.[48] The evidence is conclusive, therefore, that, though the French king had previously supported Robert and had actually established him at Gerberoy, he nevertheless joined with the Conqueror early in 1079 in besieging the Norman rebels in his own stronghold.[49] How King William had wrought this change of mind in his jealous overlord we have no means of knowing. But it is evident that, while meeting his son's rebellion by force of arms, he had not been forgetful of his mastery of the diplomatic art.

The presence of so great an ally, however, could not disguise the fact of the Conqueror's defeat; and before the struggle was allowed to go to further extremes, influences were brought to bear upon the king which led to a reconciliation. After his humiliating discomfiture William had retired to Rouen.[50] Robert is said to have gone to Flanders,[51] though this seems hardly likely in view of his decisive victory over the royal forces. In any case, intermediaries now began to pass back and forth between them. Robert was very willing to make peace and be reconciled with his father. The barons, too, had little mind for a continuation of this kind of warfare. Robert's rebellion had divided many a family, and it was irksome to the nobles to have to fight against " sons, brothers, and kinsmen." Accordingly, Roger of Montgomery, Hugh of Gournay, Hugh of Grandmesnil, and Roger of Beaumont and his sons Robert and Henry went to the king and besought him to be reconciled with his son. They explained that Robert had been led astray by the evil counsels of depraved youth — were the ' depraved youth ' in question the ' sons and brothers ' of our respectable negotiators? — that he now repented of his errors and acknowledged his fault and humbly implored the royal clemency. The king at first remained obdurate and complained bitterly against his son. His conduct, he de-

---

[48] Prou, *Actes de Philippe Ier*, no. 94.

[49] Friendly relations between the Conqueror and Philip are implied in the statement of Ordericus (ii, p. 390) that the king of France sent ambassadors to urge a reconciliation between William and Robert. *Infra*, p. 29.

[50] Ordericus, ii, p. 388.

[51] *A.-S. C., a.* 1079.

clared, had been infamous. He had stirred up civil war and led away the very flower of the young nobility. He had also brought in the foreign enemy; and, had it been in his power, he would have armed the whole human race against his father! The barons, however, persisted in their efforts. Conferences were renewed. Bishops and other men of religion, among them St. Simon of Crépy,[52] an old friend and companion of the Conqueror, intervened to soften the king's heart. The queen, too, and ambassadors from the king of France, and neighboring nobles who had entered the Conqueror's service all added their solicitations. And " at last the stern prince, giving way to the entreaties of so many persons of rank, and moved also by natural affection, was reconciled with his son and those who had been leagued with him." With the consent of the assembled barons he renewed to Robert the grant of the succession to Normandy after his death, upon the same conditions as he had granted it on a former occasion at Bonneville.[53]

[52] *Vita Beati Simonis Comitis Crespeiensis Auctore Synchrono*, in Migne, clvi, col. 1219. We have here chronological data of some importance. St. Simon was present at Compiègne at the translation of the Holy Shroud from its ivory casket to the magnificent golden reliquary which Queen Matilda had presented to the church of Saint-Corneille; and on the next day (*in crastino itaque solemnitate peracta*) he proceeded to Normandy, where he acted as mediator between the Conqueror and his rebellious son. A charter by Philip I informs us that the translation of the Holy Shroud at Compiègne took place on the fourth Sunday of Lent. Prou, *Actes de Philippe I*er, no. 126. St. Simon, therefore, left Compiègne for Normandy on the Monday after Midlent. The year, however, remains in doubt. Presumably it was 1079 or 1080, probably the latter. Philip's charter (dated 1092) refers to the translation only incidently and gives no information as to the year in which it occurred. Ordericus Vitalis (ii, p. 389) indicates that the peace negotiations were protracted: " Frequenti colloquio Normannici proceres regem allocuti sunt." It cannot certainly be said that the reconciliation had been consummated earlier than Easter (12 April) 1080, on which date Robert joined with the king in the attestation of a charter. Davis, *Regesta*, no. 123. Gregory VII, writing on 8 May 1080, speaks of it as a recent event. *Infra*, n. 55. Émile Morel, editor of *Cartulaire de l'abbaye de Saint-Corneille de Compiègne* (Montdidier, 1904–09), i, p. 53, says that the translation of the relic took place on 3 April 1082, but he cites no authority, and I have been able to find none. Jean Pillet says: " Il est constant par des manuscrits qui parlent de cette translation, qu'elle a été faite . . . en 1081." *Histoire du château et de la ville de Gerberoy* (Rouen, 1679), p. 85. But he does not indicate where these ' manuscripts ' are to be found, and his method of dealing with chronological problems is so arbitrary as to inspire little confidence.

[53] Ordericus, ii, pp. 388–390.

It is not clear over how long a period the foregoing negotiations had been drawn out, though it is not improbable that they were continued into the spring of 1080; [54] for on 8 May of that year Gregory VII wrote Robert a letter of fatherly counsel in which he referred to the reconciliation as good news which had but recently reached him. The Pope rejoiced that Robert had acquiesced in his father's wishes and put away the society of base companions; while at the same time he solemnly warned him against a return to his evil courses in the future. [55]

Whether or not the Pope's admonition had anything to do with it, Robert seems, for a time at least, to have made an earnest effort to acquiesce in his father's wishes. The reconciliation was, so far as can be seen, complete and cordial. Again Robert's name begins to appear frequently in the charters of the period, indicating a full and friendly coöperation with his parents and his brothers. [56] The king, too, seems so far to have had a change of

---

[54] *Supra*, n. 52. It may also be noted that the raid of King Malcolm, though it occurred in 1079, did not cause the king to go to England until 1080. *Infra*, p. 31.

[55] Registers of Gregory VII, bk. vii, no. 27, in Jaffé, *Bibliotheca*, ii, pp. 420–421. The letter is of more than passing interest, since it throws much light upon the matters which had been in controversy and is strongly confirmatory of the narrative sources. " Insuper monemus et paternę precamur, ut menti tuae semper sit infixum, quam forti manu, quam divulgata gloria, quicquid pater tuus possideat, ab ore inimicorum extraxerit; sciens tamen, se non in perpetuum vivere, sed ad hoc tam viriliter insistere, ut eredi alicui sua dimitteret. Caveas ergo, fili dilectissime, admonemus, ne abhinc pravorum consiliis adquiescas, quibus patrem offendas et matrem contristeris. . . . Pravorum consilia ex officio nostro praecipimus penitus dimittas, patris voluntati in omnibus adquiescas. Data Rome 8 idus Maii, indictione 3." It may also be noted that on the same day Gregory wrote letters of courtesy to William and Matilda. But in both he confined himself to generalities and said nothing of consequence, tactfully avoiding all reference to Robert or to the recent family discord. *Ibid.*, nos. 25, 26.

[56] E.g., 1080, April 12, [Rouen ?] (Davis, *Regesta*, no. 123); 1080, July 14, Caen (*ibid.*, no. 125); 1080, [presumably in Normandy] (*ibid.*, nos. 126, 127); 1081, February, [London] (*ibid.*, no. 135); [1078–83, perhaps 1081], February 2, Salisbury (*Historia et Cartularium Monasterii S. Petri Gloucestriae*, ed. W. H. Hart, London, 1863–67, i, no. 411); 1081, Winchester (Davis, *Regesta*, no. 140); 1082, June 24, Oissel (*ibid.*, nos. 145, 146); 1082, Downton (*ibid.*, no. 147); 1082 (*ibid.*, nos. 149, 150); [c. 1082] (*ibid.*, no. 158); 1083, July 18 (*ibid.*, no. 182); 1083 (*Chartes de S.-Julien de Tours*, no. 37); [1079–82] (Davis, *Regesta*, nos. 168–173); cf. *ibid.*, 165, 175, 183a.

heart as to be willing for the first time in his life to intrust his son with important enterprises.

In the late summer of 1079, King Malcolm of Scotland had taken advantage of the Conqueror's preoccupation with his continental dominions to harry Northumberland as far south as the Tyne,[57] and King William had been obliged for the moment to forego his vengeance. But in the late summer or autumn of 1080 he crossed over to England with Robert,[58] and prepared to square accounts with his Scottish adversary. Assembling a large force, which included Abbot Adelelm of Abingdon and a considerable number of the great barons of England, he placed Robert in command and sent him northward against the Scottish raider.[59] Advancing into Lothian, [60] Robert met Malcolm at Eccles, [61] but found him in no mood for fighting. Ready enough for raids and plundering when the English armies were at a safe distance, the Scottish king had no desire for the test of a decisive engagement. Unless the language of the Abingdon chronicle is misleading, he again recognized the English suzerainty over his kingdom and gave hostages for his good faith.[62] Thus enjoying an easy triumph, Robert turned back southward. Laying the foundations of 'New Castle' upon the Tyne[63] as he passed, he came again to his father and was duly rewarded for his achievement.[64]

[57] *A.-S. C.*, a. 1079; Florence of Worcester, ii, p. 13.

[58] Presumably they went over together, though we have no record of their actual crossing. They were still at Caen in Normandy 14 July 1080. Davis, *Regesta*, no. 125.

[59] *Chronicon Monasterii de Abingdon*, ed. Joseph Stevenson (London, 1858), ii, p. 9; Simeon, *H. R.*, p. 211.

[60] *Chronicon de Abingdon*, ii, p. 9. [61] Simeon, *H. R*, p. 211.

[62] ". Proinde ut regno Angliae principatus Scotiae subactus foret, obsides tribuit." *Chronicon de Abingdon*, pp. 9-10. Simeon of Durham says rather contemptuously that Robert returned from Eccles " nullo confecto negotio." *H. R.*, p. 211. But this statement is hardly inconsistent with the Abingdon account. A Durham writer, thirsting for vengeance, might very well use it in spite of the results accomplished by Robert's peaceful negotiations. William of Malmesbury uses very similar language of the expedition of William Rufus eleven years later: " Statimque primo contra Walenses, post in Scottos expeditionem movens, nihil magnificentia sua dignum exhibuit." *G. R.*, ii, p. 365. The Abingdon account is circumstantial, and the presence of the abbot indicates a sure source of information, though perhaps a biassed one.

[63] Simeon, *H. R.*, p. 211. [64] *Chronicon de Abingdon*, ii, p. 10.

Charters indicate that Robert remained in England throughout
the following winter and spring; [65] but before the end of 1081
important events had taken place on the borders of Maine which
called both the king and his son back in haste to the Continent.

Norman rule was always unpopular in Maine, and it created
grave problems. As has already been explained, it had been
temporarily overthrown during the critical years which followed
the Norman conquest of England, and it had been reëstablished
only by force of arms in 1073. [66] But the restoration of Norman
domination in Maine was a serious check to the ambition of Fulk
le Réchin, count of Anjou, who seized every opportunity to cause
embarrassment to his Norman rival. Thus, in the autumn of
1076, [67] he assisted the beleaguered garrison at Dol and was at
least in part responsible for the Conqueror's discomfiture. [68] So,
too, he made repeated attacks upon John of La Flèche, one of the
most powerful supporters of the Norman interest in Maine. [69]
Though the chronology and the details of these events are exceedingly obscure, there is reason to believe that Fulk's movements
were in some way connected with the rebellion of Robert Curthose. [70] And while it is impossible to be dogmatic, it is perhaps
not a very hazardous conjecture that upon the outbreak of
Robert's rebellion, late in 1077, or in 1078, Fulk seized the opportunity of the king's embarrassment and preoccupation on the
eastern Norman frontier to launch an expedition against his
hated enemy, John of La Flèche. [71] But Fulk's hopes were sadly

[65] Davis, *Regesta*, nos. 135, 140; cf. *Hist. et Cart. S. Petri Gloucestriae*, i, no. 411,
a charter of 1078–83, perhaps of 1081.

[66] *Supra*, p. 14.

[67] On the date (September–October 1076) see Halphen, *Anjou*, p. 182; Prou,
Actes de Philippe Ier, nos. 83, 84; *Annales dites de Renaud*, in *Recueil d'annales
angevines et vendômoises*, ed. Louis Halphen (Paris, 1903), p. 88.

[68] *Ibid.* On the Norman siege of Dol in general see Fliche, *Philippe Ier*, pp. 271–
272.

[69] Ordericus, ii, p. 256.

[70] " Turbulentis tempestatibus, quas a Cenomannensibus et Normannis permo-
tas esse diximus, fomes (ut ferunt) et causa fuit Rodbertus regis filius." *Ibid.*,
p. 294; cf. p. 297.

[71] Halphen, relying upon the *Annales de Saint-Aubin*, has assigned Fulk's first
attack upon La Flèche to 1076, suggesting that Fulk launched it while the Con-

disappointed; for John of La Flèche learned of the impending stroke in time to obtain reënforcements from Normandy,[72] and Fulk was obliged to retire, severely wounded, from the siege.[73] It was probably after these events that a truce was concluded between King William and Count Fulk at an unidentified place called " castellum Vallium," [74] a truce which appears to have relieved the Conqueror from further difficulties in Maine until after his reconciliation with Robert Curthose. In 1081, however, taking advantage of the absence of the king and Robert in England, Fulk returned to the attack upon Maine; and this time his

queror was engaged in the north at the siege of Dol. *Anjou*, pp. 182–183. These conclusions, however, seem too dogmatic. There is no evidence which indicates a connection between the attack upon La Flèche and the king's Breton enterprise; and it seems hardly likely that Fulk would have entered upon an undertaking against La Flèche which proved beyond his powers, while he was also operating against the Conqueror in Brittany. Further, the date 1076 from the *Annales de Saint-Aubin* (Halphen, *Annales*, p. 5) is not to be relied upon: because (1) the numeral " mlxxvi " is entered twice in the MS., the entry concerning La Flèche being the second of the two, and no such repetition appears elsewhere in these annals. We are, therefore, forewarned of a scribal error. And (2) the probability of such an error is made stronger by the fact that MSS. C, A, and B all read " mlxxvii," while the *Annales de Saint-Florent* (*ibid.*, p. 119) read " mlxxviii." Having no other chronological data than are furnished by these meagre and uncertain annals, it is impossible to fix the date of the first attack upon La Flèche. It may have taken place in 1076, 1077, or 1078. On the whole, one of the later dates seems more probable than 1076, in view of the vague indications of some connection with Robert's rebellion (*supra*, n. 70), and in view of the fact that Fulk was involved in Breton affairs in 1076.

[72] Ordericus, ii, p. 256. Ordericus says that Fulk had the support of Hoël, duke of Brittany; but his narrative is confused — he apparently puts together the first and second sieges of La Flèche and treats them as one — and it is impossible to say whether Breton aid was given during Fulk's first or second expedition.

[73] " Blessé grièvement à la jambe, à la suite d'un accident de cheval, et quittant le siège de la Flèche pour se faire transporter par eau à Angers." Halphen, *Anjou*, p. 311, no. 233 — from an eighteenth century copy of an undated notice in the cartulary of Saint-Nicolas of Angers.

[74] " Eo tempore quo Willelmus rex Anglorum cum Fulcone Andegavensi comite iuxta castellum Vallium treviam accepit." *Cartulaire de Saint-Vincent*, no. 99. The document is undated, but it is witnessed by Abbot William of Saint-Vincent, who was appointed bishop of Durham 5 November 1080 and consecrated 3 January 1081. The ' trevia ' of this document, therefore, cannot refer to the treaty of La Bruère (1081) and it seems probable that it refers to a truce concluded after the failure of the first attack upon La Flèche.

efforts seem to have met with more success. Again laying siege to
La Flèche, he took it and burned it.[75]

It was apparently this reverse sustained by the Norman supporters in Maine which caused the king and Robert to hasten
back from England in 1081. Levying a great army — sixty
thousand, according to Ordericus![76] — they hastened towards
La Flèche to meet the victorious Angevins. But when the hostile
armies were drawn up facing each other and the battle was about
to begin,[77] an unnamed cardinal priest [78] and certain monks inter-
posed their friendly offices in the interest of peace. William of
Évreux and Roger of Montgomery ably seconded their efforts,
and after much negotiation terms were finally agreed upon in the
treaty of La Bruère or Blanchelande (1081). Fulk abandoned
his pretensions to direct rule in Maine and recognized the rights
of Robert Curthose. Robert, on the other hand, recognized the
Angevin overlordship of Maine and formally did homage to Fulk
for the fief. Further, a general amnesty was extended to the
baronage on both sides. John of La Flèche and other Angevin
nobles who had been fighting in the Norman interest were reconciled with Fulk, and the Manceaux who had supported the
Angevin cause were received back into the good graces of the
king.[79] Finally, there probably was an interchange of hostages
as an assurance of good faith. The so-called Annals of Renaud,

[75] "MLXXXI. . . . Fulcho Rechim castrum Fisse cepit et succendit." *Annales
de Saint-Aubin*, in Halphen, *Annales* p. 5. "MLXXXI. In hoc anno . . . comes
Andecavorum Fulcho iunior obsedit castrum quoddam quod Fissa Iohannis dicitur
atque cepit necnon succendit." *Annales dites de Renaud, ibid.*, p. 88. Ordericus
Vitalis does not admit that La Flèche was taken, doubtless because of the confusion
which he makes between the two sieges. Ordericus, ii, p. 256.

[76] On the exaggeration of numbers by mediaeval chroniclers, see J. H. Ramsay,
"Chroniclers' Estimates of Numbers and Official Records," in *E. H. R.*, xviii
(1903), pp. 625–629; and cf. the same, "The Strength of English Armies in the
Middle Ages," *ibid.*, xxix (1914), pp. 221–227.

[77] Ordericus (ii, pp. 256–257) has given a spirited account; but he manifestly
wrote without any clear conception of the geographical or topographical setting of
the proposed engagement, and all efforts to render his account intelligible have
proved in vain. For a discussion of the problems involved and of the conjectures
which have been made, see Halphen, *Anjou*, p. 184.

[78] Freeman conjectures that this is the "ubiquitous Hubert," cardinal legate
of Gregory VII. *Norman Conquest*, iv, p. 562.

[79] Ordericus, ii, pp. 257–258.

at any rate, assert that the king's half-brother and nephew, Robert of Mortain and his son, and many others were given as hostages to Fulk.[80]

With the conclusion of peace in 1081 the relations between the Conqueror and the count of Anjou with regard to Maine entered upon a happier era,[81] though difficulties between them were by no means at an end. The death of Arnold, bishop of Le Mans, for example, on 29 November 1081, gave rise to a long dispute as to the right of patronage over the see. Fulk strongly opposed Hoël, the Norman candidate, and it was not until 21 April 1085 that Hoël was finally consecrated by Archbishop William at Rouen and the Norman rights over the see of Le Mans definitely vindicated.[82] During this same period King William had also to contend with a very troublesome local insurrection among the Manceaux. Under the leadership of Hubert, *vicomte* of Maine, the rebels installed themselves in the impregnable fortress of Sainte-Suzanne and maintained themselves there for several years against all the king's efforts to dislodge them. At last, in 1085, or early in 1086, he practically acknowledged his defeat, and received Hubert, the leader of the rebels, back into his favor.[83]

If Robert Curthose played any active part in the dispute with Count Fulk as to the right of patronage over the see of Le Mans, or in the siege of Sainte-Suzanne, or, indeed, if he had any actual share in the government of Maine during this period, the record of it has not been preserved. Whatever intention the king may have had of taking his son into a closer coöperation in the management of his affairs was evidently short-lived, and he continued to keep the exercise of all authority directly in his own hands.

Such a policy, however, was fatal to the good understanding that had been established after the siege of Gerberoy, and inev-

---

[80] " Qui et ipse a Fulcone bello lacessitus, obsidibus pacis pro fide datis fratre suo, consule videlicet Mauritanie, et filio suo et multis aliis, recessit." Halphen, *Annales*, p. 88.

[81] " Haec nimirum pax, quae inter regem et praefatum comitem in loco, qui vulgo Blancalanda vel Brueria dicitur, facta est, omni vita regis ad profectum utriusque provinciae permansit." Ordericus, ii, p. 258.

[82] Halphen, *Anjou*, pp. 185–186; Latouche, *Maine*, p. 79.

[83] Halphen, *Anjou*, p. 186; Latouche, Maine, p. 39.

itably led to further difficulties. Indeed, it is altogether possible
that Robert was again in exile before the end of 1083. After the
peace of La Bruère he can be traced in a number of charters of
1082 and 1083. On 24 June 1082, he was at Oissel in Normandy.[84]
Once in the same year he was at Downton in England.[85] He was
certainly back in Normandy in association with the king and
queen and William Rufus as late as 18 July 1083.[86] And then
he disappears from view until after the Conqueror's death in
1087. Evidently another bitter quarrel had intervened and been
followed by a second banishment.

It seems impossible from the confused narrative of Ordericus
Vitalis and the meagre notices of other chroniclers to disentangle
the details of this new controversy. It is clear that the points at
issue had not changed materially since the earlier difficulties.[87]

[84] Davis, *Regesta*, nos. 145, 146; cf. nos. 149, 150, 158.   [85] *Ibid.*, no. 147.

[86] *Ibid.*, no. 182. He also attests with the king, queen, and William Rufus, in
1083, a charter in favor of Saint-Julien of Tours. *Chartes de S.-Julien de Tours*,
no. 37.

Davis cites a " confirmation by William I " in favor of the abbey of Lessay,
which is attested by Robert, along with King William, Bishop Odo of Bayeux,
Henry " the king's son," and others, and which he assigns to 1084, remarking,
" The appearance of Bishop Odo is strange, considering that he was at this time in
captivity." *Regesta*, no. 199. It cannot, of course, be supposed that the Conqueror really gave a confirmation in company with Odo of Bayeux while he was
holding the latter in close confinement as a most bitter and dangerous enemy; and
some other explanation of the apparent inconsistency must be found. A glance at
the document as printed in full in *Gallia Christiana* (xi, instr., cols. 228–229) makes
it clear that we have to do here not with a single diplòma of known date, but rather
with a list of notices of gifts. At the head of the list stands the record of a grant
by Roger d'Aubigny, dated 1084, and accompanied by a list of witnesses. Then
follow no less than six separate notices of grants, each with its own witnesses; and
finally come the attestations of King William, Bishop Odo, Henry the king's son,
Count Robert, and others. There is no reason to suppose that these attestations are
of the year 1084 — a date which applies certainly only to the first grant in the list —
and they are evidently of a later period, perhaps of the year 1091, when the abbey
of Lessay might naturally seek a confirmation from the three brothers after the
pacification which followed the siege of Mont-Saint-Michel. The king in question, therefore, is probably William Rufus rather than the Conqueror. The style
of Henry " filii regis " is certainly surprising, but it can be matched in another document, also probably of the year 1091. Davis, *Regesta*, no. 320; cf. The New
Palaeographical Society, *Facsimiles of Ancient Manuscripts*, etc. (London, 1903–),
1st series, pt. 2, plate 45a and text.

[87] *Interpolations de Robert de Torigny*, in William of Jumièges, pp. 265, 267–268;
William of Malmesbury, *G. R.*, ii, p. 332; Ordericus, iii, p. 268.

Robert, long since formally recognized as the Conqueror's heir and successor designate, to whom the baronage had repeatedly done homage, could not remain content with the wholly sub- ordinate position and with the limitations which the king imposed upon him. His youth, prospects, and affable manners, his generosity and unrestrained social propensities won him a numerous following among the younger nobility; and these am- bitious companions in turn spurred him on to make importunate demands upon his father for larger powers and enjoyments. The king, on the other hand, could not bring himself to make the desired concessions. It was no part of the Conqueror's nature to share his powers or prerogatives with anyone. Doubtless there was blame on both sides. Even Ordericus Vitalis hardly justifies the king. Robert, he says, refused to be obedient, and the king covered him with reproaches publicly.[88] And so the old contro- versy was renewed, and Robert again withdrew from Normandy. Knight errant that he was, he set out to seek his fortune in foreign parts — like Polynices the Theban in search of his Adrastus![89]

As to the period of these wanderings, we have no indication beyond the negative evidence of the charters, in which Robert does not appear after 1083. It may, perhaps, be conjectured that the death of the queen (2 November 1083), who had be- friended him during his earlier difficulties with his father, had removed the support which made possible his continued residence at the court.[90]

Robert's second exile was evidently longer than the first,[91] and less filled with active warfare on the frontiers of Normandy. It

[88] " Serenitas pacis diu quaesitae inter regem et filium eius celeriter obnubilata est. Protervus enim iuvenis patrem sequi, vel ei obedire dedignatus est. Animo- sus vero princeps ob ignaviam eius crebris eum redargutionibus et conviciis palam iniuriatus est. Unde denuo post aliquod tempus, paucis sodalibus fretus, a patre recessit, nec postea rediit; donec pater moriens Albericum comitem, ut ducatum Neustriae reciperet, in Galliam ad eum direxit." Ordericus, ii, p. 390.

[89] *Ibid.*, p. 380.

[90] Robert appears in no reliable charter between the queen's death and his own accession to the duchy.

[91] Because of the extended period during which he is not to be found in the charters, and because Ordericus (ii, p. 381) speaks of his being in exile " ferme quinque annis." Cf. *supra*, n. 12.

seems natural, therefore, to suppose that the distant wanderings and vicissitudes of which we hear, ' in Lorraine, Germany, Aquitaine, and Gascony,' [92] should be assigned to this period. Of more value, perhaps, than the vague indications of Ordericus Vitalis, and certainly of greater interest, if true, is the statement of William of Malmesbury that Robert made his way to Italy and sought the hand of the greatest heiress of the age, the famous Countess Matilda of Tuscany, desiring thus to gain support against his father. In this ambitious project, however, the courtly exile was doomed to disappointment, for Matilda rejected his proposal.[93]

Failing of his quest in Italy, Robert seems to have returned to France, and to the satisfaction of his desires among baser associates. Long banishment and vagabondage had brought on deterioration of character and led him into habits of loose living [94] from which the Conqueror was notably free. At some time during his long exile, he became the father of several illegitimate children. Ordericus Vitalis puts the story as baldly as possible, asserting that he became enamored of the handsome concubine of an aged priest somewhere on the borders of France and had two sons by her.[95] Both were destined to a tragic death before their father. One of them, Richard, fell a victim to the evil spell which lay upon the New Forest, being accidentally slain by an arrow while hunting there in the year 1100.[96] The other, William,

---

[92] Ordericus, ii, p. 381.

[93] " Robertus, patre adhuc vivente, Normanniam sibi negari aegre ferens, in Italiam obstinatus abiit, ut, filia Bonifacii marchionis sumpta, patri partibus illis adiutus adversaretur: sed, petitionis huiusce cassus, Philippum Francorum regem contra patriam excitavit." William of Malmesbury, *G. R.*, ii, p. 332.

[94] " Porro ille, quae ab amicis liberalibus ad subsidium sui accipiebat, histrionibus et parasitis ac meretricibus insipienter distribuebat; quibus improvide distractis, egestate gravi compressus mendicabat, et aes alienum ab externis foeneratoribus exul egenus quaeritabat." Ordericus, ii, p. 382. Ordericus reserves his worst criticisms for Robert's later life, but doubtless the moral decay set in early. Cf. *ibid.*, iv, pp. 105–106.

[95] *Ibid.*, iv, pp. 81–82. The author embellishes his account with a further tale of how the boys were brought up in obscurity by their mother, who in later years took them to Robert, then become duke, and proved their parentage by undergoing the ordeal of hot iron.

[96] Ordericus, iv, p. 82; Florence of Worcester, ii, p. 45; William of Malmesbury, *G. R.*, ii, p. 333.

after his father's final defeat at Tinchebray in 1106, went to Jerusalem and died fighting in the holy wars.[97] Robert also had an illegitimate daughter, who lived to become the wife of Helias of Saint-Saëns, most sturdy and loyal of all the supporters of Robert Curthose in the victorious days of Henry I.[98]

Whatever the field of Robert's obscure wanderings and whatever the vicissitudes through which he passed, he returned eventually to France, where he enjoyed the friendship and support of King Philip.[99] The king of France had momentarily fought upon the side of the Conqueror at Gerberoy in 1079; but such an alliance was unnatural and could not last. Hostility between the two kings was inevitable; and almost the last act of the Conqueror's life was a revival of the ancient feud and an attempt to take vengeance upon the hated overlord who had given asylum and succor to his rebellious son.[100]

The struggle this time raged over the debatable ground of the Vexin. In the late summer of 1087 King William assembled his forces and appeared suddenly before the gates of Mantes. The inhabitants and the garrison, scattered about the countryside, were taken completely by surprise; and as they fled in wild confusion back within the walls, the king and his men rushed in after them, plundered the town, and burned it to the ground.[101]

But from that day of vengeance and destruction the Conqueror returned to Rouen a dying man. There, lingering for some weeks

[97] Ordericus, ii, p. 82.

[98] *Ibid.*, iii, p. 320.

[99] *Ibid.*, ii, p. 390; iii, p. 228; William of Malmesbury, *G. R.*, ii, p. 338.

[100] It is clear that the war grew out of the inevitable antagonism between the interests of the two monarchs, and particularly out of the determination on King William's part to reassert the Norman claim to the Vexin. Ordericus, iii, pp. 222–225. As to the immediate provocation, Ordericus explains that the Conqueror's attack upon Mantes was in retaliation for predatory incursions which certain lawless inhabitants of the city had been making across the border into Normandy (*ibid.*, p. 222); William of Malmesbury attributes it to an insulting jest which Philip had made about William's obesity (*G. R.*, ii, p. 336); while Robert of Torigny ascribes it to the aid which Philip had been giving Robert Curthose against his father (*Interpolations de Robert de Torigny*, in William of Jumièges, p. 265).

[101] Ordericus, iii, pp. 222–226; William of Malmesbury, *G. R.*, ii, p. 336; *A.–S. C.*, a. 1086; Florence of Worcester, ii, p. 20; *Interpolations de Robert de Torigny*, in William of Jumièges, p. 265.

at the priory of Saint-Gervais outside the city, he made his final
earthly dispositions. Robert, his undutiful son, was still in
France and at war against him.[102] Whether from conviction of
his incompetence or from resentment at his treason, the king had
arrived at the unalterable decision that Robert, his firstborn,
should not succeed him in England. For that honor he recom-
mended William Rufus, his second son. Indeed, the dying king,
it seems, would gladly have disinherited his eldest son altogether.[103] But there were grave difficulties in the way of such a
course. Robert had been formally and repeatedly designated as
his heir and successor.[104] In the last awful moments of his earthly
existence the Conqueror recognized that he did not hold the English kingdom by hereditary right; he had received it through the
favor of God and victorious battle with Harold.[105] Robert, his
heir, therefore — so he is said to have reasoned — had no claim
upon England. But Normandy he had definitely conceded to him;
and Robert had received the homage of the baronage. The grant
thus made and ratified he could not annul.[106] Moreover, there
were men of weight and influence present at the royal bedside
to plead the exile's cause. Fearing lest their lord should die with
wrath in his heart against the son who had injured him so deeply,
the assembled prelates and barons, Archbishop William being
their spokesman, endeavored to turn the king's heart into the
way of forgiveness. At first he was bitter and seemed to be recounting to himself the manifold injuries that Robert had done

---

[102] William of Malmesbury, *G. R.*, ii, pp. 332, 338; Ordericus, iii, p. 228; cf.
Chronicon in *Liber de Hyda*, p. 298. Robert of Torigny is more specific: " Cum
igitur in Pontivo apud Abbatisvillam, cum sui similibus iuvenibus, filiis scilicet
satraparum Normanniae, qui ei, quasi suo domino futuro, specie tenus obsequeban-
tur, re autem vera novarum rerum cupiditate illecti, moraretur et ducatum Normanniae, maxime in margine, excursionibus et rapinis demoliretur." *Interpolations de Robert de Torigny*, in William of Jumièges, p. 268.

[103] This is the plain inference from Ordericus, iii, p. 242; William of Malmesbury, *G. R.*, ii, pp. 332, 337; *De Obitu Willelmi*, in William of Jumièges, pp. 146–147.

[104] That is, (1) before the Conquest (*supra*, p. 12), (2) after the Conquest on the
occasion of the king's illness at Bonneville (*supra*, p. 15), (3) at the reconciliation
after the siege of Gerberoy (*supra*, p. 29). Cf. also the charter of Stigand de Mézidon, 1063, in Le Prévost, *Eure*, i, p. 562.

[105] Ordericus, iii, pp. 239, 242–243.

[106] *Ibid.*, p. 242.

him; he had sinned against him grievously and brought down his gray hairs to the grave. But finally, yielding to persuasion and making the supreme effort of self-conquest, the king called on God and the assembled magnates to witness that he forgave Robert all his offences and renewed to him the grant of Normandy [107] and Maine.[108] A messenger was despatched to France to bear to Robert the tidings of paternal forgiveness and of his succession to the duchy.[109] And with these and other final dispositions, William the Conqueror ended his career upon earth (9 September 1087). His undutiful and rebellious son was not present at the royal bedside at the end,[110] nor later at the burial in the church of St. Stephen at Caen.[111]

[107] *De Obitu Willelmi*, in William of Jumièges, pp. 146–147.

[108] That Maine was included is clear from the fact that Robert's right to rule there was not questioned. Wace, too, is specific:

> E quant *Guilleme* trespassa,
> Al duc Robert le Mans laissa.

Roman de Rou, ed. Hugo Andresen (Heilbronn, 1877–79), ii, p. 416. The *Annales de Wintonia* are clearly wrong in stating that the Conqueror left Maine to Henry. *Annales Monastici*, ii, p. 35. .

[109] Ordericus, ii, p. 390: "pater moriens Albericum comitem, ut ducatum Neustriae reciperet, in Galliam ad eum direxit "; *Interpolations de Robert de Torigny*, in William of Jumièges, p. 268.

[110] William of Malmesbury, *G. R.*, ii, p. 338.

[111] *Interpolations de Robert de Torigny*, in William of Jumièges, p. 265.

CHAPTER III

INDEPENDENT RULE, 1087-95

WHILE William Rufus was hurrying to England to claim the royal crown, and the young Prince Henry was piously attending his father's funeral at Caen, Robert Curthose, hearing the news of the Conqueror's death, hastily returned from his long exile, and upon arriving at Rouen took possession of his inheritance without encountering any opposition.[1] At last the duchy of Normandy and the county of Maine, so long denied him by his imperious father, were within his grasp. No doubt the news of the king's death was very welcome to the incorrigible exile; yet it is pleasant to learn that Robert, upon entering into his inheritance, was not neglectful of filial duty toward his father's memory or of those charitable acts which were regarded as necessary for the weal of the departed soul. The Conqueror upon his deathbed had made provision for the distribution of his treasures [2] and for the release of prisoners from his gaols.[3] These dispositions the duke was careful to carry out, making bounteous distribution of such treasure as he found to monasteries and churches and to the poor; while two captives of royal descent — Wulf, son of King Harold, and Duncan, son of King Malcolm — he not only allowed to go their way in peace, but honored with the arms of knighthood.[4] Filial piety and the chivalrous impulses of Robert

---

[1] *Interpolations de Robert de Torigny*, in William of Jumièges, p. 268: " Cum igitur in Pontivo apud Abbatisvillam, cum sui similibus iuvenibus . . . moraretur . . . audito nuntio excessus patris, confestim veniens Rotomagum, ipsam civitatem et totum ducatum sine ulla contradictione suscepit "; *Chronicon*, in *Liber de Hyda*, p. 298; cf. Ordericus, ii, p. 374; iii, p. 256; *A.-S. C.*, a. 1086.

[2] " Omnesque thesauros suos ecclesiis et pauperibus Deique ministris distribui praecepit. Quantum vero singulis dari voluit, callide taxavit, et coram se describi a notariis imperavit." Ordericus, iii, p. 228.

[3] *Ibid.*, p. 245.

[4] " Rotbertus in Normanniam reversus, thesauros quos invenerat monasteriis, ecclesiis, pauperibus, pro anima patris sui, largiter divisit; et Ulfum, Haroldi quondam regis Anglorum filium, Duneschaldumque, regis Scottorum Malcolmi

Curthose were never more happily united. Some of the rare charters of the duke's early reign are also indicative of a similar spirit. Thus we find him confirming to Saint-Étienne of Caen a grant of the manor of Vains which the Conqueror had made during his last illness.[5] Perhaps not quite the same motive, though assuredly no spirit of rancor, led him on 7 July 1088 to restore to La Trinité of Fécamp the lands which his father had taken away in his wrath.[6]

The news of the Conqueror's death spread with incredible swiftness,[7] and the new duke can hardly have reached Rouen before a new era (*nimia rerum mutatio*) had dawned in Normandy.[8] The days of stern government, of enforced peace, of castles garrisoned and controlled by the duke had passed — at least until Normandy should again be brought under the heavy hand of an English king. Robert of Bellême was on his way to the royal bedside, and had got as far as Brionne, when the news of the king's death reached him. Instantly he wheeled his horse, and, galloping back to Alençon, he took the royal garrison by surprise, drove it out, and established his own retainers in the castle. Then, pressing on, he repeated this performance at Bellême and at other of his strongholds. He also turned upon his weaker neighbors, and either expelled their garrisons and installed his own troops in their stead, or razed their castles to the ground in order that none might stand against him. So, too, William of Évreux, William of Breteuil, Ralph of Conches, and other lords — most of them old friends and supporters of Robert Curthose in rebellious days — expelled the garrisons of King William from their fortresses and took them into their own hands.[9] Already the stage was set for the private warfare, the pillage, and the

filium, a custodia laxatos, et armis militaribus honoratos, abire permisit." Florence of Worcester, ii, p. 21.

  [5] " Donum de manerio de Vain quod idem pater meus in infirmitate qua defunctus est eidem ecclesie fecit." Haskins, p. 285, no. 1.

  [6] *Ibid.*, pp. 287–288, no. 4 *a*.

  [7] " Mors Guillelmi regis ipso eodem die, quo Rotomagi defunctus est, in urbe Roma et in Calabria quibusdam exheredatis nunciata est, ut ab ipsis postmodum veraciter in Normannia relatum est." Ordericus, iii, p. 249.

  [8] *Ibid.*, p. 261.

  [9] *Ibid.*, pp. 261–262.

harrying that were to reduce Normandy to the verge of chaos. The monk of Saint-Évroul, whose house was unfortunately located amid the very worst dens of iniquity, sends up a wail of lamentation. Robert was duke of Normandy and prince of the Manceaux in name, indeed; but so sunk was he in sloth and idleness that his government knew neither virtue nor justice.[10] But to these things it will be necessary to recur in another connection. It was, in any event, clear from the beginning that the barons were to enjoy a position of influence, independence, and power under the new régime such as had been denied them by the Conqueror.

For some four years before the death of the late king, Bishop Odo of Bayeux had been held a royal prisoner in the castle of Rouen. Very reluctantly had the Conqueror, as he lay upon his deathbed, been prevailed upon to release him.[11] But under the new duke the fortunes of the bishop again rose rapidly. Not only did he enjoy freedom, but all his former possessions and honors in Normandy were restored to him, and he took his place among the duke's chief counsellors.[12] Soon afterwards he crossed over to England, and was reëstablished in his former earldom of Kent.[13] And then, with vaulting ambition, he began to plot the overthrow of William Rufus and the reuniting of England and Normandy under the rule of Robert Curthose.

The position of Odo of Bayeux, with his broad holdings and honors on both sides of the Channel, was typical of that of many of the Anglo-Norman barons. They had been held by William the Conqueror under a tight rein, but at least they had had a single master. Now, however, the two realms were divided, and the service of two lords presented grave inconveniences. " If we do our duty to Robert, the duke of Normandy," they said, " we shall offend his brother William, and so lose our great revenues and high honors in England. On the other hand, if we keep our

---

[10] Ordericus, iii, p. 256; cf. pp. 262–263.

[11] *Ibid.*, pp. 245–248.

[12] " Postquam de carcere liber egressus est, totum in Normannia pristinum honorem adeptus est, et consiliarius ducis, videlicet nepotis sui, factus est." *Ibid.*, p. 263; William of Malmesbury, *G. R.*, ii, p. 360.

[13] *Ibid.*; cf. Florence of Worcester, ii, p. 21; Henry of Huntingdon, p. 211.

fealty to King William, Duke Robert will take from us our patrimonial estates in Normandy." [14]   Further, the accession of two young and inexperienced princes, after the stern rule and rigorous repression of the preceding reign, offered a peculiarly tempting opportunity for rebellion.   And aś between the two princes, there could be little doubt on which side the support of most of the barons would be thrown.   Robert was affable, mild, and pliable — for the turbulent nobles of the eleventh century such a ruler as they most desired.   William, on the other hand, was arrogant and terrible and likely to be a harsh, unbending master.   Moreover, Robert, as the eldest son, was deemed to have the better right.[15] William Rufus had gained the kingdom largely by virtue of his own decisive action and the support of Archbishop Lanfranc. Though publicly acknowledged, his tenure of the English crown was by no means unreservedly accepted by the baronage in England.[16]   Accordingly, late in 1087, or more probably early in the spring of 1088,[17] a conspiracy with wide ramifications was formed for his overthrow and for the transfer of the kingdom to Robert Curthose.   " In this year," says the Chronicler, " this land was much disturbed and filled with great treason, so that the most powerful Frenchmen that were in this land would betray their lord the king, and would have for king his brother Robert who was count of Normandy." [18]

The beginnings of this treasonable enterprise are obscure, and it is impossible to say with certainty on which side of the Channel the plot was hatched.[19]   Bishop Odo of Bayeux was unquestion-

---

[14] Ordericus, iii, pp. 268–269. The speech is doubtless imaginary, but the argument must surely be contemporary.

[15] *Ibid.*, p. 269; William of Malmesbury, *G. R.*, ii, p. 360.

[16] Cf. E. A. Freeman, *The Reign of William Rufus* (London, 1882), i, pp. 9 ff.

[17] Ordericus (iii, pp. 268–270) ṣpeaks as though the conspiracy was started late in 1087, but his account lacks convincing precision and definiteness; and the *Anglo-Saxon Chronicle* (*a.* 1087 for 1088) which is followed by Florence of Worcester (ii, p. 22), makes the positive statement that the plot was formed during Lent. Further, we know from Henry of Huntingdon (p. 211) that the bishop of Bayeux was present at the king's Christmas court in 1087.

[18] *A.-S. C.*, *a.* 1087.

[19] Ordericus Vitalis (iii, pp. 268–270) seems to indicate that it was begun in Normandy at some sort of a secret gathering of the barons; but the English writers

ably its prime mover, and of his activities we have some knowledge. Having risen to honor and power in Normandy, he had
crossed over to England before the end of 1087 and was in attendance at the king's Christmas court,[20] apparently in the full enjoyment of his English earldom.[21] But he may even then have
been contemplating treason. Certainly the inception of the great
conspiracy both in England and in Normandy can hardly have
been delayed long afterwards. During the early spring secret
negotiations were active, and frequent messages must have been
exchanged between England and the Continent.[22] One after
another the great nobles and prelates were won over. Even William of Saint-Calais, bishop of Durham, who had been raised by
William Rufus to the position of chief trust in the kingdom, was
widely believed to have joined the conspiracy.[23] Before the close
of Lent [24] the greater part of the Anglo-Norman baronage had
strengthened the defences of their castles and broken into open
revolt. The rebellion extended from the south coast to North-

convey the impression that it originated in England. Cf. William of Malmesbury,
G. R., ii, p. 360; Florence of Worcester, ii, p. 21; Henry of Huntingdon, p. 214. It
may, of course, have had a double origin.

[20] Henry of Huntingdon, p. 211.

[21] William of Malmesbury, *G. R.*, ii, p. 360; cf. Florence of Worcester, ii, p. 21;
Ordericus, iii, p. 270; Freeman, *William Rufus*, ii, pp. 466–467.

[22] William of Malmesbury *G. R.*, ii, p. 360.

[23] The early writers are sharply divided in their account of William of Saint-
Calais in connection with the rebellion of 1088. The southern English writers
believed him guilty of treason. *A.-S. C.*, a. 1087; Florence of Worcester, ii, pp. 21–
22; Henry of Huntingdon, p. 214; William of Malmesbury, *G. R.*, ii, p. 360. But
a contemporary narrative by a Durham writer, who was an eyewitness of the bishop's trial, represents him as the persecuted victim of malicious enemies who had
poisoned the king's mind against him. *De Iniusta Vexatione Willelmi Episcopi
Primi*, in Simeon of Durham, *Opera Omnia*, ed. Thomas Arnold (London, 1882–
85), i, pp. 170–195. And it should be remembered that his condemnation by the
curia regis was not for the treason with which he was charged, but for his refusal
to acknowledge the jurisdiction of the court. On the treatise *De Iniusta Vexatione*
see Appendix B.

[24] The *Anglo-Saxon Chronicle* (a. 1087) and Florence of Worcester (ii, p. 22) make
the positive statement that the revolt broke out after Easter (16 April); but we
know from a more reliable source that William Rufus took the first active measures
against the bishop of Durham on 12 March, and it is clear that the rebellion was
already under way at this time. *De Iniusta Vexatione*, in Simeon, *Opera*, i, p. 171;
cf. p. 189.

umberland and from East Anglia to the Welsh border.[25] But the centre and heart of the movement, so far, at any rate, as it concerns the life of Robert Curthose, lay in the southeast of England, where Bishop Odo and his immediate supporters had established themselves in strategic positions in the strongholds of Rochester [26] and Pevensey.[27]

Duke Robert's connection with the great rebellion of 1088 in its early stages is by no means clear. According to one of the later writers, upon learning that his brother had gone to England to claim the royal crown, Robert had sworn a great oath by the angels of God, declaring that though he were in distant Alexandria, the English would await his coming and make him king.[28] Actually, however, he seems to have reconciled himself to the accomplished fact,[29] and not to have contemplated an attack upon England until the barons, taking the initiative, informed him of their plan for the overthrow of William Rufus.[30] Upon hearing this good news, however, he promptly approved the project and promised the conspirators every possible aid and support.[31] As an earnest of his intention, he sent Eustace of Boulogne and Robert of Bellême with their retainers on in advance to England, where they were installed by Bishop Odo in the great fortress of Rochester. Meanwhile, he undertook to collect a fleet and to prepare for an invasion in force.[32]

[25] Florence of Worcester, ii, p. 21: "pars etenim nobiliorum Normannorum favebat regi Willelmo, sed minima; pars vero altera favebat Rotberto comiti Normannorum, et maxima "; *A.-S. C.*, a. 1087; Henry of Huntingdon, p. 214. In general on the rebellion of 1088 and all the problems connected with it see Freeman, *William Rufus*, i, pp. 22 ff.; ii, appendices b, c, d, e.

[26] Ordericus, iii, p. 272.

[27] Pevensey, of course, was fundamental because on the coast where Robert's fleet was expected to make land.

[28] " Per angelos Dei, si ego essem in Alexandria, expectarent me Angli, nec ante adventum meum regem sibi facere auderent. Ipse etiam Willelmus frater meus, quod eum presumpsisse dicitis, pro capite suo sine mea permissione minime attentaret." *Interpolations de Robert de Torigny*, in William of Jumièges, p. 268.

[29] " Haec primo dicebat, sed, postquam rei gestae ordinem rescivit, non minima discordia inter se et fratrem suum Willelmum emersit." *Ibid.*

[30] This is the plain inference from both the Norman and the English writers. E.g., Ordericus, iii, pp. 269–270; Florence of Worcester, ii, p. 22.

[31] Ordericus, iii, pp. 269–270.

[32] *A.-S. C.*, a. 1087; Florence of Worcester, ii, p. 22; Henry of Huntingdon

But the levy and equipment of an expedition for a second Norman conquest of England was an undertaking for which the resources of the duke were little able to provide. Careless, prodigal, incurably fond of good living, Robert was by nature impecunious. The unsettling transformation that had come over the duchy upon his accession was little likely to recruit his financial resources. The sudden increase in the power and independence of the nobility, the disturbed state of the country, the lavish grant of emoluments to all who asked, the charitable distribution of the Conqueror's treasure to religious houses, all these things inevitably depleted the ducal resources. And further, under the terms of the late king's will, 5000 livres had been paid out to make provision for Prince Henry.[33]

As compared with Robert, who had squandered his treasure in reckless extravagance, Prince Henry enjoyed a certain opulence. Pious attendance at the Conqueror's obsequies had not prevented his having his treasure weighed out to the last farthing, "in order that nothing should be lacking," and putting it in a place of security among friends upon whom he could rely.[34] Without land which he could call his own, and placed in a somewhat difficult position between the rival interests of his brothers, he had stood carefully upon his guard, frugally husbanding his resources, and holding himself in readiness to take sides with either of his brothers, or with neither, as his own interests should decide.[35] He was more drawn to Robert, however, because of his mildness and good nature,[36] and for a time he remained with him in Normandy.[37] To Henry, accordingly, Robert appealed in 1088 for

p. 215; cf. William of Malmesbury, *G. R.*, ii, pp. 362, 468; Ordericus, iii, pp. 272–273; Simeon, *H. R.*, p. 216; *Des miracles advenus en l'église de Fécamp*, ed. R. N. Sauvage, in Société de l'Histoire de Normandie, *Mélanges*, 2d series (Rouen, 1893), p. 29.

[33] Ordericus, iii, p. 244; *Interpolations de Robert de Torigny*, in William of Jumièges, pp. 268–269; *A.-S. C.*, a. 1086; cf. William of Malmesbury, *G. R.*, ii, pp. 468, 337, where it is said that the Conqueror bequeathed to Henry "maternas possessiones."

[34] Ordericus, iii, p. 244.

[35] William of Malmesbury, *G. R.*, ii, p. 468.   [36] *Ibid.*

[37] *Interpolations de Robert de Torigny*, in William of Jumièges, p. 268. His presence is further proved by his attestation of charters, e.g., 30 March 1088, charter

funds to be used in the invasion of England. But gifts without reward Henry would not give. Soon, however, fresh messengers from the duke brought the welcome news that Robert was willing to sell him a part of his lands; whereupon Henry became more pliable, and a bargain was soon struck. For 3000 livres the duke handed over to him the whole of the Cotentin, Avranches, and Mont-Saint-Michel, together with the great Norman lordship of Earl Hugh of Chester.[38] Thus Robert obtained a supply of ready cash to equip his forces for the invasion of England, though at the expense of alienating a part of his birthright. This was but the beginning of a policy of short-sighted expedients in lieu of effective government, which in the end was to prove fatal to his rule.

Meanwhile, the rebellion had taken a course which was disastrous for Robert's cause in England. William Rufus, finding that the greater part of the Anglo-Norman baronage had deserted him, turned for support to his native English subjects, and his appeal to them was not made in vain.[39] Gathering together such forces as he could, he marched straight upon Tunbridge and took the place by storm. Then he pushed on towards Rochester, expecting to find Odo of Bayeux and the main body of the rebel forces. But the bishop had learned of his coming and had slipped out of Rochester and gone to Pevensey, where he joined Robert of Mortain in the defence of the castle, while they awaited the arrival of Robert Curthose with the expedition from Normandy. But the king was informed of the bishop's movement, and, abandoning his proposed attack upon Rochester, he marched southward upon Pevensey and began a protracted siege of the castle.[40]

by Ralph Fitz Anseré in favor of Jumièges (Haskins, pp. 290–291, no. 6; also in *Chartes de l'abbaye de Jumièges*, ed. J.-J. Vernier, Paris, 1916, i, no. 37); 7 July 1088, charter by the duke in favor of the abbey of Fécamp (Haskins, pp. 287–289, no. 4 a); shortly after September 1087, charter by the duke in favor of Saint-Étienne of Caen (*ibid.*, p. 285, no. 1).

[38] Ordericus, iii, p. 267; Henry of Huntingdon, p. 211. Robert of Torigny raises a question as to whether Robert conveyed the Cotentin to Henry outright or whether he only pledged it to him as surety for a loan. *Interpolations de Robert de Torigny*, in William of Jumièges, p. 269.

[39] *A.–S. C.*, a. 1087; Florence of Worcester, ii, p. 23; Simeon, *H. R.*, p. 215; William of Malmesbury, *G. R.*, ii, pp. 361, 362; Ordericus, iii, pp. 273, 277–278.

[40] *A.–S. C.*, a. 1087; Florence of Worcester, ii, pp. 22, 23; William of Malmes-

Meanwhile, the long expected fleet from Normandy did not appear. One writer complains that the duke dallied away his time with amusements ill befitting a man.[41] Indeed, so widespread was the English rebellion that the kingdom appeared to be almost within his grasp, if only he had bestirred himself to seize it.[42] Yet with William Rufus loyally supported by an English army and pushing his campaign with the utmost vigor, everything depended upon the promptness with which the duke could land troops in England to support the rebels. It was doubtless the knowledge of this pressing need which induced Robert to send forward a part of his forces in advance, while he himself remained in Normandy to make more extended preparations.[43] But the vanguard of the ducal fleet met with a disaster which proved fatal to the whole insurrectionary movement. While William Rufus himself maintained a close investment of Pevensey, he had sent his ships to sea to ward off the threatened attack. And as the Norman fleet approached the English coast, the rival forces joined in battle, and the invaders were overwhelmingly defeated. To add to the catastrophe, a sudden calm cut off every possibility of escape to the Norman forces. According to contemporary writers the multitude that perished was beyond all reckoning.[44]

Disaster followed hard upon disaster. Bishop Odo, the count of Mortain, and the garrison of Pevensey were reduced by starvation and obliged to surrender after a six weeks' resistance.[45] The bishop gave himself up, and solemnly promised upon oath to procure the surrender of Rochester and then depart the kingdom forever. Upon this understanding the king, suspecting no ruse or

bury, *G. R.*, ii, p. 362; Henry of Huntingdon, pp. 214–215; Simeon, *H. R.*, pp. 215–216.

[41] " Tunc temporis ultra quam virum deceat in Normannia deliciabatur." *Interpolations de Robert de Torigny*, in William of Jumièges, p. 270.

[42] Florence of Worcester, ii, p. 22; Simeon, *H. R.*, p. 216; *Interpolations de Robert de Torigny*, in William of Jumièges, pp. 269–270.

[43] *A.-S. C.*, a. 1087; Florence of Worcester, ii, p. 23; Simeon, *H. R.*, p. 216; Henry of Huntingdon, p. 215.

[44] *A.-S. C.*, a. 1087; Simeon, *H. R.*, p. 216; Henry of Huntingdon, p. 215; William of Malmesbury, *G. R.*, ii, pp. 362–363.

[45] *A.-S. C.*, a. 1087; Simeon, *H. R.*, p. 216; Henry of Huntingdon, p. 215; William of Malmesbury, *G. R.*, ii, p. 362.

bad faith, sent him off with a small force to receive the submission of Rochester. But the great fortress, the chief stronghold of the rebels in southeastern England, was held by a strong garrison and able leaders whom the duke had sent from Normandy,[46] such warriors as Eustace of Boulogne and Robert of Bellême and two of his brothers, men of intrepid courage, who were unwilling to admit the hopelessness of their cause. And when Odo appeared before the castle with the royal troops and summoned them to surrender, they suddenly sallied forth, seized both the bishop and his captors, and carried the whole party within the walls.[47] Outwitted by this clever ruse, the king was again obliged to summon his English supporters [48] and lay siege to Rochester. But still no reënforcements arrived from Normandy, and again the royal arms enjoyed a triumph. The defenders of Rochester were obliged to surrender; [49] and the traitor bishop was now at last deprived of all his revenues and honors in England and driven over sea forever.[50] Doubtless other rebels were sent into exile with him.[51] But William Rufus with politic foresight tempered his animosity against many and admitted them to reconciliation.[52]

[46] *Supra*, p. 47.

[47] *A.-S. C.*, a. 1087; Simeon, *H. R.*, p. 216· William of Malmesbury, *G. R.*, ii, p. 362; Henry of Huntingdon, p. 215; *De Iniusta Vexatione*, in Simeon, *Opera*, i, p. 191. At the trial of William of Saint-Calais the king says: "Bene scias, episcope, quod nunquam transfretabis, donec castellum tuum habeam. Episcopus enim Baiocensis inde me castigavit . . . "

[48] *A.-S. C.*, a. 1087; William of Malmesbury, *G. R.*, ii, p. 362.

[49] *A.-S. C.*, a. 1087; Simeon, *H. R.*, p. 216; William of Malmesbury, *G. R.*, ii, p. 362; Henry of Huntingdon, p. 215. Ordericus Vitalis (iii, pp. 273-278) gives a highly embroidered account of the siege of Rochester and of its surrender, making it the outstanding event of the period — he knows nothing of the six weeks' siege of Pevensey — but Simeon of Durham says that Rochester surrendered " parvo peracto spatio."

[50] He returned to Normandy and to his see at Bayeux. Ordericus, iii, p. 278; *A.-S. C.*, a. 1087; William of Malmesbury, *G. R.*, ii, p. 362; Henry of Huntingdon, p. 215. According to Simeon of Durham (*H. R.*, p. 216) he was intrusted by Duke Robert with the administration of the duchy, but this is an error. See Appendix B, *infra*, pp. 214-215.

[51] *A.-S. C.*, a. 1087; Simeon, *H. R.*, p. 116.

[52] William of Malmesbury, *G. R.*, ii, p. 362: " Ceteri omnes in fidem recepti "; Ordericus, iii, pp. 279-280; cf. pp. 276, 291. We are without specific information as to the date of the surrender of Rochester. According to Ordericus (iii, p. 279), it took place " in initio aestatis." A charter by Duke Robert in favor of La Trinité

With the destruction of Duke Robert's fleet, the reduction of Pevensey and Rochester, and the expulsion of Odo of Bayeux from England, the force of the rebellion had been broken. Whatever plans the duke may have had to follow with a greater fleet were perforce abandoned. Through his own weakness and procrastination, coupled with the vigor and resourcefulness of William Rufus and the loyalty of the native English, the attempt to place Robert Curthose upon the throne of England, at one time so promising, had ended in utter failure.

But Robert's failure did not end the hostility between the two brothers. No peace negotiations intervened. William Rufus continued to nurse his indignation and to thirst for vengeance. He professed to fear some further mischief from the duke.[53] Robert, too, remained suspicious and apprehensive. Prince Henry, learning of the fall of Rochester, and eager to conciliate the victor, had hastened across the Channel to visit the king and crave from him " the lands of his mother " to which he laid claim.[54] The duke regarded this move with little favor; and when, soon after,[55] Henry had accomplished his mission and was returning to Normandy in company with Robert of Bellême, who had also been reconciled with William Rufus, the duke had him seized at the landing and placed in custody. Malicious enemies, we are told, had poisoned the duke's mind with the belief that Henry and

of Fécamp is dated 7 July 1088, " quando in Angliam transire debui." Haskins, p. 288.

[53] At the trial of Bishop William of Durham before the *curia regis* at Salisbury, 2 November 1088, the king refused to allow the bishop to depart from the kingdom unless he gave pledges " quod naves meas, quas sibi inveniam, non detinebit frater meus, vel aliquis suorum, ad dampnum meum." *De Iniusta Vexatione*, in Simeon, *Opera*, i, p. 190. Some color seems to be given to the king's fears by a statement in *Des miracles advenus en l'église de Fécamp*: " Adhibuit etiam mari custodes, quos illi *piratas* vocant, qui naves ab Anglia venientes caperent, captos si redderent, capturam suis usibus manciparent." Société de l'Histoire de Normandie, *Mélanges*, 2d series, p. 29.

[54] Ordericus, iii, p. 291. William of Malmesbury (G. R., ii, 468) is not in agreement, but the statement of Ordericus seems fully confirmed by the fact that Henry attested a charter by William Rufus in favor of the church of St. Andrew at Rochester: " This grant was made to repair the damage which the king did to the church of St. Andrew, when he obtained a victory over his enemies who had unjustly gathered against him in the city of Rochester." Davis, *Regesta*, no. 301.

[55] " In autumno," according to Ordericus, iii, p. 291.

Robert of Bellême had not only made their peace with the king, but had entered into a sworn agreement to his own hurt.[56] Henry was released from prison some six months later, at the solicitation of the Norman barons,[57] and the incident is not, perhaps, of great importance — for, if Henry and the king had arrived at any understanding, it must have been of short duration — yet it serves to illustrate the strained relations which continued to exist between Robert Curthose and William Rufus.

Meanwhile, the king, at last secure in his possession of the English throne, began to develop plans for taking vengeance upon the duke. If we can rely upon the unsupported statement of Ordericus Vitalis in such a matter, he held a formal assembly of his barons at Winchester, apparently in 1089,[58] and laid before them proposals for an attack upon Normandy. He harangued the assembled magnates upon the faithless conduct of his brother and upon the state of unchecked anarchy into which he had allowed his duchy to fall. The whole country, he declared, had become a prey to thieves and robbers, and the lamentations of the clergy had reached him from beyond the sea. It behooved him, therefore, as the son of his father, to send to Normandy for the succor of holy church, for the protection of widows and orphans, and for the just punishment of plunderers and assassins. Upon being asked their advice, the assembled nobles promptly approved the king's project.[59] Perhaps some of the quondam

---

[56] Ordericus, iii, pp. 291–292; cf. William of Malmesbury, *G. R.*, ii, p. 468; *Interpolations de Robert de Torigny*, in William of Jumièges, p. 269. According to Ordericus, Henry's place of confinement was Bayeux, under the custody of Bishop Odo; according to William of Malmesbury and Robert of Torigny it was Rouen.

[57] Ordericus, iii, p. 305; William of Malmesbury, *G. R.*, ii, p. 468. Ordericus Vitalis recounts the event as if it came just after the death of Abbot Durand of Troarn, 11 February 1088. Cf. Ordericus, iii, p. 303; R. N. Sauvage, *L' abbaye de Saint-Martin de Troarn* (Caen, 1911), p. 288. But Ordericus has already spoken of Henry's captivity as beginning "in autumno," 1088. *Supra*, n. 55. According to William of Malmesbury, he was released after a half-year's detention. If we could rely upon this statement, and couple it with the earlier statement of Ordericus that the imprisonment began in the autumn of 1088, we could assign Henry's release to the late winter or spring following (1089).

[58] *Infra*, n. 62.

[59] Ordericus, iii, p. 316. The English writers make no mention of the Winchester council. Ordericus indicates that appeals had been coming to William Rufus

rebels reasoned that, since the two realms could not be reunited under the weak and pliable Robert, it would still be worth their while to attempt to bring about the desired union under his more masterful brother.[60]

The king's plan evidently did not involve immediate open war upon Robert Curthose. It was not the way of William Rufus to attempt upon the field of battle that which might more expeditiously be accomplished through diplomacy. This was a form of attack which the impoverished duke was little qualified to combat. Choosing as the field of his activities the Norman lands lying north and east of the Seine, William Rufus began by winning over by bribery the garrison of Saint-Valery at the mouth of the Somme, thus gaining a strong castle and a commodious seaport in a position most advantageously located for the further prosecution of his design. It must have been at about the same time that Stephen of Aumale yielded to the same golden argument, and opened the gates of his stronghold to the soldiers of King William. From these convenient bases plundering raids were then carried into the surrounding country.[61] Soon the contagion spread farther. Gerard of Gournay placed his castles of Gournay, La Ferté-en-Bray, and Gaillefontaine at the disposal of the king, and actively devoted himself to the promotion of the English cause among his neighbors. His example was promptly followed by Robert of Eu and Walter Giffard, lord of Longueville, and by Ralph of Mortemer. In short, by an effective blending of bribery and diplomacy, William Rufus had succeeded in detaching the greater part of the Norman nobles dwelling upon the right bank of the Seine from their allegiance to the duke.[62]

from the Norman church: " Ecce lacrymabilem querimoniam sancta ecclesia de transmarinis partibus ad me dirigit, quia valde moesta quotidianis fletibus madescit, quod iusto defensore et patrono carens, inter malignantes quasi ovis inter lupos consistit." And in a later connection (iii, p. 421) he says specifically that Abbot Roger of Saint-Évroul sought aid from William Rufus.

[60] Freeman, *William Rufus*, i, pp. 225-226.

[61] *A.-S. C.*, a. 1090; Florence of Worcester, ii, p. 26; William of Malmesbury, *G. R.*, ii, p. 363; Ordericus, iii, p. 319.

[62] *Ibid.*, pp. 319-320; *De Controversia Guillelmi Rotomagensis Archiepiscopi*, in *H. F.*, xiv, p. 68, and in *Gallia Christiana*, xi, instr., col. 18. The work of corrupting the Norman baronage and winning them away from their allegiance to the duke

The single notable exception appears to have been Helias of Saint-Saëns, to whom Robert had given his illegitimate daughter, and with her the castles of Arques and Bures and their appurtenant lands as a marriage portion. Firmly establishing his son-in-law at Saint-Saëns, Arques, and Bures, the duke intended that he should stand as a counterpoise to the rapidly growing English influence east of the Seine.[63] And his expectations were not disappointed. Through every adversity, Helias of Saint-Saëns remained staunchly loyal to the cause of Robert Curthose and of his son, long after the final triumph of Henry I at Tinchebray.

Of other measures taken by the duke to combat the insidious aggression of his more resourceful rival, we have only the most fragmentary knowledge. From one of Robert's charters, it appears that he besieged and captured the castle of Eu in 1089.[64] This, it seems not improbable, was one of his early and successful efforts against the Norman traitors and their English ally. We know, too, that in his extreme need he appealed to his overlord, the king of France. Yet here again our information is discouragingly fragmentary. Of the relations between the duke and his overlord after the death of William the Conqueror we know nothing except that on 24 April 1089 Robert was at Vernon on the Seine frontier, engaged in some sort of hostile enterprise against France.[65] Certain it is, however, that before the close of

was accomplished in 1089-90. Freeman assumes the Winchester assembly above mentioned to have been the Easter Gemot of 1090. *William Rufus*, i, pp. 222, and n. 1. But Ordericus seems to assign it to 1089—he records the death of William of Warenne, 24 June 1089, immediately after it — and we know from the *De Controversia Guillelmi* that the struggle had already begun in Normandy in 1089, when Robert Curthose and King Philip besieged La Ferté-en-Bray. Further, the siege of Eu by Duke Robert in 1089 is probably to be connected in some way with the activities of William Rufus against him. Davis, *Regesta*, no. 310.

[63] Ordericus, iii, p. 320.

[64] Davis, *Regesta*, no. 310, a charter of confirmation by Duke Robert for Bishop Odo of Bayeux, dated 1089, " secundo anno principatus Roberti Guillelmi regis filii ac Normanniae comitis, dum idem Robertus esset ad obsidionem Auci ea die qua idem castrum sibi redditum est." This would necessarily be not later than September.

[65] *Ibid.*, no. 308, a confirmation by Duke Robert in favor of Bayeux cathedral, dated 24 April 1089, " dum esset idem Robertus comes apud Vernonem . . . iturus in expeditionem in Franciam."

this year he had sought and obtained the aid of King Philip against his Anglo-Norman enemies in the lands east of the Seine.[66] Together they laid siege to La Ferté-en-Bray,[67] the castle of Gerard of Gournay. But again the golden diplomacy of William Rufus proved more than a match for the vanishing resources of the duke. " No small quantity of money having been transmitted secretly to King Philip," he was readily induced to abandon the siege and return home.[68]

In 1090 difficulties continued to multiply around Duke Robert. In the city of Rouen itself William Rufus had contrived through bribery to gain a following, and had set himself to promote civic discord as a means of undermining the duke's authority.[69] In November 1090 a factional conflict broke out in Rouen between two parties of the burghers, the *Pilatenses* and *Calloenses*. Of the latter we know no more than that they were the supporters of the duke and that they were the weaker of the two factions.[70] The *Pilatenses* were ably led by a certain Conan, son of Gilbert Pilatus, described as the wealthiest citizen of Rouen. His great riches enabled him to maintain a large household of retainers in opposition to the duke and to draw into his faction the greater part of the citizens. As a further resource, Conan had covenanted with William Rufus to deliver up to him the city. An insurrection was planned to take place on 3 November; and at the appointed hour the king's hirelings were to come from Gournay and other neighboring fortresses to support the rising. Some of the king's ad-

---

[66] The *De Controversia Guillelmi* gives the specific date 1089. *H. F.*, xiv, p. 68. William of Malmesbury, though vague, is in agreement. *G. R.*, ii, p. 363. The *Anglo-Saxon Chronicle* (a. 1090) and Florence of Worcester (ii, p. 26) assign King Philip's intervention vaguely to 1090.

[67] We learn the name of the castle from the *De Controversia Guillelmi*, in *H. F.*, xiv, p. 68. The *Chronicle* (a. 1090) and Florence (ii, p. 26) both refer to it without name.

[68] Florence of Worcester, ii, p. 27; *A.-S. C.*, a. 1090; cf. William of Malmesbury, *G. R.*, ii, p. 363.

[69] Ordericus, iii, p. 351; William of Malmesbury, *G. R.*, ii, p. 469.

[70] The name is found in the record of a suit before the court of Henry I in 1111: " in urbe Rothomagensi gravis dissensio inter partes Pilatensium scilicet et Calloensium exorta est que multa civitatem strage vexavit et multos nobilium utriusque partis gladio prostravit." Haskins, pp. 91–92. Ordericus (iii, p. 252) indicates that the loyalists were clearly outnumbered by the rebels.

herents had already secretly been brought within the walls, ready to join the rebels at the appointed moment.[71]

The duke learned late of the events that were impending and had barely time to call up reënforcements. Hasty summonses were sent to William of Évreux, Robert of Bellême, William of Breteuil, and Gilbert of Laigle. More important still, Prince Henry was induced to forget past wrongs and come to the duke's assistance in this hour of need. These measures were taken barely in time to avert a disaster. Henry, apparently, was already within the city before the outbreak; but as Gilbert of Laigle with a troop of horse galloped across the bridge over the Seine and entered Rouen from the south, Reginald of Warenne with three hundred supporters of William Rufus was already battering at the western gate. Meanwhile, within the city the insurrection had broken out amid scenes of wild confusion. Robert and Henry issued from the citadel and began to attack the rebels upon front and rear. Robert was personally brave and a sturdy fighter, and on later occasions he proved himself an excellent leader in emergencies. But in the wild confusion and uncertainties of the Rouen insurrection, his friends became alarmed lest some serious mishap should befall him, and persuaded him to retire to a place of safety and not expose himself to such grave perils until the issue of the conflict should be decided. Accordingly, he withdrew by the eastern gate into the Faubourg Malpalu, and, there taking a boat across the Seine to Émendreville, he found shelter in the priory of Notre-Dame-du-Pré.[72] Meanwhile, within the city, Henry and Gilbert of Laigle and their supporters put down the insurrection with a great slaughter of the inhabitants. Conan and many other rebels were captured, and the hirelings of William Rufus were obliged to withdraw in confusion and seek the shelter of a neighboring wood, until under the cover of darkness they were able to make good their escape. With the triumph of his forces, the duke returned to the city, and, with his habitual mildness, was for throwing Conan into a dungeon and showing

---

[71] Ordericus, iii, pp. 351–353.

[72] This, at any rate, is the account given by Ordericus Vitalis, who seems, however, at this point to feel rather more than his usual rancor towards the duke.

clemency to the rest of the rebels. But his barons had other
views, and insisted upon taking a savage vengeance upon the
burghers who had been involved in the treason. William, son of
Ansger, one of the richest men in the city, was led away into
captivity by William of Breteuil and held for a ransom of 3000
livres. As for Conan, the archtraitor, Prince Henry craved leave
of the duke to dispose of him in his own way. Taking him up to
the upper story of the tower of Rouen, where a window commanded a view of the surrounding country, he called upon the
wretch to view the beauties of the landscape as it stretched away
across the Seine; and then, swearing by the soul of his mother
that a traitor should not be admitted to ransom, he thrust him
backwards through the window. The place, says Ordericus
Vitalis, is known as Conan's Leap " unto this day." [73]

The failure of William Rufus to overthrow the authority of
Robert Curthose in Rouen by stirring up an insurrection did not
put a check upon his ambitious projects elsewhere. In this same
month of November 1090 private war broke out between William of Évreux and Ralph of Conches. The latter appealed to
the duke for aid, but got no encouragement; whereupon he
turned to William Rufus, and found him altogether too alert to
let slip so good an opportunity of extending his influence. The
king promptly directed his Norman allies, Stephen of Aumale
and Gerard of Gournay, to send reinforcements to Conches.[74]
And so the English sphere of influence was extended to the
left bank of the Seine. But William Rufus was now preparing
for more direct action against the waning power of the duke.
By long and patient diplomacy, coupled with a liberal expenditure of English treasure, he had succeeded in undermining
his authority in a large portion of the duchy. At the close of
January, or early in February 1091 [75] he himself crossed to

---

[73] Ordericus, iii, pp. 352–357; William of Malmesbury, *G. R.*, ii, p. 469.

[74] Ordericus, iii, pp. 344–346.

[75] According to Ordericus (iii, pp. 365, 377) the crossing was made in the week
of 19–25 January 1091; the *Anglo-Saxon Chronicle* (a. 1091) dates it 2 February,
while Florence of Worcester (ii, p. 27) more vaguely says " mense Februario."
William Rufus dated a charter at Dover 27 January 1091, probably soon before
sailing for Normandy. Davis, *Regesta*, no. 315. The dating clause of this charter,

Normandy with a considerable fleet and established his head-quarters at Eu.[76]

The news of the king's landing came like a thunderclap to the duke, who at the moment was engaged with Robert of Bellême in the siege of Courcy. The siege was immediately abandoned, but the barons, instead of standing with their own ruler against the invader, departed each to his own castle; and presently " almost all the great lords of Normandy," began paying their court to William Rufus, who received them with great cordiality and gave them handsome presents. But the movement in support of the English king was not confined to the barons of Normandy alone. Adventurers from Brittany, France, and Flanders also gathered at Eu to swell the royal forces.[77] Again, as in 1089, Robert in his extreme need appealed to his overlord, the king of France. And again King Philip responded to his call; and together they marched against the invaders at Eu.[78] But apparently there was no serious fighting. Whether William Rufus again contrived to weaken the king's determination, as he had done on a similar occasion at La Ferté, with a fresh supply of English gold, we have no knowledge. In any case, a peace [79] was soon negotiated be-

" anno Dominicae incarnationis mill. xc, regni vero mei iiii, indictione xiii, vi kal. Feb., luna iii," is not consistent throughout; but the year of the reign and of the lunation both compel us to assign it to 1091. Moreover, Ralph, bishop of Chichester, and Herbert, bishop of Thetford, both of whom attest, were not raised to their sees till 1091. Cf. Freeman, *William Rufus*, ii, pp. 484-485. Ralph appears to have been consecrated 6 January 1091. Stubbs, *Registrum Sacrum Anglicanum*.

[76] Ordericus, iii, pp. 365-366, 377; *Interpolations de Robert de Torigny*, in William of Jumièges, p. 270; cf. *A.-S. C.*, a. 1091; Florence of Worcester, ii, p. 27; William of Malmesbury, *G. R.*, ii, p. 363.

[77] Ordericus, iii, pp. 365-366, 377.

[78] *Interpolations de Robert de Torigny*, in William of Jumièges, p. 270.

[79] According to Robert of Torigny (*loc. cit.*), " adminiculante Philippo rege Francorum." It is a plausible hypothesis that William of Saint-Calais, the exiled bishop of Durham, played a part in these peace negotiations. Upon his expulsion from England, between 27 November 1088 and 3 January 1089, he went to Normandy and was received by Duke Robert " rather as a father than as an exile " (Simeon, *H. D. E.*, p. 128) and had the administration of the duchy committed to his charge (*De Iniusta Vexatione*, in Simeon, *Opera*, i, p. 194); and he remained in Normandy and enjoyed a position of honor for three years. In 1089 he attested two of Duke Robert's charters (Davis, *Regesta*, nos. 308, 310), and he also attested with the duke a charter by Hugh Painel [1089-91] (Haskins, p. 69, no. 16). Then in the

tween the brothers, apparently at Rouen [80] during the month of February.[81]

The sources are not in complete accord as to the terms of this pacification; but they seem to be mutually supplementary rather than contradictory. Apparently William Rufus smoothed the way for the negotiations with *ingentia dona* [82] — it always seems to have been beyond the power of Robert Curthose to resist the temptation of such ephemeral advantages — but it was the duke who made the fatal concessions. He gave up the abbey of Fécamp,[83] the counties of Eu and Aumale,[84] and the lands of Gerard of Gournay and Ralph of Conches, together with their strongholds (*municipia*) and the strongholds of their vassals (*subjecti*) [85] — in a word, all the lands which the king had won from the duke and had occupied with his adherents on both banks of the Seine in eastern Normandy.[86]   Further, in the west the king was to have the important seaport of Cherbourg and the great abbey stronghold of Mont-Saint-Michel,[87] con-

third year of his expulsion, when the king's men were being besieged in a ' certain castle in Normandy ' and were on the point of being taken, he saved them from their peril, and by his counsel the siege was raised (Simeon, *H. D. E.*, p. 128.   Can this refer to the siege of Eu and to the pacification of February (?) 1091 ?) See Appendix B, *infra*, p. 215 and n. 14.

[80] Ordericus, iii, p. 366.   Robert of Torigny gives Caen as the meeting place. *Interpolations de Robert de Torigny*, in William of Jumièges, p. 270.   But may he not have confused the peace negotiations with the general inquest into ducal rights and customs which the brothers held at Caen on 18 July of the same year ?   For this inquest see Haskins, pp. 277–278.

[81] The date of the treaty is not given specifically, but according to Ordericus Vitalis (iii, p. 378) William and Robert, after they had made peace, besieged Henry at Mont-Saint-Michel for two weeks in the middle of Lent — according to Florence of Worcester (ii, p. 27), during the whole of Lent.   The treaty, therefore, could hardly have been concluded later than the end of February.

[82] Ordericus, iii, p. 366.

[83] *A.-S. C.*, a. 1091; Florence of Worcester, ii, p. 27; William of Malmesbury, *G. R.*, ii, p. 363; *Interpolations de Robert de Torigny*, in William of Jumièges, p. 270.

[84] Ordericus, iii, p. 366; *Interpolations de Robert de Torigny*, in William of Jumièges, p. 270; *A.-S. C.*, a. 1091; Florence of Worcester, ii, p. 27.

[85] Ordericus, iii, p. 366.

[86] Specific mention of all the lordships which we know to have been won over by the king is not made in our accounts of the treaty, but they are all covered by general statements. Henry of Huntingdon, pp. 215–216; and the references given in nn. 83, 84, *supra*.

[87] Florence of Worcester, ii, p. 27; *A.-S. C.*, a. 1091.

cessions which looked ominous for Henry, count of the Cotentin. On his side, William Rufus pledged himself to help Robert recover the county of Maine,[88] then in revolt against Norman rule, and all Norman lands which the Conqueror had ever held and whose lords were then resisting the duke's authority, except, of course, the lands just noted which by the terms of the present treaty were ceded to the king.[89] For the benefit of the barons on both sides who had treasonably supported the king or the duke in their recent quarrels, a general amnesty was added. The Norman barons whose defection had brought about the duke's downfall and whose allegiance was now being transferred to the king, were to occupy their Norman fiefs in peace and to be held guiltless. And all the nobles who had been deprived of their English lands for supporting the duke were now to receive them back.[90] Further, an attempt was made to forestall a possible succession controversy by providing that if either of the brothers should die without a son born in lawful wedlock, the survivor should become sole heir of all his dominions.[91] And finally, in order to give the treaty the most solemn and binding character, it was formally confirmed by the oaths of twelve great barons on behalf of the king and of an equal number on behalf of the duke.[92]

It may, perhaps, be doubted whether William Rufus seriously intended to exert himself to carry out the provisions of this treaty, except in so far as his own interests dictated; although William of Malmesbury affirms that the king and the duke in pursuance of their agreement immediately took in hand the preparation of an expedition against Maine, and were only turned back from it by

[88] *A.-S. C.*, a. 1091; Florence of Worcester, ii, p. 27; William of Malmesbury, *G. R.*, ii, p. 363.

[89] *A.-S. C.*, a. 1091; Florence of Worcester, ii, p. 27; Henry of Huntingdon, pp. 215–216.

[90] *A.-S. C.*, a. 1091; Florence of Worcester, ii, p. 27. Florence and the *Chronicle* both add here a puzzling provision which seems to indicate that the king undertook to compensate Robert for his losses in Normandy with lands in England: " et tantum terrae in Anglia quantum conventionis inter eos fuerat comiti daret."

[91] *A.-S. C.*, a. 1091; Florence of Worcester, ii, p. 27; Henry of Huntingdon, p. 216.

[92] *A.-S. C.*, a. 1091; Florence of Worcester, ii, p. 27; William of Malmesbury, *G. R.*, ii, p. 363; Henry of Huntingdon, p. 216.

the disconcerting action of their younger brother, Prince Henry.[93]
The details of Henry's movements after the death of the Conqueror are obscure and uncertain, though the main lines of his
policy and conduct seem clear enough. His relations had not been
uniformly harmonious with either of his brothers. As has already
been pointed out, his early friendship with the duke and his
acquisition of the Cotentin had been followed by a period of
imprisonment.[94] Apparently, too, Duke Robert, after he had
squandered the money which he had obtained from Henry in
exchange for the Cotentin, had endeavored to dispossess the
young prince of the lands he had granted him, and had only been
prevented from so doing by a show of force.[95] It was only a temporary reconciliation which had gained for the duke the important services of Henry during the insurrection at Rouen in
November 1090. Fresh misunderstandings soon followed, and
Henry was again obliged to retire to his lands in the Cotentin,[96]
where he gained the warm friendship of his father's old vassals,
Hugh of Avranches and Richard de Redvers, and devoted himself
with energy to the strengthening of his castles at Avranches,
Cherbourg, Coutances, and Gavray.[97] With William Rufus, too,
he had a quarrel of long standing. The early hopes raised by his
visit to the king after the fall of Rochester in 1088 [98] had not been
fulfilled. The English lands of Matilda to which he laid claim had
been granted to Robert Fitz Hamon, and he had been able to
obtain no redress.[99] It was even said that he had assisted the
duke at Rouen out of a desire for vengeance upon the king.[100]
Finally, the treaty of peace which William and Robert had

---

[93] *G. R.*, ii, pp. 363–364; *Annales de Wintonia*, in *Annales Monastici*, ii, p. 36.

[94] *Supra*, p. 52.

[95] Henry of Huntingdon, p. 211; *Interpolations de Robert de Torigny*, in William
of Jumièges, p. 269; William of Malmesbury, *G. R.*, ii, p. 468; cf. Ordericus, iii,
p. 350.

[96] William of Malmesbury, *G. R.*, ii, p. 468.

[97] " Comes Henricus pedagium accepit de Chetelhulmo et de omni Constantino
et super hoc facit operari homines Sanctę Trinitatis de eadem villa et patria ad
castella suorum hominum." Cartulary of La Trinité of Caen, extract, in Haskins,
p. 63.

[98] Ordericus, iii, pp. 350–351, 378.

[99] *Ibid.*, p. 350; cf. pp. 318, 378; cf. also William of Malmesbury, *G. R.*, ii, p. 468.

[100] *Ibid.*

recently concluded was manifestly aimed directly against him. They had planned between themselves for an exclusive partition of all the Conqueror's dominions, and for a recovery of ducal authority at all points where it was being defied. That obviously meant, among other places, in the Cotentin; and the clauses ceding Mont-Saint-Michel and Cherbourg to William Rufus were not likely to remain a dead letter. Henry realized the menace and protested vigorously against the injustice of a plan to deprive him of all share in the dominions of his glorious father.[101] He collected troops wherever he could find them in Brittany or Normandy, reënforced the defences of Coutances and Avranches with feverish energy, and prepared for war.[102]

Whatever the original destination of the expedition which the duke and the king had prepared, they suddenly turned it against their obstreperous brother who was presuming to resist them, and soon drove him to the last extremity.[103] Henry's resistance was a forlorn hope from the beginning. Hugh of Avranches and other nobles who had previously been his enthusiastic supporters against the duke, but who had important holdings across the Channel, now prudently reflected that it would be unwise to incur the wrath of William Rufus, and in view of the meagreness of Henry's resources they discreetly surrendered their strongholds.[104] Thus deserted and overwhelmed on every side, Henry was driven from the mainland; but by favor of some of the monks [105] he gained entrance to the monastery of Mont-Saint-Michel, and there in the famous abbey fortress he determined to make a last stand.

For two weeks, about the middle of Lent,[106] William Rufus and

[101] Ordericus, iii, p. 378; William of Malmesbury, *G. R.*, ii, p. 363-364; Florence of Worcester, ii, p. 27; *Interpolations de Robert de Torigny*, in William of Jumièges, p. 270.

[102] Ordericus, iii, p. 378.

[103] William of Malmesbury, *G. R.*, ii, p. 364; Ordericus, iii, p. 378; Florence of Worcester, ii, p. 27.

[104] Ordericus, iii, p. 378.

[105] Florence of Worcester, ii, p. 27.

[106] Ordericus, iii, p. 378. Lent in 1091 extended from 26 February to 13 April. According to Florence of Worcester (ii, p. 27) the siege continued through the whole of Lent.

Robert Curthose besieged him.[107] Stretching their forces about
the bay of Mont-Saint-Michel from Genêts on the north past
Ardevon to the Couesnon on the south, they completely invested
the Mount upon the landward side, and, as Henry was without
naval resources, this constituted an effective blockade. The duke
had his headquarters at Genêts, while the king established himself
at Avranches.[108] The scene was enlivened from day to day by the
knightly joustings of the opposing forces upon the sandy beach.[109]
William Rufus himself was once engaged in these feats of arms to
his grave humiliation, being unhorsed by a simple knight.[110]
Meanwhile, the besieged garrison was rapidly being reduced to
desperate straits. Though the food supply was adequate, there
was great lack of water. Manifestly a close maintenance of the
blockade would quickly have forced a surrender. But Robert
Curthose had too chivalrous a heart to let his brother suffer from
thirst. He directed the guards to keep their watch a little carelessly in order that Henry's servants might occasionally pass
through the lines and fetch water.[111] Wace affirms that he even
sent Henry a tun of wine.[112] Such chivalrous and impractical
generosity was beyond the comprehension of William Rufus, who
upbraided the duke and came near disrupting their alliance and
withdrawing from the siege.[113] But Henry soon saw the hopelessness of his plight, and, " reflecting upon the changing fortunes

[107] Ordericus, iii, p. 378; *Interpolations de Robert de Torigny*, in William of
Jumièges, pp. 270–271; *Annales de Mont-Saint-Michel*, in *Chronique de Robert de
Torigni*, ed. Léopold Delisle (Rouen, 1872–73), ii, pp. 222, 232; William of Malmesbury, *G. R.*, ii, pp. 364, 469–470; Florence of Worcester, ii, p. 27; *Annales de Wintonia*, in *Annales Monastici*, ii, p. 36; Wace, *Roman de Rou*, ed. Andresen, ii, p. 409.

[108] *Ibid.* Freeman remarks, " We may trust the topography of the Jerseyman."
William Rufus, i, p. 286, n. 1.

[109] Wace, *Roman de Rou*, ii, p. 409; cf. Florence of Worcester, ii, p. 27.

[110] William of Malmesbury, *G. R.*, ii, p. 364; Wace, *Roman de Rou*, ii, p. 410.

[111] William of Malmesbury, *G. R.*, ii, p. 365; Wace, *Roman de Rou*, ii, p. 411.

[112] *Ibid.*

[113] William of Malmesbury, *G. R.*, ii, p. 365; Wace, *Roman de Rou*, ii, p. 412;
Interpolations de Robert de Torigny, in William of Jumièges, p. 271; cf. Florence of
Worcester, ii, p. 27. These sources do indeed indicate an abandonment of the
siege before its object was accomplished; but against them stands the very positive
statement of Ordericus Vitalis, which is confirmed by the Annals of Winchester
(*infra*, n. 114). Robert and William evidently did not enjoy a very complete
triumph. Still there seems no doubt of Henry's expulsion from the Cotentin.

of mortals, determined to save himself for better times." He offered to capitulate upon honorable terms, and William and Robert readily agreed to his proposals, and allowed him to march out with his garrison under arms.[114] Henry's subsequent fortunes are obscure. Ordericus Vitalis recounts some heroic details of his wanderings and vicissitudes in exile.[115] But it is clear that some definite reconciliation was arranged with his brothers before the end of summer, for early in August we find him crossing with them to England to join in an expedition against the king of Scotland.[116]

Meanwhile, having disposed of the factious opposition of the would-be count of the Cotentin, the allied brothers turned their attention to other problems within the duchy. Ordericus Vitalis affirms that for almost two years after the siege of Mont-Saint-Michel Normandy was free from wars,[117] though it must be confessed that his own more detailed record on other pages does not bear him out in this general assertion. The mere fact, however, that William Rufus had changed from an insidious enemy into an active ally, present in the duchy, was in itself a guarantee of more vigorous government. But more convincing evidence that William and Robert had determined upon a programme of greater rigor in the enforcement of ducal rights, and upon a systematic recovery of the ducal prerogatives which had been usurped by the baronage during the recent disorders, has been preserved in a unique document which records the Norman *Consuetudines et Iusticie* as they existed under William the Conqueror. On 18 July 1091, the allied brothers assembled the bishops and lay barons at Caen and held a formal inquest into the ducal rights and customs which had prevailed in their father's lifetime. The prohibition upon the building of adulterine castles, the ducal right to garrison private strongholds and take hostages of their

---

[114] Ordericus, iii, pp. 378–379; *Annales de Wintonia*, in *Annales Monastici*, ii, p. 36; *Interpolations de Robert de Torigny*, in William of Jumièges, p. 271.

[115] Ordericus, iii, p. 379.

[116] William of Malmesbury, *G. R.*, ii, p. 365. He attests a charter of confirmation by William Rufus for the bishop of Durham, evidently while on the Scottish expedition late in 1091. Davis, *Regesta*, no. 318.

[117] " Fereque duobus annis a bellis Normannia quievit." Ordericus, iii, p. 379.

holders, the limitations upon private warfare, all these things and much besides, which had been firm custom in the Conqueror's time, were now revived and carefully reduced to writing.[118] If these measures were not in exact pursuance of the provisions of the treaty of the previous spring, they certainly were in accord with its spirit. Manifestly a new régime was in contemplation.

Quite unexpectedly, however, these plans for a restoration of public order in Normandy were interrupted by the arrival of news from across the Channel which demanded the immediate presence of the king and his ally in England.[119] Serious disturbances had broken out on the Welsh border, and King Malcolm of Scotland had made a destructive raid into the north of England. The inquest at Caen had been held on 18 July. Early in August, or perhaps even before the end of July,[120] William and Robert, accompanied by Prince Henry,[121] departed for England. So unexpectedly had these changes of plan been made as to provoke general consternation.[122]

Of the king's campaign against the Welsh we know nothing save that he met with small success,[123] and there is no evidence that Duke Robert played any part in it. It was the Scotch expedition, coming after it, which claimed the interest of contemporary

[118] Haskins, pp. 277–284.

[119] William of Malmesbury, G. R., ii, p. 365; Ordericus, iii, pp. 381, 394; A.-S. C., a. 1091; Florence of Worcester, ii, p. 28; Henry of Huntingdon, p. 216.

[120] Florence of Worcester (ii, p. 28) gives the date of the crossing as " mense Augusto "; and Ordericus Vitalis (iii, pp. 366, 377) indicates that 1 August was the date. Roger du Sap was elected abbot of Saint-Évroul on 21 July. Apparently he went immediately to the duke to seek investiture and found that the latter had already departed. Ibid., p. 381. The Rotulus Primus Monasterii Sancti Ebrulfi dates the crossing of William and Robert in 1090. Ibid., v, p. 189. But this is evidently the error of a copyist.

[121] Supra, p. 65, and n. 116.

[122] " Ambo fratres de Neustria in Angliam ex insperato tranfretaverant, mirantibus cunctis." Ordericus, iii, p. 381.

[123] William of Malmesbury, G. R., ii, p. 365. Freeman rejects the testimony of William of Malmesbury regarding this Welsh campaign of 1091. William Rufus, ii, pp. 78–79. But I see no reason for so doing — especially since the statements coupled with it regarding Henry and the Scottish expedition are demonstrably accurate —; and how else explain the lateness of the Scottish campaign ? William of Malmesbury says specifically: " Statimque primo contra Walenses, post in Scottos expeditionem movens."

writers. Large preparations were made for a northern war both
by land and by sea.[124] But the fleet which was sent northward in
September was wrecked a few days before Michaelmas; [125] and the
land forces led by the king and the duke were evidently still later
in advancing. If we can trust our dating, they did not reach Durham till 14 November.[126] On that day the king formally reinstated William of Saint-Calais in the bishopric of Durham.[127]
Then pushing on northward into Lothian,[128] he found that Malcolm had come to meet him with a formidable army. The situation was strikingly like that of eleven years earlier when Robert
Curthose at the head of the Conqueror's forces had crossed the
Tweed to avenge King Malcolm's raid of 1079.[129] The hostile
armies stood facing each other, but again there was no battle.
And again, as formerly, it was Robert Curthose who procured a
peaceful renewal of the Scotch king's homage. Supported by
Edgar Atheling, scion of the old English royal line, who was then
with Malcolm's forces, he undertook negotiations.[130] Malcolm,
we are told, was not unmindful of his old friendship for the duke,
and even admitted that, at the Conqueror's bidding, he had done
homage to Robert as his eldest son and heir.[131] This obligation
he would fully recognize; but to William Rufus, he declared, he
owed nothing. This was shrewd diplomacy, but Robert, un-

[124] Ordericus, iii, p. 394; Florence of Worcester, ii, p. 28; A.-S. C., a. 1091.
[125] Ibid.
[126] See Appendix B, infra, pp. 215-216.
[127] De Iniusta Vexatione, in Simeon, Opera, i, p. 195. The bishop was believed
to have regained the king's favor through services which he rendered him in Normandy. Simeon, H. D. E., p. 128. In any case, under the amnesty provision of
the treaty between Robert Curthose and William Rufus he was entitled to a restoration of his estates and honors in England.
[128] A.-S. C., a. 1091; Florence of Worcester, ii, p. 28. For the reading 'Lothian,' instead of Leeds, see Freeman, William Rufus, ii, p. 541. Ordericus (iii, p.
394), in an obviously embroidered account, represents the two kings as facing one
another from opposite sides of the Firth of Forth. But the English writers say
specifically that Malcolm had advanced into Lothian to meet the English forces.
[129] Supra, p. 31.
[130] A.-S. C., a. 1091; Florence of Worcester, ii, p. 28; William of Malmesbury,
G. R., ii, p. 366; Ordericus, iii, pp. 394-395.
[131] We have no other record of this homage. Can it have taken place in 1080,
when Malcolm made his submission to Robert, who was then leading the Conqueror's army against him?

moved by it, tactfully explained that the times had changed; and after some further parley, Malcolm consented to an interview with the English king and to the conclusion of a peace [132] upon the basis of the old agreement which had bound him to the Conqueror. To William Rufus he renewed his homage and received from him a regrant of all his English lands. Florence of Worcester adds that the English king undertook to pay him an annual pension of twelve marks of gold.[133] It was never the way of William Rufus to hazard in battle what he could more surely gain through a politic expenditure of English treasure.

From the meeting with Malcolm in Lothian the allied brothers moved back southward into Wessex.[134] Robert remained in England almost until Christmas. He had rendered important services in the negotiations with Malcolm, and he might justly look to William Rufus for continued friendly coöperation under the terms of the treaty which they had concluded in Normandy the previous spring. But he now discovered that the king's friendship was " more feigned than real." [135] William Rufus was no longer minded to abide by the terms of their alliance — probably, that is, he was not willing again to cross the Channel with Robert and assist him in the work of reëstablishing his authority in the lands of Normandy and Maine which had fallen away from their obedience. Accordingly, the duke withdrew in dudgeon, and, taking ship from the Isle of Wight, returned to Normandy, 23 December 1091.[136]

During the four years of Robert's reign which we have so far passed in review, his attention had been in the main absorbed by his relations with William Rufus, first in an effort to overthrow him and obtain the English crown, then in a struggle to preserve

---

[132] Ordericus, iii, pp. 394–396.

[133] Florence of Worcester, ii, p. 28; *A.-S. C.*, a. 1091.

[134] Florence of Worcester, ii, p. 29; *A.-S. C.*, a. 1091. At some point on the homeward march the three brothers joined with a distinguished company of nobles and prelates in the attestation of a charter of the lately restored Bishop William of Durham. Davis, *Regesta*, no. 318; cf. Freeman, *William Rufus*, i, p. 305; ii, p. 535.

[135] Henry of Huntingdon, p. 216.

[136] *A.-S. C.*, a. 1091; Florence of Worcester, ii, p. 29.

his own duchy from English conquest, and finally in an effort to coöperate with his brother in a friendly alliance which, after drawing him away on distant enterprises, had proved a hollow mockery. During this same period other problems had pressed upon the duke, in the solution of which he had met with little better success. Indeed, the county of Maine had already slipped entirely from his grasp.

The historian of the bishops of Le Mans records that the death of William the Conqueror produced a ferment throughout the whole of Maine;[137] and there is some reason for believing that very early in his reign Robert Curthose had led a Norman army against the Manceaux and had suppressed an incipient rebellion.[138] In the absence of convincing evidence, however, it seems more probable that Maine was not disturbed during the first year of Robert's rule by more than local disorders, and that his first expedition into the county did not take place until the late summer of 1088. Upon the fall of Rochester and the failure of his attempted invasion of England, the duke — acting, it is said, upon the advice of Odo of Bayeux,[139] who had now returned to Normandy to pursue his restless ambition [140] — assembled an army and determined to march into Maine and assert his authority. Probably the expedition was intended primarily as a formal progress for receiving the homage of the lords of Maine, for the county was disturbed by no general revolt at that time. Robert's garrison still held the castle of Le Mans securely, and Bishop Hoël and the clergy and people of the city were loyal.[141] Placing

---

[137] " In illis namque diebus, Willelmus, Anglorum rex strenuus, mortuus est, eiusque morte tota Cenomannorum regio perturbata." *Actus Pontificum*, p. 385.

[138] *Interpolations de Robert de Torigny*, in William of Jumièges, p. 273: " Unde factum est, ut paulo post mortem ipsius regis idem dux Robertus, de quo nunc sermo est, in principio sui ducatus, iam tunc rebellionis contumaciam attentantes in ipsis suis finibus ducto exercitu Normannorum, eos compescuit "; Ordericus, iii, p. 327: " ipso [i.e., the Conqueror] mortuo statim de rebellione machinari coeperunt." The statement of the *Actus Pontificum* (*supra*, n. 137) is not convincing because the next sentence opens with the rebellion of 1090. Robert of Torigny shows himself poorly informed in these matters. The statement of Ordericus is vague, and his record elsewhere does not point to any serious disturbances till later in the reign.

[139] Ordericus, iii, pp. 293, 296. [140] *Ibid.*, pp. 289, 292. [141] *Ibid.*, p. 293.

Bishop Odo, William of Évreux, Ralph of Conches, and William of Breteuil at the head of his forces, the duke moved southward, apparently in August 1088, and, encountering no opposition, entered Le Mans, where he was received by the clergy and people with demonstrations of loyalty.[142]   The great barons, Geoffrey of Mayenne, Robert the Burgundian, and Helias, son of John of La Flèche, whatever their secret feelings, came forward promptly with offers of loyal service.[143]   Only Pain de Mondoubleau, collecting his retainers in the castle of Ballon, dared to offer resistance; and early in September [144] he was reduced to submission. Everywhere Robert's authority appeared to be firmly established; [145] and as he returned to Normandy to wage war against the rebellious house of Talvas, he was able to recruit his army from the Manceaux as well as from the Normans.[146]

Yet the following year there appear to have been fresh disturbances in Maine.   By this time Robert had his hands full with the hostile activity of William Rufus and with the growing defection of the Norman barons in the lands east of the Seine; and as he appealed to his overlord, King Philip, for aid in Normandy,[147] so he turned to his other overlord, Fulk le Réchin, for assistance against the Manceaux.[148]   If we could accept the hardly credible account of Ordericus Vitalis,[149] Fulk came to visit Robert in Normandy, where he found him convalescing after a serious illness,

[142] Ordericus, iii, p. 296. The fragment of a charter by Robert " Normannie princeps et Cenomannorum comes," granting the tithe of his customs and rents at Fresnay to Saint-Vincent of Le Mans, should probably be assigned to this visit. *Cartulaire de S.-Vincent*, no. 532.

[143] Ordericus, iii, p. 269.

[144] Osmond de *Gaprée* was killed at the siege on 1 September. Ordericus, iii, p. 297: Ordericus was probably well informed, since Osmond was buried at Saint-Évroul. This date makes it possible to say definitely that this expedition into Maine did not take place in 1087, for William the Conqueror did not die till 9 September of that year. It is not so clear that it did not take place after 1088; yet between this and the successful rebellion of 1090 there were the threatened disturbances which Fulk is said to have repressed for a year. Cf. Latouche, *Maine*, p. 40, n. 2.

[145] Ordericus, iii, pp. 296–297.

[146] *Ibid.*, iii, p. 297.

[147] *Supra*, p. 55.

[148] Ordericus, iii, p. 320.   [149] *Ibid.*, pp. 320–323.

and revealed to him his passion for Bertrada de Montfort, niece and ward of Robert's vassal, William of Évreux. If the duke would only gain for him the hand of the beautiful Bertrada, he, Fulk, would keep the Manceaux in obedience. Accordingly, so runs the account, Robert undertook the delicate negotiations for this famous amour. But William of Évreux was far from pliable, and not until the duke had made him enormous concessions [150] did he agree to the marriage of his ward to the notorious count of Anjou. But with such sacrifices the hand of Bertrada was won, and, true to his undertaking, Fulk prevented a revolt of the Manceaux for a year, " rather by prayers and promises than by force."

In the year 1090, Robert by this time having become still more deeply involved in his struggle with William Rufus, new and far more serious troubles broke out in Maine.[151] Helias of La Flèche, grandson of Herbert Éveille-Chien through his daughter Paula, set up a claim to the county, and in furtherance of his ambition seized the castle of Ballon, which Duke Robert had besieged and taken two years before. Within the city of Le Mans, however, the cause of Helias made little progress, thanks mainly to Bishop Hoël, who remained staunchly loyal to Robert Curthose and used his great influence to keep the citizens true to their allegiance.[152] But when Helias perceived that the bishop was the chief obstacle to his plan of throwing off the Norman yoke, he did not scruple to seize him and hold him in captivity at La Flèche amid circumstances of great indignity. He could hardly have made a greater mistake. So great was Hoël's popularity that the persecution provoked a remarkable popular demonstration in his favor. Within the city and the suburbs of Le Mans holy images and crosses were laid flat upon the ground, church doors were blockaded with brambles in sign of mourning, bells ceased to ring, and all the customary religious services and solemnities were

---

[150] He granted Bavent, Noyon-sur-Andelle, Gacé, and Gravençon to William of Évreux, and Pont-Saint-Pierre to William of Breteuil, his nephew. Ordericus, iii, pp. 321-322.

[151] Ordericus, iii, pp. 327-332; *Actus Pontificum*, pp. 385 ff.; *Interpolations de Robert de Torigny*, in William of Jumièges, pp. 272-273.

[152] *Actus Pontificum*, p. 385.

suspended.   Before such a demonstration Helias yielded and set the bishop free.[153]

Meanwhile, Geoffrey of Mayenne and other revolutionaries had brought from Italy a third claimant to the county of Maine in the person of Hugh of Este, another grandson of Herbert Éveille-Chien.[154]   And with his arrival, the rebellion made more rapid progress.   Helias of La Flèche, forgetful for the moment of his own claims, joined with Geoffrey of Mayenne and other prominent Manceaux in welcoming the new count.   Oaths of fealty to Robert Curthose weighed for nothing.[155]

But Bishop Hoël stood firmly against the revolution.   His loyalty could not be shaken.   Withdrawing from Le Mans, he hastened to Normandy and laid the whole state of affairs before the duke.   But Robert was " sunk in sloth and given over to the pursuit of pleasure," and showed himself little worthy of the bishop's loyalty and devotion.   The rebellion in Maine disturbed him little; and he showed no disposition to act with vigor for its suppression.   It was enough, he thought, if he could preserve his right of patronage over the bishopric.   He directed the bishop at all costs to avoid making any concessions to the rebels in the matter of patronage, and with no better satisfaction sent him away.[156]   Returning to Le Mans, Hoël found Hugh in possession of the city and occupying the episcopal palace.   Hugh opened negotiations and tried to persuade the bishop to receive the temporalities of his office as a grant from himself; but Hoël remained true to Duke Robert, and would make no concessions.   An agreement proved impossible.   Meanwhile Hugh had succeeded in stirring up a formidable faction against the bishop among the clergy.   Soon the disorders became so aggravated that Hoël was obliged to retire from his diocese and seek asylum in England, where he

[153] Ordericus, iii, pp. 328–329; *Actus Pontificum*, pp. 385–386.

[154] He was the son of Azzo II, marquis of Este, and Gersent, eldest daughter of Herbert Éveille-chien.

[155] *Actus Pontificum*, p. 386; Ordericus, iii, pp. 327–328.

[156] " Ipse autem Rotbertus, ultra modum inertie et voluptati deditus, nichil dignum ratione respondens, que Cenomannenses fecerant, pro eo quod inepto homini nimis honerosi viderentur, non multum sibi displicuisse monstravit." *Actus Pontificum*, p. 386.   This is a remarkable corroboration of Ordericus Vitalis in his view of Robert's character.

received a cordial welcome from William Rufus and remained for some four months.[157] But in the spring of the following year (1091) he returned to his diocese, and, after further controversy, was finally reconciled with Hugh and his enemies among the clergy, and welcomed back to Le Mans amid much ceremony and rejoicing (29–30 June).[158] Apparently he had at last come to regard Duke Robert and his rights with complete indifference.

[157] *Actus Pontificum*, pp. 387–390. Hoël's presence in England early in 1091 is proved by his attestation of two charters by William Rufus, at Dover (27 January) and at Hastings. Davis, *Regesta*, nos. 315, 319. It is not unlikely that Hoël returned to Normandy with the king, who was evidently about to sail at the time the Dover charter was issued.

[158] *Actus Pontificum*, pp. 391–392. He celebrated Easter (13 April) and Pentecost (1 June) at Solesmes; and arriving at La Couture 28 June, he observed the day of the Apostles on the 29th; and the ceremony in the cathedral church took place the day following. *Chartularium Insignis Ecclesiae Cenomanensis quod dicitur Liber Albus Capituli* (Le Mans, 1869), no. 178; cf. *Cartulaire de S.-Vincent*, no. 117. The year in which these events occurred requires some further discussion. Latouche, though admitting with Ordericus Vitalis (iii, p. 327) that the revolt began in 1090, still believes that Hugh did not arrive in Maine until after Easter 1091, that Hoël was in England from November to March 1091–92, and that his return and reconciliation with Hugh took place at the end of June 1092. *Maine*, pp. 41–44. Latouche bases his chronological deductions upon a charter by Hugh in favor of Marmoutier, given at Tours, according to Latouche, on 13 April 1091. Bibliothèque Nationale MSS., Collection Baluze, 76, fol. 14. Since Hugh does not bear the title of count in this document, Latouche argues that he had not yet arrived in Maine, and, therefore, that the subsequent events of the revolution must be carried forward through 1091 into 1092. The dating clause of the charter in question, as kindly furnished me by M. Henri Omont, is as follows: " Factum hoc m° anno et lxxxxi. ab incarnatione Domini, indictione xiiii. anno xxxiiii. Philippi regis, primo anno R. archiepiscopatus, secundi Aurelianensis. Aderbal scolae minister secundarius scriptsit." Granting that this is a document of the year 1091 — which is by no means likely, in view of the year of the reign and of Ralph, archbishop of Tours — there still appears to be no reason why Latouche should assign it to the Easter date (13 April); and upon other evidence it is clear that Hugh arrived in Maine at a much earlier period: (1) It is not clear from the *Actus Pontificum* (pp. 386–387), as Latouche supposes (p. 42, n. 6), that Hoël was already in Normandy upon Hugh's arrival in Maine, but quite the contrary. (2) Ordericus Vitalis (iii, pp. 328, 330) indicates that Hugh was induced to come to Maine because Robert Curthose and William Rufus were at war, and that a strong argument in favor of his return to Italy was the fact that they had recently made peace and were meditating an attack upon Maine. This we know to have been in the spring and summer of 1091, and not in 1092 after William Rufus had returned to England. (3) A charter by William Rufus proves the presence of Hoël in England 27 January 1091, and not

But by this time the popularity of Count Hugh had vanished among the Manceaux, who had found him to be " without wealth, sense, or valor." [159]   And when the soft Italian learned that Robert Curthose and William Rufus had composed their difficulties and, as allies, were planning the reëstablishment of Norman rule in Maine,[160] he had no stomach for remaining longer to cope with the difficulties that were gathering around him.   A few days after he had made peace with Bishop Hoël, he sold all his rights in Maine to Helias of La Flèche for 10,000 *sous manceaux*, and departed for Italy.[161]   Count Helias now quickly gained the recognition and support of Hoël and of Fulk le Réchin,[162] and became henceforth the sole opponent of Norman rights in Maine. Hard fighting was yet in store for him against William Rufus, and only in the time of Henry I was he to obtain universal recognition; but for the time being his trials were at an end.   The plans which William and Robert were maturing for a combined invasion of the county were, as has been seen,[163] suspended by their sudden departure for England in August 1091.   And when Robert returned to the Continent, he made, so far as is known, no effort to recover his authority in Maine.   Through weakness and inertia he had allowed a splendid territory, which the Conqueror had been at much pains to win, to slip from his hands without striking a blow.   Indeed, without any formal abrogation of his rights he seems to have dropped all pretension to ruling in Maine.   In four extant charters he bears the title of count or prince of the Man-

November–March 1091–92, as Latouche supposes.   Davis, *Regesta*, no. 315. (4) Finally, two charters in favor of Saint-Julien of Tours, dated 11 November 1091, prove that Helias was already at that time count of Maine with Hoël's approval, and incidentally show that Hoël was not then in England.   *Chartes de S.-Julien de Tours*, nos. 43, 44.

[159] Ordericus, iii, pp. 329–330; cf *Actus Pontificum*, p. 393.

[160] Ordericus, iii, p. 330.   This gives an important synchronism for dating.

[161] *Ibid.*, iii, pp. 331–332; *Actus Pontificum*, p. 393; *Cartulaire de S.-Vincent*, no. 117.

[162] Bishop Hoël and Count Helias join in confirming a charter by Alberic de la Milesse, 11 November 1091. *Chartes de S.-Julien de Tours*, nos. 43, 44.   Count Helias attests a confirmation by Fulk le Réchin, 27 July 1092. Halphen, *Anjou*, p. 320, no. 262.

[163] *Supra*, pp. 66–67.

ceaux.[164] But they all belong to the early period of his reign (1087–91), and, so far as their evidence goes, it is not clear that he used the title after 1089.

It was not only in his dealings with William Rufus and in his government of Maine that Robert's reign was one long record of weakness and failure. He showed himself equally incompetent to curb and control the feudal baronage within the duchy. We have already remarked the general expulsion of royal garrisons from baronial castles upon the death of the Conqueror.[165] It is not recorded that Robert made any protest against this, and his own reckless grants of castles to the barons aggravated a situation which had been dangerous from the first. He gave Ivry to William of Breteuil; and for recompense to Roger of Beaumont, who had previously had castle guard at Ivry, he gave Brionne, "a most powerful fortress in the very heart of his duchy." [166] To William of Breteuil, he also gave Pont-Saint-Pierre, and to William of Évreux, Bavent, Noyon, Gacé, and Gravençon, apparently for no better reason than to gratify Fulk le Réchin in the matter of Bertrada de Montfort and gain his friendly support in Maine.[167] When Robert had reduced Saint-Céneri by a successful siege, he immediately gave it away to Robert Géré,[168] upon whom he later had to make war to compel the destruction of an adulterine castle.[169] He established Gilbert of Laigle at Exmes,[170] and to Helias of Saint-Saëns he granted several strongholds on the east bank of the Seine.[171] The almost independent establishment of Prince Henry in the Cotentin and the Avranchin has been noted elsewhere. Some of these favored barons, it is true, remained faithful to their trusts; but such reckless prodigality meant ex-

---

[164] Davis, *Regesta*, nos. 308, 310, 324; Haskins, p. 285, no. 1.

[165] *Supra*, p. 43.

[166] Ordericus, iii, p. 263; *Interpolations de Robert de Torigny*, in William of Jumièges, p. 288.

[167] Ordericus, iii, pp. 321–322.

[168] *Ibid.*, pp. 297–298.

[169] Castle of Montaigu. *Ibid.*, p. 420.

[170] *Ibid.*, p. 333.

[171] Castles of Saint-Saëns, Arques, and Bures. *Ibid.*, p. 320. These grants to Helias proved to be a source of strength rather than of weakness.

haustion of resources, and too often it meant license for private
war, plunder of the unarmed populace, and an open defiance of
ducal authority.

Against rebellious barons, the duke could on occasion act with
great vigor. In 1088 he threw Robert of Bellême into prison,[172]
and accepted the challenge of Roger of Montgomery to a decisive
contest. He laid siege to the impregnable stronghold of Saint-
Céneri, and when he had reduced it by starvation, he blinded
Robert Quarrel, the castellan, and had other members of the garrison condemned to mutilation by judgment of his *curia*.[173] He
also imprisoned Robert of Meulan for factious opposition to the
grant of Ivry to William of Breteuil; and, in the sequel of this
controversy, between three in the afternoon and sunset, he took
Brionne by assault, a great fortress which it had taken the Conqueror three years to reduce with the aid of the king of France.[174]

But with all this fitful energy, the duke's love of ease and his
desire ' to sleep under a roof ' called him home too often in mid-
campaign.[175] He lacked the resolution to carry a difficult and
laborious enterprise through to the end. Seeking mere temporary
advantages, he was prone to adopt the easy but fatal expedient of
allying himself with the turbulent barons whose lawlessness it
should have been his first concern to curb. Upon the fall of
Saint-Céneri he seemed to be in mid-course of victory over the
notorious house of Talvas. The shocking punishment visited
upon the surrendered garrison had caused fear and consternation
to spread among the supporters of Roger of Montgomery. The
garrisons of Bellême and Alençon are said to have been ready to
surrender at the mere approach of the ducal forces. Yet to the
general amazement the war went no further. The duke suddenly

---

[172] Ordericus, iii, pp. 291–296.

[173] " Verum deficiente alimonia castrum captum est, et praefatus municeps iussu
irati ducis protinus oculis privatus est. Aliis quoque pluribus, qui contumaciter
ibidem restiterant principi Normanniae, debilitatio membrorum inflicta est ex
sententia curiae." *Ibid.*, p. 297. This is the only instance I have met with where
Robert might be charged with cruelty. The distinction between the blinding of
Robert Quarrel by the duke's command and the mutilation of others by sentence
of the *curia* is curious.

[174] *Ibid.*, pp. 337–342.

[175] See, e.g., Ordericus, iii, p. 299.

made peace with Roger and released Robert of Bellême from captivity.[176]

And the peace then made with the rebel was a lasting one. Not again, until after his return from the Crusade, did the duke fight against Robert of Bellême. Evidently he had decided that in his future difficulties it would be better to have the house of Talvas for him rather than against him. Not a check was placed hereafter by the duke upon this most notorious tyrant of the age. Robert of Bellême was " a subtle genius, crafty and deceitful." His ability challenged admiration. But his cruelty, avarice, and lawlessness knew no bounds. Plundering and oppressing all over whom he had power, he came to be regarded by contemporaries as the veritable incarnation of Satan.[177] He built a castle in a dominating position at Fourches, and forcibly transferred the inhabitants of Vignats thither. He also erected Château-Gontier in a strong position on the Orne, and thus placed his yoke upon the district of Le Houlme.[178] Against Geoffrey of Mortagne he waged a war for the possession of Domfront.[179] He did not hesitate to besiege Gilbert of Laigle, the duke's loyal vassal, at Exmes.[180] His intolerable violence drew down upon him a concerted attack by his neighbors in the Hiémois. But he was able to bring the duke to his aid and to besiege his enemies at Courcy, in January 1091.[181] Later he waged a successful war against Robert Géré of Saint-Céneri and a formidable combination of the lords of Maine. Again on this occasion he gained the assistance of the duke, and so compelled the destruction of a castle which Géré was attempting to fortify at Montaigu.[182] He was said to be the possessor of thirty-four strong castles, [183] and he was, perhaps, more powerful than the duke himself. Indeed, in his dealings with the duke the relation of lord and vassal seems at times almost to have been inverted, as when Robert Curthose acted as his ally in private warfare.

One might perhaps suppose that considerations of policy led the duke to adopt a conciliatory attitude towards Robert of Bel-

---

[176] Ordericus, iii, p. 299.
[177] *Ibid.*, pp. 299–300.
[178] *Ibid.*, p. 358.
[179] *Ibid.*, pp. 301–302.
[180] *Ibid.*, pp. 333–334.
[181] *Ibid.*, pp. 361–366.
[182] *Ibid.*, pp. 417–420.
[183] *Ibid.*, v, p. 4.

lême, his most powerful subject. But in his dealings with other barons Robert showed himself equally weak and vacillating. He made no effort to check the long and desperate war by which William of Breteuil was seeking to bring his rebellious vassal, Ascelin Goël, back to his allegiance.[184] Indeed, he sought rather to gain some temporary financial advantage from it. When Ascelin, in defiance of feudal right and honor, seized Ivry, the castle of his lord, Robert did not scruple to take it from him and to compél William of Breteuil to redeem it by a payment of 1500 livres.[185] And a little later he took the other side in the struggle, and, in exchange for ' large sums,' joined with Robert of Bellême, King Philip of France, and other hirelings whom William of Breteuil was gathering from every quarter, in the overthrow of Ascelin at the siege of Bréval.[186] When a bitter feud broke out between William of Évreux and Ralph of Conches, Robert sought to avoid becoming involved in the struggle. But his failure to respond to the appeal of the lord of Conches merely drove the latter into the arms of William Rufus.[187]

The expulsion of Prince Henry from the Cotentin and the Avranchin after the siege of Mont-Saint-Michel had been no lasting victory for the duke. In 1092 Henry suddenly reappeared in western Normandy in secure possession of the town and castle of Domfront. The inhabitants had revolted against the intolerable oppression of Robert of Bellême, and, recalling Henry from exile, had accepted him as their lord.[188] Secure in the possession of this impregnable stronghold, Henry set himself to recover the lands from which he had been expelled and to establish himself in an independent position in the southwest. He defied Robert of Bellême,[189] and made war upon the duke with much burning, pillage, and violence.[190] With the aid of Earl

---

[184] Ordericus, ii, p. 469; iii, pp. 332–333, 335–336, 412–416.

[185] *Ibid.*, iii, pp. 332–333, 412.

[186] *Ibid.*, pp. 415–416. Robert of Torigny calls this " quamdam rem dignam memoria." *Interpolations de Robert de Torigny*, in William of Jumièges, p. 290.

[187] Ordericus, iii, pp. 344–348; *supra*, p. 58.

[188] Ordericus, iii, pp. 384–385; *Interpolations de Robert de Torigny*, in William of Jumièges, p. 271; Wace, *Roman de Rou*, ii, p. 413.

[189] *Ibid.*, p. 414; Ordericus, iii, p. 418.

[190] " Ille vero contra Rodbertum, Normanniae comitem, viriliter arma sumpsit,

Hugh of Chester, to whom he gave the castle of Saint-James, and of Richard de Redvers, Roger de Mandeville, and others, he gradually won back the greater part of the Cotentin.[191]

The pages of Ordericus Vitalis are filled with lamentations over the evil times that had fallen upon the duchy. Through the indolence of a soft and careless duke all that the Conqueror had created by his vigor and ability was allowed to fall into decay and confusion. The whole province was in a state of dissolution. Bands of freebooters overran villages and country, and plundered the unarmed peasantry. The church's possessions were wrung from her by force. Monasteries were filled with desolation, and the monks and nuns were reduced to penury. Adulterine castles arose on every hand to become the dens of robbers who ravaged the countryside with fire and sword. A depopulated country remained for years afterwards a silent witness to the evil day.[192]

That the indignant outbursts of Ordericus Vitalis are not mere rhetoric, is amply proved by a more prosaic narrative of the nuns of La Trinité of Caen.[193] In the cartulary of their abbey they have tersely recorded the long list of their injuries and losses in men and revenues and lands and cattle. " After the death of King William," they say, " William, count of Évreux, took from Holy Trinity and from the abbess and the nuns seven arpents of vineyard and two horses and twenty sous of the coinage of Rouen and the salt pans at Écrammeville and twenty livres annually from Gacé and from Bavent. Richard, son of Herluin, took the two manors of Tassilly and Montbouin. William the chamberlain, son of Roger de Candos, took the tithe of Hainovilla. William Baivel took twenty oxen which he had seized at Auberville. Robert de Bonebos plundered the same manor . . .; " and so the complaint continues through a long list of some thirty offenders, among them such well known names as Richard de Courcy, William Bertran, and Robert Mowbray. Even Prince Henry takes his place in this remarkable catalogue of sinners. It is a

incendiis et rapinis expulsionis suae iniuriam vindicavit, multosque cepit et carceri mancipavit." Ordericus, iii, p. 385.

[191] *Interpolations de Robert de Torigny*, in William of Jumièges, pp. 271-272.

[192] Ordericus, iii, pp. 289, 303, 332, 357.

[193] Haskins, pp. 63-64.

little startling to learn that in his government of the Cotentin he
was not altogether worthy of the polite compliments which have
been paid him by the chroniclers. The nuns complain that he
" took toll (*pedagium*) from Quettehou and from all the Cotentin,
and forced the men of Holy Trinity in the said vill and county to
work upon the castles of his men." It is significant that in this
extraordinary entry in the Caen cartulary the record of violations
of right stands alone. We hear nothing of suits for the recovery
of the alienated lands and goods. The distressed nuns appear to
have been patiently preserving the record of their grievances
against the day when there should be a government and courts
to which they could appeal with some prospect of obtaining
redress.

Indeed, orderly government and the regular operation of courts
of law seem to have been suspended almost entirely during
Robert's reign. With the exception of a fragment of a charter of
donation in favor of Saint-Vincent of Le Mans,[194] no single record
of an administrative or judicial act by the duke for Maine has
been preserved. And for Normandy we have nothing but a few
scattered references to the *curia ducis* [195] and one imperfect record
of a suit before that court in 1093.[196] The study of Robert's
charters, which have now at last been collected and set in order,[197]
reveals a state of disorder and of irregularity hardly conceivable
so soon after the reign of the Conqueror. The duke had a chancellor and evidently some semblance of a centralized administration. Yet the chancery seems hardly ever to have performed the
most common functions of such an office, viz., the issuing of ducal
charters. Most of Robert's acts were drawn up locally and according to the prevailing forms of the religious houses in whose
favor they were issued. Evidence of any systematic taxation is
wholly lacking; and the extent to which Robert was neglectful
of ducal customs and rights of justice stands patently revealed by
the inquest of Caen, held when, for a moment, with the assistance

---

[194] *Cartulaire de S.-Vincent*, no. 532.

[195] Ordericus, iii, pp. 297, 303, 381; Milo Crispin, *Vita Willelmi Abbatis Beccensis Tertii*, in Migne, cl, col. 717.

[196] Round, *C. D. F.*, no. 1115; Davis, *Regesta*, no. 342; Haskins, p. 70, no. 36.

[197] Haskins, pp. 66–70.

of William Rufus, a more vigorous régime was in contemplation.[198] Rare occasions when the duke asserted himself to compel
the destruction of an adulterine castle [199] or the submission of a
refractory noble stand out as wholly exceptional in a reign of
weakness, indifference, and indecision.[200]

It was, of course, the clergy who suffered most from this reign
of lawlessness and who were at the same time able to make their
woes articulate. The lamentful narrative of Ordericus Vitalis
and the bare record of the nuns of Caen have already been
sufficiently dwelt upon. Yet it should in justice be noted that
Robert Curthose was not a wilful oppressor of the church. He
was no impious tyrant such as William Rufus or Ranulf Flambard. His offences against the clergy were rather the sins of
weakness than of malice. His sale of lay rights over the sees of
Coutances and Avranches to Prince Henry [201] when he was preparing for the invasion of England was doubtless dictated by the
sudden needs of the moment. So, too, in 1089 he granted the
manor of Gisors, a property of the church of St. Mary of Rouen,
to his overlord, King Philip, " non habens de proprio quod posset
dare." [202] On the other hand, the duke often acted in a perfectly
just and cordial coöperation with the clergy. There is every
indication of harmony in the relations between Robert and the
bishops and abbots at the synod held at Rouen in June 1091, for
the election of Serlo as bishop of Séez.[203] So, too, soon after, he
gave his willing assent to the election of Roger du Sap as abbot
of Saint-Évroul, and " committed to him by the pastoral staff the
care of the monastery in worldly affairs." [204] So, also, upon the
election of Anselm, abbot of Bec, as archbishop of Canterbury, he
gladly consented to his resignation of the abbey, [205] and afterwards entirely accommodated himself to Anselm's wishes with
regard to his successor at Bec. There is a note of real affection in

[198] *Supra*, p. 65.

[199] Ordericus, iii, p. 420; Charter by Duke Robert in favor of La Trinité of
Fécamp, in Haskins, p. 289, no. 4 *c*.

[200] For a full discussion of Robert's government, see Haskins, pp. 62–78.

[201] *Gallia Christiana*, xi, instr., col. 221.   [203] Ordericus, iii, p. 379.

[202] *H. F.*, xiv, p. 68.   [204] *Ibid.*, p. 381.

[205] Eadmer, *Historia Novorum in Anglia*, ed. Martin Rule (London, 1884), p. 37;
Epistolae Anselmi, bk. iii, no. 10, in Migne, clix, col. 31.

the words with which Anselm in a letter to the prior and monks of Bec refers to Robert on this occasion: " By the grace of God, our lord the prince of the Normans has sent me a most kindly letter asking pardon if his love of me and his sorrow at my loss have caused him to think or say of me anything unseemly because of my election to the archiepiscopate. In the same letter he has graciously sought my counsel concerning the appointment of an abbot for you, and has promised to accept it gladly not only in this matter but in other things as well." [206]

Of the duke's relations with the papacy in this period we know almost nothing, except that his attitude, on the whole, was one of obedience and accommodation. The violence which Robert had done to the property of St. Mary of Rouen in granting the manor of Gisors to King Philip caused Archbishop William to lay the whole province under an interdict. This, in turn, brought on a controversy between the archbishop and the abbey of Fécamp, and in the sequel the Pope suspended the metropolitan from the use of his pallium for having exceeded his authority. At this point the duke intervened, and at the expense of acknowledging himself subject to the jurisdiction of the apostolic see, " saving only the privileges of his ancestors," he obtained for the archbishop at least a temporary restoration of his pallium, while further investigations were pending.[207] The church and clergy often suffered from Robert's weakness, or his sudden temptation to gain some temporary advantage, but rarely, if ever, from his ill will.

Inexcusable weakness and the steady disintegration of ducal authority, either through his own rash grants, or through the

[206] *Epistolae Anselmi*, bk. iii, no. 15, in Migne, clix, col. 39; cf. *ibid.*, nos. 8, 14; Milo Crispin, *Vita Willelmi Abbatis*, in Migne, cl, col. 717.

[207] *De Controversia Guillelmi*, in *H. F.*, xiv, pp. 68–69; Heinrich Böhmer, *Kirche und Staat in England und in der Normandie im xi. und xii. Jahrhundert* (Leipsic, 1899), p. 146. According to Böhmer, the suspension of Archbishop William took place towards the end of 1093. There is an unpublished tract by the ' Anonymous of York ' upon the exemption of the monastery of Fécamp in Corpus Christi College, Cambridge, MS. 415, pp. 264–265. Cf. Karl Hampe, in *Neues Archiv der Gesellschaft für ältere deutsche Geschichtskunde*, xxii (1897), pp. 669–672; Böhmer, *op. cit.*, pp. 177, 180.

usurpations of his turbulent subjects, or through the insidious aggressions of William Rufus, these are the outstanding features of Duke Robert's unfortunate reign.

Two days before Christmas, 1091, Robert had departed from England and returned to Normandy, feeling much vexed because the Red King would not abide by the terms of their alliance.[208] Yet an open breach between the brothers was long delayed. William Rufus had his hands full with domestic affairs in 1092 and 1093, and he had little opportunity either for advancing his own interests in Normandy or for aiding the duke against his enemies as he had agreed to do. Robert, on his part, so far as can be seen, did not fail in his obligations under the provisions of the treaty. In the reservation which he attached to a grant to the abbey of Bec in February 1092 he was careful to guard the rights of William Rufus as well as of himself.[209] The readiness with which he accommodated himself to the king's wishes in releasing Anselm, abbot of Bec, to become archbishop of Canterbury in 1093 is indicative of a similar spirit of coöperation. But it appears that he sought in vain the king's promised assistance in Normandy until his patience was exhausted; and when, finally, the rupture came between them, it was the duke who took the initiative in terminating an agreement from which he could no longer hope to derive any good. Towards the close of 1093, he addressed to William Rufus a formal defiance. " This year at Christmas," says the Chronicler, " King William held his court at Gloucester; and there came messengers to him out of Normandy, from his brother Robert, and they said that his brother renounced all peace and compact if the king would not perform all that they had stipulated in the treaty; moreover they called him perjured and faithless unless he would perform the conditions, or would go to the place where the treaty had been concluded and sworn to, and there clear himself." [210]

---

[208] *Supra*, p. 68.

[209] " This power he reserves for his brother, King William, as well as for himself." Davis, *Regesta*, no. 327.

[210] *A.-S. C.*, *a.* 1094; cf. Florence of Worcester, ii, p. 33, MS. C, in note; Henry of Huntingdon, p. 217.

In the spring of 1094, William Rufus took up this challenge and prepared for an invasion of Normandy. It is characteristic of the Red King that we hear more of the vast quantities of money which he gatheied in from all sides than of the men whom he brought together for the expedition. The barons were called upon to contribute heavily to the expenses of the campaign, and strong pressure was put upon them in order to insure that their offerings should not be too sparing. Archbishop Anselm thought to make a contribution of five hundred pounds of silver, but the king rejected his offer as being too small.[211] On 2 February the forces were assembled at Hastings for the crossing.[212] But the winds were contrary and the expedition was delayed for more than a month,[213] and it did not succeed in sailing till Midlent.[214]

After the landing in Normandy, active hostilities were still further delayed by negotiations. William and Robert met in a conference, but a reconciliation proved impossible between them. Then a more formal meeting was held at an unidentified place called *Campus Martius*, and the dispute was laid before the great nobles who had confirmed the earlier treaty with their oaths. Unanimously they gave their decision in favor of the duke and laid the whole responsibility for the present discord upon the king. But William Rufus, ' a fierce king,' would have none of their condemnation. He would not accept responsibility for the breach, neither would he abide by the terms of the treaty. The conference was accordingly broken off, and the brothers separated in wrath, the king going to his headquarters at Eu, the duke to Rouen.[215]

[211] Eadmer, p. 43.

[212] *A.-S. C.*, a. 1094; Florence of Worcester, ii, p. 33, MS. C, in note; cf. Eadmer, p. 47.

[213] *Ibid.*; cf. Davis, *Regesta*, nos. 347, 348.

[214] *A.-S. C.*, a. 1094; Florence of Worcester, ii, p. 33, MS. C, in note. In 1094 Lent extended from 22 February to 9 April. If by ' Midlent' an exact day is designated, it was probably Sunday, 19 March.

[215] *A.-S. C.*, a. 1094; Florence of Worcester, ii, p. 33, and MS. C, in note; Henry of Huntingdon, p. 217. Florence of Worcester is the sole authority for ' Campus Martius' and for the fact that after the conferences Robert went to Rouen and William Rufus to Eu. Henry of Huntingdon mentions only the final meeting. A phrase in a letter of Bishop Ivo of Chartres makes it not improbable that King Philip was present at this conference: " iturus vobiscum ad placitum

Then, or more likely even before this, William Rufus turned to that brand of diplomacy in which he was so eminently skilful and which had gained him such successes in his earlier Norman policy. With the treasure which he had brought from England, he began to collect great numbers of mercenaries; and also, by lavish expenditure of gold and silver, and by grants and promises of Norman lands, he succeeded in corrupting more of the Norman baronage and in winning them away from their allegiance to the duke. And as rapidly as he gained possession of their strongholds he filled them with garrisons upon whom he could rely.[216] But he was not content with mere diplomacy and bribery. He also took the field, and laying siege to Bures, a castle of Helias of Saint-Saëns, he reduced it, and took many of the duke's men captive.[217]

But meanwhile, Robert had not been idle, and the success of his operations suggests that he had not ventured to defy William Rufus without making greater preparations than have been recorded by the contemporary writers. As he had done previously when confronted with an English invasion, he brought in his overlord, King Philip, and a French army.[218] Philip and Robert appear to have opened their campaign in the south and west of Normandy with two remarkable victories. Philip invested Argentan,[219] and, on the very first day of the siege, Roger le Poitevin

quod futurum est inter regem Anglorum et comitem Normannorum." *H. F.*, xv, p. 82, no. 28; cf. Fliche, *Philippe Iᵉʳ*, p. 299. But the letter is undated, and proof is lacking that it refers to the conference of 1094. There is no basis for Fliche's assumption that the meeting between William and Robert took place at Pontoise or at Chaumont-en-Vexin. Ivo's letter contains no such evidence. The above mentioned places are named only as a rendezvous for Philip and Ivo preparatory to proceeding to the meeting between Robert and William.

[216] Florence of Worcester, ii, p. 34.

[217] *A.-S. C.*, *a.* 1094; Florence of Worcester, ii, p. 34; Henry of Huntingdon, p. 217.

[218] References as in n. 217, *supra*.

[219] Argentan is pretty clearly, though not certainly, the place designated. Florence of Worcester (ii, p. 34), who seems generally best informed on these events, has " Argentinum," about which there can be no question. The readings of the *Anglo-Saxon Chronicle* (*a.* 1094) and of Henry of Huntingdon (p. 217) are " castel aet Argentses " and " Argentes," which might refer to Argentan or Argences. Thomas Stapleton says that the place in question was Argentan. *Magni Rotuli Scaccarii Normaniae sub Regibus Angliae* (London, 1840-44), ii, p. xxx. I cannot discover that there was any castle at Argences in the eleventh century.

and an enormous garrison of seven hundred knights and fourteen hundred esquires surrendered without any blood being shed, and were held by the king to ransom. Soon after, the duke won a victory of almost equal importance by the reduction of Le Homme and the capture of William Peverel and a garrison of eight hundred knights.[220]

These reverses came as a staggering surprise to William Rufus. Immediately he sent off to England and ordered the assembling of a great army of English foot soldiers — some twenty thousand, it is said — for the invasion of Normandy. But when they came to Hastings for the crossing, Ranulf Flambard, at the king's order, took from each of them the ten shillings that he had brought for maintenance during the campaign; and then sent them back home, while he forwarded the money to William Rufus in Normandy.[221] The king had need of this fresh supply of English treasure. For by this time Philip and Robert, after their double victory in the south and west, were advancing on William's headquarters at Eu,[222] in the very heart of the district which he had controlled since 1089 or 1090. But at Longueville King Philip halted.[223] William Rufus had found a way to repeat the measure which had turned the French king back from La Ferté in 1089, if not from Eu in 1091. " There was the king of France turned back by craft, and all the expedition was afterwards dispersed." [224] Again the resources of Duke Robert had proved unequal to the greater stores of English treasure which the Red King was able to command.[225]

---

[220] Florence of Worcester, ii, pp. 34–35; *A.–S.C.*, a. 1094; Henry of Huntingdon, p. 217.

[221] *A.–S.C.*, a. 1094; Florence of Worcester, ii, p. 35; Henry of Huntingdon, p. 217.

[222] According to Henry of Huntingdon (p. 217), they actually besieged Eu.

[223] *A.–S.C.*, a. 1094.

[224] *Ibid.*, a. 1094; Henry of Huntingdon, p. 217.

[225] Fliche sets forth the extraordinary hypothesis that there was no war between William Rufus and Robert Curthose in 1094, though he admits the meeting between them and the unsuccessful attempt at a reconciliation. He bases his hypothesis upon the fact that Ordericus Vitalis makes no mention of the war of 1094, and that the account of the campaign of 1094 as set forth in the English sources bears certain resemblances to that of 1091. He argues that the English writers in their

Yet the strength of Robert's resistance was by no means broken. William Rufus sent to Domfront to call Prince Henry to his aid, and such was Robert's strength that it proved impossible for Henry to make his way by land to Eu. The king sent ships to fetch him.[226] But instead of proceeding to Eu, he crossed the Channel, and, landing at Southampton at the end of October, he went to London for Christmas, evidently with a view to meeting the king upon his return from the Continent.[227] Meanwhile, William Rufus remained in Normandy almost to the end of the year. But clearly he met with no great success in his projects. He had spent vast sums of money, yet little or nothing had come of it — so ran the contemporary judgment: " Infecto itaque negotio, in Angliam reversus est." [228] On 29 December he crossed from Wissant to Dover.[229]

The progress of the Norman war in 1095 is obscure in the extreme. The king's whole attention was absorbed by pressing affairs within the limits of his own realm; and he seems to have committed his continental interests almost wholly to Prince Henry. Henry remained in England until Lent, and then crossed over to Normandy ' with great treasure '; and during the months which followed, he waged war against Duke Robert.[230] But in what part of the duchy, or how, or with what success, we have no information.

confusion have assigned events to 1094 which really belong to 1091 — in brief, that there was only one campaign, that of 1091: " Et alors ne faudrait-il pas reporter toute la campagne racontée ici à l'année 1090–1091 ? " *Philippe I*, pp. 298–300. In point of fact there is far less duplication between the events of 1090–91 and 1094 than Fliche supposes, and such resemblances as exist are readily accounted for by the fact that William Rufus had his headquarters at Eu on both occasions and pursued the same general policy throughout his dealings with Robert Curthose and King Philip. It may be admitted as extraordinary that the events of 1094 have escaped the attention of Ordericus Vitalis; but to reject the highly circumstantial accounts of the English writers is to betray a strange lack of appreciation of the range and accuracy of their information.

[226] *A.-S. C.*, a. 1094.

[227] *Ibid.* According to Henry of Huntingdon (p. 218), the king's original order had been to proceed to London.

[228] Eadmer, p. 52.

[229] *A.-S. C.*, a. 1095; Florence of Worcester, ii, p. 35.

[230] *A.-S. C.*, a. 1095; Henry of Huntingdon, p. 218.

The close of the year 1095 saw Robert Curthose in a difficult situation, but the issue of the contest had not yet been decided. Meanwhile, the famous sermon of Pope Urban II before the council of Clermont had thrilled all Europe with a new impulse and turned the course of Robert's life into a new and unexpected channel.

CHAPTER IV

THE CRUSADE

THE year 1096 marks the beginning of a new era in the history of western civilization as well as in the life of Robert Curthose. On 27 November 1095,[1] Pope Urban II had preached his momentous sermon before the assembled multitude at Clermont, and ' the gates of the Latin world were opened '[2] upon the East. " It was the miracle of the Lord in our time," writes Henry of Huntingdon, " and a thing before unheard of in all the ages, that such divers peoples and so many distinguished princes, leaving their splendid possessions, their wives, and their children, set forth with one accord and in scorn of death to seek the most unknown regions." [3]

It was natural that the stirring words of Pope Urban should find a ready hearing among the ' untamed race of the Normans.' [4] The great adventurers of their age, they were destined to play the most vigorous and aggressive, if not the most devout and single-minded, part in the supreme adventure of the Latin world in the Middle Ages. Moreover, the situation of Duke Robert at home was such that new fields of opportunity and adventure offered peculiar attractions to him. Lacking the indomitable energy of his great forbears and the Norman genius for organization, government, and law, surrounded by enemies both within and without his dominions, his tenure of the duchy had become a heavy burden. His war with William Rufus still dragged on. Disloyal barons continued to desert to the English cause; and twenty Norman castles were said to be in the Red King's hands. Prince Henry, long firmly established at Domfront, and now backed by the strong arm and the long purse of his older brother, had gained control of ' a great part of Normandy '; and the ' soft

---

[1] Hagenmeyer, *Chronologie*, no. 9.
[2] Matthew of Edessa, *Chronique*, in *H. C. A.*, i, p. 24.
[3] P. 219.
[4] " Indomita gens Normannorum." Ordericus, iii, p. 474.

duke' had fallen into contempt among his turbulent subjects. Disobedience and disorder were everywhere on the increase, and the unarmed population lacked a protector.[5] An expedition to the Holy Land at the head of a splendidly equipped band of knights, with new scenes and new adventures and plenary indulgence for past sins, offered a welcome prospect of escape from the trying situation in which Duke Robert found himself in the spring of 1096.[6]

Yet the First Crusade was a papal, not a Norman, enterprise.[7] At the provincial council of Rouen which was convened in February, 1096, for the purpose of ratifying the canons of the council of Clermont, there is, oddly enough, no evidence that the projected Crusade was taken under consideration by the Norman clergy.[8] The initiative of the Pope, on the other hand, was clear-cut and vigorous, and his activity can be traced with some fulness. From Clermont Urban proceeded on a tour of western France; and passing northward through Poitou and Anjou early in 1096, he arrived at Le Mans in the middle of February and was at Vendôme near the end of the month. Then turning back southward, he was still occupied with the Crusade in a council at Tours in March.[9] The Pope seems not to have entered Normandy at all; but he was close to the border while in Maine and at Vendôme, and it is not improbable that it was during this period that he took the first steps towards launching the Crusade in the Norman lands.

Pope Urban's first duty, if he wished to raise large forces in Normandy for the Crusade, was obviously the promotion of peace between the warring sons of William the Conqueror. It was not

---

[5] Ordericus, iii, pp. 475–476.

[6] *Ibid.*, p. 476. Ordericus evidently believes that the duke's unfortunate situation in Normandy was his chief reason for taking the cross: " Denique talibus infortuniis, Rodbertus dux, perspectis anxius, et adhuc peiora formidans, ut pote ab omnibus pene destitutus, . . . decrevit terram suam fratri suo regi dimittere; et cruce Domini sumpta, pro peccatis suis Deo satisfacturus, in Ierusalem pergere."

[7] Cf. Louis Bréhier, *L'église et l'Orient au moyen âge: les croisades* (Paris, 1907), pp. 52–62.

[8] Cf. Ordericus, iii, pp. 470 ff.

[9] For the papal itinerary see Philipp Jaffé, *Regesta Pontificum Romanorum* (2d ed., Leipsic, 1885–88), i, pp. 681–685.

to be thought of that Robert Curthose should lead a Norman army to the liberation of the Holy Sepulchre while William Rufus continued the struggle to deprive him of his duchy. Accordingly, the Pope sent Abbot Gerento of Saint-Bénigne of Dijon as his special agent to undertake the delicate task of negotiating a peace.[10] The abbot was with William Rufus in England at Easter (13 April) 1096.[11] He crossed to Normandy before the end of May;[12] and remaining there throughout the summer, brought the peace negotiations to a successful termination, and accompanied the crusading host upon the initial stages of its journey as it departed in the autumn.[13] It may be conjectured that during this whole period Gerento was engaged in the work of promoting the Crusade in Normandy; and this conclusion is fully in accord with the statements of the chroniclers that Duke Robert took the cross " at the admonition of Pope Urban "[14] and " by the counsel of certain men of religion." [15]

The treaty which had been concluded at the abbot's instance was wisely drawn to meet the exigencies of Robert's situation. Not only did it bring about the necessary peace, but upon such terms as to provide the impecunious duke with ample funds for his distant enterprise. Normandy was to be taken in pledge by William Rufus, and in exchange Robert was to receive a loan of 10,000 marks of silver.[16] The date at which this bargain was struck cannot be exactly determined, but, in any case, it was early enough to allow the king time to extort money from his unfortu-

---

[10] Hugh of Flavigny, *Chronicon*, in *M. G. H.*, Scriptores, viii, p. 475.

[11] *Ibid.*

[12] Hugh of Flavigny, the abbot's companion and secretary, drew up a charter for Duke Robert at Bayeux 24 May 1096. Haskins, p. 67, no. 4, and n. 19; cf. p. 76, n. 34; and *supra*, p. 18, n. 6.

[13] Haskins, pp. 75–76, and the sources there cited.

[14] William of Malmesbury, *G. R.*, ii, p 371.

[15] Ordericus, iii, p. 476.

[16] Hugh of Flavigny, in *M. G. H.*, Scriptores, viii, p. 475; *Interpolations de Robert de Torigny*, in William of Jumièges, pp. 274–275; Ordericus, iii, p. 476; iv, p. 16; Eadmer, p. 74; *A.–S. C.*, a. 1096; Florence of Worcester, ii, p. 40; William of Malmesbury, *G. R.*, ii, p. 371; *Annales de Wintonia*, in *Annales Monastici*, ii, p. 38. There is disagreement as to the term of the loan. According to Hugh of Flavigny it was to be for three years, according to Ordericus five, and according to Robert of Torigny until the duke's return from the Crusade.

nate subjects by means which provoked a general outcry.[17] An aid (*auxilium*) was demanded of the barons, and an extraordinary Danegeld was levied at the rate of four shillings to the hide throughout the kingdom. Though the clergy had from early times been exempted from this tax, their privileges were not now respected; and they were obliged to pay their full share along with the lay nobles.[18] Churches were stripped of their ornaments in order that the sum might be raised.[19]

Meanwhile, in Normandy and the surrounding lands, preparations for the Crusade had been going steadily forward; though it must be owned that we have but slight information concerning the measures which were taken, beyond what may be inferred from the occasional record of a mortgage of lands to a religious house in exchange for a loan of ready cash for the journey,[20] or from the names of a relatively small number of men and women [21] — less than fifty in all — who, stirred by religious impulse, the spirit of adventure, or the hope of gain, followed the duke's example and took the cross.

[17] Eadmer, pp. 74–75; Florence of Worcester, ii, p. 40; William of Malmesbury, *G. R.*, ii, pp. 371–372.

[18] *Leges Edwardi Confessoris*, in *Die Gesetze der Angelsachsen*, ed. Felix Liebermann (Halle, 1898–1912), i, pp. 636–637; " Et hanc libertatem habuit sancta ecclesia usque ad tempus Willelmi iunioris, qui de baronibus totius patrie auxilium petiit ad Normanniam retinendam de fratre suo Rodberto eunte in Ierusalem. Ipsi autem concesserunt ei quatuor solidos de unaquaque hyda, sanctam ecclesiam non excipientes.

" Quorum dum fieret collectio, clamabat ecclesia, libertatem suam reposcens; sed nichil sibi profuit." A later recension adds that the grant was made, " non lege statutum tamen neque firmatum, sed hac necessitatis causa."

[19] It is difficult to see why this should have been such a burden, but the contemporary writers leave no doubt as to the resentment which it aroused. William of Malmesbury (*G. P.*, p. 432) is very bitter against the abbot of Malmesbury because of his action on this occasion and very specific as to the sufferings of his church: " Denique die uno .xii. textus Evangeliorum, .viii^{to}. cruces, .viii^{to}. scrinia argento et auro nudata et excrustata sunt." Eadmer (p. 75) tells how Anselm was obliged to borrow two hundred marks from the cathedral treasury, placing his demesne vill of Peckham in *vif gage* for seven years as security. — On *vif gage* see R. Génestal, *Rôle des monastères comme établissements de crédit* (Paris, 1901), pp. 1–2.

[20] E.g., a charter published by Léopold Delisle in *Littérature latine et histoire du moyen âge* (Paris, 1890), pp. 28–29. All such documents as have come to light are cited in connection with individual crusaders in Appendix D.

[21] For the women with Duke Robert's forces see Appendix D, nos. 6, 10, 13, 14.

So far as it is possible to describe it at this distance, Robert Curthose certainly travelled at the head of an interesting and honorable company, which, drawn not only from Normandy but from the surrounding lands, was altogether worthy of the dignity of the Conqueror's eldest son. To attempt a comprehensive enumeration would be tedious, but the names of at least the more important of the duke's companions should be recorded.[22] Of the Norman bishops, the only ones who took the cross were Odo of Bayeux and Gilbert of Évreux. Both had been present at the council of Clermont as 'legates' of their fellow bishops; and Odo, at any rate, had been in touch with Abbot Gerento in Normandy during the summer of 1096. Yet it is doubtful whether he was a very active promoter of the Crusade, for some, at least, believed that he had taken the cross for personal reasons rather than out of zeal for the Holy War. He had been driven from England after the failure of the rebellion against William Rufus in 1088, and the king's wrath against him had not been appeased. Rather than remain in Normandy to become the subject of his bitter enemy, he preferred to undertake the hardships of the distant pilgrimage. Among the lay nobles from Normandy who accompanied Robert on the Crusade we meet with no very great names; but it is interesting to note that the list contains not only such life-long friends of the duke as Ivo and Alberic of Grandmesnil, but also — a fruit of the recent pacification — his late enemies Count Stephen of Aumale and Gerard of Gournay. The great house of Bellême was represented by Philip the Clerk, one of its younger scions. Mention should also be made of Roger of Barneville, an obscure knight from western Normandy, who was destined to lose his life in a skirmish with the Turks at Antioch, and whose noble character and unexampled bravery made him a great favorite with the army.

The neighboring lands of northern France contributed an equally distinguished company to Duke Robert's forces. His cousin, Count Robert of Flanders, and his less heroic brother-in-law, Count Stephen of Blois and Chartres, both found it to

---

[22] For a full list of Robert's known companions on the Crusade, with all the evidence concerning them, see Appendix D. ˙

their advantage to travel with him, as did also Alan Fergant, duke of Brittany, and a notable list of Bretons. Among these latter may be mentioned Alan, the steward of Archbishop Baldric of Dol;[23] Ralph de Gael, the one-time earl of Norfolk whose treason had caused the Conqueror to drive him forth from England; Conan de Lamballe, who was killed by the Turks at Antioch; and Riou de Lohéac, who died while on the Crusade, but sent back to the church of his lordship a casket of precious relics which included a portion of the true cross and a fragment of the Sepulchre. From Perche came Rotrou of Mortagne, son of the then reigning Count Geoffrey. And from the Flemish border came old Hugh, count of Saint-Pol, and his brave son Enguerrand, who gave his life for the Christian cause at Marra in Syria; Walter of Saint-Valery and his valiant son Bernard, who according to one account was the first to scale the wall of Jerusalem. The forces of Duke Robert also included a number of Manceaux,[24] but Helias of La Flèche, the count of Maine, was not among them. Stirred by the common impulse, he had taken the cross, apparently designing to travel with Robert Curthose. But when he learned that William Rufus would grant him no peace, but proposed to bring Maine back under Norman domination by force of arms, he was obliged to abandon his undertaking and remain at home to defend his county.[25]

From England, strangely enough, only two crusaders of known name and history have come to light among the followers of

[23] It was perhaps through this Alan that the names of so many Breton crusaders have been preserved in the history of Baldric of Dol, from which they have been copied by Ordericus Vitalis.

[24] They are mentioned in a general way as taking part in the battle with Kerboga at Antioch, 28 June 1098: " In tertia Rodbertus dux Normannorum, cum xv milibus Cenomannorum, Andegavorum, Britonum, et Anglorum." Ordericus, iii, p. 555. There is a good deal of documentary evidence bearing upon crusaders from Maine, which, however, is in no case quite sufficient to prove that any individual Manceau whom we can identify actually went on the First Crusade. It will be found in Appendix D, nos. 22–24, 27, 30, 38, 47. An anonymous work entitled *Noblesse du Maine aux croisades* (Le Mans, 1859), pp. 13–14, gives a list of twenty-five noble Manceaux who answered Pope Urban's call. The list is valueless, however, since no evidence or authority is cited in any case, and the work is obviously based upon no sufficient criticism.

[25] Ordericus, iv, pp. 37–38.

Robert Curthose: the Norman William de Percy, the great benefactor of Whitby abbey, and Arnulf of Hesdin, a Fleming. Neither, it will be observed, was a native Englishman. The Anglo-Saxon chronicler remarks that the preaching of Pope Urban caused " a great excitement through all this nation," [26] and English mariners are known to have coöperated with the crusaders on the Syrian coast.[27] Yet England still lay largely beyond the range of continental affairs and the great movements of world history, and the part played by the English in the First Crusade appears to have been of minor importance. William of Malmesbury observes truly that ' but a faint murmur of Asiatic affairs reached the ears of those who dwelt beyond the British Ocean.' [28]

The standard-bearer of Duke Robert throughout the Crusade is said to have been Pain Peverel, the distinguished Norman knight who later was granted a barony in England by Henry I and became the patron of Barnwell priory. As his chaplain, or chancellor, Robert took Arnulf of Chocques, the clever Flemish adventurer who had long served in the ducal family as preceptor of his eldest sister, Princess Cecilia, and who later rose to the dignity of patriarch of Jerusalem.[29] And finally mention should be made of Fulcher of Chartres, the well known historian of the Crusade, who travelled with the ducal forces as far as Marash in Armenia, and who up to that point may almost be regarded as the official historiographer of the northern Norman contingent.

While preparations for the Crusade were being pushed forward in Normandy and the adjoining lands, William Rufus had completed the work of collecting English treasure for the Norman loan, and in September 1096 [30] he crossed the Channel. Meeting the duke, apparently at Rouen,[31] he paid over the 10,000 marks

[26] *A.-S. C.*, a. 1096.
[27] See Appendix E, pp. 231–232.
[28] *G. R.*, ii, p. 431.
[29] See Appendix C.
[30] Florence of Worcester, ii, p. 40.
[31] Cf. Ordericus, iv, p. 37: " Ea tempestate qua Rodbertus dux fratri suo Normanniam commisit, et ab eo magnam argenti copiam, ad explendum iter ad sepulchrum Regis nostri, recepit, Helias comes ad curiam regis Rotomagum venit. Qui, postquam diu cum duce consiliatus fuit, ad regem accessit, eique humiliter dixit . . ." Freeman places the meeting " at some point of the border-land of the Vexin,

which had been agreed upon, and received the duchy in pledge.[32] Thus was Robert supplied with funds for his distant journey, and when this most necessary matter had been arranged, final preparations were speedily brought to an end, and the duke took his place at the head of his forces.

Near the end of September, or early in October,[33] amid tearful but courageous leave-takings from friends and loved ones,[34] the crusaders set forth upon their long pilgrimage. As they moved forward over the first stages of the march, their numbers were considerably augmented by additional forces which flowed in from districts along the way.[35] At Pontarlier on the upper waters of the Doubs, Abbot Gerento of Dijon and his faithful secretary, Hugh of Flavigny, who had accompanied the host thus far, and must have viewed with much satisfaction the successful culmination of their enterprise, took their leave of the leaders and turned back.[36]

From Pontarlier the route probably lay by the well known road of pilgrimage and commerce past the great monastery of Saint-Maurice and over the Alps by the Great St. Bernard to Aosta, and thence across the valley of the Po and over the Apennines to Lucca.[37] At Lucca the crusaders were met by Urban II, who conferred with the leaders, Robert of Normandy

at Pontoise or at Chaumont," citing as authority a letter of Ivo of Chartres (*H. F.*, xv, p. 82); but he has quite arbitrarily assigned to 1096 a letter which clearly does not belong to that period. *William Rufus*, i, p. 559; cf. *supra*, p. 84, n. 215.

[32] Cf. *supra*, n. 16.

[33] Fulcher of Chartres, *Historia Hierosolymitana* (*1095–1127*), ed. Heinrich Hagenmeyer (Heidelberg, 1913), p. 159, and n. 21. Fulcher first wrote 'September' and later changed it to 'October.' Ordericus Vitalis (iii, p. 483) and William of Malmesbury (*G. R.*, ii, p. 402) both place the departure in September. Hagenmeyer probably explains the discrepancy correctly when he remarks that all did not depart at exactly the same time.

[34] Fulcher, pp. 162–163. The passage is highly rhetorical, but Fulcher, it should be remembered, was an eyewitness. [35] *Ibid.*, p. 161.

[36] Hugh of Flavigny, in *M. G. H.*, Scriptores, viii, p. 475.

[37] For the stages of this route see the remarkable itinerary of Abbot Nicholas Saemundarson of Thingeyrar (in northern Iceland) who made the pilgrimage to the Holy Land between 1151 and 1154. E. C. Werlauff, *Symbolae ad Geographiam Medii Aevi ex Monumentis Islandicis* (Copenhagen, 1821), pp. 18–25. It is summarized by Paul Riant, *Expéditions et pèlerinages des Scandinaves en Terre Sainte* (Paris, 1865), pp. 80 ff.

and Stephen of Blois, and gave his blessing to the departing host as it moved on southward and came to Rome 'rejoicing.' [38] But in the basilica of St. Peter the crusaders found little joy, for the great church, with the exception of a single tower, was in the hands of the men of the anti-Pope, who, sword in hand, seized the offerings of the faithful from off the altar, and from the roof hurled down stones upon the pilgrims as they prostrated themselves in prayer.[39] Saddened by such outrages, but not delaying to avenge them, they pushed on southward, pausing at Monte Cassino to ask a blessing of St. Benedict as they passed,[40] and came to the port of Bari.[41]

Already tidings of the great enterprise which Pope Urban had launched had stirred one of the ablest chiefs of the southern Normans to action. Bohemond, prince of Taranto, the oldest son of Robert Guiscard, was engaged in the siege of Amalfi with his uncle, Count Roger of Sicily, when news reached him that early contingents of French crusaders had already arrived in Italy. The possibilities of the great adventure fired his ardent imagination, and, " seized with a divine inspiration," he took the cross. Then, dramatically ordering his magnificent cloak to be cut into crosses, he distributed them among such of the knights present as were willing to follow his example; and so great was the rush of men to his standard, that Count Roger found himself almost deserted, and was obliged to abandon the siege and retire in dudgeon to Sicily.[42] Before the arrival of Robert Curthose and

---

[38] Fulcher, p. 164; cf. Baldric of Dol, in *H. C. Oc.*, iv, p. 20; Ordericus, iii, p. 486.

[39] Fulcher, pp. 164–166.

[40] Petrus Diaconus, *Chronica Monasterii Casinensis*, in *M. G. H.*, Scriptores, vii, p. 765; cf. the letter of Emperor Alexius to Abbot Oderisius of Monte Cassino, in *Kreuzzugsbriefe*, pp. 140–141.

[41] Fulcher, p. 166; Petrus Diaconus, *loc. cit.*

[42] *G. F.*, pp. 147 ff.; Lupus Protospatarius, in *M. G. H.*, Scriptores, v, p. 62; cf. Ferdinand Chalandon, *Histoire de la domination normande en Italie et en Sicilie* (Paris, 1907), i, pp. 301–302. William of Malmesbury (*G. R.*, ii, pp. 390, 453), on the other hand, represents the crafty Bohemond as responsible for the inception of the whole crusading movement, a view which is accepted and developed at great length by Sir Francis Palgrave, *History of Normandy and England* (London, 1851–64), iv, p. 484 *et passim*. H. W. C. Davis is also tempted by it. *England under the Normans and Angevins* (London, 1905), p. 102. But in the face of the positive testimony of the *Gesta Francorum* and of Lupus Protospatarius it is untenable.

the northern Normans, Bohemond had already crossed the Adriatic at the head of a splendid band of knights and entered upon the road to Constantinople.

The hopes of Robert and his followers to make an immediate crossing and push on in the footsteps of Bohemond were doomed to disappointment. When they arrived at Bari, winter was already close at hand, and the Italian mariners were unwilling to undertake the transport of such an army in the inclement season.[43] Duke Robert and Count Stephen, therefore, were obliged to turn aside and winter in Apulia and Calabria.[44] Only the more active Robert of Flanders with his smaller forces managed to make the winter passage and push on towards Constantinople.[45] Meanwhile, Roger Bursa, duke of Apulia, received Robert of Normandy with much honor " as his natural lord " and supplied him with abundant provisions for himself and his noble associates.[46] Many of the poorer crusaders, however, were confronted with a grave problem. To winter peacefully in a friendly country which they could not plunder seemed quite out of the question; and, fearing lest they should fall into want, they sold their bows, and, resuming pilgrims' staves, turned back ' ignominiously ' to their northern homes.[47] Their more fortunate comrades, the nobles, however, found generous hospitality among friends; [48] and the winter months must have passed pleasantly for these northern Normans in the sunny Italian climate among their distinguished kinsmen. Bishop Odo of Bayeux, still vigorous and active, in spite of his advanced years, crossed over to Sicily, and paid a visit to Count Roger's beautiful capital at Palermo. There he was taken with a fatal illness, and died early in 1097.

---

[43] Fulcher, p. 167.

[44] *Ibid.*, pp. 167–168; Baldric of Dol, in *H. C. Oc.*, iv, p. 20; Ordericus, iii, p. 486.

[45] Fulcher, p. 168.

[46] Ordericus, iii, p. 486.

[47] Fulcher, p. 168. But probably many had only intended to make the pilgrimage to the shrine of St. Nicholas of Bari. Cf. *Miracula S. Nicolai conscripta a Monacho Beccensi*, in *Catalogus Codicum Hagiographicorum Latinorum in Bibliotheca Nationali Parisiensi*, ed. the Bollandists (Brussels, 1889-93), ii, p. 422. Fulcher of Chartres (p. 167) notes that many of the crusaders turned aside to pray at the church of St. Nicholas.

[48] William of Malmesbury, *G. R.*, ii, p. 409.

His fellow bishop, Gilbert of Évreux, buried him in the great cathedral church of St. Mary; and Count Roger reared a splendid monument over his grave.[49]

With the return of spring, in the month of March, Robert of Normandy and Stephen of Blois assembled their forces at Brindisi and prepared to push on to Constantinople, the general rendezvous of all the crusading armies. The embarkation was marred by a tragic accident. One of the vessels broke up and went to pieces almost within the harbor with some four hundred souls on board, besides horses and mules and quantities of money. Overwhelmed by fear in the presence of such a catastrophe, some of the more faint-hearted landsmen abandoned the Crusade altogether and turned back homeward, declaring that they would never entrust themselves to the deceitful waves. Doubtless more would have followed their example, had it not been discovered that the bodies washed ashore after the wreck bore upon their shoulders the miraculous imprint of the cross. Encouraged by this token of divine favor, the crusaders place their trust in the omnipotent God, and, raising sail on Easter morning (April 5) amid the blare of many trumpets, pushed out to sea.[50]

Sailing before a gentle breeze, they made the passage without further accident, and landed on the fourth day at two small ports some ten miles distant from Durazzo. Thence, passing Durazzo, they advanced along the ancient Roman road, the Via Egnatia, with few adventures and by relatively rapid marches towards Constantinople.[51] The route lay up the valley of the

---

[49] See Appendix D, no. 29.   [50] Fulcher, pp. 168-171.

[51] Fulcher of Chartres (pp. 172-175) gives a full itinerary: " ante urbem praefatam [i.e., Durazzo] transivimus. Itaque Bulgarorum regiones per montium praerupta et loca satis deserta perreximus. Daemonis ad flumen rapidum tunc venimus omnes. . . . Mane autem aurora clarescente, . . . iter nostrum adripuimus conscendendo montem, quem Bagulatum nuncupant. Postea montanis postpositis urbibusque Lucretia, Botella, Bofinat, Stella, pervenimus ad flumen, quod vocatur Bardarium. . . . Quo transito, sequenti die ante urbem Thessalonicam . . . tentoria tetendimus nostra. . . . Deinde Macedoniam transeuntes, per vallem Philippensium et per Crisopolim atque Christopolim, Praetoriam, Messinopolim, Macram, Traianopolim, Neapolim et Panadox, Rodosto et Eracleam, Salumbriam et Naturam Constantinopolim pervenimus." For identification of place names see Hagenmeyer's notes, ibid.

Skumbi and through a mountainous region to Ochrida, the ancient capital of Bulgaria, and then on past Monastir and across the Vardar to Salonica on the Aegean, a city ' abounding in all good things.' There the crusaders pitched their tents and rested for four days, and then pushed on by the coast road through Kavala and Rodosto to Constantinople, where they encamped outside the city and rested for a fortnight in the latter half of May.[52]

The magnificent oriental capital with its noble churches and stately palaces, its broad streets filled with works of art, its abounding wealth in gold and silver and rich hangings, its eunuchs, and its busy merchants from beyond sea,[53] made a deep impression upon the minds of the crusaders, although they were not permitted to view it at great advantage. For earlier bands who had gone before them had not passed through the city without plundering, and the Greeks had learned to be wary. The Emperor Alexius ordered the crusaders to be well supplied with markets outside the walls, but only in bands of five or six at a time would he permit them to enter the city of wonders and pray in the various churches.[54]

Meanwhile, the leaders, Robert of Normandy and Stephen of Blois, were being sumptuously entertained and assiduously flattered by the Emperor.[55] The real contest between him and the crusading chieftans had already taken place and been practically settled before the arrival of the northern Normans.[56] After the greater leaders, Godfrey of Bouillon and Bohemond, had yielded to the Emperor's demands and entered into treaty relations with him, he had clearly gained his point, and it was not to be supposed that he would meet with serious obstacles in dealing with the princes who came later. Least of all were such difficulties to be expected in Robert Curthose and Stephen of Blois.

[52] Fulcher, pp. 175–176.

[53] *Ibid.*, pp. 176–177.

[54] *Ibid.*, pp. 175–176.

[55] Letter of Stephen of Blois to his wife Adela, in *Kreuzzugsbriefe*, pp. 138–139; cf. Fulcher, p. 178.

[56] For the relations of Alexius with the crusaders see the admirable discussion by Ferdinand Chalandon, *Essai sur le règne d'Alexis I*er *Comnène* (Paris, 1900), ch. vi, especially pp. 175–186.

Both promptly took the oath that was required of them; [57] for, explains Fulcher of Chartres — evidently voicing a sentiment which had become general — it was necessary for the crusaders to consolidate their friendship with the Emperor, since without his support and coöperation they could not advance freely through his dominions, and it would be impossible for fresh recruits to follow by the route which they had taken.

When Robert and Stephen had satisfied the demands of the Emperor, he loaded them with gifts of money and silks and horses, and, providing ships, had them ferried over with their forces to the Asiatic shore. [58] As they advanced beyond Nicomedia past the battle field where the forces of Peter the Hermit had met disaster the previous winter, the Normans were moved to tears at the sight of the whitening bones which still lay unburied; [59] but pressing on without pausing, they reached Nicaea in the first week of June. [60] There they received an enthusiastic welcome from the crusaders who had preceded them and who, since the middle of May, had been besieging the city; and, passing around to the southern side, they took up their position before the walls between the forces of Robert of Flanders and Raymond of Toulouse. [61]

For the remainder of the expedition the exploits of Robert are for the most part merged in the general action of the Crusade and must, for want of detailed information, be narrated briefly. Though a leader of the first rank, Robert was hardly to be compared with Godfrey of Bouillon, Bohemond, or Raymond of Toulouse. He has, therefore, received but an incidental treatment at the hands of the contemporary writers.

It is not recorded that Robert and his forces in any way distinguished themselves at the siege of Nicaea. They had arrived too late to share in the splendid victory over Kilij Arslan (Soli-

---

[57] Fulcher, p. 178; William of Malmesbury, *G. R.*, ii, p. 413; Albert of Aix, in *H. C. Oc.*, iv, p. 314.

[58] Fulcher, p. 179; letter of Stephen of Blois, in *Kreuzzugsbriefe*, p. 139.

[59] Fulcher, p. 180.

[60] *Ibid.*, pp. 182–183; letter of Stephen of Blois, in *Kreuzzugsbriefe*, p. 139; Raymond of Aguilers, in *H. C. Oc.*, iii, p. 239; cf. Hagenmeyer, *Chronologie*, no. 153.

[61] Fulcher, p. 181, and n. 4; *G. F.*, pp. 186–187.

man II), sultan of Iconium, on 16 May.[62]   Doubtless they were
also too late to play an important part in the construction of
the elaborate siege machinery which formed so marked a feature
in the operations against the city.   On 19 June Nicaea surrendered;[63] and Robert hurried away with the other leaders to
congratulate the Emperor upon the victory and to share in the
rich gifts which Alexius was bestowing upon the Franks as a reward for their services.[64]

Events moved rapidly after the fall of Nicaea.   By 26 June
some of the crusaders were already on the march.   Robert with
his habitual slackness took a more leisurely leave of the Emperor[65] and did not advance till two days later.   But he quickly
came up with the rest of the forces at a bridge over a small tribu-
tary of the Sangarius; and from that point the whole crusading
host moved forward on the morning of 29 June before daybreak.[66]
Either by accident or design the army was separated into two
divisions,[67] which advanced by different, but roughly parallel,
routes.   At the head of the smaller force, mainly composed of
Normans, marched the Norman leaders, Robert Curthose, Bohemond, and Tancred.   Raymond, Godfrey, Hugh of Vermandois, and Adhemar, bishop of Le Puy, with their followers made
up the larger division.   As the Normans pitched camp on the
second evening their scouts reported the enemy's presence ahead,
and special watches were set to guard the tents; but the night
passed without incident.   When, however, on the following

---

[62] Albert of Aix reports Robert as taking part in this battle; but he is in direct
disagreement with the testimony of eyewitnesses, and is clearly wrong. *H. C. Oc.*,
iv, p. 320.

[63] See the sources collected in Hagenmeyer, *Chronologie*, no. 160.

[64] Letter of Stephen of Blois, in *Kreuzzugsbriefe*, p. 140; cf. Anna Comnena,
in *H. C. G.*, i, 2, p. 46.

[65] Fulcher, p. 189, and n. 3.   [66] Hagenmeyer, *Chronologie*, no. 167.

[67] According to the *Gesta Francorum* (p. 196) the division was accidental and
due to darkness; and this appears to be the meaning of Raymond of Aguilers
(*H. C. Oc.*, iii, p. 240).   Fulcher of Chartres (p. 194) confesses that he does not
know the cause of the separation.   Ralph of Caen (*H. C. Oc.*, iii, pp. 620–621) explains that there were two opinions, but leans to the view that the division was accidental.   Albert of Aix (*ibid.*, iv, pp. 328–329), on the other hand, says that it was
intentional.   Cf. Hagenmeyer's note in Fulcher, p. 194; Reinhold Röhricht,
Geschichte des ersten Kreuzzuges, p. 90.

morning (1 July) the march was resumed, the way was soon barred by the enemy in force under the command of Kilij Arslan. The Normans hastily prepared for battle; and towards eight or nine o'clock an engagement was begun which continued with uninterrupted fury till well after midday. Though the Normans fought valiantly, they could not long maintain the unequal contest. The mounted knights were hurled back in disorder upon the foot soldiers; and the heroic efforts of Bohemond and Robert to rally their forces and resume the offensive were of no avail. The crusaders, greatly outnumbered, and terrified by the outlandish modes of warfare practiced by their enemies, were overwhelmed and thrown back in wild confusion upon their camp. It was a desperate moment. The Christian forces were packed together " like sheep in a fold." Priests were praying, knights were prostrate confessing their sins. The panic was general. But suddenly, when all seemed lost, relief came. Earlier in the day a messenger had been despatched to the crusaders of the other division, who were advancing at some distance by a separate route. When they learned of the desperate plight of the Normans, they rushed to arms, and, by hard riding across country, arrived upon the scene of battle barely in time to save their companions from annihilation. Strengthened by these reënforcements, the Normans quickly re-formed their battle order and renewed the contest; and the Turks, unexpectedly confronted by an enemy doubled in numbers, turned in flight and were swept from the field. The crusaders pursued them till nightfall, plundered their camp, and took quantities of booty.[68]

There can be no doubt that Robert Curthose fought bravely, as befitted one of his ancestry,[69] on the field of Dorylaeum. But the accounts, nearly contemporary though they be, which picture him as the supremely brave leader, whose heroic action checked the rout of the Christians and saved the day, belong rather to the realm of legend than of sober history.[70] A just estimate based

[68] Fulcher, pp. 190–198; *G. F.*, pp. 196–205; Raymond of Aguilers, in *H. C. Oc.*, iii, p. 240; letter of Anselm de Ribemont, in *Kreuzzugsbriefe*, p. 145; Ralph of Caen, in *H. C. Oc.*, iii, 620–622, 625 ff.; Albert of Aix, *ibid.*, iv, pp. 329–332.

[69] Guilbert of Nogent, *ibid.*, iv, p. 160; Ralph of Caen, *ibid.*, iii, p. 622.

[70] See Chapter VIII, pp. 193–194.

upon strictly reliable sources must recognize that Robert divided the honors of Dorylaeum with Bohemond and the other leaders, but must assign him a part in the battle somewhat subordinate to that played by the great leader of the southern Normans.

The rout of the Turks at Dorylaeum opened the way through Asia Minor; and on 4 July,[71] after a two days' halt to rest and to bury the dead,[72] the crusaders entered upon the long march to Antioch, the great Seljuk stronghold in northern Syria.[73] No serious opposition was encountered from the enemy; and on 20 October,[74] after three and a half months of varied hardships, they arrived at the so-called Iron Bridge (Djisr el-Hadid) over the Orontes a few miles above Antioch. Robert Curthose led the vanguard [75] which encountered outposts of the enemy at the bridge and defeated them in a sharp engagement; and that night the crusaders camped beside the river.[76] Next day (21 October) they pushed on to Antioch and took up their positions before the city.[77]

The siege of Antioch was a problem fit to try the resources, spirit, and endurance of the greatest commander. Its massive walls and towers, far superior to anything then known in western Europe, rendered it impregnable by assault. It was held by a strong garrison under the command of a resourceful emir; and the

---

[71] Hagenmeyer, *Chronologie*, no. 172.

[72] Albert of Aix, in *H. C. Oc.*, iv, pp. 332–333; cf. Hagenmeyer, *Chronologie*, no. 170.

[73] On the route and the events of the march in general see Hagenmeyer, *Chronologie*, nos. 172, 175–179, 181–204, and the sources there collected. At Heraclea the army was divided, Baldwin and Tancred with their followers taking the southern route through the Cilician Gates, Robert and the other leaders with their forces making a long detour to the northward through Caesarea Mazaca, Coxon (the ancient Cocussus), and Marash, and finally approaching Antioch from the northeast. Albert of Aix, in *H. C. Oc.*, iv, pp. 357–358: the fact is also implied in the other sources, especially Fulcher of Chartres, who writes in the first person until his separation from the Norman forces at Marash and his departure for Edessa as chaplain of Baldwin.

[74] Hagenmeyer, *Chronologie*, no. 200.

[75] Albert of Aix, in *H. C. Oc.*, iv, p. 362.

[76] *G. F.*, pp. 239–241; letter of Anselm de Ribemont, in *Kreuzzugsbriefe*, p. 145; Albert of Aix, in *H. C. Oc.*, iv, pp. 362–363.

[77] Hagenmeyer, *Chronologie*, no. 203. On the positions taken up by the various contingents see Röhricht, *Geschichte des ersten Kreuzzuges*, p. 110.

besiegers were in constant danger from a sortie in force. Moreover, the beleaguered garrison was not to be left without assistance; and more than once the crusaders had to meet and drive off a relief force in greatly superior numbers. And finally, the food problem soon became so acute as to threaten the besiegers with starvation; and to hunger were added the hardships of the winter season. Plainly this was not the kind of warfare which appealed to the easy-going, pleasure-loving Robert of Normandy. During the early stages of the siege, while the abundant supplies of a fertile district still held out, he played his part with courage and spirit, as, for example, when he joined with Bohemond and Robert of Flanders in a victorious fight against the Turks on the Aleppo road near Harim in November.[78] But when, in December, the crusaders began to feel the pinch of famine,[79] Robert could not withstand the temptation to withdraw to more pleasant winter quarters at Laodicea.[80]

Though the preaching of the Crusade had aroused little enthusiasm among the upper classes in England, it had met with a curious response among the English seamen. Assembling a considerable fleet, they had passed the Straits of Gibraltar and arrived off the Syrian coast well in advance of the crusading forces which were making their way across the highlands of Asia Minor; and in concert with the Emperor — who, it must not be forgotten, was coöperating with the crusaders both by land and sea — they had captured Laodicea and established themselves there before the land forces had arrived at Antioch. Well stocked with provisions from Cyprus, and protected from pirates by the English fleet, which secured its trade communications with the islands, Laodicea offered tempting quarters for one who had tired of the rigors of the winter siege at Antioch. Moreover, the English mariners appear to have been menaced in their possession by wandering bands of the enemy in the surrounding country and

[78] Raymond of Aguilers, in *H. C. Oc.*, iii, p. 242; cf. *G. F.*, pp. 245–247; letter of Anselm de Ribemont, in *Kreuzzugsbriefe*, p. 145.

[79] Hagenmeyer, *Chronologie*, no. 214.

[80] Laodicea ad Mare (modern Latakia), the seaport on the Syrian coast directly opposite the island of Cyprus. For all that follows concerning Laodicea and Robert's connection therewith see Appendix E.

in need of reënforcements. Accordingly, they appealed to Robert of Normandy as their most natural lord among the crusading chieftains, and besought him to come to Laodicea as their protector.

Accepting this invitation with alacrity, Robert retired from Antioch in December 1097, and, joining his friends at Laodicea, gave himself up to sleep and idleness, content with forwarding a part of the abundant provisions which he enjoyed to his suffering comrades at the siege. The situation of the besiegers, however, was precarious, and they could not long remain indifferent to the absence of so important a leader as Robert. Soon they summoned him to return; and when their appeal met with no response, they repeated it and finally threatened him with excommunication. Thus pressed, Robert had no choice but to yield, and, very reluctantly turning his back upon the comforts of Laodicea, he returned to the hardships of the siege.

Robert was back at Antioch for the crisis of 8 and 9 February 1098, which was brought on by the arrival of Ridwan of Aleppo at the head of a large Turkish relief force. He attended the war council of 8 February which determined upon a plan of action; [81] and next day, while Bohemond and the mounted knights were winning their splendid victory over the forces of Ridwan,[82] he assumed command, along with the bishop of Le Puy and the count of Flanders, over the foot soldiers who remained behind to maintain the siege and guard the camp.[83] And though the Turkish garrison attempted a sortie in force from three gates, Robert and his comrades kept up a hard but victorious struggle throughout the day, and at nightfall drove the enemy back within the walls.[84]

From the defeat of Ridwan of Aleppo until the capture of Antioch, 3 June 1098, we lose sight of Robert completely; and it must remain a matter of doubt whether he was privy to the

---

[81] Tudebode, *Historia de Hierosolymitano Itinere*, in *H. C. Oc.*, iii, p. 43.

[82] Hagenmeyer, *Chronologie*, no. 233.

[83] Tudebode, *loc. cit.* Albert of Aix (*H. C. Oc.*, iv, pp. 381,385) and Henry of Huntingdon (pp. 223, 224) erroneously make him lead one of the six divisions of knights under Bohemond.

[84] Hagenmeyer, *Chronologie*, no. 233.

secret negotiations by which Bohemond, corrupting a Turkish guard, succeeded at last in opening the gates of the impregnable fortress.[85] Robert was certainly present at the capture of Antioch [86] and played his part honorably in the trying days which followed.

The month of June brought the crusaders face to face with the gravest crisis with which they had yet been confronted. The citadel of Antioch still held out against them; and, within two days after their victorious entrance into the city, advance guards of a vast Moslem army under the command of Kerboga of Mosul arrived before the gates. By the 8th of the month the Franks were compelled to burn their outworks and retire within the walls, themselves to stand a siege.[87] Though not especially mentioned, Robert doubtless took his part in the all-day struggle of 10 June; and when, next morning, it was discovered that a panic was spreading through the ranks, and that some of the forces, followers of Robert among them, had already let themselves down over the wall and fled,[88] he promptly joined with the other leaders in the

---

[85] Hagenmeyer, *Chronologie*, nos. 260, 262, 264, 265. According to Bruno of Lucca, Robert Curthose and Robert of Flanders both had a hand in the secret negotiations. Letter of the clergy and people of Lucca, in *Kreuzzugsbriefe*, p. 166. But Bruno, though present at the capture of Antioch, was clearly not well informed about these matters, and great importance cannot be attached to his statement. According to Baldric of Dol (*H. C. Oc.*, iv, p. 55) and Ordericus Vitalis (iii, p. 537), Robert was among the chiefs to whom Bohemond confided his plans on the eve of putting them into execution. This is in no way unlikely, but Baldric and Ordericus are not independent, and it must be acknowledged that they are a very uncertain authority for such a point as this. The writers who were on the ground make no mention of Robert Curthose in this connection.

[86] Letter of the clergy and people of Lucca, in *Kreuzzugsbriefe*, p. 166; Ralph of Caen, in *H. C. Oc.*, iii, p. 657.

[87] Hagenmeyer, *Chronologie*, nos. 267, 269–274, 276, 278.

[88] The brothers William and Alberic of Grandmesnil were among the fugitives. *G. F.*, pp. 332–334; Raymond of Aguilers, in *H. C. Oc.*, iii, p. 256; Baldric of Dol, *ibid.*, iv, p. 64; Ordericus, iii, p. 545; Guibert of Nogent, in *H. C. Oc.*, iv, p. 194; Ralph of Caen, *ibid.*, iii, p. 662; Tudebode, *ibid.*, iii, p. 67; *Historia Belli Sacri*, *ibid.*, iii, p. 200. (In citing the last work I follow the practice of Hagenmeyer's *Chronologie* in retaining the caption of Mabillon's edition, though the title given in the Academy edition to which reference is made is *Tudebodus Imitatus et Continuatus*. The author is conjectured to have been a Norman from southern Italy who took part in the Crusade and afterwards settled at Antioch. He wrote after 1131.) William of Grandmesnil did not set out with Robert from Normandy, but

solemn oath by which they mutually bound themselves to stand firm to the end.[89]   And when finally, on 28 June, it was decided to stake all on a battle with Kerboga in the open, he led the third division[90] in the action and shared in the greatest victory of the Christians during the First Crusade.   A few days later he attended the council at which it was determined, in view of the summer heat and the scarcity of water, to postpone the advance upon Jerusalem until 1 November;[91] and with that the leaders parted company.

How Robert passed the summer months, it is impossible to say. Probably he sought cooler and more healthful quarters away from pest-ridden Antioch.   But he was evidently there again on 11 September, for he joined the other leaders in the letter to Urban II in which they recounted the progress of the Crusade, reported the death of Bishop Adhemar of Le Puy, and urged the Pope himself to come and join them.[92]   Robert was certainly at Antioch on 1 November, the day set for the general advance upon Jerusalem.[93]

But the advance was again delayed by a bitter quarrel which had broken out between Bohemond and Raymond of Toulouse

went from southern Italy.   According to Tudebode, Ralph of Caen, and the *Historia Belli Sacri*, Ivo of Grandmesnil was also among the fugitives.   This act of cowardice made a deep impression upon contemporaries.   Ralph of Caen writes: " At fratres, pudet, heu!   pudet, heu!   Normannia misit."   Guibert of Nogent, as a friend of the family, declines to mention the family name in connection with the incident.

[89] *G. F.*, p. 340; Guibert of Nogent, in *H. C. Oc.*, iv, p. 196; cf. Raymond of Aguilers, *ibid.*, iii, p. 256.   The purpose of the measure was to restore the morale of the rank and file.

[90] *G. F.*, pp. 368-370; Raymond of Aguilers, in *H. C. Oc.*, iii, p. 259.   Or possibly he led the second division, the count of Flanders leading the third.   The two Roberts evidently fought in close coöperation.   Letter of Anselm de Ribemont, in *Kreuzzugsbriefe*, p. 160; Fulcher, p. 255; Ralph of Caen, in *H. C. Oc.*, iii, p. 666; Albert of Aix, *ibid.*, iv, p. 422.   During the battle a new division was formed from the forces of Robert Curthose and Godfrey in order to checkmate an attempt of the Turks to outflank the crusaders.   *G. F.*, p. 373.

[91] *Ibid.*, pp. 382-385; Guibert of Nogent, in *H. C. Oc.*, iv, p. 208; cf. Hagenmeyer, *Chronologie*, no. 298.

[92] *Kreuzzugsbriefe*, p. 161.

[93] *G. F.*, p. 394-395; Tudebode, in *H. C. Oc.*, iii, p. 87; cf. Raymond of Aguilers, *ibid.*, iii, p. 266; Albert of Aix, *ibid.*, iv, p. 448; Hagenmeyer, *Chronologie*, no. 321.

over the possession of Antioch.[94]   And now we find Robert, in the rôle of peacemaker, joining with the other disinterested leaders who desired to respect their pledges to the Emperor in an effort to arbitrate the difficulties.[95]   But all these efforts were in vain, for when the arbitrators had arrved at a decision on the merits of the case, they lacked authority to enforce their judgment, and dared not announce it lest matters should be made worse. Finally, however, a truce was agreed upon in the hope of continuing the Crusade;[96] and Robert departed with Raymond and others to lay siege to Marra.[97]   But hardly had this place been taken (11 December),[98] when the quarrel between Bohemond and Raymond flamed up afresh; and now the controversy spread from the leaders to the ranks, and the army was divided into two bitter factions.[99]   Again Robert joined the other leaders in council at Rugia in an attempt to bring about a reconciliation;[100] but again all efforts failed, and Raymond and Bohemond remained at enmity.

Meanwhile, the count of Toulouse, yielding to popular pressure in the army, determined upon an independent advance to Jerusalem; and in order to isolate his rival the more effectually, he undertook to hire other leaders to follow him.   To Godfrey of Bouillon and to Robert Courthose he offered 10,000 *solidi*, to the count of Flanders 6000, to Tancred 5000, and to others in accordance with their dignity.[101]   Tancred definitely closed with the offer,[102] and there is reason for believing that Robert Curthose

[94] Raymond of Aguilers, in *H. C. Oc.*, iii, pp. 261–268; *G. F.*, pp. 379–380, 394–395.

[95] At a series of conferences held in the basilica of St. Peter at Antioch. *Ibid.*, pp. 394–395; Albert of Aix, in *H. C. Oc.*, iv, p. 434; cf. Hagenmeyer, *Chronologie*, no. 323.

[96] *G. F.*, pp. 395–396; Raymond of Aguilers, in *H. C. Oc.*, iii, pp. 267–268.

[97] Ralph of Caen, in *H. C. Oc.*, iii, p. 674; Albert of Aix, *ibid.*, iv, p. 448; cf. *G. F.*, pp. 402–403, and n. 9.

[98] Hagenmeyer, *Chronologie*, no. 329.

[99] Raymond of Aguilers, in *H. C. Oc.*, iii, pp. 270–271; *G. F.*, p. 410; Fulcher, pp. 267–268.

[100] *G. F.*, p. 411; cf. Hagenmeyer, *Chronologie*, no. 335.

[101] Raymond of Aguilers, in *H. C. Oc.*, iii, p. 271.

[102] *Ibid.*, p. 278.

also accepted it.[103]   In any case, Robert joined Raymond and
Tancred at Kafartab, 14 January 1099, and two days later the
three leaders moved southward with their followers towards
Jerusalem, Robert and Tancred leading the vanguard while
Raymond brought up the rear.   As they moved southward up the
beautiful valley of the Orontes, panic-stricken emirs along their
line of march sent to purchase peace at any price and poured out
their wealth in gifts, while the plunder of a fertile countryside
supplied the crusaders with still greater abundance.[104]   Crossing
the river at a ford a short distance above Shaizar, they made their
way over the mountainous divide and descended towards the sea
into the rich valley of El-Bukeia.[105]   Halting there for a fortnight's rest and the celebration of the Purification,[106] they crossed
the valley and encamped before the great fortress of Arka on the
northern slopes of Lebanon (14 February).   The neighboring
port of Tortosa fell into their hands almost immediately, and
when easy communication with the sea had thus been secured,
they settled down to the siege of Arka.[107]   This caused another
delay of three months, and though Robert, Raymond, and
Tancred each built siege towers,[108] no progress was made towards
reducing the fortress.   Even with the aid of Godfrey and Robert
of Flanders, who came up with their forces 14 March, all their
efforts were unavailing.[109]

Meanwhile, fresh disputes arose within the ranks of the army;
and the Provençals, who at Marra had vented their rage upon

[103] This is made probable by the fact that Robert alone of all the important
leaders joined Raymond and Tancred in the advance upon Jerusalem. Robert was
still in the company of Raymond at Caesarea. Albert of Aix, in *H. C. Oc.*, iv, p. 460.
But upon the arrival of the crusaders before Jerusalem, the point at which the con-
tract should have terminated, he promptly separated from Raymond; and thereafter during the siege he acted in close association with Godfrey of Bouillon and
Robert of Flanders. Cf. *infra*, p. 112.
[104] *G. F.*, pp. 414 ff.; Raymond of Aguilers, in *H. C. Oc.*, iii, pp. 272–273; cf.
Fulcher, p. 268.
[105] Hagenmeyer, *Chronologie*, nos. 341–345. For a detailed study of this itinerary see Hagenmeyer's notes in *G. F.*, pp. 414–419.
[106] *G. F.*, pp. 419 ff.
[107] *Ibid.*, pp. 425–428; Raymond of Aguilers, in *H. C. Oc.*, iii, pp. 275–276.
[108] Ralph of Caen, *ibid.*, p. 680.
[109] Hagenmeyer, *Chronologie*, nos. 352–354, 359–360.

Bohemond and his followers, now turned against Robert and the northern Normans. The genuineness of the so-called Holy Lance had been called in question.[110] Many of the Normans believed that the discovery of the Lance at Antioch had been a mere hoax got up by the vision-loving followers of Count Raymond; and on this question opinion in the army was sharply divided.[111] Arnulf of Chocques, Duke Robert's chaplain, was regarded as the "chief of all the unbelievers," [112] and upon him the bitter hatred of the Provençals was concentrated. An attempt was made to settle the controversy by an ordeal; but this resulted indecisively, and each side continued to believe as before. Arnulf was firmly supported by the duke and the Norman party generally, and the attacks of his enemies met with no success.[113]

While time was thus being wasted in disputes and recriminations the season was rapidly advancing; and since Arka showed no signs of capitulating, the leaders, Duke Robert among them, decided to abandon the siege and push on forthwith to Jerusalem.[114] Breaking camp 13 May, they advanced along the coast road by rapid marches, and on 7 June arrived before the Holy City,[115] ' rejoicing and exulting.' [116]

Of the multitudes who had set out from Europe three years before, comparatively few had endured to complete this last stage of the pilgrimage. Not only were the ranks of the army greatly thinned, but half of the leaders had either fallen behind or turned back. The bishop of Le Puy had died at Antioch the previous August; Baldwin, Duke Godfrey's brother, had turned aside to

[110] For the discovery of the Lance at Antioch and the use to which it was put during the critical days of the struggle between the crusaders and Kerboga, see Hagenmeyer, *Chronologie*, nos. 277, 284, 285, 288, 291, and the sources there cited.

[111] *Ibid.*, no. 363.

[112] " Arnulfum, capellanum comitis Normanniae, qui quasi caput omnium incredulorum erat." Raymond of Aguilers, in *H. C. Oc.*, iii, p. 281.

[113] Hagenmeyer, *Chronologie*, nos. 364, 367.

[114] *G. F.*, pp. 436–437; Fulcher, pp. 270–271.

[115] Hagenmeyer, *Chronologie*, nos. 371–385. Guibert of Nogent says that Robert Curthose laid siege to Acre during the advance upon Jerusalem; but that he was called away by Godfrey. *H. C. Oc.*, iv, p. 257. Ibn el-Athir also reports an attack upon Acre as the crusaders advanced upon Jerusalem. *Kamel-Altevarykh*, in *H. C. Or.*, i, p. 198.

[116] *G. F.*, p. 448.

become count of Edessa; Bohemond had remained to pursue his ambitious schemes at Antioch; Hugh of Vermandois had been sent upon a mission to the Emperor; and Stephen of Blois had deserted and returned to Europe to face the reproaches of his more heroic Norman wife.

With forces so diminished, a complete investment of Jerusalem was out of the question. If the city was to be taken at all, it would have to be carried by storm. The crusaders, therefore, selected approaches and prepared for an assault upon the walls. If, as has been suggested, Robert Curthose had been, since the previous January, in the hire of Raymond of Toulouse,[117] the connection between them was now severed; and during the siege of Jerusalem Robert's operations were strategically combined with those of Duke Godfrey and Robert of Flanders. With them he took up his position before the northern wall to the west of St. Stephen's church.[118]

The assault upon the city on 13 June failed miserably through the almost complete lack of siege machinery; and it became clear that far more elaborate preparations would have to be made. It was decided, therefore, to construct at all costs two movable wooden siege towers and other apparatus.[119] Count Raymond assumed responsibility for one of the towers; the providing of the other was undertaken by Godfrey, Robert Curthose, and Robert

---

[117] *Supra*, p. 109, and n. 103.

[118] *G. F.*, pp. 449–450; Raymond of Aguilers, in *H. C. Oc.*, iii, p. 293; Fulcher, p. 297; Ralph of Caen, in *H. C. Oc.*, iii, p. 687; Albert of Aix, *ibid.*, iv, p. 463.
It was evidently at this point that, according to Ordericus Vitalis, Robert was joined by Hugh Bunel, son of Robert de Jalgeio, the fugitive assassin of Countess Mabel, the cruel wife of Roger of Montgomery. Hugh had been provoked to the crime in 1082 because Mabel had violently deprived him of his lawful inheritance, and he had been obliged to flee for his life. He had gone first to Apulia and Sicily and then to Constantinople. But still being pursued by the spies whom William the Conqueror and Mabel's powerful family had employed to take his life wherever they might find him, he had fled from Christendom altogether; and for many years had dwelt among the Moslems, whose language and customs he had learned. He now offered his services to Robert Curthose, who received him kindly; and, being an excellent warrior and familiar with all the deceptions and stratagems which the pagans practised against the Christians, he was able to be of great service to the crusaders. Ordericus, iii, pp. 597–598.

[119] Hagenmeyer, *Chronologie*, nos. 388–389, 391.

of Flanders.[120] Owing to the barrenness of the region around Jerusalem, wood for the construction was not to be had near at hand; but guided by a friendly Syrian Christian, the two Roberts with a band of knights and foot soldiers made their way to a distant forest in the hills 'in the direction of Arabia', and, loading wood upon camels, brought it back to Jerusalem, where the building operations were pushed forward with feverish activity for almost four weeks.[121] When the work had almost reached completion, Godfrey and his associates determined upon a sudden change of plan; and, during the night of 9–10 July, they had their tower and other engines taken apart and moved a mile eastward towards the valley of Jehoshaphat, to a point where level ground offered a good approach, and where the wall was weaker, not having been reënforced by the beleaguered garrison.[122]

During the next three days the siege tower and other apparatus were again assembled and set in order for action; and at dawn 14 July the assault was begun.[123] All day long it was pressed with vigor, and though the defenders fought with the heroism of desperation, endeavoring to set fire to the tower as it was moved forward,[124] all their efforts failed. Next morning at daybreak the attack was renewed, Robert Curthose and Tancred operating the mangonels which cleared the way for the tower to be rolled up close to the wall.[125] 'The garrison still stood stoutly to the defence and let down bags filled with straw to break the shock of the missiles hurled from the mangonels. The Christians were filled with discouragement.[126] But as the hour approached at which the

[120] Raymond of Aguilers, in *H. C. Oc.*, iii, p. 297; *G. F.*, pp. 461–462.

[121] Albert of Aix, in *H. C. Oc.*, iv, pp. 467–468; cf. *G. F.*, pp. 462–463; Raymond of Aguilers, in *H. C. Oc.*, iii, p. 297.

[122] *Ibid.*, p. 298; *G. F.*, pp. 462–463; Albert of Aix, in *H. C. Oc.*, iv, p. 471; cf. Hagenmeyer, *Chronologie*, no. 399.

[123] *Ibid.*, no. 403.   [124] Albert of Aix, in *H. C. Oc.*, iv, pp. 476–477.

[125] Ralph of Caen, *ibid.*, iii, pp. 692–693.

[126] *G. F.*, p. 464; Raymond of Aguilers, in *H. C. Oc.*, iii, p. 299; Guibert of Nogent (*ibid.*, iv, p. 226) particularizes as to Robert Curthose and Robert of Flanders: " Est etiam mihi non inferiore relatione compertum Rotbertum Northmanniae comitem, Rotbertumque alterum, Flandriarum principem, iunctis pariter convenisse moeroribus, et se cum fletibus uberrimis conclamasse miserrimos, quos suae adoratione Crucis et visione, immo veneratione Sepulchri tantopere Ihesus Dominus iudicaret indignos."

Saviour was raised upon the cross (9 A.M.), their mighty effort at last was crowned with success.[127]   With burning arrows they managed to fire the sacks of straw with which the wall was protected; and as the flames burst forth the defenders were compelled to retire.   Then dropping a bridge from the tower to the wall, the crusaders rushed across and carried all before them.[128] Soon the gates were opened and the city was given over to carnage and plunder.[129]   With victory assured, the blood-stained warriors paused momentarily in their work of destruction, and, " rejoicing and weeping from excess of joy," turned aside to render adoration at the Sepulchre and fulfil their vows; [130] but not for two days were the pillage and slaughter ended.[131]

It remained for the crusaders to elect a ruler of the newly conquered city and territory.   After two conferences [132] and much discussion the choice of the leaders fell upon Godfrey of Bouillon, the position having first been offered to Raymond of Toulouse.[133] " Though unwilling," Godfrey was elected " advocate of the church of the Holy Sepulchre." [134]   A generation later the belief was widely current that the honor had also been offered to Robert Curthose and declined by him; [135] but it rests upon no acceptable contemporary authority, and appears to have been a later invention.

Hardly had Godfrey been raised to his new dignity when he became involved in a dispute with the count of Toulouse, not unlike the quarrel which had arisen between Raymond and Bohemond after the capture of Antioch.   Raymond was holding the Tower of David and declined to hand it over to the new ruler.   But God-

---

[127] *G. F.*, pp. 464-465, and n. 15.

[128] Raymond of Aguilers, in *H. C. Oc.*, iii, pp. 299-300; William of Malmesbury, *G. R.*, ii, p. 427.

[129] Hagenmeyer, *Chronologie*, no. 405.

[130] *G. F.*, pp. 473-474.

[131] Hagenmeyer, *Chronologie*, no. 407.

[132] *Ibid.*, nos. 408-409.

[133] Raymond of Aguilers, in *H. C. Oc.*, iii, p. 301.

[134] Letter of the leaders to the Pope, in *Kreuzzugsbriefe*, p. 168; *G. F.*, pp. 478-480, n. 12.

[135] William of Malmesbury, *G. R.*, ii, p. 461; Henry of Huntingdon, p. 236; *Historia Belli Sacri*, in *H. C. Oc.*, iii, p. 225; cf. Albert of Aix, *ibid.*, iv, p. 485.

frey was strongly supported in his just demand by Robert Curthose and Robert of Flanders and by many even of Raymond's
own followers, who were eager to return home and desired the
count to lead them; and under pressure Raymond, always sensi-
tive to popular opinion, was obliged to yield.[136] It was during this
same period that Duke Robert's chaplain, Arnulf of Chocques,
was raised to the dignity of acting patriarch of Jerusalem (1 August).[137] Though only a priest — perhaps not even in sub-
deacon's orders — and of obscure birth, he had contrived by his
learning, personality, and eloquence to make himself the leader
of the anti-Provençal party; and his elevation to this high position was another notable victory for the enemies of Count
Raymond.

Meanwhile a new peril arose to menace the crusaders in the
enjoyment of their conquests. Before any of the leaders had completed their preparations for the homeward journey, news arrived
that the emir Malik el-Afdhal, grand vizier of the caliph of
Egypt, was rapidly approaching at the head of a great army.[138]
Once more the crusaders were to be put to the test of a battle in
the open with an enemy in greatly superior numbers. On 11 August the leaders concentrated their forces in the vicinity of Ascalon and prepared for battle.[139] Next morning at dawn they
advanced into a pleasant valley near the seashore and drew up
their forces in battle order. Duke Godfrey led the left wing,
farthest inland, Count Raymond the right beside the sea, while
the centre was commanded by the two Roberts, Tancred, and
Eustace of Boulogne.[140] When all was ready, the crusaders
moved forward, while the Saracens held their positions and

---

[136] Raymond of Aguilers, *ibid.*, iii, p. 301.

[137] Hagenmeyer, *Chronologie*, no. 413; cf. *G. F.*, p. 481, n. 14.

[138] *Ibid.*, pp. 485–486, and n. 21; Raymond of Aguilers, in *H. C. Oc.*, iii, pp. 302–303; Albert of Aix, *ibid.*, iv, p. 490.

[139] Hagenmeyer, *Chronologie*, no. 420. Robert Curthose with characteristic indolence remained in Jerusalem with Raymond until the enemy was almost at hand, announcing that he would not go out unless he had more certain assurance that a battle was really to take place. He and Raymond did not lead their forces out from Jerusalem till 10 August. *G. F.*, pp. 486–488; Raymond of Aguilers, in *H. C. Oc.*, iii, p. 305; Albert of Aix, *ibid.*, iv, p. 491.

[140] *G. F.*, pp. 493–494; cf. Albert of Aix, in *H. C. Oc.*, iv, p. 494.

awaited the attack.[141] As the opposing forces came together
Robert Curthose perceived the standard of the emir — a lance of
silver surmounted by a golden sphere — which served as the
rallying point for the Saracen forces; and charging the standard-
bearer at full speed, he wounded him mortally [142] and caused the
standard itself to be captured by the crusaders. Spurred on by
Robert's brilliant example, the count of Flanders and Tancred
dashed forward to the attack and carried all before them right
into the enemy's camp. The victory of the centre was complete;
and the Saracens broke and fled, many of them being slain by the
Christians who pursued them. Vast quantities of booty were
taken and borne away by the victors to Jerusalem.[143] Robert of
Normandy purchased for twenty marks of silver the standard of
the emir, which had been captured by his own heroic act, and presented it to Arnulf, the acting patriarch, to be placed in the
church of the Sepulchre as a memorial of the great victory.[144]

With the battle of Ascalon the contemporary histories of the
Crusade come abruptly to an end, and it becomes more difficult
than ever to piece together a connected account of the exploits of
Robert Curthose in the Holy Land. If the account of Ordericus
Vitalis can be trusted, he again assumed the rôle of mediator,
together with Robert of Flanders, in the fresh quarrel which
broke out between Godfrey and the count of Toulouse over the
expected surrender of Ascalon.[145] But his efforts met with no
success, and the Saracens, learning of the dissension among the
leaders, closed their gates. For more than fifty years Ascalon
remained in the hands of the enemy, a constant menace to the
peace and prosperity of the Latin Kingdom.

Nothing now remained to detain longer in the Holy Land
Robert Curthose and Robert of Flanders, and other crusaders

[141] Albert of Aix, in *H. C. Oc.*, iv, p. 494.
[142] *G. F.*, pp. 494–495; Albert of Aix, in *H. C. Oc.*, iv, p. 497; cf. William of
Malmesbury, *G. R.*, ii, pp. 429–430.
[143] *G. F.*, pp. 499–501.
[144] *Ibid.*, pp. 498–499; Albert of Aix, in *H. C. Oc.*, iv, p. 497; Baldric of Dol,
ibid., p. 110.
[145] Ordericus, iii, pp. 620–621; cf. Albert of Aix, in *H. C. Oc.*, iv, pp. 497–498;
Ralph of Caen, *ibid.*, iii, p. 703. Hagenmeyer studies the whole problem in *G. F.*,
pp. 500–502, n. 94.

who had no personal ambitions to promote. Having bathed in the Jordan and gathered palms at Jericho according to the immemorial custom of Jerusalem-farers,[146] they took leave of Godfrey and Tancred and set forth upon the homeward journey in company with Count Raymond.[147] As they proceeded northward by the coast road they learned that Bohemond had taken advantage of their absence in the south to lay siege to the friendly city of Laodicea. But making a short halt at Jebeleh, they quickly came to an understanding with the Laodiceans; and when they had compelled Bohemond to retire from his disgraceful enterprise, they were received into the city with great rejoicing.[148] It was then the month of September.[149] Raymond, who by this time — as Chalandon has made perfectly clear [150] — was acting in close agreement with Alexius, garrisoned the fortresses in the Emperor's name and remained to hold the city against the machinations of Bohemond.[151]

After a brief sojourn at Laodicea, Robert Curthose and Robert of Flanders and many of their comrades continued their homeward journey by sea,[152] embarking, apparently, upon imperial ships and sailing for Constantinople, where they were magnificently received by the Emperor.[153] To all who would enter his service he offered great rewards and honors; but the two Roberts desired to push on homeward without delay. Accordingly, he presented them with rich gifts and granted them markets and a free passage through his territories; and so they returned to Italy and were received with great rejoicing by Roger of Sicily, Roger

---

[146] Fulcher, p. 319, and n. 2.

[147] *Ibid.*, pp. 319–320; Albert of Aix, in *H. C. Oc.*, iv, p. 499; letter of Dagobert, Godfrey, and Raymond to the Pope, in *Kreuzzugsbriefe*, p. 173; Ordericus, iv, p. 69.

[148] Albert of Aix, in *H. C. Oc.*, iv, pp. 499–500, 502–503; Ordericus, iv, pp. 70–72; letter of Dagobert, Godfrey, and Raymond to the Pope, in *Kreuzzugsbriefe*, p. 173.

[149] Albert of Aix, in *H. C. Oc.*, iv, p. 503; cf. Ordericus, iv, p. 69.

[150] *Alexis I⁰ʳ*, pp. 205 ff.

[151] Albert of Aix, in *H. C. Oc.*, iv, pp. 503–504.

[152] *Ibid.*, p. 504.

[153] Ordericus, iv, pp. 72–75; Fulcher, pp. 319–320. Though Ordericus knew the work of Fulcher, which he calls " certum et verax volumen " (iii, p. 459), he appears at this point to be entirely independent of it.

Bursa, Geoffrey of Conversano, and other relatives and compatriots.[154]

Here Duke Robert paused and comfortably rested upon his
enviable reputation while he enjoyed the sumptuous entertainment of admiring friends and made plans for the future. His
position during this second sojourn in Italy was indeed an enviable
one. For once in his life he had played a distinguished part in a
great adventure worthy of the best traditions of the Normans.
It is true that he had not displayed so great energy and resourcefulness as some of the other leaders. Bohemond and Tancred,
had they been present, might in a measure have eclipsed his
fame. But for the moment he stood without a rival; and it is
little wonder that he gained the hand of one of the great heiresses
of Norman Italy together with a dower sufficiently rich to enable
him to redeem his duchy.[155]

The Crusade had been a fortunate venture in the life of Robert
Curthose. He had set out from Normandy with a record of con-
tinuous failure and a reputation for weakness and incompetence.
He was now returning with all the prestige and glory of a great
crusading prince, his past sins and failures all forgotten. He was
soon to become a hero of romance; and, among modern writers,
Freeman has not hesitated to praise him as a skilled commander,
" ever foremost in fight and council." [156] But a careful reading
of the sources hardly justifies the bestowal of such praise. Robert
had, it is true, shown some fine qualities as a crusader. He had
kept faith with the Greek Emperor and won his lasting gratitude.
His generosity and good-fellowship had gained him many friends
and followers,[157] and it is not recorded that any one was his enemy.

---

[154] Ordericus, iv, pp. 75–76, 77–78.

[155] *Ibid.*, pp. 78–79; William of Malmesbury, *G. R.*, ii, p. 461; cf. *infra*, pp. 123–124.

[156] William Rufus, i, pp. 560, 564. Palgrave goes so far as to say, "Robert had earned an entirely new reputation. The thoughtless spendthrift was transiently disciplined into prudence, the dissolute idler reformed into a happy and affectionate husband." *History of Normandy and of England*, iv, p. 673.

[157] Ralph of Caen, in describing the positions at Antioch, says: " Ab altero autem latere Blesensis, Boloniensis, Albamarensis, Montensis, Sancti-Paulensis, et Hugo Magnus; nam omnes his comitis Normanni muneribus, aliqui etiam homina-gio obligabantur." *H. C. Oc.*, iii, p. 642.

As a warrior he had always fought with distinguished bravery, and in the battle of Ascalon, at least, he had performed a greater feat of arms than any of his comrades. He had gone to the Holy Land with no ulterior ambitions, and in this respect he stands in happy contrast with the self-seeking Bohemond and the grasping count of Toulouse. His disinterestedness had gained him a certain distinction enjoyed by no other crusader, save perhaps his cousin, Count Robert of Flanders; and it is not without reason that he appears frequently among the peacemakers, who in the general interest undertook to reconcile the quarrels of rival leaders. Yet he was still the same indulgent, affable, ' sleepy duke,' [158] who had failed in the government of his duchy once and was to fail again. Though brave and active in the moment of danger, he was in no sense comparable as a general or as a statesman with such leaders as Bohemond and Godfrey; and on the whole the judgment of Freeman must be reversed. Robert was, so far as we know, never foremost in council; he was rarely foremost on the field of battle; and he showed no particular capacity for generalship. But with such qualities as he possessed, he was content to coöperate harmoniously with the more active and resourceful leaders, persevering on the way until the pagan had been vanquished and the Sepulchre had been won. Not unnaturally he returned to Europe in the enjoyment of fame and honor.

[158] This favorite characterization of Ordericus Vitalis is confirmed by Ralph of Caen and by Guibert of Nogent. *H. C. Oc.*, iii, p. 649; iv, p. 149.

CHAPTER V

FAILURE TO GAIN THE ENGLISH CROWN

WHILE Robert Curthose was loitering in southern Italy, enjoying the hospitality of Norman friends and kinsmen, events of immense importance for him were taking place beyond the Alps. On 2 August 1100 William Rufus was slain while hunting in the New Forest.[1] News of the tragedy quickly reached the ears of Henry Beauclerc, his younger brother, who was a member of the royal party; and without a moment's delay he put spurs to his horse and galloped away to Winchester, the seat of the royal treasury, and as lawful heir (*genuinus haeres*) imperiously demanded the keys of the keepers. But the interests and the superior claims of Robert Curthose did not go undefended in that hour. William of Breteuil, son of William Fitz Osbern, had also been a member of the king's hunting party; and foreseeing Henry's design, he had ridden hard upon his heels to Winchester. Arriving upon the scene before Henry had gained possession of the treasure, he protested that Robert's rights should be respected. Robert, he declared, was beyond a doubt the Conqueror's eldest son; Henry had done him homage and sworn fealty to him as his lord; Robert had long labored in the Lord's service on the Crusade; and now God was restoring to him, as if by miracle, the duchy which he had relinquished for the love of Heaven. But Henry was not to be balked in his purpose by any such scruples. The crowd which had gathered to witness the altercation clearly favored " the present heir who was claiming his right "; and with such encouragement, Henry drew his sword and exclaimed that he would never permit a " foreigner," through " frivolous delays," to anticipate him in grasping the sceptre of his father. Then friends and prudent counsellors intervened to allay the dissensions, and, without any serious rupture, the supporters of the duke gave way, and the castle and the royal hoard were

---

[1] *A.-S. C.*, a. 1100; Florence of Worcester, II, p. 44; William of Malmesbury, *G. R.*, ii, p. 378; Henry of Huntingdon, p. 232; Ordericus, iv, pp. 86–87.

handed over to Henry.[2] In that moment Robert Curthose lost a kingdom.

The rapidity with which events now moved forward, and the intelligence and sureness of judgment which were introduced into the direction of affairs, are highly indicative of the character and determination of the man who had grasped the helm. " On Thursday he [William Rufus] was slain, and on the morning after buried; and after he was buried, those of the council who were nigh at hand chose his brother Henry for king; and he straightways gave the bishopric of Winchester to William Giffard, and then went to London; and on the Sunday after, before the altar at Westminster, promised to God and all the people to put down all the injustices that were in his·brother's time; and to maintain the best laws that stood in any king's day before him. And then, after that, .the bishop of London, Maurice, hallowed him king; and all in this land submitted to him and swore oaths and became his men." [3] " And that nothing might be wanting to the aggregate of happiness, Ranulf, the dregs of iniquity, was cast into the gloom of a prison, and speedy messengers were despatched to recall Anselm." [4] The news of the king's death had, it may be supposed, taken Henry entirely unawares. Yet within less than four days he had surmounted all the difficulties connected with the seizure of the kingdom and had sketched out the programme of a reign. To Robert's claim of primogeniture he had opposed the fact that he alone had been born within the realm of England and the son of a king and queen.[5] The very real argument that Robert was still far away, and that his return could not be awaited without grave peril to the nation, was also doubtless used with telling effect.[6] The appointment of William Giffard to

[2] Ordericus, iv, pp. 87–88; William of Malmesbury, *G. R.*, ii, p. 470; cf. *Interpolations de Robert de Torigny*, in William of Jumièges, p. 279.

[3] *A.-S. C., a.* 1100, Thorpe's translation.

[4] William of Malmesbury, *G. R.*, ii, p. 470.

[5] Ordericus, iv, p. 88; *Interpolations de Robert de Torigny*, in William of Jumièges, p. 279.

[6] Suger, *Vie de Louis le Gros*, ed. Auguste Molinier (Paris, 1887), p. 8; Wace, *Roman de Rou*, ii, p. 432 :

E al realme rei estoet,

Kar sainz rei pas estre ne poet.

the vacant see of Winchester, the recall of Anselm, and the imprisonment of the infamous Ranulf Flambard, the chief oppressor of the late reign, were all measures calculated to announce in unmistakable terms to church and clergy that the evils from which they had suffered under William Rufus were at an end.[7] And the issue of the famous Charter of Liberties, in direct connection with the coronation, was a proclamation to the nation that better days were at hand.[8] Its publication in the counties must in some cases have brought almost the first news of the tyrant's death and of the inauguration of the new reign. But not content with these measures, Henry took another step well calculated to strengthen his hold upon the affections of his English subjects. Giving up ' meretricious pleasures,' he married Matilda," daughter of Malcolm, king of Scotland, and of the good queen Margaret, King Edward's kinswoman, of the true royal line of England." [9] The marriage was solemnized on Martinmas (11 November). At Christmas, Henry gained the tacit recognition of his royal title among the crowned heads of Europe. With King Philip's full permission, Louis, the king designate of France, paid him a state visit with a distinguished suite, and was received with fitting honors at Westminster.[10] But this was not only an indication that Henry had been received into the society of kings, it was an earnest of the cordial relations which were to prevail between the French and English courts until the critical years of the new reign had passed. The triumph of Henry's clear-cut, far-seeing policy could hardly have been more complete. There were rocks ahead, but at least he had made the vessel seaworthy, and with firm and careful steering he might hope to avoid all perils.

Henry I had good reason for acting with precipitate haste in making sure his hold upon the English crown, for the rumor ran

But Wace becomes quite incredible when he asserts that the bishops and barons forced the crown upon Henry, who desired to await Robert's return.

[7] Cf. *A.-S. C.*, *a.* 1100; Florence of Worcester, ii, pp. 46–47; William of Malmesbury, *G. R.*, ii, p. 470; Henry of Huntingdon, pp. 232–233.

[8] See the text in Stubbs, *Select Charters*, 9th ed. (Oxford, 1913), pp. 117–119.

[9] *A.-S. C.*, *a.* 1100; cf. Florence of Worcester, ii, p. 47; William of Malmesbury, *G. R.*, ii, p. 470; Henry of Huntingdon, p. 233.

[10] Simeon, *H. R.*, p. 232; *Annales de Wintonia*, in *Annales Monastici*, ii, p. 41; Ordericus, iv, pp. 195, 196.

that his elder brother was returning from Italy, and was already close at hand. The king had well grounded fears that unless he made his position absolutely secure the English barons might repent of their decision and withdraw their allegiance.[11]

Robert Curthose was probably already on his way home from southern Italy when William Rufus came to his tragic end in the New Forest. Late in August, or early in September,[12] he arrived in Normandy with his newly won bride, the beautiful Sibyl of Conversano, and was joyfully welcomed by his subjects.[13] Without encountering any opposition, he entered into full possession of his duchy,[14] " except the castles which were occupied by King Henry's men, against which he had many onsets and contests." [15]

There were many reasons for the cordial welcome which Normandy extended her duke upon his return from the Crusade. The old evils and abuses of his earlier reign had doubtless largely been forgotten, while the rule of William Rufus, who had " trampled Normandy under his feet " [16] by reason of his warlike undertakings and the extreme rigor of his justice,[17] had prepared men's minds for a milder régime. Robert's long labors in the Holy War had brought him much prestige and made him a European figure. The charms of his fair Italian bride [18] struck the imagination of the people. Moreover, the death of the late king had been followed by a fresh outburst of private war in Normandy; [19]

[11] William of Malmesbury, G. R., ii, p. 470.
[12] September, according to Ordericus Vitalis (iv, p. 98). Henry of Huntingdon (p. 233) gives August, which is his usual rendering of the ' in autumn ' of the Anglo-Saxon Chronicle (cf. a. 1100). The sources agree that Robert returned soon after Henry's accession. Cf. Interpolations de Robert de Torigny, in William of Jumièges, p. 282.
[13] A.-S. C., a. 1100; Henry of Huntingdon, p. 233; Wace, Roman de Rou, ii, pp. 438–439; cf. Ordericus, v. p. 2.
[14] William of Malmesbury, G. R., ii, p. 471; Interpolations de Robert de Torigny, in William of Jumièges, p. 283; Ordericus, iv, pp. 98–99; Wace, Roman de Rou, ii, p. 439.
[15] A.-S. C., a. 1100. Henry had held Domfront since 1092; the Cotentin had been granted him by William Rufus in 1096.
[16] Ordericus, iv, p. 16.
[17] Ibid., p. 98; Wace, Roman de Rou, ii, p. 416.
[18] Interpolations de Robert de Torigny, in William of Jumièges, p. 285; Ordericus, iv, p. 78; Wace, Roman de Rou, ii, p. 438.
[19] Ordericus, iv, p. 98.

and the return of the legitimate duke, ' as if by miracle,' offered at least a hope of the restoration of peace and order. But most important of all, the critical state of English affairs left Henry I no time or resources to turn his attention to the Continent; and, except in so far as his garrisons might still hold out at Domfront and in the Cotentin, he was powerless to prevent the restoration.

If Robert's absence during the critical days of early August had been fatal to his cause in England, the unexpected death of the late king had nevertheless been his rare good fortune, so far as the recovery of Normandy was concerned. Men saw in it the hand of God exercised on behalf of the crusader.[20] Probably William Rufus had never intended to restore the Norman duchy upon Robert's return from the Crusade.[21] In any case, Robert could not have hoped to recover it except by repayment of the loan for which it had been pledged. Indeed, we know that while in Italy, by means of his wife's dowry and through the gifts of friends, he had taken pains to provide himself with funds for the redemption of the duchy.[22] But the tragedy in the New Forest had obviated this unpleasant necessity. Joyfully welcomed home, the weary crusader entered into possession of his dominions without the repayment of a single penny.

Robert's first acts upon his return to Normandy are eminently characteristic, and they contrast strangely with the unparalleled energy and decision with which Henry was pressing forward to his goal in England. Far from giving his undivided attention to the grave problems of his distracted state, he went with his wife on pilgrimage to Mont-Saint-Michel to render thanks to God and the archangel for his safe return from the Crusade.[23] Then, if Wace may be trusted, he went to Caen to visit his sister, Abbess Cecilia of La Trinité, and presented her church with a splendid Saracen banner which he had captured in the Holy War.[24]

[20] Cf. Ordericus, iv, p. 88.

[21] This is the view of Freeman. *William Rufus*, i, p. 556.

[22] Ordericus, iv, pp. 78–79; *Interpolations de Robert de Torigny*, in William of Jumièges, p. 282.

[23] Ordericus, iv, p. 98.

[24] *Roman de Rou*, ii, p. 415. Wace is the only authority to mention this incident. The trophy in question cannot be the one already mentioned (*supra*, p. 116), which

While Robert was indulging in devotions and ceremonial and Henry was absorbed in the affairs of his kingdom, events in Maine were rapidly approaching a crisis which was to prove fatal to Norman dominion in the county. During Robert's absence on the Crusade, William Rufus had reasserted with the utmost vigor, but with questionable success, the Norman claim to rule in Maine. Against him Helias of La Flèche had maintained a stubborn resistance. And although towards the end of the Red King's reign he had been forced to retire beyond the frontier into his own strongholds farther south, no sooner did he receive word of the king's death·than he pushed forward again and recovered Le Mans. But the citadel with its Norman garrison still held out against him, and, obtaining reënforcements from Fulk le Réchin, his Angevin overlord, Helias began to besiege it.

The events which followed are a perfect illustration of the prevailing ideas of the feudal age. The commanders of the Norman garrison had been set to guard the castle of Le Mans by their lord, William Rufus, who was now dead. And there was a question as to who was his legitimate successor, and, therefore, as to whom they now owed allegiance. Obtaining a truce from Helias, they sent to both Robert and Henry to seek aid or instructions. Going first to Robert, their messenger found him " broken by the hardships of his long pilgrimage, and preferring the quiet of the couch to warlike exertions." The plight of the Norman garrison at Le Mans and the prospective loss of a county moved him little. " I am wearied with long labor," he is reported to have said, " and my duchy of Normandy is enough for me. Moreover, the barons of England are inviting me to cross the sea and are prepared to receive me as'their king." Robert, therefore, advised the commanders of the garrison to make an honorable peace.

was taken in the battle of Ascalon and presented by Robert to the church of the Holy Sepulchre in Jerusalem. But Robert may very well have captured more than one such trophy, and Wace's personal connection with Caen adds more than the usual weight to his authority on a point of this kind.

There is in the *Miracula* of St. Thomas Becket a record of a topaz which was reputed to have been brought back from Jerusalem by Robert, and which was later presented to the shrine of the martyr at Canterbury by Ralph Fitz Bernard in gratitude for his healing. *Materials for the History of Thomas Becket*, ed. J. C. Robertson (London, 1875–85), i, pp. 482–483.

Getting no satisfaction from the duke, the envoy hastened to
England to ask aid of the king. But Henry was engrossed in the
affairs of his realm — which Robert's return had rendered critical
— and he prudently decided not to embark upon a hazardous
foreign enterprise at that time. He thanked the Norman commanders at Le Mans for their loyalty and consideration, but sent
their messenger away empty. And when they had thus " laud-
ably proved their fidelity," they surrendered the citadel to Helias
of La Flèche, late in October, and marched out with the honors of
war.[25]

So ended the Norman domination in Maine. Helias of La
Flèche was now completely master of the county; and the betrothal of Eremburg, his only daughter, to the oldest son of Fulk
le Réchin paved the way for its later union with Anjou. Not
until an Angevin count should succeed to the Norman duchy
were the two territories again to be brought under a single ruler.

It has been suggested that Henry I, while declining to aid the
Norman garrison at Le Mans, was already secretly negotiating
with Helias of La Flèche with a view to obtaining his aid against
Robert Curthose.[26] But there is no evidence of any such negotiations, and since it is not until several years later that Maine and
Anjou appear as active supporters of the king against the duke,
this hypothesis seems unwarrantable. In the autumn of 1100,
Henry was in no position to interfere in continental affairs. He
showed his wisdom and his sense of proportion in allowing Maine
to go its way, while he dealt with the more pressing problem of

[25] The whole episode is related with much detail by Ordericus Vitalis in one of
his most pleasing chapters. Ordericus, iv, pp. 99–102. His whole account is in
general confirmed by the *Actus Pontificum* (p. 404), which, however, make no
mention of the envoy sent to Robert, and merely record that the besieged garrison
waited in vain for aid from the king. The date of the surrender of the garrison can
be placed definitely before 1 November 1100 on the evidence of a donation in favor
of Saint-Aubin of Angers. Archives départementales de la Sarthe, H 290 (*Inventaire sommaire*, iii, p. 127). The document is dated in the year of King William's
death " et recuperationis Helie comitis Cenomanorum," 1100, indiction viii, kalends
of November. According to the *Actus Pontificum*, the garrison held out for more
than three months, but this is evidently an exaggeration, as it would carry us beyond 1 November. The surrender must, it seems safe to conclude, have taken place
on or very shortly before that date.

[26] Latouche, *Maine*, pp. 51–52.

the investiture controversy with Anselm and the papacy and prepared to frustrate the projects of disaffected subjects who were
already plotting his overthrow. The interests of Robert Curthose
in Maine, on the other hand, were more immediate, and Ordericus
Vitalis charges his inaction to his habitual indolence. But the
real cause of his indifference, it seems, was the fact that visions of
a second Norman conquest of England were already floating
before his unstable mind. Within a few months he was fairly
launched in preparations for an invasion of the island kingdom
and an attempt to gain the English crown.

As soon as Robert's return from the Crusade became known in
England, " almost all the magnates of the land violated the
fealty which they had sworn " [27] and entered into secret negotiations for his elevation to the English throne.[28] Robert of Bellême
and his two brothers Roger and Arnulf, William of Warenne,
Walter Giffard, Ivo of Grandmesnil, and Robert, son of Ilbert de
Lacy, were the chief conspirators.[29] Accepting their proposals
with alacrity, Robert Curthose promptly relapsed into all the old
extravagant practices which had impoverished him and stripped
him of his inherited dominions during his earlier reign. To
Robert of Bellême he granted the castle of Argentan, the forest of
Gouffern, and lucrative rights attaching to the bishopric of Séez.[30]
Upon others he squandered the treasure which he had brought
back with him from Italy, while to others still he made extravagant promises to be fulfilled out of the spoils of England.[31] Yet

---

[27] William of Malmesbury, *G. R.*, ii, p. 471.

[28] *A.-S. C.*, a. 1101; Florence of Worcester, ii, p. 48; cf. *Annales de Wintonia*,
in *Annales Monastici*, ii, p. 40.

[29] Ordericus, iv, pp. 103–104.

[30] " Tunc Rodberto de Belismo Sagiensem episcopatum et Argentomum castrum silvamque Golferni donavit." *Ibid.*, p. 104. The meaning of " Sagiensem episcopatum " is not clear. Le Prévost says: " Nous pensons que par *episcopatus Sagiensis* il faut entendre, non pas les revenus ecclésiastiques de l'évêché
de Séez, mais la possession et les revenus féodaux du pays qui en dépendait et qui
est plus connu sous le nom d'Hiémois." *Ibid.*, p. 104, n. 2. Freeman understands
the phrase to mean the " ducal right of advowson over the bishopric of Séez " —
" a claim very dear to the house of Belesme." *William Rufus*, ii, p. 396. Ordericus
Vitalis (iv, pp. 104, 162–163, 192) mentions this grant in practically identical
language on three separate occasions.

[31] Ordericus, iv, pp. 104–105.

it is doubtless an exaggeration which pictures the king as deserted by ' almost all the magnates of the land.' Some of the ablest and most powerful of the barons remained loyal, among them Count Robert of Meulan and his brother Henry of Beaumont, earl of Warwick, Robert Fitz Hamon, Richard de Redvers, Roger Bigot,[32] and probably many others of less note.

During the autumn and winter the conspiracy smouldered, causing the king no small concern. In his letter to Anselm immediately after his coronation, Henry directed him in returning to England to avoid Normandy and travel by way of Wissant and Dover.[33] And in his negotiations with Anselm after his arrival in England (23 September 1100), he showed great anxiety lest the archbishop should go over to the support of Robert, from whom at that time it would have been easy to get full assurances on the question of investitures.[34] Clearly the king regarded the situation as critical; yet an invasion was hardly to be feared before the following spring or summer.

It was in the spring that an untoward incident occurred, which contributed not a little to bring the conspiracy to a head and to precipitate the invasion. On 2 February 1101, Ranulf Flambard, ' the dregs of iniquity,' escaped from the Tower of London and fled to Normandy.[35] Going straight to the duke, he was received with favor, and, if we may rely upon Ordericus Vitalis, he was charged with the administration of the duchy.[36] Henceforth, the sources picture him as the chief instigator of the attack upon England. Doubtless his well known talents were turned to good account in the equipment of a fleet and in the assembling of the " no small multitude of knights, archers, and foot soldiers " which was gathered at Tréport ready for the crossing.[37]

---

[32] William of Malmesbury, *G. R.*, ii, p. 471.

[33] " Laudo ergo et mando ne per Northmanniam venias, sed per Guitsand, et ego Doveram obviam habebo tibi barones meos." *Epistolae Anselmi*, bk. iii, no. 41, in Migne, clix, col. 76.

[34] Eadmer, p. 120.

[35] *A.-S. C.*, a. 1101; Florence of Worcester, ii, p. 48; William of Malmesbury, *G. R.*, ii, p. 471; Henry of Huntingdon, p. 234; Ordericus, iv, p. 109.

[36] Ordericus, iv, p. 110.

[37] Florence of Worcester, ii, p. 48.

Meanwhile, in England, the Pentecostal court (9 June) was thrown into consternation by the news of an imminent invasion.[38] The *curia* was honeycombed with treason, and king and magnates regarded one another with mutual suspicion. Not knowing how far the conspiracy had spread, Henry was in terror of a general desertion by the barons. They, on the other hand, feared an increase of royal power and the summary vengeance that would fall upon them as traitors after the restoration of peace. At this juncture, all discussion of the investiture controversy was set aside, and king and barons alike turned to Archbishop Anselm as the one man whose character commanded universal confidence and who, by his position as primate of England, was constitutionally qualified to act as mediator in such a crisis. Apparently the nobles and people renewed their allegiance by a general oath; and the king, on his part, extending his hand to the archbishop as the representative of his subjects, " promised that so long as he lived he would govern the realm with just and holy laws." [39]

When this mutual exchange of assurances had somewhat cleared the air, already thick with treason, the king proceeded with his accustomed vigor to take measures to thwart the impending attack. He sent ships to sea to head off the hostile fleet. He gathered an army from all parts of the realm, and, marching

---

[38] Eadmer, p. 126; cf. *A.-S. C., a.* 1101; Henry of Huntingdon, p. 233.

[39] Eadmer, p. 126: " . . . actum ex consulto est, ut certitudo talis hinc inde fieret, quae utrinque quod verebatur excluderet. Sed ubi ad sponsionem fidei regis ventum est, tota regni nobilitas cum populi numerositate Anselmum inter se et regem medium facerunt, quatinus ei vice sui, manu in manum porrecta, promitteret iustis et sanctis legibus se totum regnum quoad viveret in cunctis administraturum "; William of Malmesbury, *G. P.,* pp. 105–106.

It is probable that the king's promise to abide by his coronation charter and the exaction of an oath of obedience from his subjects were extended to the whole realm by means of writs addressed to the counties. One of these writs, that addressed to the shire-moot of Lincolnshire, has been preserved. It reads in part as follows: " Sciatis quod ego vobis concedo tales lagas et rectitudines et consuetudines, quales ego vobis dedi et concessi, quando imprimis coronam recepi. Quare volo ut assecuretis michi sacramento terram meam Anglie, ad tenendum et ad defendendum contra omnes homines et nominatim contra Rotbertum comitem Normannie fratrem meum usque ad natale domini; et vobis predictis precipio ut hanc securitatem recipiatis de meis dominicis hominibus francigenis et anglis, et barones mei faciant vobis habere hanc eandem securitatem de omnibus suis hominibus sicut michi concesserunt." *E. H. R.,* xxi, p. 506; facsimile, *ibid.,* xxvi, p. 488.

to Pevensey "at midsummer," he pitched a permanent camp
there and awaited the invasion.[40]   Anselm joined the levy with
the knights due from his fief; [41] but the archbishop's services were
mainly moral rather than military.

As the duke's forces for the invasion were being assembled at
Tréport, not far from Saint-Valery — the port from which the
Conqueror's fleet had sailed in 1066 — it was but natural to
expect that a landing would again be attempted at Pevensey. A
different plan, however, was adopted. Buscarls whom Henry had
sent to sea to head off the invasion were corrupted — through the
contrivance of Ranulf Flambard, it is said [42] — and, deserting the
royal cause, accepted service with the duke as pilots of his fleet.[43]
With such guides the invaders easily avoided the ships which the
king had sent out against them, and sailing past Pevensey, where
the royal forces were awaiting them, they landed safely at Portsmouth (21 July),[44] and were welcomed by their confederates
within the kingdom.[45]   Sending a defiance to the king,[46] Robert
advanced upon Winchester, the seat of the royal treasury and the

---

[40] *A.-S. C.*, a. 1101; Florence of Worcester, ii, p. 48; Henry of Huntingdon,
p. 233; cf. *Interpolations de Robert de Torigny*, in William of Jumièges, p. 282;
Eadmer, pp. 126–127.

[41] *Ibid.*, p. 127.

[42] Florence of Worcester, ii, p. 48.

[43] *A.-S. C.*, a. 1101; Florence of Worcester, ii, p. 48; Henry of Huntingdon,
p. 233; cf. Ordericus, iv, p. 110.

[44] *A.-S. C.*, a. 1101: " twelve nights before Lammas "; Henry of Huntingdon,
p. 233: " ante kalendas Augusti"; Florence of Worcester, ii, pp. 48–49: " circa ad
Vincula S. Petri"; Ordericus, iv, p. 110: " in autumno."   The sources agree that
the expedition landed at Portsmouth, though Wace gives the landing place as
Porchester. *Roman de Rou*, ii, p. 439. Freeman explains that Portsmouth is a
" vaguer name " referring to the " whole haven," and that Wace, wishing to be
more specific, names Porchester as the exact point within the harbor where the
landing took place. *William Rufus*, ii, p. 406, n. 1. But it seems more likely that
Wace's choice of the word was due to the exigencies of his verse:

> Passa mer e vint a Porcestre,
> D'iloc ala prendre Wincestre.

The *Annales de Wintonia* places the number of ships in the invading fleet at two
hundred, and record the presence of Ranulf Flambard: " Dux Robertus venit in
Angliam cum cc. navibus, et cum eo Radulfus Passeflambere." *Annales Monastici*,
ii, p. 41.

[45] Ordericus, iv, p. 110.   [46] *Ibid.*

chief administrative centre of the realm, and pitched his camp in a strong position. Apparently he meant to attack the city;[47] but such a plan, if entertained, was quickly abandoned, and Robert turned towards London and advanced as far as the forest of Alton.[48]

It was a trying moment for the king, and the chroniclers describe in moving terms the terrors which he suffered.[49] Almost despairing of his kingdom, they declare, he feared even for his life.[50] The successful landing of the invaders had given the signal for further desertions among the disaffected barons.[51] Many who until this moment had maintained the appearance of loyalty now openly aligned themselves with the duke, seeking to cloak their infamous conduct by demanding unjust and impossible concessions from the king. To this number belong Robert of Bellême and William of Warenne,[52] who clearly had been among the chief conspirators from the beginning, and probably also William of Mortain, earl of Cornwall.[53] Robert of Meulan, who on every occasion remained faithful to the king, was for paying these base traitors in their own coin. He urged the king to conciliate

---

[47] Florence of Worcester, ii, p. 49; Wace, *Roman de Rou*, ii, p. 440.

[48] *Ibid.*, ii, pp. 440–441. For the identification of Alton, see Freeman, *William Rufus*, ii, p. 408, n. 2. According to Ordericus (iv, p. 113) the armies met " in quadam planicie."

Wace, with his fondness for chivalrous detail, relates that Robert abandoned his proposed attack upon Winchester because he learned that the queen was then lying there in childbed. Only a villain, he declared, would attack a woman in such plight:

> Mais l'on li dist que la reigne,
> Sa serorge, esteit en gesine,
> Et il dist que vilains sereit,
> Qui dame en gesine assaldreit.

Roman de Rou, ii, p. 440. J. H. Ramsay remarks, "but Matilda did not give birth to her child till January or February following." *The Foundations of England* (London, 1898), ii, p. 238, n. 9. He gives no reference. Henry and Matilda were married 11 November 1100.

[49] Henry of Huntingdon, pp. 311–312 (*Epistola de Contemptu Mundi*).

[50] Eadmer, p. 127; William of Malmesbury, *G. P.*, p. 105.

[51] Florence of Worcester, ii, p. 49; Eadmer, p. 127; William of Malmesbury, *G. P.*, p. 106.

[52] Ordericus, iv, p. 110.

[53] William of Malmesbury, *G. R.*, ii, p. 473.

them, " to indulge them as a father indulges his children," to grant all their requests, even though they demanded London and York. When the storm had been weathered, he insinuated, the king might visit condign punishment upon them and reclaim the domains which they had wrung from him in his hour of need.[54]

But in this dire hour Henry found a more powerful supporter in Anselm. As treason thickened around the king, he placed his trust in almost no one except the archbishop.[55] Their quarrel over investitures was no longer allowed to stand between them. Eadmer affirms that Henry gave up his whole contention in that matter, and promised henceforth to obey the decrees and commands of the apostolic see.[56] And with such assurances Anselm threw himself heart and soul into the royal cause. Privately he undertook to inspire the disloyal barons whom the king brought before him with a holy fear of violating their plighted faith.[57] But he went further. Mounting a pulpit in the midst of the host, he harangued the forces upon their obligation to abide by their sworn allegiance. His voice was like the blast of a trumpet calling the multitude to arms. Raising their voices, they pledged their goods and their loyalty to the king, upon condition that he put away the evil customs which had come in with William Rufus and that he keep good laws.[58]

Thus the church and the English people stood firmly behind the king,[59] and many of the barons who at first had contemplated desertion seem to have been held back by the strong personal influence of the archbishop. And, with such support, Henry

---

[54] Ordericus, iv, pp. 112–113.

[55] Eadmer, p. 127.

[56] " Ipse igitur Anselmo iura totius Christianitatis in Anglia exercendae se relicturum, atque decretis et iussionibus apostolicae sedis se perpetuo oboediturum, summo opere promittebat." *Ibid.*

[57] William of Malmesbury, *G. P.*, pp. 105–106.

[58] Eadmer, p. 127; William of Malmesbury, *G. P.*, p. 106; cf. *G. R.*, ii, pp. 471–472.

[59] " Omnes quoque Angli, alterius principis iura nescientes, in sui regis fidelitate perstiterunt, pro qua certamen inire satis optaverunt." Ordericus, iv, pp. 110–111; cf. Florence of Worcester, ii, p. 49.

moved forward to intercept the invaders,[60] and came face to face with them at Alton.[61] Yet no battle ensued:

> Dote li reis, dote li dus,
> Mais io ne sai qui dota plus.[62]

In this happy couplet Wace has described the situation exactly. In spite of a very fortunate beginning, resolution failed the duke and his supporters when it came to pressing their advantage home.[63] The king, too, notwithstanding the disaffection among his barons, had been able to muster a formidable army. Probably the desertions from the royal cause had been less numerous than Robert and his supporters had anticipated.[64] The battle, if joined, would certainly be a bloody one. And, on his side, the king was in no position to force the issue: the loyalty of a considerable portion of his army was too doubtful. Moreover, it was no part of Henry's character to seek by arms what he could achieve by diplomacy, a sphere in which he enjoyed a far greater superiority. The chief supporters of both sides also hesitated. A fratricidal war was as little attractive to the barons, whose families were divided between the two opposing forces, as it was to the two brothers who were the principals in the contest.[65] And so saner counsels prevailed, and leading barons from each side opened negotiations for peace.[66]

[60] *A.-S. C.*, a. 1101; Henry of Huntingdon, p. 233; *Chronicon*, in *Liber de Hyda*, p. 305; *Interpolations de Robert de Torigny*, in William of Jumièges, p. 282.

[61] Wace, *Roman de Rou*, ii, p. 440; cf. *supra*, n. 48.

[62] Wace, *Roman de Rou*, ii, p. 441.

[63] " Rotbertus qui magis aliorum perfidia quam sua fidens industria venerat, destitit praelio, descivit a negotio." William of Malmesbury, *G. P.*, p. 106.

[64] Eadmer, pp. 127–128. Eadmer adds that Robert was also deterred by a threat of excommunication which Anselm held over him: "non levem deputans excommunicationem Anselmi, quam sibi ut invasori nisi coepto desisteret invehi certo sciebat, paci adquievit."

[65] *Chronicon*, in *Liber de Hyda*, p. 306; Wace, *Roman de Rou*, ii, pp. 441–442.

[66] William of Malmesbury, *G. R.*, ii, p. 472; *A.-S. C.*, a. 1101; Florence of Worcester, ii, p. 49; Henry of Huntingdon, p. 233; *Chronicon*, in *Liber de Hyda*, p. 306.

The account of the peace negotiations given by Ordericus (iv, pp. 113–114) differs fundamentally from that of the English sources. According to him, it was Henry and Robert personally, rather than their supporters, who came together and made peace: " remotis omnibus arbitris, soli fratres scita sua sanxerunt." The

The text of the treaty which resulted has not come down to us in documentary form, but it is possible to reconstruct its terms with some fulness from the narrative sources. Robert gave up all claim to the English crown, released Henry from the homage which he had done him on an earlier occasion — probably upon the receipt of the Cotentin in 1088 — and recognized his royal title and dignity.[67]   It was not considered fitting that an English king should remain the vassal of a Norman duke. On his side, the king undertook to pay Robert an annual subsidy of 3000 marks of silver [68] and to surrender all his holdings in Normandy except the great stronghold of Domfront.[69]   Long years before, when Henry

noble envoys through whom they at first attempted to exchange messages turned out to be base traitors, who desired war rather than peace, and who acted for their own private advantage rather than for the public good.   This led Henry to seek a personal interview with Robert.   Meeting in a great circle, around which " terribilis decor Normannorum et Anglorum in armis effulsit," their hearts were filled with " the sweetness of fraternal love," and, talking together for a little while, they made peace and exchanged " sweet kisses."   Freeman has attempted, without success as it seems to me, to reconcile this account with that of the English writers. *William Rufus*, ii, appendix xx: pp. 688–691.   I have rejected it as being essentially untrustworthy for the following reasons: (1) It is in fundamental disagreement with the English sources, which appear to be better informed.   (2) It has all the appearance of being a fancy picture, drawn from the author's notion of what ought to have happened under the circumstances.   (3) It tends greatly to eulogize the king.   This last consideration suggests the need of caution in dealing with Ordericus's statement of the terms of the treaty.

Wace says that the mediators between the king and the duke were Robert of Bellême, William of Mortain, Robert Fitz Hamon, and others whose names he has not learned. *Roman de Rou*, ii, p. 442.

[67] Ordericus, iv, p. 114.

[68] *A.-S. C.*, a. 1101; Florence of Worcester, ii, p. 49; William of Malmesbury, *G. R.*, ii, p. 472; Henry of Huntingdon, p. 233; Wace, *Roman de Rou*, ii, p. 444; *Annales de Wintonia*, in *Annales Monastici*, ii, p. 41.   Robert of Torigny places the amount of the subsidy at 4000 marks (*Interpolations de Robert de Torigny*, in William of Jumièges, p. 282); so also does the *Liber Memorandorum Ecclesie de Barnewelle* (p. 55); Ordericus Vitalis (iv, p. 114) gives it as 3000 pounds.

[69] Ordericus, iv, p. 114.   The *Anglo-Saxon Chronicle* (a. 1101) says that the king agreed to relinquish " all that he held by force in Normandy against the count." It is possible that the duke had tacitly, if not actually, recognized Henry's claim to Domfront as legitimate — he had held it since 1092 — and, therefore, that the statement quoted refers only to Henry's possessions in the Cotentin.   In that case there would be no disagreement between Ordericus and the *Anglo-Saxon Chronicle*. Wace must surely be mistaken in his statement that Henry retained the Cotentin as well as Domfront. *Roman de Rou*, ii, p. 444.

had been a wandering exile, his fortunes at their lowest, the men of Domfront had voluntarily called him in and made him their lord; and on taking possession of their town and castle he had solemnly sworn never to abandon them. The binding force of this oath was now invoked as a pretext for the king's retention of a solitary outpost in Robert's dominions. An amnesty provision was added for the benefit of the barons with holdings on both sides of the Channel who by supporting one of the brothers had jeopardized their interests with the other. Robert undertook to restore all Norman honors which he had taken from the king's supporters; [70] and Henry promised the restoration of all English lands which he had seized from partisans of the duke.[71] A special clause, of which we would gladly know the full significance, provided that Count Eustace of Boulogne should have " his paternal lands in England." [72] Further, it was agreed that, if either of the brothers should die before the other and leave no lawful heir, the survivor should succeed to his dominions whether in England or in Normandy.[73]

So far the provisions of the treaty seem reasonably certain. The remainder are more doubtful. Ordéricus Vitalis asserts — and his whole defence of Henry's dealings with Robert down to the latter's overthrow at Tinchebray, and after, is founded upon the assertion — that Robert and Henry entered into a sworn agreement to recover all of the Conqueror's domains which had been lost since his death and to visit condign punishment upon the wicked men who had fomented discord between them.[74]

---

[70] Florence of Worcester, ii, p. 49.

[71] *A.-S. C.*, a. 1101; Florence of Worcester, ii, p. 49.

[72] *A.-S. C.*, a. 1101. This is the only mention of Eustace of Boulogne in connection with these events, and it is not clear what part he had played in them.

[73] *Ibid.*; Henry of Huntingdon, p. 233.

[74] Ordericus, iv, p. 115. The phrase " omnia patris sui dominia " might refer, as in the treaty of 1091, to the recovery of Maine; or it might refer more locally to parts of the ducal demesne in Normandy which Robert had squandered upon favorites. If it refers to Maine, it must have been a purely formal provision — perhaps proposed by Henry for the diplomatic needs of the moment — for there is no evidence that an attack upon Maine was contemplated. Ordericus (iv, pp. 162–163, 192) in recounting a later stage of the quarrel between Henry and Robert, applies it to recent grants which the duke had made to Robert of Bellême in Normandy. The provision for coöperation in the punishment of traitors, if not actually incon-

Wace adds that each undertook, in case the other should be at
war, to furnish him with one hundred knights so long as the war
lasted.[75] According to the Annals of Winchester, Ranulf Flambard gave up his bishopric of Durham.[76]

The treaty, as finally agreed upon, was duly confirmed in accordance with a custom of the period by the oaths of twelve great
barons on each side.[77]

Thus ended Robert's last and greatest effort to gain the English
throne. The royal army was disbanded and sent home. A part
of the ducal forces were sent back to Normandy.[78] But with the
rest, Robert remained in England for several months upon terms
of peace and friendship with his brother.[79] May he possibly have
been awaiting the first instalment of the English subsidy ? The
Chronicler does not fail to raise a characteristic lament, though
he makes no reference to oppressive gelds: " and his men inces-
santly did much harm as they went, the while that the count con-

sistent with the amnesty clause, is, at any rate, of a piece with Ordericus's conception of the treaty as made by the brothers in spite of their followers. It ought,
therefore, to be accepted with caution. Ordericus makes frequent use of it on later
occasions to justify Henry's course of action toward Robert.

[75] *Roman de Rou*, ii, p. 444.

[76] *Annales Monastici*, ii, p. 41.

[77] *A.-S. C., a.* 1101; Henry of Huntingdon, p. 233.

[78] Florence of Worcester, ii, p. 49.

[79] We have some definite evidence concerning Robert's coöperation with King
Henry during his sojourn in England. Soon after the treaty of Alton had been concluded Anselm was summoned to appear before the *curia regis*; and we are told
that it was by the advice of Duke Robert and his friends, who hated the archbishop because he had frustrated their plans, that Henry demanded of Anselm that
he become his man and consecrate bishops and abbots whom the king had invested,
or else quit the realm. Eadmer, pp. 128, 131. On 3 September at Windsor Robert
confirmed two charters of donation by King Henry, the one in favor of Herbert,
bishop of Norwich, and the other in favor of John, bishop of Bath. W. Farrer,
" An Outline Itinerary of King Henry the First," in *E. H. R.*, xxxiv, pp. 312,
313.

At some time before the battle of Tinchebray (29 September 1106) Bishop John
of Bath obtained a separate charter from Robert confirming donations of William
Rufus and Henry I. *Two Chartularies of the Priory of St. Peter at Bath*, ed. William
Hunt (London, 1893), i, p. 47, no. 44. The document is undated. It may have
been issued during Robert's sojourn in England in 1101 or during one of his two
later visits, late in 1103 (cf. *infra*, pp. 148–149), or early in 1106 (cf *infra*, p. 169);
or, indeed, it may have been issued at some other time in Normandy.

tinued here in the country." About Michaelmas Duke Robert returned to Normandy.[80]

The treaty of Alton has been described as " the most ill considered step in the whole of Robert's long career of folly." [81] It can hardly prove a surprise, however, to one who has followed Robert's course through that long career. The real folly lay not so much in the making of the treaty as in the whole project of overthrowing Henry I, once he had got fairly seated on the English throne. It is hard to believe that the crown was within the duke's grasp as the two armies stood facing each other at Alton. Henry had the support of the church and of the mass of his English subjects. Only a faction of the nobles was against him. And a single victory gained by the ducal forces would, it seems, hardly have resulted in disaster for the royal cause. Robert had undertaken a task which was beyond his power and his resources, a fact which the king's momentary weakness cannot disguise.

[80] *A.-S. C., a.* 1101: " after St. Michael's mass "; Henry of Huntingdon, p. 234: "Usque ad festum Sancti Michaelis." Ordericus Vitalis (iv, p. 116) is more indefinite: " appropinquante hieme, in Neustriam rediit."

[81] Davis, *Normans and Angevins*, p. 124.

CHAPTER VI

THE LOSS OF NORMANDY

DUKE Robert's ambitious attempt to drive Henry I from the throne had ended in a signal failure. To be sure, he had gained the promise of an annual subsidy of 3000 marks of silver, and this must have seemed to him an important consideration. But he had also revealed his weakness and indecision; and Henry can hardly have looked upon the payment of the subsidy as more than a temporary measure which would serve his purpose until he was in a position to adopt a more aggressive course towards the duke. By accepting a money payment in lieu of his claim upon the English crown, Robert had inevitably been reduced from the offensive to the defensive; and his continued failure to give strong and effective government to Normandy was a standing invitation to Henry to attack him. The treaty of Alton marked the beginning of a path of disaster which was to lead the duke to the field of Tinchebray and the prison walls of Cardiff.

From a military standpoint there had been little of the heroic about Henry's course in meeting the invasion. But he had won a diplomatic victory of the first importance, and he was not slow to take full advantage of his success. Regardless of the amnesty which had been provided by the recent treaty, he proceeded at once to take summary vengeance upon his enemies. Robert had not yet left the realm when the first blow fell upon William of Warenne and several others who were sent out of the kingdom with him, " disinherited for his sake." [1] It soon appeared that a like fate was in store for others of the duke's late supporters. King Henry did not proceed against them directly for calling in the invader — that presumably would have been a needless violation of the treaty — nor did he court disaster by attacking them all at once. But one by one, and upon various charges, he had

[1] Ordericus, iv, p. 116.

them haled before his *curia* and condemned.[2] Ivo of Grandmesnil, the crusader, attempted to engage in private war, a thing
before almost unknown in England, and was made to pay for his
presumption with a heavy fine. Covered with shame as he was,
as a result of his cowardice at Antioch, and convinced that he
would never be able to regain the king's friendship, he found it
advisable to extricate himself from his difficulties by departing a
second time on crusade.[3] Robert Malet and Robert of Pontefract,
son of Ilbert de Lacy, were also disinherited and made to quit
the realm.[4]

Before proceeding against his more powerful enemies of the
great house of Talvas, or Bellême, Henry made more careful preparations. For the best part of a year he set his secret agents to
watch the terrible Robert, earl of Shrewsbury, and to gather
information against him, which was all carefully reduced to
writing.[5] Then suddenly, in 1102, the earl was summoned to
appear before the *curia regis*,[6] accused upon forty-five separate
counts of words spoken or acts committed against the king or his
brother, the duke of Normandy. Tacitly admitting that his case
was hopeless, the great earl fled to his strongholds without plead-
ing, and was adjudged a public enemy.[7] War followed. One by
one, the earl's fortresses, Arundel, Tickhill, Bridgenorth, and
Shrewsbury, were reduced; and before Michaelmas [8] Robert of
Bellême was driven from England, an utterly defeated and disinherited outlaw. " Filled with grief and rage," he went over sea
and " spent his fury on the Normans." [9]

[2] " Nec simul, sed separatim, variisque temporibus, de multimodis violatae
fidei reatibus implacitavit." Ordericus, iv, p. 161.

[3] *Ibid.*, pp. 167–168. He died on the way. For Ivo's flight from Antioch during the First Crusade, see *supra*, p. 107, n. 88.

[4] Ordericus, iv, pp. 161, 167.

[5] " Diligenter enim eum fecerat per unum annum explorari, et vituperabiles
actus per privatos exploratores caute investigari, summopereque litteris annotari."
Ibid., pp. 169–170; cf. Florence of Worcester, ii, p. 50.

[6] Probably the Easter court at Winchester. *A.-S. C.*, a. 1102.

[7] Ordericus, iv, p. 170; cf. Florence of Worcester, ii, p. 50.

[8] *A.-S. C.*, a. 1102; Florence of Worcester, ii, p. 51.

[9] Ordericus, iv, pp. 161, 169–177; cf. *A.-S. C.*, a. 1102; Florence of Worcester,
ii, pp. 49–50; Henry of Huntingdon, p. 234; William of Malmesbury, *G. R.*, ii,
pp. 472–473; Wace, *Roman de Rou*, ii, pp. 445–446. For a much fuller account of

It was not the king's way to do things by halves. As soon as he had finished with Robert, he took action against other members of the Bellême family. Accusations were brought against Arnulf and Roger, Robert's brothers, and they were condemned to the loss of their estates and driven from the realm.[10] But even then the king's anger was not appeased or his appetite for plunder sated; and he proceeded to confiscate the lands which the nuns of the Norman monastery of Almenèches had received in England through the generosity of Roger of Montgomery.[11] Their sole offence lay in the fact that they happened to be presided over by Abbess Emma, a sister of Robert of Bellême.

While Henry was thus engaged in extirpating his enemies in England, Normandy under Duke Robert was increasingly a prey to confusion and anarchy. As we have noted, the death of William Rufus had been the signal for an outbreak of private war in the duchy. In the very week that the news of the king's death was received, William of Évreux and Ralph of Conches made a hostile incursion into the territory of Beaumont and plundered the lands of Robert of Meulan. In a like spirit, others who had been held in check by the rigor of the Red King's justice now took up arms and desolated the wretched country.[12] It is probable that the duke's return from the Crusade and his attack upon England in some degree mitigated these conditions of disorder. The expedition against England could hardly have been fitted out and launched amid such anarchy as Ordericus describes. And as the turbulent barons prepared themselves for the foreign enterprise, their minds and hands must necessarily have been turned away from domestic feuds.

But for the same reason the failure of the attack upon England reacted disastrously upon Normandy, and brought on disorders hitherto unheard of. As Henry I expelled the outlaws from England, they invariably sought a refuge in Normandy and

the expulsion of Robert of Bellême, and for its significance in English history, see Freeman, *William Rufus*, ii, pp. 415–450.

[10] Ordericus, iv, pp. 177–178; Florence of Worcester, ii, pp. 50–51; William of Malmesbury, *G. R.*, ii, p. 473.

[11] Ordericus, iv, p. 178.

[12] *Ibid.*, p. 98.

attempted to recoup their damaged fortunes by indulging in the worst excesses.[13] For a time Robert Curthose showed some spirit in dealing with the freebooters, though, if one accept the account of Ordericus Vitalis even with considerable reservations, his efforts did him little credit. When Henry embarked upon his great struggle with the house of Bellême in 1102, he appealed to Robert under the terms of the treaty of Alton to join him in the enterprise. And the duke so far responded to his call as to assemble the forces of Normandy and lay siege to the castle of Vignats, a Bellême stronghold, which was held by Gerard de Saint-Hilaire. It is reported that the garrison were ready and even eager to surrender, had a vigorous assault been made to give them a fair excuse. But the duke had little control over his undisciplined host, and Robert de Montfort and other traitors in the ranks fired the encampment and threw the whole army into a panic. The ducal forces fled in wild confusion with none pursuing, and the astonished garrison of Vignats shouted after them in derision.[14] Realizing now that they had nothing to fear, they issued from their stronghold and carried a devastating war throughout the Hiémois, and, so far as is recorded, the duke made no effort to repress them. Nothing remained but for the local lords of the district to defend themselves. Robert of Grandmesnil and his two brothers-in-law, Hugh de Montpinçon and Robert de Courcy, assembled their vassals and did what they could to check the freebooters. But their efforts met with small success. Other Bellême garrisons from Chateau-Gontier, Fourches, and Argentan joined with the plunderers from Vignats, and their raids were carried far and wide. Only the strong could defend themselves, and the homes of the unarmed peasantry were pillaged and given over to the flames.[15]

If we have here a true account, Robert Curthose had proved unequal to the task of putting down an insignificant body of Bellême's retainers and of keeping peace in the restricted territory of the Hiémois. He was soon called upon to deal with the arch-enemy of peace and order in person. It must have been

---

[13] Cf. William of Malmesbury, *G. R.*, ii, p. 473; Ordericus, iv, p. 177.
[14] Ordericus, iv, pp. 171–172. [15] *Ibid.*, p. 172.

in the autumn of 1102 that Robert of Bellême, utterly discomfited and overwhelmed in England, crossed over to Normandy and began to vent his fury upon those of his countrymen who had dared to join the duke in attacking his garrisons.[16]

The disorders of 1102 were but a prelude to those that followed in 1103. We have only a fragmentary account of the events, but the general impression of the picture is that of a war of unparalleled violence and cruelty. Villages were depopulated, and churches were burned down upon the men, women, and children who had taken refuge in them. " Almost all Normandy " arose as by common consent against the tyrant of Bellême. But the movement was rendered ineffective for want of a strong and persistent leader.[17] Robert of Bellême, on his side, possessed almost unlimited resources. He is said to have held thirty-four strong castles, all well stocked with provisions and ready for war. Disregarding the claims of his brothers Roger and Arnulf, who had suffered outlawry and exile on his account, he retained the whole family inheritance in his own hands. While this kept his resources intact, it cost him the support of his brothers. Roger retired from the conflict and spent the rest of his life upon his wife's patrimony at Charroux. But Arnulf in high indignation deserted the family cause and threw in his lot with Robert Curthose, taking with him a considerable number of Bellême supporters. Having recently captured the castle of Almenèches, he turned it over to the duke, who assembled an army there and prepared to press his advantage.[18] With ' almost all Normandy ' in arms against him, with one of his brothers in retirement, and the other actively supporting the duke, the cause of Robert of Bellême might well seem desperate. He even doubted the fidelity of his closest friends. Yet, undismayed, he rushed to Almenèches, and, without a moment's hesitation, fired the nunnery and burned it to the ground.[19] Overwhelming the ducal

---

[16] Ordericus, iv, pp. 176, 177.   [17] *Ibid.*, pp. 178–179.

[18] *Ibid.*, p. 179.

[19] Ordericus Vitalis gives the date of these events as " mense Iunio," probably 1103. The nuns of Almenèches were dispersed, Abbess Emma with three of her associates taking refuge at Saint-Évroul. It is not improbable that Ordericus got much of his information from her. *Ibid.*, pp. 179–180; cf. pp. 182–183.

forces, he captured Oliver de Fresnay and many others, and subjected not a few of them to horrible punishments. The duke,
admitting his defeat, retired to Exmes.[20]

The necessity of crushing Robert of Bellême now became more
imperative than ever, and for a time there seemed some prospect
of success. His violence and oppression had stirred up against
him not only the Normans, but some of his powerful neighbors
across the border. Rotrou of Mortagne joined forces with William of Évreux and the men of the Hiémois. Robert of Saint-
Céneri and Hugh de Nonant also joined the movement with their
retainers. But even this swarm of enemies was unable to inflict a
crushing defeat upon the lord of Bellême. They could injure him
in numerous small engagements, but to overcome him, or inflict
any condign punishment upon him, was beyond their power.[21]

Robert of Bellême's future in Normandy was finally determined by a decisive battle with the duke, but the place and
date of the engagement are not recorded. We are without information as to the duke's movements after his retirement from
Almenèches to Exmes, though it seems clear that he reassembled
his troops and determined to renew the offensive against Robert of
Bellême. But the lord of Bellême did not wait to be attacked.
Drawing up his forces in battle order as the ducal army was approaching, he launched a furious onslaught which carried all
before it. The duke was put to flight, and William of Conversano and many others of his supporters were captured. Then,
laments the chronicler, " the proud Normans blushed for shame
that they, who had been the conquerors of barbarous foreign
nations, should now be vanquished and put to flight by one of
their own sons in the very heart of their own country." Robert
of Bellême is said to have aspired to the conquest of the whole
duchy. Many of the Normans who hitherto had resisted him now
felt constrained to bow their necks beneath the yoke, and joined
the tyrant for the sake of their own safety. Pressing his advantage home, he now gained possession of Exmes.[22] The discom-

---

[20] Ordericus, iv, p. 180. Exmes was in the keeping of Mauger Malherbe, who
had been placed there by Roger de Lacy, the duke's *magister militum*.

[21] *Ibid.*, pp. 180–181.   [22] *Ibid.*, pp. 181–182.

fiture of the duke was complete, and he had no choice but to conclude a peace with his too powerful subject upon humiliating terms.[23]

Bishop Serlo of Séez and Ralph, abbot of Saint-Martin of Séez, unable any longer to bear the oppression of the tyrant, withdrew from their posts and crossed over to England, where they were cordially welcomed by Henry I.[24] They were to be of no small service to the king in the shaping of his future policy.

While the diocese of Séez was a prey to the indescribable confusion of the struggle with Robert of Bellême, the Évrecin was not spared the horrors of a private war. There the death of William of Breteuil [25] without legitimate issue,[26] and a consequent disputed succession, had reopened an ancient local feud.[27] While William was being buried at Lire, a natural son named Eustace seized his lands and occupied the strongholds.[28] But a nephew named Renaud, of the illustrious Burgundian house of Grancey, claimed the succession as legitimate heir. Many of the Normans preferred a fellow countryman, though a bastard, to a foreigner, and supported Eustace. But the ancient enemies of Breteuil rallied around the Burgundian. William of Évreux led the

---

[23] Ordericus, iv, p. 192; cf. pp. 162–163, 200. The terms of the treaty are not recorded, except that apparently the duke conceded to Robert of Bellême " the castle of Argentan, the bishopric of Séez, and the forest of Gouffern." Inasmuch as the duke had originally made this grant before the expedition against England in 1101 (*supra*, p. 127 and n. 30), it seems evident that at some time during the struggle with Bellême he had revoked it, and that now, upon making peace, he was obliged to restore it or confirm it. Ordericus charges repeatedly that in making this peace without consulting Henry I, the duke acted in direct violation of the treaty of Alton. Ordericus, iv, pp. 162, 192, 200.

[24] *Ibid.*, p. 192.

[25] He died on 12 January, probably in 1103. *Ibid.*, ii, p. 407; iv, pp. 183, 185. Robert of Torigny gives the date of his death as 9 January 1099. *Chronique de Robert de Torigni*, ed. Léopold Delisle (Rouen, 1872–73), ii, p. 154. But this is clearly an error, since he was present at the dedication of the church of Saint-Évroul in October 1099, and since he was at Winchester in August 1100, when Henry I seized the royal treasure after the death of William Rufus.

[26] Ordericus, iv, p. 185; *Interpolations de Robert de Torigny*, in William of Jumièges, p. 290.

[27] *Supra*, pp. 76, 78.

[28] *Interpolations de Robert de Torigny*, in William of Jumièges, p. 290; Ordericus, iv, p. 186.

movement, and was promptly joined by Ralph of Conches, Amaury de Montfort, and Ascelin Goël.[29] But Eustace was supported by loyal and powerful vassals; and when he saw that he could not win single-handed, he appealed for aid to Henry I, who was quick to realize the advantages which the Breteuil succession controversy offered for the inauguration of a far-reaching policy of intervention in the internal affairs of Normandy. The king not only promised Eustace the desired assistance, but he gave him the hand of Juliana, one of his natural daughters, in marriage.[30] And further, he sent his able and trusted minister, Robert of Meulan — who as lord of Beaumont had special interests in the disturbed district — to Normandy to deal personally with the situation and to warn Robert Curthose and the Normans barons that unless they supported his son-in-law and drove out the foreign intruder, they would incur his royal displeasure. With such powerful backing, Eustace of Breteuil gradually got the better of his rival — who waged the war with such disgusting cruelty that he alienated many of his adherents — and finally made himself master of the whole of his father's honor, and expelled the foreigner from the land.[31]

It was one thing to expel the foreigner; it was quite another to overcome the local enemies of Breteuil who had rallied around the intruder for the sake of their own advantage. With these, Robert of Meulan undertook to deal, and he found them aggressive enemies, if more nearly bandits and robbers than warriors. Ascelin Goël, whose prison walls at Ivry had on a former occasion closed around William of Breteuil, ambushed and captured a certain John of Meulan, a rich burgess and usurer, when he was returning from a conference with his lord, the count of Beaumont. For four months the ' avaricious usurer ' lay in Ascelin's gaol. Doubtless the financial resources of the wealthy burgess were of no small concern to Robert of Meulan, and he made frantic efforts to procure his release. But try as he might, he could not

---

[29] Ordericus, iv, pp. 186–187.

[30] *Ibid.*, p. 187; *Interpolations de Robert de Torigny,* in William of Jumièges, pp. 290, 308.

[31] Ordericus, iv, p. 190.

extract him from the ' wolf's mouth.' Finally he was obliged to conclude a peace with William of Évreux, betrothing his infant daughter Adelina to William's nephew Amaury de Montfort. Ralph of Conches, Eustace of Breteuil, Ascelin Goël, and the other belligerent lords were included in the pacification, and John of Meulan, the usurer, was set at liberty.[32]

It is not recorded that Robert Curthose interfered in any way in this private war, or made any effort to suppress it. Perhaps he was at the time wholly occupied by the struggle with Robert of Bellême, or perhaps he may already have been on his way to England on a mission of intercession for a friend. But before following him again across the Channel, we must take some account of his domestic affairs.

The Norman heiress, Sibyl of Conversano, whom Robert brought back with him from Italy to be duchess of Normandy, has been universally praised for her surpassing beauty, refinement of manners, and excellent qualities.[33] Though she may have had a few private enemies, she enjoyed a great popularity; and Robert of Torigny affirms that at times during the duke's absence she was entrusted with the administration of the dúchy, and that in this capacity she was more successful than her husband.[34] But her beneficent career of usefulness was short indeed. Soon after the birth of her only child,[35] William the Clito, she died at Rouen,[36] and was buried, amid universal sorrow, in the cathedral church, Archbishop William Bonne-Ame performing the obsequies.[37]

The cause of Sibyl's death is shrouded in mystery. William of Malmesbury reports simply that she died shortly after the birth of

---

[32] Ordericus, iv, p. 191.

[33] *Interpolations de Robert de Torigny*, in William of Jumièges, p. 285; Ordericus, iv, p. 78; William of Malmesbury, *G. R.*, ii, p. 461; Wace, *Roman de Rou*, ii, p. 438.

[34] *Interpolations de Robert de Torigny*, in William of Jumièges, p. 285.

[35] *Ibid.*; Ordericus, iv, p. 78; Wace, *Roman de Rou*, ii, p. 438.

[36] Ordericus Vitalis (iv, p. 184) says she died ' in Lent,' probably in 1102. Cf. William of Malmesbury, *G. R.*, ii, p. 461; *Interpolations de Robert de Torigny*, in William of Jumièges, p. 285.

[37] Ordericus, iv, pp. 184–185. Her tomb in the nave of the great church was covered with a slab of white marble bearing her epitaph, which has been preserved in Ordericus Vitalis.

her son, as the result of foolish advice given by the midwife.[38] But Ordericus Vitalis does not spare us a dark scandal. According to him Agnes de Ribemont, sister of the distinguished crusader, had recently been left a widow by the death of her husband Walter Giffard, and, becoming infatuated with Robert Curthose, had entangled him in the snares of illicit love. By undertaking to gain for him the aid of her powerful family connections against his numerous enemies, she obtained from him a promise that, upon the death of his wife, he would marry her and intrust her with the administration of the duchy. Soon after, the beautiful Sibyl took to her bed and died of poison.[39] It seems almost incredible that this tale should be anything but a malicious libel got up by some of the duke's unscrupulous enemies. Duchess Sibyl was probably already dead before Agnes de Ribemont became a widow. But in the chaotic chronology of the early chapters of the eleventh book of Ordericus Vitalis, it is impossible to speak with any assurance, and a dark saying of Robert of Torigny may possible lend some color to the scandalous tale.[40]

It would seem that with domestic bereavement, and the distractions of rebellion and private war, Robert Curthose had enough to occupy him within the limits of his duchy. Yet it was apparently during this critical period that a foolish impulse of generosity towards a friend led him to embark upon an enterprise which resulted in further humiliation and disaster. William of Warenne, one of the barons who had been deprived of his possessions and honors in England after the failure of the invasion of 1101, came to the duke to complain that through loyalty to his cause he had lost the great earldom of Surrey with its annual revenue of 1000 pounds, and besought him to intercede with King Henry in order that he might regain the earldom and the royal favor. Apparently the duke had not yet realized the character of his unscrupulous brother, or the hostile plans which

---

[38] *G. R.*, ii, p. 461.

[39] Ordericus, iv, pp. 184, 473.

[40] " Vixit autem in Normannia parvo tempore, invidia et factione quorumdam nobilium feminarum decepta." *Interpolations de Robert de Torigny*, in William of Jumièges, p. 285.

Henry was maturing against him, and he readily consented to William of Warenne's request.[41]

It must have been towards the end of the year 1103 that Duke Robert crossed the Channel with a small suite of knights and squires and landed at Southampton.[42]   Henry I was quick to realize the advantages of the situation, and with perfect unscrupulousness he determined to use them to the utmost.   Feigning great indignation that Robert had presumed to enter his dominions without permission and a safe-conduct, he sent his agents — Robert of Meulan seems to have been chiefly charged with the enterprise [43] — to intimate to him that he was in grave danger of capture and imprisonment.   The duke was taken completely by surprise.   He had no armed force at his back.   He was, in fact, at the king's mercy, although the externals of an honorable reception were accorded him, and he was conducted to the royal court, where negotiations were carried on in private.   Henry charged him with a violation of the treaty of Alton in that, instead of punishing traitors with the rigor befitting a prince, he had made peace with Robert of Bellême and had confirmed him in the possession of certain of their father's domains.   The duke, appreciating his helplessness in the situation in which he found himself, humbly promised to make amends; but the king now informed him that he desired something more than this — indeed, that he would not permit him to quit the realm until he had surrendered his claim to the annual subsidy of 3000 marks which was due him under the terms of the treaty of Alton.   In order that this crowning humiliation might be cloaked in a garb of decency, the duke was allowed to see the queen, his god-daughter, and to relinquish the subsidy as if at her request.[44]   But this clever play upon his

---

[41] Ordericus, iv, pp. 161–162; Wace, *Roman de Rou*, ii, p. 448.

[42] *Ibid.*, pp. 448–449; Ordericus, iv, p. 162; *A.-S. C.*, a. 1103;   Florence of Worcester, ii, p. 52; Henry of Huntingdon, p. 234.

[43] Wace, *Roman de Rou*, ii, p. 449.

[44] The foregoing details have been drawn from Ordericus (iv, pp. 162–163) and from Wace (*Roman de Rou*, ii, pp. 449–454), the only writers who report this episode with any fulness.   They are not in complete accord, yet on the whole they confirm and support one another to a remarkable degree.   Ordericus endeavors to justify the king at every point.   Wace, on the other hand, sees the king's action in its true

chivalrous nature could not conceal the character of the trans-
action. Robert in his ineffable simplicity had been treacherously
taken and robbed. According to William of Malmesbury, the
king had even gone the length of inducing him to come to England
by a special invitation.[45] However this may be, and whatever the
uncertainty about the details of this episode, the sources are
agreed as to the character of the part which the king had played
in it.[46] Wace avers that it was only then that Robert began to
realize that his brother hated him.[47]

William of Warenne was now restored to the royal favor, and
recovered his earldom. And the duke, having given full satisfaction in all that was demanded of him, was allowed to return to
Normandy, a greater object of contempt than ever among his
subjects.[48] It can hardly be doubted that from this moment the
king had formed a deliberate project of depriving him of his
duchy and of reuniting Normandy to England. Step by step
Robert was paving the way to his own destruction, while Henry
with equal sureness was preparing himself for the final triumph.
Whatever prestige the duke had brought back with him from the
Crusade must long since have been dissipated. He had failed
lamentably in his attempt to gain the English crown, he had
failed to oust an ever encroaching enemy from the strongholds of
his duchy, he had failed to subdue his most powerful and lawless
subject, Robert of Bellême. He had placed no check upon the
anarchy of private war, he had wasted his fortune upon base
associates and barren enterprises, and he had alienated the Norman church.

light, but he adds many details which are probably imaginative. Ordericus makes
no mention of the part played by the queen; but Wace makes this a leading feature
of the episode. Can this be mere embroidery on the brief statement of William of
Malmesbury: " Porro ille, quasi cum fortuna certaret utrum plus illa daret an ipse
dispergeret, sola voluntate reginae tacite postulantis comperta, tantam massam
argenti benignus in perpetuum ignovit; acclines foeminei fastus preces pro magno
exosculatus; erat enim eius in baptismo filiola " ? *G. R.*, ii, p. 462.

[45] *Ibid.*, p. 474. The same notion finds expression in Wace, not as a fact, but as
a current opinion. *Roman de Rou*, ii, p. 448.

[46] Even Ordericus Vitalis cannot conceal it.

[47] *Roman de Rou*, ii, p. 451.

[48] Ordericus, iv, p. 163.

Since the duke's return from the Crusade, government in Normandy seems to have been almost in abeyance. Nothing could more surely have lost Robert the support of the church than the unrestrained anarchy and disorder which prevailed. Yet there were other grounds on which he was found wanting by the clergy. While dissipating his treasure upon unworthy favorites and unscrupulous courtiers, he had few favors to bestow upon religious foundations. Only a single charter by the duke has survived from the period after his return from the Crusade, a grant of a fair and a market in the village of Cheux to the monks of Saint-Étienne of Caen.[49]

But the church had greater and more positive grievances against Robert Curthose. His peace and friendship with Robert of Bellême were an unpardonable offence; and by granting lucrative rights over the bishopric of Séez to this turbulent vassal,[50] the duke had aroused enemies whose influence against him was to prove disastrous in the crisis of 1105. As has already been explained,[51] Serlo, bishop of Séez, and Ralph, abbot of Saint-Martin of Séez, deemed it intolerable longer to endure the oppression of the tyrant; and going into voluntary exile, they sought an asylum in England, where they were warmly welcomed by Henry I.[52] The value which the king attached to the support and services of Abbot Ralph may perhaps be judged by the fact that he was promoted to the see of Rochester in 1108 and made archbishop of Canterbury in 1114; and it is no mere chance that it was Bishop Serlo who was to welcome King Henry and his invading army in Normandy in 1105, and to preach the sermon which was to stand as the public justification of the king's action in dispossessing his brother of the duchy.[53]

But the duke had sinned further against the church through the practice of simony. A peculiarly flagrant case occurred in 1105 in connection with the abbey of Saint-Pierre-sur-Dives. Upon the death of Abbot Fulk, the duke sold the abbacy for one hundred and forty-five marks of silver to a certain Robert, a

[49] Haskins, pp. 286–287, no. 3.
[50] Cf. *supra*, p. 127, and n. 30.
[51] *Supra*, p. 144.
[52] Ordericus, iv, p. 192.
[53] *Infra*, pp. 161–164.

wicked monk of Saint-Denis, who like a devouring wolf drove out the monks, built a stronghold in the sacred precincts of the monastery, and garrisoned it with armed retainers whom he hired out of profits derived from the sale of ecclesiastical ornaments belonging to the abbey.[54]

More notorious still, and more fatal to the good name of the duke, was the situation which arose in the bishopric of Lisieux upon the death of Gilbert Maminot in August 1101. At first Ranulf Flambard, the notorious bishop of Durham, succeeded in gaining the vacant see for his brother Fulcher, who, in spite of his illiteracy, had some commendable qualities; and since he lived but a few months after his consecration, no active protest was raised against him.[55] But upon his death, Flambard resorted to a more scandalous measure and obtained the see for his son Thomas, a youth some twelve years of age.[56] The duke invested the boy with the sacred office, at the same time agreeing that, if he should die, another of Flambard's sons, who was still younger, should succeed to the bishopric.[57] And meanwhile Flambard himself administered the affairs of the see, " not as bishop but as steward." [58]

So matters stood for some three years, until in 1105 the great canonist and reformer, Ivo of Chartres, intervened, and through his immense influence elevated what had hitherto been but a flagrant local abuse into an affair of something like European importance. He wrote to the Norman bishops demanding that they put an end to such a scandal.[59] Meanwhile, the serious danger in which Robert Curthose stood of losing his duchy brought him for a moment to his senses, and, at the urgent warning of the archbishop of Rouen and of the bishop of Évreux, he had Flambard and his sons ejected from the see, and gave orders for a canonical election.[60] The choice of the clergy fell upon William, archdeacon

---

[54] Ordericus, iv, p. 215; *Gallia Christiana*, xi, instr., col. 155.

[55] Ordericus, iv, p. 116. Bishop Fulcher died 29 January 1102.

[56] *Ibid.*, pp. 116–117; Ivo of Chartres, *Epistolae*, no. 157, and cf. no. 149, in *H. F.*, xv, pp. 134, 131.

[57] *Ibid.*, no. 157.   [58] Ordericus, iv, p. 117.

[59] Ivo of Chartres, *Epistolae*, no. 157, in *H. F.*, xv. p. 134.

[60] *Ibid.*

of Évreux, a worthy man, who went at once to the metropolitan and demanded consecration;[61] and Ivo of Chartres wrote to congratulate the Norman bishops upon having purged the church of the ' dirty boys ' who had been thrust into the sacred office.[62] But now new complications arose. It so happened that William Bonne-Ame, archbishop of Rouen, was then under sentence of excommunication, and therefore incompetent to install the new bishop elect. Accordingly, the latter wrote Bishop Ivo to inquire whether under the circumstances he might legitimately receive consecration from the suffragans of the excommunicated archbishop. Ivo confessed himself unable to answer the question, and referred the bishop elect to Rome to deal directly with the Holy See.[63]

During this unexpected delay, Flambard executed another ' tergiversation.' He induced the duke, in return for a great sum, to confer the bishopric upon one of his clerks, a certain William de Pacy.[64] Again the venerable Ivo wrote to the archbishop of Rouen and the bishop of Évreux to protest against this new introduction of uncleanness into the church which they had so recently purged, and to warn them that unless they acted with vigor to correct this latest abuse, he would bring the " filthy, fetid rumor to the apostolic ears " to their no small disadvantage.[65] The threat was not without avail. William de Pacy was summoned to Rouen to answer before the metropolitan for his conduct, and was able to make no defence. He freely admitted that he had received the bishopric neither by election of clergy and people nor by the free gift of the duke. Judgment upon him, however, was suspended — perhaps because the archbishop was still under sentence of excommunication — and he was sent to Rome, there to be condemned for simony.[66] Bishop Ivo wrote to the Pope setting forth in detail the whole course of the disgraceful business.

[61] Ivo of Chartres, *Epistolae*, no. 157, in *H. F.*, xv, p. 134.
[62] *Ibid.*, no. 153.
[63] *Ibid.*, no. 157.
[64] *Ibid.*; Ordericus, iv, p. 117.
[65] Ivo of Chartres, *Epistolae*, no. 153, in *H. F.*, xv, p. 133.
[66] *Ibid.*, no. 157; Ordericus, iv, p. 117.

But now Ivo of Chartres went a step farther. He had put the full weight of the great moral influence which he exerted in Europe upon the Norman bishops. He had laid the scandal of Lisieux before the Pope. He now turned his gaze across the English Channel. Writing to Robert of Meulan, King Henry's trusted minister, he again protested against the disgraceful intrusion of Ranulf Flambard into the see of Lisieux. He urged him to use his well known influence with the king to induce him to do whatever he could for the liberation of the oppressed church, lest those who had welcomed Henry's intervention in the affairs of Normandy, and had predicted that good would come of it, " should willy-nilly change the serenity of their praise into clouds of vitupera-tion." " For," said he, " kings are not instituted that they may break the laws, but that, if the destroyers of laws cannot other-wise be corrected, they may strike them down with the sword." [67] Could even a more scrupulous monarch than Henry I have resisted such a call to arms ? [68]

As a returned crusader, Robert Curthose might possibly have looked to the Holy See for some support against his enemies. Indeed, he had done so. Before embarking upon the invasion of England in 1101, he had written to the Pope complaining that Henry had violated his oath in assuming the English crown; and

[67] Ivo of Chartres, *Epistolae*, no. 154, in *H. F.*, xv, pp. 133–134.

[68] It does not appear that the duke was seriously involved in the ecclesiastical controversy over Thorold, the appointee of William Rufus to the see of Bayeux after the death of Bishop Odo. On 8 October, apparently 1104, Pascal II wrote to the clergy and people of Bayeux announcing the condemnation of Thorold because, among other things, he had failed to keep his promise to King Henry not to receive investiture from Duke Robert: "Pro his igitur omnibus pro fide etiam non accipiendi a Normannorum comite honoris aecclesiastici ante conspectum Anglici regis data depositionis in eum erat promenda sententia." " Lettre inédite de Pascal II," ed. Germain Morin, in *Revue d'histoire ecclésiastique*, v (1904), pp. 284–285. But the execution of the sentence was delayed for a long period, and the Pope satisfied him-self that Thorold had not received investiture from the duke. *Epistolae Paschalis*, in Migne, clxiii, col. 188. Thorold was deposed, however, upon other grounds, ap-parently in 1107. Ordericus, iv, p. 18; Morin, in *Revue d'histoire ecclésiastique*, v, pp. 286–288. For an exhaustive discussion of all that is known and for many con-jectures about Thorold, see Wilhelm Tavernier, " Beiträge zur Rolandsforschung," in *Zeitschrift für französiche Sprache und Litteratur*, xxxvii, pp. 103–124; xxxviii, pp. 117–135; xxxix, pp. 133–151. Tavernier believes that Thorold was the author of the *Chanson de Roland*.

Pascal had felt constrained to write Anselm a mild letter[69] in which he recognized the special obligations of the papacy to one who had labored " in the liberation of the church of Asia." He asked Anselm to join with the legates he was sending in mediating between the warring brothers, ' unless peace had already been made between them.' [70] But at best this was only a perfunctory and belated recognition of an inconvenient obligation, and Pascal can hardly have seriously expected to influence the situation in Duke Robert's favor.

And as time elapsed, the attitude of Pascal did not become more favorable to the duke. In the summer of 1105 the relations between the papacy and Henry I suddenly improved greatly, and from that time rapid progress was made towards a definite settlement of the investiture controversy in England.[71] This removed the last possible consideration which might have induced the Pope to support the duke against the king in Normandy. Moreover, a fragment of Pascal's correspondence with Robert Curthose, which has recently been brought to light,[72] reveals the fact that at this very time the Pope was engaged in an investiture struggle with the duke. We would gladly know more of this controversy, but this single surviving letter is enough to show that the Pope had complained that, contrary to the law of the church, Robert was performing investitures with staff and ring; that, treating the church not as the spouse of Christ but as a handmaiden, he was giving her over to be ruled by usurping enemies. Probably Pascal referred to the notorious scandals of Lisieux and of Saint-Pierre-sur-Dives. Something also of the duke's reply may be gathered from the papal letter. Taking his stand upon the rights and customs of his ancestors, he had boldly claimed for himself

---

[69] *Epistolae Paschalis*, in Migne, clxiii, col. 81.

[70] " Nosti quia eidem comiti debemus auxilium pro laboribus quos in Asianae Ecclesiae liberatione laboravit. Idcirco volumus ut, si necdum inter eos pax composita est, te satagente, nostris nuntiis intervenientibus, componatur."

[71] *Infra*, pp. 168–169.

[72] A letter discovered by Wilhelm Levison in the British Museum (Harleian MSS., 633) and published in *Neues Archiv der Gesellschaft für ältere deutsche Geschichtskunde*, xxxv (1909), p. 427. Reprinted by Léopold Delisle, in *Bibliothèque de l'École des Chartes*, lxxi, p. 466.

the right of investiture. This was sound ducal policy, but it would not be accepted in Rome from such a prince as Robert Curthose. It could only serve to complete the breach between the ex-crusader and the Holy See and leave the duke without support in his hour of need.

Meanwhile, in what striking contrast with the weak and blundering policy of Robert Curthose, were the careful, methodical preparations which Henry I was making for the struggle upon which he had determined! With him all was wisdom, foresight, largeness of view, self-control.

The friendly relations between the courts of France and England, established at the beginning of Henry's reign by the state visit of Louis, the king designate of France, have already been remarked upon.[73] Henry I took good care to preserve and cultivate this diplomatic cordiality during the critical years of his struggle for Normandy. And, as will appear in the sequel, his efforts were abundantly rewarded when Prince Louis officially recognized his conquest of the duchy shortly after it was completed.[74] In the same spirit the king prepared for all eventualities on the side of Flanders. In the archives of the English exchequer there has been preserved an original chirograph of a treaty which he concluded, apparently in 1103, with Count Robert of Flanders.[75] By its terms the count bound himself, in exchange for an annual subsidy of four hundred marks, to furnish the king with a

[73] *Supra*, p. 122.
[74] *Infra*, p. 180.
[75] Thomas Rymer, *Foedera*, ed. Record Commission (London, 1816–69), i, p. 7, *ex originali*, but incomplete and fragmentary; *Liber Niger Scaccarii*, ed. Thomas Hearne, 2d ed. (London, 1771), i, pp. 7–15. The original, though very badly damaged, is still extant in the Public Record Office. The document itself is dated 10 March at Dover; and a reference in Eadmer (p. 146) seems to fix it in the year 1103. Cf. J. M. Lappenberg, *Geschichte von England* (Hamburg, 1834–37), ii, pp. 240–241; Freeman, *Norman Conquest*, v, pp. 850–851; Henri Pirenne, *Histoire de Belgique*, 3d ed. (Brussels, 1909), i, p. 102. The treaty of 1103 is but one of a series of similar agreements beginning with the original grant of a money fief by the Conqueror to Count Baldwin V (William of Malmesbury, *G. R.*, ii, p. 478) and extending to the reign of Henry II (*Foedera*, i, pp. 6, 7, 22; *Liber Niger*, i, pp. 7–34). All these agreements, and especially the one of 1103, are being studied by Dr. Robert H. George in a work on the relations of England and Flanders. Harvard doctoral dissertation, 1916.

force of a thousand knights — for service in Normandy, among other places, be it noted — and to do his utmost to dissuade the king of France from any attack upon the king of England. Further, as the decisive struggle approached, Henry entered into agreements with the princes of Maine, Anjou, and Brittany for contingents to be furnished from those regions to his army for the conquest of Normandy. The record of the negotiations has not been preserved; but we shall meet with these contingents rendering effective service in the campaigns of 1105 and 1106.[76]

But Henry prepared himself against the duke not only by the careful manipulation of his relations with foreign powers; he spared no effort to undermine him in the duchy. His intervention in the war of the Breteuil succession and the marriage of his daughter Juliana to Eustace of Breteuil have already been alluded to.[77] A similar purpose must have prompted him to arrange the marriage of another of his natural daughters to Rotrou of Mortagne,[78] one of the chief enemies of Robert of Bellême, and an old companion in arms of Robert Curthose on the Crusade. Some hint, at least, of the nature of the pacification which Robert of Meulan was intended to make when he was sent to Normandy as the king's special agent in 1103 may be gathered from the efforts which he made to procure the liberation of the ' avaricious usurer,' John of Meulan.[79] It can hardly be doubted that Henry was making free use of money in the corruption of the duke's influential subjects and in the upbuilding of an English party in Normandy. And in this policy he was very successful. Not only were important Norman churchmen imploring his aid and working for his intervention; but many great nobles were either openly or secretly deserting the duke and offering their services to the English cause. The movement is well illustrated by the case of Ralph III of Conches. His father, Ralph II, had been among the Norman barons who upon the death of William Rufus had taken up arms and plundered the lands of Robert of Meulan at Beaumont.[80] He was certainly no friend of Henry I. But upon

[76] *Infra*, pp. 164, 165, 167, 172, 174–175.   [77] *Supra*, pp. 145–146.
[78] Ordericus, iv, pp. 187, 418; v, p. 4; *Interpolations de Robert de Torigny*, in William of Jumièges, p. 307.
[79] *Supra*, pp. 145–146.   [80] *Supra*, p. 140.

his death, probably in 1102,[81] his son saw new light. Crossing to England, he was cordially welcomed by the king, who granted him his father's lands and the hand of an English heiress who was connected with the royal family.[82] Such a shining example was not lost upon other Norman barons who now deserted the duke and besought King Henry ' with tears ' to come to the aid of the suffering church and of their wretched country.[83]

By the beginning of 1104, Henry I had acquired a strong party, both lay and ecclesiastical, in Normandy, which eagerly awaited his coming and stood ready to aid him in the overthrow of Robert Curthose and in the conquest of the duchy. He had never given up Domfront, and he apparently retained possession of certain strongholds in the Cotentin,[84] the treaty of Alton notwithstanding. Upon these he could rely as a secure base while his friends rallied around him after he had landed on Norman soil. Henry's diplomacy, however, could not remove all enemies from his path, and he sometimes chose to defy them. William of Mortain, earl of Cornwall, had been among the duke's most powerful supporters against the king in 1101. Yet, for some unexplained reason, he did not suffer the prompt banishment to which the Bellêmes and other traitors were condemned when the crisis of the invasion had passed. The king temporized and kept up at least an appearance of friendship. It is even intimated that in 1104 he sent the earl to Normandy to act on his behalf. However this may be, when William of Mortain arrived in Normandy, he worked against the king rather than for him, and, as a result, was promptly deprived of all his English honors.[85] The duke had gained at least one supporter who would not desert him.

The year 1104 was for Henry I a period of active preparation for an enterprise which he was not yet ready publicly to avow.

[81] Ordericus, ii, p. 404, n. 6.

[82] *Ibid.*, iv, p. 198; *Interpolations de Robert de Torigny*, in William of Jumièges, p. 327.

[83] Ordericus, iv, pp. 198–199.

[84] Wace, *Roman de Rou*, ii, pp. 455–459; cf. p. 444.

[85] William of Malmesbury, *G. R.*, ii, pp. 473–474; *A.-S. C.*, *a.* 1104; Florence of Worcester, ii, p. 53; Henry of Huntingdon, pp. 234–235; *Chronicon*, in *Liber de Hyda*, p. 307; cf. Wace, *Roman de Rou*, ii, p. 445.

His trusted agents were busy in Normandy preparing the way
with English treasure. Gradually and quietly he was sending men
and equipment to reënforce the garrisons of his Norman strongholds.[86] Indeed, if Ordericus Vitalis can be trusted,[87] Henry himself crossed the Channel with a fleet and paid a visit to Domfront
and his castles in Normandy in great state, and was welcomed by
Robert of Meulan, Richard earl of Chester, Stephen of Aumale,
Henry of Eu, Rotrou of Mortagne, Robert Fitz Hamon, Robert
de Montfort, Ralph de Mortimer, and many others who held
estates in England and were ready to support him in an attack
upon the duchy. The list shows strikingly the proportions to
which the English party in Normandy had grown. Encouraged
by his enthusiastic reception, the king is said to have taken a lofty
tone in his dealings with the duke. He summoned him to a conference and lectured him upon his incompetence. Again, as the
year before in England, he upbraided him for making peace with
Robert of Bellême and for granting to him the domains of the
Conqueror, contrary to their agreements. He charged him with
abetting highwaymen and brigands, and with dissipating the
wealth of his duchy upon the impudent scamps and hangers-on
who surrounded him. He declared him neither a real prince nor a
shepherd of his people, since he suffered the defenceless population to remain a prey to ravening wolves. This eloquent indict-
ment, we are told, quite overwhelmed the duke. Though he
placed the blame for his misdeeds upon his turbulent associates,
he craved the king's pardon and offered to compensate him by
surrendering the homage of William of Évreux together with his
county and his vassals. Henry accepted the offer, William of
Évreux agreed, and a formal transfer of the homage was effected,
the duke placing the count's hands between the hands of the
king. And with this reward for his pains, Henry returned to
England "before winter," doubtless more than ever convinced of

<hr/>

[86] *A.-S. C.*, a. 1104; Henry of Huntingdon, p. 234.

[87] Ordericus, iv, p. 199. No other writer mentions the journey of Henry I to
Normandy in 1104; and it is not clear that Ordericus is wholly trustworthy at this
point, though his testimony is too specific to be rejected. He treats the campaigns
of 1105 and 1106 together in a most confusing manner.

the weakness of Robert Curthose and of the feasibility of his overthrow and of the conquest of the duchy.[88]

Henry's visit had given a further shock to the duke's prestige, and his return to England was followed by a renewed outbreak of anarchy and disorder in the duchy. Robert of Bellême and William of Mortain, in high indignation at the new advantages which the king had gained, began to attack his adherents, and such was the harrying and burning and wholesale murder which ensued that many of the unarmed peasants fled into France with their wives and children.[89] Robert Fitz Hamon, lord of Torigny and Creully, one of the duke's chief supporters in 1101, had thrown in his lot with the king, and his treason against the duke had been of so black a character as to render him particularly odious among loyal subjects and to arouse intense indignation against him. He now took to plundering the countryside, and as he was harrying the Bessin, Gontier d'Aunay and Reginald of Warenne with the forces from Bayeux and Caen managed to cut him off and surround him in the village of Secqueville. He sought refuge in the church tower, but the sanctuary did not protect him; for the church was burned, and he was taken prisoner. As his captors led him away to Bayeux, they had great difficulty to keep him from the hands of the mob which crowded after them, shouting

> La hart, la hart al traitor
> Qui a guerpi son dreit seignor![90]

Such were the chaotic conditions in Normandy as they are depicted for us in the spring of 1105. Yet we should beware of exaggeration. They may not have been general. Indeed, they probably were not. Our evidence, at best, is but fragmentary, and it rests in the main upon the testimony of Ordericus Vitalis, who was no friend of Robert Curthose, and who dwelt in the debatable region of the south, where the lawless elements were most unbridled, and where the disturbing influence of English aggression had made most headway. Even though we accept at

---

[88] Ordericus, iv, pp. 199–201.

[89] *Ibid.*, pp. 201–202.

[90] Wace, *Roman de Rou*, ii, p. 470. He tells the story with much picturesque detail. He is in the main confirmed by Ordericus, iv, pp. 203–204.

its face value the testimony concerning the diocese of Séez, the Bessin, and the Cotentin, it seems reasonable, in the absence of such evidence for other parts of the duchy, to conclude that conditions elsewhere were almost certainly better.

It is impossible to form anything like a complete picture of the state of the defences of the duchy upon the eve of the English invasion. Robert of Bellême and William of Mortain, by far the most powerful of the duke's supporters, were still in undisputed possession of their hereditary Norman dominions. Robert d'Estouteville had charge of the duke's troops and castles in the pays de Caux.[91] Hugh de Nonant was in command at Rouen.[92] His nephew Gontier d'Aunay was charged with the defence of Bayeux;[93] and, apparently, Enguerran, son of Ilbert de Lacy, with that of Caen.[94] Others of the duke's chief supporters were Reginald of Warenne,[95] brother of the earl of Surrey, and William of Conversano,[96] brother of the late Duchess Sibyl. The ducal forces were evidently too weak to offer effectual resistance in the open. Robert's hope lay in the strength of his fortresses; and it appears that he made a spirited effort to put them in a state of defence, though his financial resources were near exhaustion. Wace is specific with regard to the works which were undertaken at Caen. In his day, it was still possible to trace one of the great trenches which had been dug

> par la rue Meisine,
> Qui a la porte Milet fine,

and which was connected with the waters of the Orne. So long as the duke could raise money by laying taxes upon the burgesses, he hired mercenaries, and for the rest he made promises. But his exactions only served to stir up the townsmen against him, without being in any way adequate to keep his forces together. In a steady stream they deserted to the king, and the helpless duke could only remark characteristically:

[91] Ordericus, iv, p. 214. [92] *Ibid.*, p. 206.
[93] *Ibid.*, pp. 203, 206, 219, 401; Wace, *Roman de Rou*, ii, p. 469.
[94] Ordericus, iv, pp. 219, 401.
[95] *Ibid.*, pp. 203, 222–223.
[96] *Ibid.*, p. 206.

Laissiez aler!
Ne poon a toz estriver;
Laissiez aler, laissiez venir!
Ne poon pas toz retenir.[97]

Meanwhile, Henry I, having fitted out his expedition for the invasion of Normandy, crossed the Channel in Holy Week 1105,[98] and landed without opposition at Barfleur in the Cotentin; and on Easter eve he found quarters in the village of Carentan.[99]

Then, according to the account of Ordericus Vitalis, there followed an amazing piece of acting. The venerable Serlo, bishop of Séez, "first of the Normans to offer his services to the king," came to Carentan to celebrate Easter in the royal presence. Clothing himself in his sacred vestments, he entered the church. And while he sat awaiting the assembling of the people and of the king's followers before beginning the service, he observed that the church was filled with all sorts of chests and utensils and various kinds of gear which the peasants had brought in for protection from the war and anarchy which were devastating the Cotentin. It was probably in the main from pillage by the king's forces that the frightened peasantry were seeking protection,[100] but this fact did not prevent the facile bishop from making the scene before him his point of departure for a ringing appeal to arms, and for a public justification of Henry's attack upon Normandy. Observing the king with a group of his nobles seated humbly among the peasants' panniers at the lower end of the church, Serlo heaved a deep sigh for the misery of the people and rose to speak.

The hearts of all the faithful, he said, should mourn for the distresses of the church and for the wretchedness of the people. The Cotentin was laid waste and depopulated. For lack of a governor all Normandy was a prey to thieves and robbers. The church of God, which ought to be a place of prayer, was now, for want of a righteous defender, turned into a storehouse for the peasants' belongings. There was no room left in which to kneel reverently

---

[97] Wace, *Roman de Rou*, ii, pp. 461–463.
[98] Ordericus, iv, p. 204; *A.-S. C.*, *a.* 1105; cf. Henry of Huntingdon, p. 235; Florence of Worcester, ii, p. 53.
[99] Ordericus, iv, p. 204.
[100] Wace, *Roman de Rou*, ii, pp. 460–461.

or to stand devoutly before the Divine Majesty because of the
clutter of goods which the helpless rustics for fear of plunderers
had brought into the Lord's house.   And so, where government
failed, the church had perforce become the refuge of a defenceless
people.   Yet not even in the church was there security; for that
very year, in Serlo's own diocese of Séez, Robert of Bellême had
burned the church of Tournay to the ground, and men and
women to the number of forty-five had perished in it.   Robert,
the king's brother, did not really possess the duchy or rule his
people as a duke who walked in the path of justice.   He was an
indolent and an abandoned prince, who had made himself sub-
servient to William of Conversano, Hugh de Nonant, and Gontier
d'Aunay.   He had dissipated the wealth of his fair duchy in
vanity and upon trifles.   Often he fasted till three in the afternoon for lack of bread.   Often he dared not rise from bed and
attend mass for want of trousers, stockings, and shoes; for the
buffoons and harlots who infested his quarters had carried them
off during the night while he lay snoring in drunkenness; and
then they impudently boasted that they had robbed the duke.
So, the head languishing, the whole body was sick, and a prince
without understanding had placed the whole duchy in peril.   Let
the king arise, therefore, in God's name, and obtain his paternal
inheritance with the sword of justice.   Let him snatch his ances-
tral possessions from the hands of base men.   Let him give rein to
his righteous anger, as did David of old, not from any worldly
desire for territorial aggrandizement, but for the defence of his
' native soil.' [101]

Moved by this stirring appeal, the king gravely arose. " In the
Lord's name," he said, " I will rise to this labor for the sake of
peace, and with your aid I will seek peace for the church."
Robert of Meulan and other barons present applauded the
momentous decision.

And now, behold another wonder! King Henry had become
the defender of the church. In order that his virtue might appear
the more transcendent, he was now to join the ranks of the re-

[101] Normandy now becomes the *solum natale* of King Henry!

formers of morals. The venerable Serlo, resuming his discourse, proceeded to harangue the king and his suite upon the evils of the outlandish fashions which had recently been take up in high society, to the great scandal of the clergy and of decent Christians. Like obdurate sons of Belial, the men of fashion had taken to dressing their hair like women and to wearing things like scorpion's tails at the extremities of their feet, so that they resembled women because of their effeminacy, and serpents by reason of their pointed fangs. This kind of men had been foretold a thousand years before by St. John the Divine, under the figure of locusts. Let the king offer his subjects a laudable example, in order that they might see in his person a model by which to regulate their own.

Again Henry was convinced by episcopal eloquence and readily assented to Serlo's proposal. The bishop had come prepared. Amid a general consternation which may well be imagined, he drew shears from his wallet and proceeded to crop the royal locks. Robert of Meulan was the next victim to be sacrificed to the bishop's reforming zeal. And by this time the rest of the royal household and the congregation, anticipating a positive order from the king, began to vie with one another as to which should be shorn first; and soon they were trampling under foot as vile refuse the locks which a few moments before they had cherished as their most precious possessions.[102]

The reader may, perhaps, be left to judge for himself as to the amount of credibility to be attached to the highly colored and obviously strongly prejudiced narrative of Ordericus Vitalis which has here been paraphrased. It clearly has a significance of its own, quite apart from the question of strict historical veracity. The speech of Bishop Serlo, as we have it, is, of course, not his at all, but a literary creation of the monk of Saint-Évroul. Yet it must pretty faithfully represent the contemporary point of view of the Norman clergy and of royal apologists generally. It sets forth the king's ' platform,' to borrow a very modern term, and contains the grounds on which contemporaries attempted to

[102] Ordericus, iv, pp. 204-210.

justify what was in reality an unjustifiable act of aggression. Moreover, in spite of much imaginary coloring, there must be a certain residuum of truth in Ordericus's narrative, which illustrates again in a striking manner the extreme care and almost endless detail with which Henry I prepared his way for the conquest of Normandy. In spite of the mediaeval trappings, there is something almost modern about this elaborate attempt to manipulate public opinion and to crystallize a party. Further, it is not a little significant that the Easter scene at Carentan could have been enacted at all. That Henry should have been able to land an invading army at Barfleur, advance without opposition to an unprotected village, and there delay at will in all security, is a striking proof of the defenceless condition of the duchy. The duke's sole reliance was in his strongholds. There is no evidence that he had any force assembled to oppose the invader in the open.

King Henry had no need to hurry. While he delayed at Carentan, his supporters in Normandy rallied around him, and his forces gained greatly in strength. His landing at Barfleur had been the signal for further desertions among the duke's vassals. English gold and silver were all-powerful.[103] Wace says the king had ' bushels ' of the precious treasure. He carried it about with him in ' hogsheads ' loaded upon carts, and by its judicious distribution among barons, castellans, and doughty warriors, he readily persuaded them to desert their lord the duke.[104] Meanwhile, Henry sent envoys to King Philip of France,[105] and summoned his allies, Geoffrey Martel and Helias of La Flèche, to join him with their Angevins and Manceaux.[106]

The military events of the campaign which followed are obscure, and can be traced with little chronological certainty. We hear of some sort of hostile encounter at Maromme near Rouen

---

[103] " Omnes igitur ferme Normannorum maiores illico ad regis adventum, spreto comite domino suo, et fidem quam ei debebant postponentes, in aurum et argentum regis cucurrerunt, eique civitates castra et urbes tradiderunt." Eadmer, p. 165; cf. Florence of Worcester, ii, p. 54.

[104] Wace, *Roman de Rou*, ii, p. 460.

[105] Ordericus, iv, p. 210.

[106] *Ibid.*; Wace, *Roman de Rou*, ii, p. 461.

shortly after Easter, but we know nothing about it, save that a certain knight in the service of Robert d'Estouteville was slain.[107] The chief military undertaking of the campaign was undoubtedly the siege of Bayeux. Against Bayeux and its commander, Gontier d'Aunay, the king had a particular grievance because of the capture and imprisonment of his supporter Robert Fitz Hamon.[108] Accordingly, he assembled all his forces, including his allies from Maine and Anjou, and laid siege to Bayeux.[109] Gontier d'Aunay went out to meet him and promptly handed over his prisoner, Robert Fitz Hamon. He declined, however, to make any further concessions, and Henry refused to raise the siege.[110] But the garrison failed to justify the confidence which their commander had placed in them,[111] and, in an assault, Henry managed to fire the city.[112] A high wind carried the flames from roof to roof, and soon the whole place was swept by the conflagration. Bishop Odo's beautiful cathedral and several other churches, the house of the canons attached to the cathedral, the house of a distinguished citizen named Conan, almost all the buildings in the town, in fact, except a few poor huts, were destroyed. Many of the inhabitants, who in their terror had fled to the cathedral, perished in the flames. The place was given over to be plundered by the Manceaux and the Angevins, and Gontier d'Aunay and many of the garrison were taken captive.[113]

---

[107] Ordericus, iv, pp. 214–215. A charter in favor of St. Mary of Bec, attested by Hugh d'Envermeu " in obsidione ante Archas," not improbably belongs to this year, and indicates that military operations were undertaken against Arques. Round, C. D. F., no. 393.

[108] Supra, p. 159.

[109] Ordericus, iv, p. 219; Annales de Saint-Aubin, in Recueil d'annales angevines et vendômoises, ed. Halphen, p. 44; Henry of Huntingdon, p. 235; Versus Serlonis de Capta Baiocensium Civitate, in H. F., xix, pp. xci, xciii. On this poem and its author see the exhaustive study by Heinrich Böhmer, " Der sogenannte Serlo von Bayeux und die ihm zugeschriebenen Gedichte," in Neues Archiv, xxii, pp. 701–738.

[110] Ordericus, iv, p. 219.

[111] Versus Serlonis, in H. F., xix, p. xciv.

[112] Ordericus, iv, p. 219; Florence of Worcester, ii, p. 54; Annales de Saint-Aubin, in Halphen, Annales, p. 44; Wace, Roman de Rou, ii, p. 471.

[113] Versus Serlonis, in H. F., xix, pp. xci ff.; Ordericus, iv, p. 219; Wace, Roman de Rou, ii, p. 471; cf. Florence of Worcester, ii, p. 54. Wace's account of the siege of Bayeux is elaborate, and credits the city with a long and stubborn resistance.

Caen was the next important place to fall into Henry's hands; but here no siege was necessary. The fate of Bayeux had spread consternation throughout the duchy, and served as a terrible warning of what might be expected, if resistance proved unsuccessful; and the burgesses of Caen had little love for the duke, who had made them feel the weight of his exactions. Accordingly, a conspiracy was formed among certain of the leading citizens, Enguerran de Lacy and the ducal garrison were expelled, and the town was basely surrendered to the English, to the intense indignation of the common people, among whom the duke appears to have been popular.[114] Robert Curthose was himself in Caen at the time, and, learning of the plot at the last moment, he fled headlong to the Hiémois. His attendants, who followed closely after him, were held up at the gate, and his baggage was rifled.[115]

But in the absence of all evidence to this effect in the other sources, and in the face of the positive testimony of the poet Serlo, an eyewitness, that the defence was weak and cowardly on the part of both garrison and inhabitants, Wace's view cannot be accepted.

[114] Ordericus, iv, pp. 219-220; Wace, *Roman de Rou*, ii, pp. 473-479; cf. Henry of Huntingdon, p. 235; William of Malmesbury, *G. R.*, ii, pp. 462-463. Wace gives an elaborate account of the conspiracy, which is perhaps worth summarizing. Thierry, son of Ralph Fitz Ogier, and several other citizens of Caen had been ambushed and captured by Robert of Saint-Rémy-des-Landes at Cagny in the Hiémois while travelling home from Argences; Robert of Saint-Rémy had taken his prisoners to Torigny and sold them for a great price to Robert Fitz Hamon; who, in turn, surrendered them to the king, in exchange for the grant of Caen as a fief to be held by himself and his heirs forever. The king was delighted over the acquisition of these prisoners, " riches homes de Caan nez," for he saw in them the possibility of gaining Caen without striking a blow. A convention was quickly agreed upon. Henry promised to free the prisoners and to enrich them with lands and goods; and they undertook to deliver Caen into his hands. And to seal the bargain, they gave hostages, " filz e nevoz de lor lignages." Great precautions were taken to deceive " la gent menue ";

> Kar se la povre gent seust
> Que l'ovre aler issi deust,
> Ia li reis Caan nen eust,
> Que grant barate n'i eust,

though many prominent burgesses were involved in the conspiracy, and treason was spreading far and wide throughout the city before the duke got wind of it. Then, with the king's men from the Bessin close at hand, and desertion general among the citizens, Robert had no choice but to flee by the Porte Milet to the Hiémois, leaving his baggage behind to be ransacked at the gate.

[115] Wace, *Roman de Rou*, ii, p. 478; William of Malmesbury, *G. R.*, ii, p. 463.

In grateful appreciation of this easy conquest, the king conferred the manor of Dallington, in England, upon the wealthy burgesses who had betrayed the second town of Normandy into his hands.[116]

Having gained possession of Bayeux and Caen, the king marched upon the strong castle of Falaise. But at this moment he temporarily lost the powerful support of the count of Maine. " At the request of the Normans," it is not said of what Normans, Helias of La Flèche withdrew from the contest; and Henry found his forces so weakened that he was obliged to abandon the attack upon Falaise until the following year. Some desultory fighting occurred, however, in which one of the king's knights, Roger of Gloucester, was mortally wounded by a shaft from a crossbow.[117] Almost simultaneously, apparently, with the operations about Falaise, Robert and Henry attempted to make peace. In the week of Pentecost (21–28 May), they met in conference at the village of Cintheaux near Falaise and endeavored for two days to arrive at an agreement. But the king was prepared to offer no terms which the duke could accept, and the negotiations were broken off.[118]

There was, indeed, no good reason why Henry should have made peace, except to gain time while he reëquipped himself for the completion of the enterprise upon which he had embarked. The sources speak specifically only of the conquest of Bayeux and of Caen during the campaign of 1105. Yet it is certain that the extension of the king's domination through the influence of English gold and through the voluntary surrender of numerous minor strongholds had gone much further than this.[119] Eadmer, writing of the situation as he himself saw it in Normandy in July

---

[116] Ordericus, iv, pp. 219–220; cf. Wace, *Roman de Rou*, ii, p. 476.

[117] Ordericus, iv, p. 220; William of Malmesbury, *G.R.*, ii, p. 475. The fact that the attack upon Falaise belongs to the campaign of 1105 is definitely established by a charter of donation by Roger to St. Peter's, Gloucester: " Anno Domini millesimo centesimo quinto, Rogerus de Gloucestria miles, apud Waleyson graviter vulneratus . . ." *Hist. et Cart. S. Petri Gloucestriae*, i, p. 69.

[118] Ordericus, iv, pp. 220–221.

[119] *A.-S. C.*, a. 1105: " and almost all the castles and chief men there in the land became subject to him "; cf. Henry of Huntingdon, p. 235.

1105, was able to say that almost all Normandy had been subjected to the king. The power of the duke had been reduced to such a point that hardly any one obeyed him or rendered him the respect due to a prince. Almost all the barons spurned his authority and betrayed the fealty which they owed him, while they ran after the king's gold and silver and surrendered towns and castles on every side.[120] Yet with all his success, Henry was unable to complete the conquest of Normandy in a single campaign. Even hogsheads may be drained, and the method of waging war with gold and silver, as well as with the sword, had been costly. Before completing his task, he found it necessary to return to England and replenish his supplies.[121]

But before returning to England, Henry had a diplomatic problem of great importance to solve. Since 1103 Anselm had been living in exile, and the investiture controversy had been in abeyance. But the archbishop had at last grown restive and had decided to resort to the extreme measure of excommunicating the king. Rumor of the impending sentence spread throughout France, England, and Normandy, and caused not a little uneasiness.[122] In the midst of his struggle for Normandy with Robert Curthose, Henry could not but view this new danger with grave concern; and he never showed to better advantage than in the broad and statesmanlike way in which he met the crisis. Through the mediation of Ivo of Chartres and of the king's sister, Countess Adela of Blois, a conference was arranged between him and the archbishop, to be held on 22 July at Laigle on the Norman frontier. There he received Anselm with the utmost courtesy, and, since he was in no position to drive matters to a rupture, he showed himself sincerely desirous of arriving at an amicable adjustment. Anselm, too, was disposed to compromise; and they were soon able to agree upon the broad lines of a final settlement of the long controversy. Messengers were despatched to

[120] Eadmer, p. 165.

[121] "Rex enim ipse a Normannia digressus, quia eam totam eo quo supra diximus modo sibi subiugare nequierat, reversus in Angliam est, ut, copiosiori pecunia fretus rediens, quod residuum erat, exhaeredato fratre suo, subiiceret." *Ibid.*, p. 171; cf. Florence of Worcester, ii, p. 54.

[122] Eadmer, p. 166.

Rome by both the king and the archbishop to secure the ratification of the Holy See.[123] The details of a formal concordat had yet to be arranged; but friendly relations were now completely restored between Henry and Anselm, and the ecclesiastical crisis was averted. In August [124] the king returned to England, " and what he had won in Normandy continued afterwards in peace and obedient to him, except those who dwelt anywhere near Count William of Mortain." [125]

In point of fact, William of Mortain and Robert of Bellême appear to have been almost the only really powerful barons in Normandy who still supported the duke, and the loyalty even of the Bellême interests could probably have been shaken had the king so desired. Before Christmas Robert of Bellême paid a visit to England and sought an interview with the king. It would be hazardous to infer that he, too, was contemplating a desertion of the ducal cause; but whatever his mission, he failed to accomplish it, and, departing from the king's Christmas court 'unreconciled,' he returned to Normandy.[126]

It was not long before the king had a more important visitor from beyond the sea. Early in 1106 Robert Curthose himself crossed the Channel, and, in an interview with the king at Northampton, besought him to restore the conquests which he had won from him in Normandy.[127] The duke must have felt his situation almost desperate, yet it is difficult to imagine what inducements he expected to offer, or how, in the light of his past experience, he could have dreamed of gaining a concession or any consideration from his unscrupulous brother. Henry could well afford to be obdurate, and he returned a flat refusal to the duke's demands. Robert withdrew in anger, and returned to his duchy;[128] and

---

[123] Eadmer, pp. 165–166; cf. *G. B. Adams, History of England from the Norman Conquest to the Death of John* (London, 1905), pp. 141–142.

[124] Henry of Huntingdon, p. 235; *A.-S. C., a.* 1105.

[125] *Ibid., a.* 1105.

[126] *Ibid., a.* 1106.

[127] *Ibid., a.* 1106; Henry of Huntingdon, p. 235; Florence of Worcester, ii, p. 54. The place of the interview is further established by Henry's letter to Anselm which ends: " Teste W. Cancell. apud Northamptonem." *Epistolae Anselmi*, bk. iv, no. 77, in Migne, clix, col. 240.

[128] References as in n. 127, *supra.*

Henry wrote immediately to Anselm, who was still in Normandy, announcing his own crossing for 3 May following. It is not quite easy to see why he should have stated in his letter that Robert had parted with him amicably,[129] but the ways of diplomacy are often obscure.

Robert Curthose now knew beyond all question what he had to expect, and, as formerly in the crisis of his struggle with William Rufus, he sought aid from without. If the unsupported statement of William of Malmesbury may be accepted, he appealed to his overlord, the king of France, and to Robert of Flanders in a conference at Rouen; [130] but the far-seeing diplomacy of Henry I had anticipated him,[131] and he was able to obtain no assistance.

Meanwhile, Henry had completed his preparations for a second invasion of Normandy, and " before August " [132] he crossed the Channel. He landed without opposition, but soon afterwards, apparently, an attempt was made to take him in an ambush. Abbot Robert of Saint-Pierre-sur-Dives, the notorious simoniac, entered into a secret compact with the duke and some of his barons at Falaise to betray the king into their hands. Then, while Reginald of Warenne and the younger Robert d'Estouteville, with a considerable body of knights, installed themselves in the fortress which the abbot had constructed within the precincts of his monastery, he paid a visit to the king at Caen and treacherously agreed to surrender the fortress to him, at the same time advising him to come quietly with but a few knights to take it, in order to avoid giving the alarm. But Henry did not ride blindly into the trap that was set for him. Placing himself at the head of a force of seven hundred horse, he came suddenly upon the monastery at daybreak after an all night's ride; and, as soon as he had apprised himself of the true situation, he launched an in-

---

[129] *Epistolae Anselmi*, bk. iv, no. 77, in Migne, clix, col. 240.

[130] *G. R.*, ii, p. 463.   [131] Cf. *supra*, pp. 155-156.

[132] *A.-S. C.*, a. 1106; Florence of Worcester, ii, p. 54; Henry of Huntingdon, p. 235. Though Henry's original intention had been to cross at Ascension (3 May) (*Epistolae Anselmi*, bk. iv, no. 77, in Migne, clix, col. 240), it is clear from the *Chronicle* that he was still in England at Pentecost (13 May). The phrase ' before August ' used by the sources would seem to point to a crossing in the latter part of July.

THE LOSS OF NORMANDY

stant attack, burned both the monastery and the fortress, and took Reginald of Warenne, Robert d'Estouteville, and many of their men captive. Reënforcements on their way from Falaise saw the conflagration and turned back in flight. The attempted ambush had been turned into a notable royal victory. The treacherous Abbot Robert was also taken. Thrown across a horse ' like a sack,' he was brought before the king, who expelled him from the land with the declaration that, if it were not for his sacred orders, he would have him torn limb from limb.[133]

As we have noted, the duke's power was in the main confined to scattered strongholds such as Falaise and Rouen.[134] Through the open country Henry was able to move about practically at will. He went to Bec and had a cordial interview with Anselm (15 August). Much progress had been made towards the settlement of the investiture controversy since their meeting at Laigle the year before, and they were now completely reconciled. Anselm returned to England disposed to give the king his full support.[135] Every moral obstacle now seemed removed from Henry's path.[136]

Meanwhile, or soon after, [137] the king began operations against the castle of Tinchebray. Adopting the well known expedient of

[133] Ordericus, iv, pp. 215, 223–224; *Annales de Wintonia,* in *Annales Monastici,* ii, p. 42. The chronology of Ordericus is confused. Abbot Fulk, predecessor of the simoniac Robert, is said to have died at Winchester 3 April 1105. *Gallia Christiana,* xi, instr., col. 155; Ordericus, iv, p. 19, and n. 2; p. 215, and n. 2. Henry's destruction of the abbey must, therefore, be referred to 1106, since it would have been impossible for Abbot Robert to have gained possession of the monastery and to have erected a fortress in it while Henry was still in Normandy in the previous summer, the king having returned to England in August. This conclusion is confirmed by the Annals of Winchester: " MCVI. Hoc anno rex in Normanniam duxit exercitum; et veniens ad Sanctum Petrum super Divam, abbatiam redegit in pulverem, et centum homines et eo amplius interfecit."

[134] Cf. *Interpolations de Robert de Torigny,* in William of Jumièges, p. 283: " Rex autem Henricus, non diutius hoc ferens, maximeque indigne ferens, quod frater suus ita paternam hereditatem, ducatum scilicet Normanniae, dissipaverat, quod, preter civitatem Rothomagensem, nichil pene in dominio haberet; quam etiam forsitan alicui ut cetera dedisset, si hoc sibi licitum propter cives ipsius fuisset." This is doubtless an exaggerated statement, but it is not without significance.

[135] Eadmer, pp. 182–183; Florence of Worcester, ii, p. 55.

[136] The Pope was clearly no longer supporting the crusader against the king. William of Malmesbury goes so far as to say that Pascal wrote to Henry urging him on to the fratricidal conflict. *G. R.,* ii, p. 474.

[137] The operations before Tinchebray, such as they are described, must have ex-

the siegecraft of the period, he erected a counter fortress against the place, and installed in it Thomas de Saint-Jean with a garrison of knights and foot soldiers. Thereupon William of Mortain, lord of Tinchebray, collected forces which were more than a match for Thomas de Saint-Jean and his men, and threw food and necessary supplies into the stronghold.[138] But by this time the king had been powerfully reënforced with auxiliary troops from Maine and Brittany, under the command of Helias of La Flèche and of Alan Fergant,[139] and he began the siege of Tinchebray in earnest.[140]

Robert Curthose, now reduced to desperate straits, and urged on by the importunity of William of Mortain,[141] decided to stake all on the issue of a battle in the open.[142] Collecting all his forces, he marched upon Tinchebray and challenged the king to raise the siege or prepare for battle.[143] Again, as at Alton in 1101, the two brothers stood facing one another, about to engage in a fratricidal struggle. But again there were negotiations. Certain men of religion, the venerable hermit Vitalis among them, intervened to prevent the conflict.[144] The king, as always, was careful to justify himself before the public eye; and, if we can trust our authority, he offered terms of peace. Protesting loudly that he was actuated by no worldly ambition, but only by a desire to succor the poor and to protect the suffering church, he proposed

tended over a considerable period before the decisive battle, which was fought on or about 29 September.

[138] Ordericus, iv, pp. 224–225.

[139] *Ibid.*, pp. 229–230; letter of a priest of Fécamp to a priest of Séez, in *E. H. R.*, xxv, p. 296; Henry of Huntingdon, p. 235; Dom Morice, *Preuves*, i, col. 129; cf. William of Malmesbury, *G. R.*, ii, p. 478. Henry of Huntingdon mentions the presence also of Angevins, but this is probably an error.

[140] Ordericus, iv, p. 225; *Interpolations de Robert de Torigny*, in William of Jumièges, p. 283; *A.-S. C.*, a. 1106; Florence of Worcester, ii, p. 55; Henry of Huntingdon, p. 235.

[141] Ordericus, iv, p. 225.

[142] William of Malmesbury, *G. R.*, ii, p. 463: "ad bellum publicum venit, ultimam fortunam experturus."

[143] Ordericus, iv, p. 225; cf. letter of Henry I to Anselm, in Eadmer, p. 184; *A.-S. C.*, a. 1106; Florence of Worcester, ii, p. 55; Henry of Huntingdon, p. 235; William of Malmesbury, *G. R.*, ii, p. 475; *Interpolations de Robert de Torigny*, in William of Jumièges, p. 283.

[144] Ordericus, iv, pp. 226–227.

that the duke surrender to him all the castles in Normandy and the whole financial and judicial administration of the duchy, reserving for himself one half of the revenues. Henry, on his side, would undertake to pay the duke, out of the English treasury, an annual subsidy equal to the other half of the Norman revenues; and, for the future, Robert might revel in feasts and games and all delights, in perfect security and in freedom from all care. Such terms, if indeed they were ever really proposed, were in themselves an insult. And, moreover, the duke had already had bitter experience of Henry's devotion to treaties. The monk of Saint-Évroul, therefore, becomes quite incredible when he would have us believe that Robert laid these proposals seriously before his council, and insinuates that he was inclined to accede to them. In any case, the duke's supporters rejected them with violent language, and negotiations were broken off.[145] Both sides now prepared for battle.

The sources are by no means clear, or in perfect accord, as to the exact disposition of the forces in the battle of Tinchebray; but the general plan of the engagement is clear,[146] as is also the very considerable numerical superiority which the king enjoyed.[147] The forces on either side were composed of both mounted knights and foot soldiers;[148] and, so far as it is possible to say from the evi-

[145] Ordericus, iv, pp. 227-228. Henry did not fail to propitiate the Almighty. He released Reginald of Warenne from prison — to the great satisfaction of William of Warenne, his brother, who now became a more enthusiastic royal supporter than ever — and made a vow to rebuild the church which he had burned at Saint-Pierre-sur-Dives. *Ibid.*, p. 229. The Hyde *Chronicle* is doubtless in error in stating that Reginald of Warenne was captured at Tinchebray and later released at the request of his brother. *Liber de Hyda*, p. 307.

[146] See Appendix F.

[147] It is hardly worth while to discuss the numbers engaged in the battle, since mediaeval figures are not to be relied upon. Cf. *E. H. R.*, xviii, pp. 625-629. The estimate of the priest of Fécamp (*E. H. R.*, xxv, p. 296), placing the king's forces at 40,000 and the duke's at 6000, of which 700 were knights, is doubtless an exaggeration. It is good evidence, however, of the king's numerical superiority, which is also indicated by Henry of Huntingdon (p. 235). Ordericus Vitalis grants that the duke was inferior to the king in knights, but asserts that he had more foot soldiers.

[148] *E. H. R.*, xxv, p. 296; Eadmer, p. 184; Ordericus, iv, pp. 226, 230; cf. *Interpolations de Robert de Torigny*, in William of Jumièges, p. 283; Henry of Huntingdon, p. 235.

dence, they were arranged in columns of successive divisions, called *acies*, drawn up one behind another.[149] William of Mortain commanded the vanguard of the ducal forces, and Robert of Bellême the rear.[150] It is not clear what position the duke held in the battle formation.[151] Our information as to the disposition of the royal forces is fuller, but confusing. The first division, or *acies*, was composed in the main of foot soldiers from the Bessin, the Avranchin, and the Cotentin — probably under the command of Ranulf of Bayeux [152] — but they were supported by a considerable body of mounted knights. The second division, under the immediate command of King Henry, was likewise made up of both mounted knights and men fighting on foot, the latter in this case being the king in person and a considerable number of his barons who had dismounted in order to give greater stability to the line.[153] A further division of some sort may have been placed in reserve in the rear.[154] Most important of all, the auxiliary knights from Maine and Brittany, under the command of Helias of La Flèche and Alan Fergant, were stationed on the field at some distance to one side [155] in readiness for a strategic stroke at the proper moment.

[149] See Appendix F.

[150] Ordericus, iv, p. 230.

[151] The statement of J. D. Drummond that he held the foot soldiers in reserve in the distant rear behind the forces of Robert of Bellême (*Kriegsgeschichte Englands*, p. 40), is based upon pure conjecture. C. W. C. Oman (*Art of War*, p. 379), adopting the view of a line formation, asserts, equally without authority, that Robert Curthose held the centre between William of Mortain and Robert of Bellême.

[152] " Primam aciem rexit Rannulfus Baiocensis; secundam Rodbertus comes Mellentensis; tertiam vero Guillelmus de Guarenna." Ordericus, iv, p. 229. It certainly is impossible to reconcile this statement completely with the letter of the priest of Fécamp, but perhaps the leadership of the first division may be accepted.

[153] Letter of the priest of Fécamp, in *E. H. R.*, xxv, p. 296: " In prima acie fuerunt Baiocenses, Abrincatini, et Constantinienses, omnes pedites; in secunda vero rex cum innumeris baronibus suis, omnes similiter pedites. Ad hec septingenti equites utrique aciei ordinati ". Also Henry of Huntingdon, p. 235: " rex namque et dux, et acies caeterae pedites erant, ut constantius pugnarent."

[154] Ordericus, iv, p. 229.

[155] *Ibid.*, pp. 229–230: " Cenomannos autem et Britones longe in campo cum Helia consule constituit "; letter of the priest of Fécamp, in *E. H. R.*, xxv, p. 296: " preterea comes Cenomannis et comes Britonum Alanus Fregandus circumcin-

The action was opened by William of Mortain, who charged at the head of Robert's vanguard;[156] and for a time the ducal forces gained a considerable advantage and pushed the royal van back at several points. But they were unable to gain a decision; and while the opposing forces were locked together in a great mêlée of hand-to-hand encounters, the Bretons and the Manceaux charged impetuously from their distant position, and, falling upon the flank of the ducal forces, cut them in two and wrought great havoc among the foot soldiers.[157] Robert of Bellême, seeing which way the battle was going, saved himself by flight; and the forces of the duke thereupon dissolved in a general rout.[158]

Robert Curthose was captured by Waldric, the king's chancellor, who, though a cleric, had taken his place among the knights in the battle.[159] The Bretons captured William of Mortain and were with some difficulty persuaded to surrender their prize to the king. Robert d'Estouteville, William de Ferrières, William Crispin, Edgar Atheling, and many others were also taken prisoners.[160] Henry pardoned some, including the Atheling, and set them at liberty; but others he kept in confinement for the rest of

gentes exercitum, usque ad mille equites, remotis omnibus gildonibus et servis "; Henry of Huntingdon, p. 235.

[156] Ordericus, iv, p. 230. But cf. Henry of Huntingdon, p. 235: " dux Normanniae cum paucis multos audacissime aggressus est, assuetusque bellis Ierosolimitanis aciem regalem fortiter et horrende reppulit. Willelmus quoque consul de Moretuil aciem Anglorum de loco in locum turbans promovit." This statement would seem to give some color to Oman's view of a line formation, but it is not convincing in the face of other evidence. Cf. Appendix F.

[157] Ordericus, iv, p. 230; Henry of Huntingdon, p. 235; cf. Dom Morice, *Preuves*, i, col. 129.

[158] Letter of the priest of Fécamp, in *E. H. R.*, xxv, p. 296; Henry of Huntingdon, pp. 235–236; Ordericus, iv, p. 230; cf. *A.–S. C.*, a. 1106; Florence of Worcester, ii, p. 55; William of Malmesbury, *G. R.*, ii, p. 475; *Chronicon*, in *Liber de Hyda*, p. 307.

[159] Ordericus, iv, p. 230; cf. *E. H. R.*, xxv, p. 296; Henry of Huntingdon, p. 236; Eadmer, p. 184; *A.–S. C.*, a. 1106; Florence of Worcester, ii, p. 55; William of Malmesbury, *G. R.*, ii, p. 463; the same, *G. P.*, p. 116; *Interpolations de Robert de Torigny*, in William of Jumièges, p. 283; *Chronicon*, in *Liber de Hyda*, p. 307. On Waldric the Chancellor see H. W. C. Davis, in *E. H. R.*, xxvi, pp. 84–89.

[160] Ordericus, iv, pp. 230–231; *E. H. R.*, xxv, p. 296; Henry of Huntingdon, p. 236; Eadmer, p. 184; Florence of Worcester, ii, p. 55; *A.–S. C.*, a. 1106; William of Malmesbury, *G. R.*, ii, p. 475; *Interpolations de Robert de Torigny*, in William of Jumièges, p. 283; *Chronicon*, in *Liber de Hyda*, p. 307.

their lives.[161]   A considerable number of the duke's foot soldiers
had been slain, and many more had been captured.[162]   But the
casualties among the king's forces had been negligible.   " Hardly
two " of his men had been killed, while " only one," Robert de
Bonebos, had been wounded.[163]   The battle had been joined at
about nine o'clock in the morning, probably on the 29th of
September [164] 1106.   It had lasted " barely an hour," [165] yet it
deserves to rank among the decisive battles of the twelfth century, for it had settled the fate of Normandy and of Robert
Curthose.

[161] Ordericus, iv, p. 231.

[162] *Ibid.*, p. 230; Eadmer, p. 184.   Robert of Torigny places the number of slain
among the duke's forces at " vix sexaginta." *Interpolations de Robert de Torigny*,
in William of Jumièges, p. 284.

[163] *E. H. R.*, xxv, p. 296; cf. Eadmer, p. 184; *Interpolations de Robert de Torigny*,
in William of Jumièges, p. 284; *Chronicon*, in *Liber de Hyda*, p. 307.

[164] *E. H. R.*, xxv, p. 296: " iii kal. Octobris hora tertia."   The date usually
given by modern writers is 28 September.   Le Prévost, in Ordericus, iv, 228, n. 2;
Davis, *Normans and Angevins*, p. 129; Adams, *History of England from the Norman
Conquest to the Death of John*, p. 145; Le Hardy, p. 164; Fliche, *Philippe I*er*, p. 311.
It is based upon the authority of the *Anglo-Saxon Chronicle* (a. 1106), which is
copied by Florence of Worcester (ii, p. 55), and upon the *Chronicon Breve Fon-
tanellense* (*H. F.*, xii, p. 771).   But, in view of the explicit statement of the priest
of Fécamp, 29 September is probably the correct date.   William of Malmesbury
(*G. R.*, ii, p. 475) confusingly dates the battle " sabbato in Sancti Michaelis vigilia."
Michaelmas in 1106 fell upon Saturday.   A further variation is introduced by
Robert of Torigny, who dates the battle 27 September. *Interpolations de Robert
de Torigny* in William of Jumièges, p. 284.

[165] *E. H. R.*, xxv, p. 296.

CHAPTER VII

LAST YEARS AND DEATH

Soon after the battle of Tinchebray Henry I wrote exultingly to Anselm, announcing the great victory and boasting that he had captured four hundred knights and ten thousand foot soldiers, and that the number of slain was legion.[1] It was a pardonable exaggeration, for indeed the battle had ended all resistance and decided the fate of Normandy. The duke seems to have had no thought of a continuance of the struggle, and meekly submitted to his conqueror. Henry hastened to the great stronghold of Falaise, which had successfully defied him the year before, and at the duke's own command it was promptly surrendered into his hands.[2] Then he pressed on with his captive to Rouen, where he received a cordial welcome from the burgesses, to whom he restored the laws of the Conqueror and all the honors which their city had previously enjoyed.[3] And, again at the duke's command, Hugh de Nonant handed over the citadel to the king. The duke, too, formally absolved the fortified towns (*municipia*) throughout all Normandy from their allegiance, and their defenders hastened to make peace with the victor.[4] Even the king's most bitter enemies sought a reconciliation. Ranulf Flambard, the exiled bishop of Durham, who had caused such a scandal in the see of Lisieux, and who was still residing there as lord of the city (*princeps in urbe*), humbly sent to seek peace, and, upon surrendering Lisieux, was restored to his bishopric of Durham.[5] The terrible Robert of Bellême still boasted the possession of thirty-four strong castles, and for a moment he seems to have contemplated

---

[1] Eadmer, p. 184. The letter was written from Elbeuf-sur-Andelle near Rouen, according to H. W. C. Davis before 15 October. *E. H. R.*, xxiv, p. 729, n. 4.

[2] Ordericus, iv, pp. 231–232.

[3] " Rex siquidem cum duce Rotomagum adiit, et a civibus favorabiliter exceptus, paternas leges renovavit, pristinasque urbis dignitates restituit." *Ibid.*, p. 233.

[4] *Ibid.*   [5] *Ibid.*, p. 273.

further resistance. But an appeal for aid to Helias of La Flèche met with no encouragement; and at the advice and through the mediation of the latter, he chose the prudent course of making peace with Henry upon the best terms possible. By the surrender of all the ducal domain which he had occupied illegally, he managed to obtain Argentan and the *vicomté* of Falaise, together with certain other possessions which had formerly been held by his father, Roger of Montgomery.[6] But these temporary concessions to Robert of Bellême were almost the only ones which the king felt it necessary to make. For, while he favored the clergy and gave peace and protection to the humble and unarmed population, he made it his first business to curb the restless baronage. He ordered the destruction of adulterine castles throughout the duchy.[7] Summoning a council of magnates at Lisieux in the middle of October, he proclaimed a royal peace, asserted his title to all the ducal domain which Robert Curthose through extravagance or weakness had let slip from his hands, and guaranteed to the churches and other legitimate holders all the possessions which they had lawfully enjoyed at the time of the Conqueror's death.[8] Such measures brought despair to outlaws and evil men, but they inaugurated a new era of vigorous and orderly government which was welcomed with the utmost gratitude by all peace-loving subjects, especially by the clergy.[9] Anselm wrote to the king, saluting him as ' duke,' to congratulate him upon his splendid victory, and to thank him for the promise of good and considerate government.[10]

Henry remained in Normandy during the autumn and winter to complete the organization of the new régime. In January 1107 he called the nobles together at Falaise, and in March he held another council at Lisieux, and promulgated many important decrees for the administration of the duchy.[11] And then, in

[6] Ordericus, iv, pp. 234–236.   [7] *Ibid.*, pp. 236–237.
[8] *Ibid.*, pp. 233–234.
[9] Letter of the priest of Fécamp, in *E. H. R.*, xxv, p. 296: " Et nunc pax in terra reddita est, Deo gratias "; Ordericus, iv, p. 232; cf. William of Malmesbury, *G. R.*, ii, p. 476; *Interpolations de Robert de Torigny*, in William of Jumièges, p. 284.
[10] *Epistolae Anselmi*, bk. iv, no. 82, in Migne, clix, cols. 242–243.
[11] Ordericus, iv, p. 269; cf. *A.-S. C.*, a. 1107.

Lent, " when he had either destroyed his enemies or subdued them, and had disposed of Normandy according to his will," [12] he returned to England, and held his Easter court at Windsor.[13] And there " both Norman and English barons were present with fear and trembling." [14]

Apparently the king had sent his prisoners, including the duke, on before him to England, lest the turbulent Normans, under the guise of aiding Robert Curthose, should break the peace.[15] And once he had them safely across the Channel he took good care that they should never escape him. William of Mortain, at least, was placed in close confinement for the rest of his life; and, if Henry of Huntingdon can be trusted, he was blinded.[16] Robert Curthose, it seems, was kept in free custody and provided with certain comforts and even luxuries; [17] but his confinement was not made less secure for that. According to the Annals of Winchester, he was first imprisoned at Wareham; [18] but he was afterwards

[12] Henry of Huntingdon, p. 236; cf. *A.-S. C.*, *a.* 1107; Eadmer, p. 184; Ordericus, iv, p. 274.

[13] *A.-S. C.*, *a.* 1107; Eadmer, p. 184. On Henry's itinerary in Normandy, cf. Haskins, pp. 309–310; W. Farrer, in *E. H. R.*, xxxiv, pp. 340–341.

[14] Henry of Huntingdon, p. 236.

[15] Ordericus. iv, pp. 232, 237; but cf. *Interpolations de Robert de Torigny*, in William of Jumièges, p. 284, where it is stated that the king took the prisoners to England with him upon his return. Cf. also *A.-S. C.*, *a.* 1106.

[16] Henry of Huntingdon, pp. 236, 255; William of Malmesbury, *G. R.*, ii, p. 475; Ordericus, iv, p. 234.

[17] *Ibid.*, p. 237: " Fratrem vero suum . . . xxvii annis in carcere servavit, et omnibus deliciis abundanter pavit "; *ibid.*, p. 402: " Fratrem vero meum non, ut captivum hostem, vinculis mancipavi, sed ut nobilem peregrinum, multis angoribus fractum, in arce regia collocavi, eique omnem abundantiam ciborum et aliarum deliciarum, ·variamque suppellectilem affluenter suppeditavi"; *Interpolations de Robert de Torigny*, in William of Jumièges, p. 284. Two entries in the Pipe Roll of 31 Henry I record the king's expenditures for Robert's entertainment: " Et in liberat*ione* Archie*piscopi* Rothoma*gensis*, et in pannis Com*itis* Normann*orum* .xxiij. lib*ras* et .x. sol*idos* nu*mero*"; "Et in Soltis. *per* bre*ve* Re*gis* Fulchero fil*io* Walt*heri* .xij. lib*ras* pro estruc*tura* Com*itis* Normann*orum*." *Magnus Rotulus Pipae de Anno Tricesimo-Primo Regni Henrici Primi*, ed. Joseph Hunter for the Record Commission (London, 1833), pp. 144, 148; cf. Le Prévost, in Ordericus, iv, 402, n. 2. In later years an ugly rumor was current to the effect that Henry had Robert blinded; but it rests upon no contemporary or early authority. Cf. *infra*, pp. 200–201.

[18] *Annales Monastici*, ii, p. 42. These annals also state that William of Mortain was imprisoned in the Tower of London.

given into the custody of the great Bishop Roger of Salisbury, who kept him in his magnificent castle at Devizes.[19]

In 1107 King Henry's triumph seemed complete. He was now master both in England and in Normandy as he had never been before.[20] His conquest of the duchy had been willingly accepted by both clergy and people. And even Louis, the king designate of France — contrary, it may be observed, to his father Philip's advice — had officially ratified his action.[21] Yet Henry's troubles in Normandy had hardly begun, and the following years were a period of almost incessant warfare for the maintenance of his conquest. Hostility between him and his continental neighbors was, indeed, inevitable. With the accession Louis VI (le Gros) to the throne of France in 1108, the Capetians entered upon an era of royal ascendancy which necessarily made them look with jealous eyes upon their great feudatories, particularly the dukes of Normandy. The union of England and Normandy brought an increase of strength and of ambition to Henry I which rendered him dangerous not only to his overlord, the king of France, but also to his neighbors on the north and south in Flanders and Anjou; while in Normandy itself, the turbulent baronage soon grew restive under the stern rule of the 'Lion of Justice,' and were ever ready to ally themselves with anyone who would make common cause with them against him. And, unfortunately for Henry, he had made one fatal mistake in his settlement of Normandy after Tinchebray, which left a standing temptation in the way of the disaffected Norman baronage and of his jealous neighbors beyond the frontier.

The son of Robert Curthose, William surnamed the Clito, had fallen into the king's hands at the surrender of Falaise in 1106,[22]

---

[19] Ordericus, iv, p. 486; *A.-S. C.*, a. 1126.

[20] Cf. Henry of Huntingdon, p. 236.

[21] *La Chronique de Morigny*, ed. Léon Mirot (Paris, 1909), p. 21: " Ludovicus, rex designatus et adhuc adolescens, quorumdam suorum collateralium consilio deceptus, ut talia gererentur assensit, patre, sapiente viro, sibi contradicente, et malum, quod postea accidit, spiritu presago sibi predicente "; Suger, *Vie de Louis le Gros*, p. 47: " fretusque domini regis Francorum auxilio "; William of Malmesbury (*G. R.*, ii, p. 480) explains that Louis's favor was gained " Anglorum spoliis et multo regis obryzo."

[22] Ordericus, iv, p. 232. William Clito was born in 1101 at Rouen and was

and it would have been possible for Henry to have made away with him or to have placed him in permanent confinement, just as he had imprisoned the duke. But William Clito was still a child of tender years, and Henry feared public sentiment. Rather than bear the responsibility if any evil should befall the lad while in his hands, he placed him in ward with Helias of Saint-Saëns, Duke Robert's son-in-law, to be brought up and educated.[23] Henry soon repented of this indiscretion, however, and, at the advice of certain of his counsellors, he gave orders for the Clito to be taken into custody. But before Robert de Beauchamp, the *vicomte* of Arques, who was charged with the execution of the king's command, could carry out his mission, friends of the child learned of the impending stroke, and carried him away sleeping from his bed and hid him; and soon after the stanch Helias of Saint-Saëns fled with him into exile.[24] Abandoning all that they had in Normandy,[25] Helias and the Clito's tutor, Tirel de Mainières, devoted their lives to their charge,[26] finding a refuge now here, now there, among King Henry's enemies in France and Flanders and Anjou.[27]

It would lead us too far afield to trace in detail the tragic career of William Clito. But its salient features may, at least, be indicated; for he was the last hope of the lost cause of Robert Curthose.

The Clito rapidly grew to be a youth of uncommon attractions —"mult fu amez de chevaliers" [28] — and his pathetic story made an irresistible appeal to the discontented and ambitious, both in Normandy and beyond the frontiers.[29] Robert of Bellême, until he was captured in 1112 and sent to end his days in an English prison,[30] made himself in a special way the patron and

baptized by Archbishop William Bonne-Ame, after whom he was named. *Ibid.*, pp. 78, 98. Cf. *supra*, p. 146.

[23] Ordericus, iv, p. 232.

[24] *Ibid.*, pp. 292–293, 473; *Chronicon*, in *Liber de Hyda*, p. 308.

[25] Ordericus, iv, pp. 292–293.

[26] *Ibid.*, pp. 464, 477, 482; *Chronicon*, in *Liber de Hyda*, p. 308.

[27] Cf. Ordericus, iv, p. 294.   [28] Wace, *Roman de Rou*, ii, p. 439.

[29] Ordericus, iv, pp. 293–294, 465, 472–473; *Chronicon*, in *Liber de Hyda*, p. 308.

[30] Ordericus, iv, pp. 305, 376–377; William of Malmesbury, *G. R.*, ii, p. 475; Henry of Huntingdon, p. 238; *A. S.–C.*, a. 1112.

'supporter of the Clito;[31] and the cause of the injured exile, mere child that he was, undoubtedly lay back of much of the desultory warfare in which King Henry was involved in Normandy and on the French frontier between 1109 and 1113. Count Robert of Flanders lost his life fighting in Normandy in 1111,[32] and his successor, Baldwin VII, gave an asylum to the Clito and conferred on him the arms of knighthood in his fourteenth year.[33]

It was between the years 1117 and 1120, however, that the opponents of King Henry's continental ambitions first organized themselves in support of William Clito upon a formidable scale. Louis VI had repented of his earlier friendship for Henry I,[34] and in 1117 he entered into a sworn alliance with Baldwin of Flanders and Fulk of Anjou to overthrow the English rule in Normandy and place the Clito on the ducal throne.[35] Simultaneously, a widespread revolt broke out among the Norman baronage, and for three years Henry was involved in a formidable war, which he conducted with characteristic vigor and success.[36] The death of Count Baldwin eliminated Flanders from the contest.[37] Henry succeeded in making peace and forming an alliance with Fulk of Anjou in June 1119.[38] And in the decisive battle of Brémule in the same year, the English overwhelmed the French, and Louis VI fled from the field.[39] But from arms the French king turned to diplomacy. He appeared with the Clito before the council of Rheims (October 1119), and laid the cause of Robert Curthose

---

[31] Ordericus, iv, pp. 293–294.   [32] *Ibid.*, p. 290.

[33] Hermann of Tournay, *Liber de Restauratione S. Martini Tornacensis*, in *M. G. H.*, Scriptores, xiv, p. 284; cf. Ordericus, iv, p. 294.

[34] *Supra*, pp. 122, 180.

[35] Henry of Huntingdon, pp. 239–240; *Chronicon*, in *Liber de Hyda*, p. 308; Suger, *Vie de Louis le Gros*, pp. 85–86; Ordericus, iv, pp. 315 ff.; William of Malmesbury, *G. R.*, ii, p. 479.

[36] Ordericus, iv, *passim*.

[37] Ordericus, iv, pp. 291, 316; William of Malmesbury, *G. R.*, ii, p. 479; Suger, *Vie de Louis le Gros*, p. 90; *A.–S. C.*, a. 1118, 1119; Henry of Huntingdon, pp. 240, 242.

[38] Ordericus, iv, p. 347; Suger, *Vie de Louis le Gros*, p. 91; *A.–S. C.*, a. 1119.

[39] Ordericus, iv, pp. 354–363; Suger, *Vie de Louis le Gros*, p. 92; *A.–S. C.*, a. 1119; Henry of Huntingdon, pp. 241–242. William Clito fought among the French forces and lost his palfrey, but it was returned to him next day by his cousin William Atheling as an act of courtesy.

and of his exiled son before the assembled prelates with such telling effect [40] that Pope Calixtus set out for Normandy to deal in
person with the English king. But Henry showed himself as apt
at diplomacy as he had been successful in arms. Meeting the
Pope at Gisors (November 1119), he welcomed him with the utmost courtesy and with an extraordinary show of humility.[41]
He provided elaborately for his entertainment.[42] And when
Calixtus arraigned him for his unjust conduct, and, in the name of
the council, called upon him to release Robert Curthose from
prison and to restore him and the Clito to the duchy,[43] Henry
replied in an elaborate speech, placing the whole responsibility
upon the duke. He declared that he had been obliged to conquer
Normandy in order to rescue it from anarchy, and that he had
offered to confer three English counties upon the Clito and to
bring him up in all honor at his court.[44] Strange to say, the Pope
professed himself entirely convinced by Henry's assertions and
declared that " nothing could be more just than the king of England's cause." But William of Malmesbury explains that the
royal arguments were " well seasoned with rich gifts." [45] Henry
had won the Pope, and through the latter's mediation a peace was
soon arranged with Louis VI upon the basis of mutual restitu-
tions; and William Atheling, Henry's son, did homage to the

[40] Ordericus, iv, pp. 376–378 (probably Ordericus was himself present at the
council and heard the king's speech — *ibid.*, p. 372, n. 2); *Chronicon*, in *Liber de
Hyda*, p. 310. The archbishop of Rouen arose to reply, but was howled down and
refused a hearing.

[41] Ordericus, iv, pp. 398–399. The purpose of the Pope in going to Gisors was
not merely to support the interests of the Clito but to bring about a settlement of
all the difficulties between the kings of France and England, and reëstablish peace.
The Pope also endeavored, though without success, to induce King Henry to make
some concession in the ecclesiastical controversy concerning the profession of obedience by the archbishop of York to the archbishop of Canterbury. *The Historians
of the Church of York and its Archbishops*, ed. James Raine (London, 1879–94), ii,
pp. 167–172, 376–377.

[42] William of Malmesbury, *G. R.*, ii, p. 482.

[43] " Synodus ergo fidelium generaliter decernit, et a sublimitate tua, magne rex,
humiliter deposcit ut Rodbertum, fratrem tuum, quem in vinculis iamdiu tenuisti,
absolvas, eique et filio eius ducatum Normanniae, quem abstulisti, restituas."
Ordericus, iv, p. 399.

[44] *Ibid.*, pp. 399–403.

[45] *G. R.*, ii, p. 482.

king of France for Normandy (1120).[46] The Norman rebels, too, seeing that their cause was hopeless, hastily made peace with Henry, and at his command did homage and swore fealty to the Atheling.[47] William Clito was deserted on almost every hand, and his cause did indeed seem hopeless. If we can trust the chronicle of Hyde monastery, he sent messengers to King Henry and humbly besought him to release his father from captivity, and promised, if his request were granted, to depart with him for Jerusalem, abandoning Normandy to the king and his heirs forever, and never again to appear this side the Julian Alps.[48]

King Henry, we are told, treated these overtures with arrogant contempt, as well he might in view of his victory over all his enemies. Yet before the end of the year the loss of the Atheling on the *White Ship* put all his well laid plans awry, and left William Clito, his bitter enemy, as the most direct heir of all his dominions both in Normandy and England.[49] Soon his old enemies began to rally to the Clito's cause; and he was again confronted with a formidable revolt of the Norman baronage (1123-25), which had at least the tacit support of the king of France.[50] Fulk of Anjou, in league with the rebels, abandoned the English alliance and conferred the county of Maine, together with the hand of his younger daughter Sibyl, upon the Clito.[51] Though Henry succeeded in having this marriage annulled by papal decree in 1124 upon the

---

[46] Achille Luchaire, *Louis VI le Gros: annales de sa vie et de son règne* (Paris, 1890), p. 139, and the references there given.

[47] Ordericus, iv, p. 398; *Chronicon*, in *Liber de Hyda*, pp. 319-320.

[48] *Ibid.*, pp. 320-321.

[49] " Solus regius esset haeres." Henry of Huntingdon, p. 305 (*Epistola de Contemptu Mundi*); cf. Ordericus, iv, p. 438; William of Malmesbury, *G. R.*, ii, pp. 497-498.

[50] Ordericus, iv, pp. 438-462; *Interpolations de Robert de Torigny*, in William of Jumièges, pp. 294-296; Henry of Huntingdon, p. 245; cf. Davis, *Normans and Angevins*, p. 150.

[51] " All this hostility was on account of the son of Count Robert of Normandy named William. The same William had taken to wife the younger daughter of Fulk, count of Anjou; and therefore the king of France and all these counts and all the powerful men held with him, and said that the king with wrong held his brother Robert in durance and unjustly drove his son William out of Normandy." *A.-S. C.*, a. 1124; cf. Ordericus, iv, p. 440; William of Malmesbury, *G. R.*, ii, p. 498.

ground of consanguinity,[52] Louis VI continued to support the Clito. At his Christmas court in 1126 he called upon the assembled barons to assist the young prince.[53] Shortly thereafter he gave him the half-sister of his own queen in marriage and conferred upon him Pontoise, Chaumont, Mantes, and the whole of the Vexin. Before Lent 1127 the Clito appeared at Gisors at the head of an armed force, and laid claim to Normandy.[54] And soon afterwards the foul murder of Count Charles the Good opened the question of the Flemish succession, and gave the king of France, as overlord of the county, an opportunity to raise his protégé to the throne of Flanders, although the king of England was himself a candidate for the honor.[55] The fortunes of the Clito were now decidedly in the ascendant, and it behooved Henry I to bestir himself to check his progress. He crossed the Channel and began active military operations against the Franco-Flemish alliance.[56] He sent his agents into Flanders to distribute bribes and build up a combination against the new count. He freely subsidized the rival claimants to the county.[57] But Henry's problem was soon solved for him by a civil war in which, so far as we know, he had no part or influence. William Clito had allied himself with the feudal aristocracy of Flanders, but he had failed to comprehend the spirit of the progressive bourgeoisie, to whom his predecessor, Charles the Good, had made important

---

[52] William of Malmesbury, *G. R.*, ii, pp. 527–528; *Bullaire du pape Calixte II*, ed. Ulysse Robert (Paris, 1891), ii, no. 507; Ordericus, iv, pp. 294–295, 464; *A.-S. C.*, a. 1127. The pair were separated by eleven degrees of kinship, the Clito being descended in the fifth and Sibyl in the sixth generation from Richard the Fearless, third duke of Normandy. The pedigree is given by Ordericus, *loc. cit.* The king resorted to high-handed bribery in order to bring about the divorce. Cf. Le Prévost, in Ordericus, iv, p. 295, n. 1.

[53] Ordericus, iv, p. 472.   [54] *Ibid.*, p. 474.

[55] *Ibid.*, pp. 474–477; Suger, *Vie de Louis le Gros*, pp. 110–112; *A.-S. C.*, a. 1127; Galbert of Bruges, *Histoire du meurtre de Charles le Bon, comte de Flandre*, ed. Henri Pirenne (Paris, 1891), *passim*; cf. Luchaire, *Louis VI le Gros*, pp. 175–176, and the references there given.

[56] *A.-S. C.*, a. 1128; Henry of Huntingdon, pp. 247–248; letter of William Clito to Louis VI, in *H. F.*, xv, p. 341. On the date of this letter (March 1128) see Luchaire, *Louis VI le Gros*, p. 188.

[57] *Ibid.*; Walter of Thérouanne, *Vita Karoli Comitis Flandriae*, in *M. G. H.*, Scriptores, xii, p. 557; Galbert of Bruges, pp. 144–147; Ordericus, iv, pp. 480–484; Henry of Huntingdon, p. 249.

concessions.[58] Increasing friction with the burgesses soon led to an insurrection, and the Clito was wounded at the siege of Alost, late in July 1128, and died soon after.[59] That night, Robert Curthose, we are told, lying in his distant English prison, dreamed that he had himself been wounded in the right arm; and waking, " Alas! " he said, with telepathic vision, " my son is dead." [60] It was, indeed, the end of all hope for the captive duke; and thereafter Henry I ruled in peace in Normandy as well as England.

Of the vicissitudes of Robert Curthose during the long years of his imprisonment we know almost nothing. A curious notice in the chronicle of Monte Cassino for the year 1117 styles him ' king of the English,' and avers that his ' legates ' had visited the monastery, and, presenting the monks with a precious golden chalice, had besought their prayers for himself and his realm.[61] In 1126, upon his return from Normandy, Henry I transferred the duke from the custody of Bishop Roger of Salisbury to that of Earl Robert of Gloucester, who placed him in confinement at first in his great stronghold at Bristol.[62] But later he moved him to Cardiff castle in his Welsh lordship of Glamorgan; [63] and there, in this wild frontier stronghold, in full view of the ' Severn

---

[58] Pirenne, *Histoire de Belgique*, i, pp. 183–185. For a full discussion of the relations between the Clito and the Flemish burghers see Arthur Giry, *Histoire de la ville de Saint-Omer et de ses institutions jusqu'au XIVe siècle* (Paris, 1877), pp. 45 ff.

[59] Ordericus, iv, pp. 481–482; *A.-S. C.*, a. 1128; Florence of Worcester, ii, pp. 90–91; Galbert of Bruges, pp. 170–171, and n. 2, where the chronological problem is fully discussed.

[60] Ordericus, iv, p. 486.

[61] " His porro diebus Robbertus rex Anglorum legatos ad hoc monasterium direxit, petens ut pro se atque pro statu regni sui Domini clementiam exorarent, calicemque aureum quantitatis non modicae beato Benedicto per eos dirigere studuit." Petrus Diaconus, *Chronica Monasterii Casinensis*, in *M. G. H.*, Scriptores, vii, p. 791. This may very possibly be a scribal error, and the reference may really be to Henry I.

[62] *A.-S. C.*, a. 1126: " In this same year the king caused his brother Robert to be taken from the bishop Roger of Salisbury, and committed him to his son Robert, earl of Gloucester, and had him conducted to Bristol, and there put into the castle. That was all done through his daughter's counsel, and through her uncle, David, the Scots' king "; cf. *Interpolations de Robert de Torigny*, in William of Jumièges, p. 292.

[63] Ordericus, iv, p. 486; v, pp. 18, 42; Florence of Worcester, ii, p. 95; *Hist. et Cart. S. Petri Gloucestriae*, i, p. 15.

Sea,' Robert Curthose ended his days. If we can rely upon our evidence, he took advantage of his long imprisonment to master the Welsh language, and amused himself with verse-making. And he appears to have left behind him a poem of no mean order. It was extracted by the Welsh bard, Edward Williams,[64] "from a MS. of Mr. Thomas Truman, of Pant Lliwydd (Dyer's valley), near Cowbridge, Glamorgan, containing, in the Welsh language, ' An Account of the Lords Marchers of Glamorgan from Robert Fitz Hamon down to Jasper, Duke of Bedford,' and written about the year 1500," [65] and was published in the *Gentleman's Magazine* in 1794, from which it seems worth while to quote it in full, together with the attribution of authorship:

Pan oedd Rhobert Tywysog Norddmanti yngharchar Ynghastell Caerdyf, gan Robert ap Amon, medru a wnaeth ar y iaith Gymraeg; ac o weled y Beirdd Cymreig yno ar y Gwyliau efe a'u ceris, ac a aeth yn Fardd; a llyma englynion a gant efe.

Dar a dyfwys ar y clawdd,
Gwedi, gwaedffrau gwedi ffrawdd;
Gwae! wrth win ymtrin ymtrawdd.

Dar a dyfwys ar y glâs,
Gwedi gwaedffrau gwyr a lâs;
Gwae! wr wrth y bo ai câs.

Dar a dyfwys ar y tonn,
Gwedi gwaedffrau a briw bronn;
Gwae! a gar gwydd amryson.

Dar a dyfwys ym meillion,
A chan a'i briw ni bi gronn;
Gwae! wr wrth ei gaseion.

Dar a dyfwys ar dir pen
Gallt, ger ymdonn Mor Hafren
Gwae! wr na bai digon hên.

Dar a dyfwys yngwynnau,
A thwrf a thrin a thrangau;
Gwae! a wyl na bo Angau.
Rhobert Tywysog Norddmanti ai Cant.

[64] Known as Iolo Morganwg (1746–1826).
[65] The manuscript referred to is apparently no longer extant, the Truman Collection having been scattered early in the nineteenth century, and almost every trace of it having now disappeared. We are therefore solely indebted to Edward Williams for the preservation of this poem and its brief introduction, which to-

In English thus:

When Robert, duke of Normandy, was held a prisoner in Cardiff castle by Robert Fitz Hamon, he acquired a knowledge of the Welsh language; and, seeing the Welsh bards there on the high festivals, he became a bard; and was the author of the following stanzas:

Oak that hast grown up on the mound,
Since the blood-streaming, since the slaughter;
Woe! to the war of words at the wine.

Oak that hast grown up in the grass,
Since the blood-streaming of those that were slain;
Woe! to man when there are that hate him.

Oak that hast grown up on the green,
Since the streaming of blood and the rending of breasts,
Woe! to him that loves the presence of contention.

Oak that hast grown up amid the trefoil grass,
And, because of those that tore thee, hast not attained to rotundity;
Woe! to him that is in the power of his enemies.

Oak that hast grown up on the grounds
Of the woody promontory fronting the contending waves of the Severn sea; [66]
Woe! to him that is not old enough [to die].

Oak that hast grown up in the storms,
Amid dins, battles, and death;
Woe! to him that beholds what is not death.
The Author Robert Duke of Normandy.[67]

Whether these lines be actually by Robert Curthose or not, they are in their tragic pathos no inapt epitome of his misdirected career, which had begun with such bright promise and ended in

gether constitute the only evidence that Robert became acquainted with the Welsh language and wrote verses. The poem has been several times printed, but all texts of it derive from a single source, viz., Williams's transcript of the Pantlliwyd manuscript. According to Mr. John Ballinger, librarian of the National Library of Wales, to whom I am indebted for the foregoing information, Williams's statements as to the sources from which he made his copies are usually accurate, but his deductions are often uncritical and faulty.

[66] " The Severn sea, or Bristol channel, and the woody promontory of Penarth, are in full view of Cardiff castle, at the distance, in a direct line, of no more than two miles. There are on this promontory the vestiges of an old camp (Roman, I believe), on one of the banks or mounds of which, these verses suppose the apostrophized oak to be growing." Williams, in *Gentleman's Magazine*, lxiv (1794), 2, p. 982.

[67] *Ibid.*, p. 981.

such signal disaster. 'Woe to him that is in the power of his enemies,' 'woe to him that is not old enough to die' — often must these sentiments have haunted him during the long years of his captivity. But his melancholy longings at last found satisfaction. Early in February 1134 he died at Cardiff,[68] a venerable octogenarian, and was buried before the high altar in the abbey church of St. Peter at Gloucester.[69] Henry I piously made a donation to the abbey, in order that a light might be kept burning perpetually before the great altar for the good of the soul of the brother whom he had so deeply injured.[70]

[68] Ordericus, iv, p. 486; v, pp. 18, 42; Florence of Worcester, ii, p. 95; *Hist. et Cart. S. Petri Gloucestriae*, i, p. 15. Robert of Torigny is in error in stating that he died at Bristol. *Interpolations de Robert de Torigny*, in William of Jumièges, p. 292. The date of Robert's death is probably 3 February, as stated by the local Gloucester annals, though Robert of Torigny places it on 10 February.

[69] *Hist. et Cart. S. Petri Gloucestriae*, i, p. 15: " in ecclesia Sancti Petri Gloucestriae honorifice coram principali altari sepelitur "; Ordericus, iv, p. 486; v, p. 18; *Interpolations de Robert de Torigny*, in William of Jumièges, p. 292. The well known effigy of Robert Curthose in wood with which his tomb was later adorned is still preserved in Gloucester cathedral — the abbey church having become the cathedral upon the institution of the bishopric in 1541. It is no longer in its original position, but is in the northeast chapel, called Abbot Boteler's chapel, off the ambulatory. It was broken into several pieces during the civil wars of Charles I, but was repaired and restored to the cathedral through the generosity of Sir Humphrey Tracey of Stanway. It was evidently still in its original position when Leland saw it in the sixteenth century. He says: " Rob[tus]. Curthoise, sonne to K. William the Conquerour, lyeth in the midle of the Presbitery. There is on his Tombe an Image of Wood paynted, made longe since his Death." *The Itinerary cf John Leland the Antiquary*, ed. Thomas Hearne, 3d ed. (Oxford, 1769), iv, p. 80. According to W. V. Guise the effigy is of "a date not very remote from the period at which the duke lived." He bases his opinion upon the fact that the hauberk of chainmail and the long surcote, as represented in the effigy, ceased to be worn after the thirteenth century. *Records of Gloucester Cathedral*, ed. William Bazeley (Gloucester, n. d.), i, 1, p. 101. Nothing appears to be known as to who provided for the effigy or as to the circumstances under which it was wrought. See H. J. L. J. Massé, *The Cathedral Church of Gloucester: a Description of its Fabric and a brief History of the Episcopal See* (London, 1910), pp. 85–86.

[70] " Rex Henricus senior dedit Deo et Sancto Petro Gloucestriae manerium suum de Rodele cum bosco et piscaria ibidem, ad inveniendum lumen ante altare magnum ibidem iugiter arsurum pro anima Roberti Curthose germani sui ibidem sepulti tempore Willelmi abbatis." *Hist. et Cart. S. Petri Gloucestriae*, i, pp. 110–111. " Willelmi " is probably a scribal error for Walteri.

CHAPTER VIII

ROBERT CURTHOSE IN LEGEND[1]

THOUGH Robert's life had been filled with failures and had ended in a signal disaster, his memory by no means perished with him. As a leader in the Holy War he had earned an enviable fame, which was early enhanced by legend; and if modern writers have been guilty of some exaggeration in their estimates of his merit as a crusader,[2] they have merely perpetuated unconsciously a tradition which was already well established in the literature of the later Middle Ages. William of Malmesbury, writing as early as 1125, declared that Robert gave proof of his valor on the Crusade by many wonderful feats of arms, for "neither Christian nor pagan could ever unhorse him," and he goes on to add details about his exploits at Antioch and the honor of the kingship which was offered him at Jerusalem.[3] The more extended account of Wace is equally flattering:

> Robert Ierusalem requist,
> Bel se contint, maint bien i fist;
> A Antioche prendre fu,
> D'armes i a grant pries eu.
> Pois fu a Ierusalem prendre,
> Ne s'i porent paiens deffendre.
> De l'estandart qu'il abati,

---

[1] This chapter makes no pretence of being based upon an exhaustive examination of all the sources. Scattered as these are through the historical and romantic literature of several centuries, it is not unlikely that important printed materials have been overlooked, while many manuscripts of the poetic cycle of the Crusade still lie unprinted. It is hoped, however, that enough material has been found and used to give an adequate view of the legendary accretions which gathered about Robert's name, and to throw an interesting light upon the repute in which he was held in after times.

[2] See *supra*, p. 118, and n. 156.

[3] *G. R.*, ii, pp. 460–461; cf. the superlatives of William of Newburgh, writing at the end of the twelfth century: " Qui tamen armis tantus fuit, ut in illa magna et famosa expeditione Ierosolymitana in fortissimos totius orbis procres clarissimae militiae titulis fulserit." *Historia Rerum Anglicarum*, ed. H. C. Hamilton (London, 1856), i, p. 15.

Ou Corberan se combati,
E des paiens que il ocist
E de l'enseigne qu'il conquist,
Qu'il pois a l'iglise dona
Que sa mere a Chaem funda,
Out il grant pries e grant enor,
E mult en parlerent plusor.[4]

And by Geoffrey Gaimar, writing about the middle of the twelfth century, he is pictured as the supreme leader of the First Crusade, disposing of the cities and lands of the conquered territory according to his pleasure:

Suz ciel nen out meillor baron.
Celui fu duc de Normendie,
Sur Normans out la seignurie.
Maint bonte e maint barnage
E maint estrange vasselage
Fist i cest duc de Normendie,
E mainte bele chevalerie.
Co fu cil ki mult bien fist,
Ierusalem sur paens prist,
Il conquist la bone cite,
Des crestiens fust alose.
Pur Curbarant kil out oscis
Entrat li duc si halt pris,
Ka rei le voleient eslire;
Esguarde ont kil seit lur sire
A Antioche la cite,
La fust tenu pur avoue.
Il la conquist com ber vaillant;
Puis la donat a Normant;
E les altres bones citez,
Si com li ducs ad divisez,
Furent parties e donees,
E les pais e les contrees.
Duc Godefrai, par son otrei,
Fust feit en Ierusalem rei;
Pur co kil ni volt remaneir,
Lui lessat; si en fist son air.[5]

The foregoing illustrations, written during the duke's lifetime or within a generation after his death, offer a convincing demon-

[4] *Roman de Rou*, ii, pp. 415–416.
[5] *Lestorie des Engles*, ed. T. D. Hardy and C. T. Martin (London, 1888–89), i, pp. 244–245.

stration of the extraordinary rapidity with which legend set to
work to rehabilitate the memory of the vanquished of Tinchebray; and it will not be without interest to make at least a cursory examination of these unhistorical traditions, in so far as they
reflect the duke's reputation among the writers of the later Middle
Ages. Gaston Paris has not hesitated to affirm that Robert, as a
crusader, became the hero of a whole poetic cycle which has since
been lost, though not without leaving traces in the literature of
after times.[6] Stated in this sweeping form, the pronouncement
of this distinguished scholar is perhaps an unwarrantable exaggeration; at any rate, in the present state of the evidence it can
hardly be regarded as more than a bold hypothesis.[7] But if there
was not, properly speaking, a Norman cycle of the Crusade of

[6] " Le duc de Normandie a été, en tant que croisé, le héros de tout un cycle
poétique qui s'est perdu, mais non sans laisser des traces." " Robert Court-Heuse
à la première croisade," in *Comptes rendus des séances de l'Académie des Inscriptions
et Belles-Lettres*, 1890, 4th series, xviii, p. 208.

[7] Gaston Paris (*op. cit.*, p. 211, n. 3) believes that the Robert legend was extinguished first by Robert's disastrous and inglorious end, and second by the growing popularity of the Godfrey cycle. He thinks that the " lutte des deux traditions
poétiques, de provenances différentes, dont l'une avait pour héros Robert et l'autre
Godefroi" can be seen in an episode of the *Chanson d'Antioche* which may be
briefly paraphrased as follows. Godfrey, " because he is *preux* and courageous and
of the lineage of Charlemagne," has just been chosen to represent the Christian
army in a proposed single combat with a champion from Kerboga's host; on hearing which Robert is so incensed at being himself passed over that he prepares to
withdraw with his forces from the crusading army. Compared with his own splendid lineage, the ancestors of Godfrey, he declares, are not worth a button. Thereupon the descent of Godfrey from the Chevalier au Cygne is explained to him. And
then Godfrey himself comes and humbles himself before Robert and expresses his
willingness to yield the honor to him. At that Robert is mollified and consents to
remain. *La Chanson d'Antioche*, ed. Paulin Paris (Paris, 1848), ii, pp. 177–183. It
is difficult to see where support for Paris's theory can be found in the matter thus
summarized. All that concerns Robert, it seems clear, exists not for itself at all, but
as a mere literary foil for setting off the merits of Godfrey and his descent from the
Chevalier au Cygne. The evidence of the Saint-Denis window which Gaston Paris
cites must be ruled out. See Appendix G.

The *Chanson d'Antioche*, in the form in which we now have it, is held to have been
composed early in the reign of Philip Augustus by Grandor of Douai, a Flemish
trouvère, upon the basis of an earlier poem, now lost, by Richard le Pèlerin, a min-
strel who actually took part in the First Crusade. *Histoire littéraire de la France*,
xxii (1852), pp. 355–356; Auguste Molinier, *Les sources de l'histoire de France*
(Paris, 1901–06), no. 2154.

which Robert was the hero, there certainly were numerous legends which it seems worth while to bring together in such order as is possible in the arrangement of matter so scattered and fragmentary.

William of Malmesbury has sounded the keynote of Robert's later fame as a crusader: [8] it was his personal prowess on the field of battle which most impressed itself upon the imagination of later generations. With one exception of minor importance, [9] later writers tell us little or nothing of a legendary character respecting the position and achievements of Robert at the siege of Nicaea; but his imaginary exploits in the battle of Dorylaeum (1 July 1097) begin to meet us in accounts which are almost contemporary. Robert the Monk, writing before 1107, pictures him as the saviour of the day. The Franks were all but overwhelmed and had turned in flight, and the contest would surely have ended in disaster for them, had not the count of Normandy quickly turned his charger and checked the rout by waving aloft his golden banner and calling out the inspiring battle cry, *Deus vult! Deus vult!* [10] In the *Gesta Tancredi* of Ralph of Caen, written but a few years later, Robert appears as a hero whose valor surpassed even that of the great Bohemond; for in the crisis of the battle, remembering who he was and the royal blood which flowed in his veins, he turned upon his fleeing comrades and shouted: " O Bohemond! why do you fly ? Apulia and Otranto and the confines of the Latin world are far away. Let us stand fast. Either the victor's crown or a glorious death awaits us: glory will there be in either fate, but it will be the greater glory

[8] *Supra*, p. 190.

[9] *Li estoire de Jérusalem et d'Antioche*, in *H. C. Oc.*, v, pp. 629–630. This chronicle, in old French prose of the second half of the thirteenth century, is based ultimately upon Fulcher of Chartres, but it is filled with matter of a purely imaginary character. It seems to contain almost no points of contact with the other sources from which the Robert legends are to be drawn. It represents Robert as taking part in the battle with Kilij Arslan at Nicaea — actually Robert had not yet arrived at Nicaea — and overthrowing him and taking his horse. It also portrays Robert as the principal leader at Nicaea, and the one to whom Kilij Arslan sent the messenger Amendelis to open negotiations.

[10] *H. C. Oc.*, iii, p. 761; cf. the fifteenth century *Anonymi Rhenani Historia et Gesta Ducis Gotfredi*, ibid., v, p. 454.

which makes us sooner martyrs. Therefore, strike, O youths, and let us fall upon them and die if need be!"[11] And with that the flight was halted. Henry of Huntingdon puts a similar speech into the mouth of Robert, and gives an even more wonderful account of his exploits in the battle. In Henry's story, when Robert had finished speaking, he charged upon a paynim king and with one mighty thrust of his lance pierced his shield, armor, and body; then he felled a second and a third of the infidels.[12] And from Henry of Huntingdon the account of Robert's prowess on the field of Dorylaeum was handed on with slight modification from writer to writer throughout the mediaeval period.[13]

The further legendary exploits of Robert Curthose are in the main connected with the great battles at Antioch by which the Christians drove off the successive relief forces which the Moslems sent against them, first the army of Ridwan of Aleppo (9 February 1098) and then the host of Kerboga of Mosul (28 June 1098). Actually Robert seems to have taken no part in the earlier battle;[14] but in the account of the admiring Henry of Huntingdon, we find him leading the first division in the action, and, with a single blow of his mighty sword, splitting head, teeth, neck, and even the shoulders (*usque in pectora*) of a pagan warrior.[15] And while this feat of arms, like the exploits at Dorylaeum, appears to be unknown to the poems of the Godfrey cycle, it was taken up and passed on by English and Norman writers to the close of the Mid-

---

[11] *H. C. Oc.*, iii, p. 622. Ralph's whole account of the battle is almost epic in character; cf. the poems (pp. 625–629) devoted to the exploits of individual heroes, and especially the two lines on p. 627:

> Rollandum dicas Oliveriumque renatos,
> Si comitum spectes hunc hasta, hunc ense, furentes.

[12] P. 221.

[13] *Chronique de Robert de Torigni*, i, pp. 82–83; Ralph de Diceto, *Opera Historica*, ed. William Stubbs (London, 1876), i, p. 222; Roger of Wendover, *Flores Historiarum*, ed. H. O. Coxe (London, 1841–44), ii, p. 87; Matthew Paris, *Chronica Maiora*, ed. H. R. Luard (London, 1872–83), ii, p. 64; idem, *Historia Minor*, ed. Frederick Madden (London, 1866–69), i, pp. 85–86; *Flores Historiarum*, ed. H. R. Luard (London, 1890), ii, p. 29; *Le livere de reis de Brittanie e le livere de reis de Engletere*, ed. John Glover (London, 1865), p. 166; Robert of Gloucester, *Metrical Chronicle*, ed. W. A. Wright (London, 1887), ii, pp. 585–586; Thomas Walsingham, *Ypodigma Neustriae*, ed. H. T. Riley (London, 1876), p. 79.

[14] *Supra*, p. 106.   [15] P. 224.

dle Ages.[16] Indeed, new and grotesque exaggerations were added
to it. Presently we learn that Robert not only split the paynim's
head and a portion of his body, but his shield and his helmet also;
that he slew him even as one slaughters a sheep; and that as the
body fell to earth the victor cried aloud commending its blood-
stained soul to all the minions of Tartarus![17] One would have
thought this sufficient, surely, but another version tells us that
Godfrey came to Robert's assistance, and with a second blow cleft
the unfortunate pagan in twain, so that one half of his body fell to
the ground while his charger bore the other in among the infidels![18]

It was however in the later battle with Kerboga that, according
to the legends, Robert performed his greatest feat of arms. The
trustworthy accounts tells us merely that he led the third division
in action.[19] But William of Malmesbury has represented him as
attacking the great Kerboga himself, while the latter was rallying
the Moslem forces, and slaying him.[20] And this tradition was preserved in England and in Normandy without elaboration throughout the twelfth century.[21] Wace seems to mention the incident,
but without any indication that Kerboga was killed by Robert; [22]
and in this he is in agreement with the earliest extant version of
the Godfrey cycle, the so-called *Chanson d'Antioche*, which narrates the exploit in truly epic form:

> The count of Normandy was of right haughty mien;
> Full armed he sat upon his steed of dappled gray.
> He dashed into the mêlée like a leopard;
> And his doughty vassals followed him;
> There was wrought great slaughter of accursed Saracens.
> Kerboga was seated before his standard;
> Richly was he armed, he feared neither lance nor dart;

[16] *Chronique de Robert de Torigni*, i, p. 84; Ralph de Diceto, i, p. 223; Matthew Paris, *Chronica Maiora*, ii, p. 74; *Flores Historiarum*, ii, p. 29; Robert of Gloucester, ii, p. 591; Walsingham, *Ypodigma*, p. 80. See also the references given in nn. 17 and 18 *infra*.

[17] Roger of Wendover, ii, p. 103; Matthew Paris, *Historia Minor*, i, p. 102.

[18] *Le livere de reis*, p. 168.

[19] *Supra*, pp. 107–108.   [20] *G. R.*, ii, p. 460.

[21] Geoffrey Gaimar, in the extract quoted on p. 191, *supra*; *Gesta Regis Henrici Secundi*, ed. William Stubbs (London, 1867), i, p. 329; cf. Roger of Hoveden, i, p. 274.

[22] *Roman de Rou*, as quoted on p. 191, *supra*.

From his neck a rich buckler was suspended;
His helmet was forged in the city of ' Baudart ';
A carbuncle burned upon the nasal;
A strong, stiff lance he bore, and a scimitar;
Upon the shield which swung from his neck a parrot was painted.[23]
Kerboga advanced with serried ranks.
When the count saw him he too advanced upon him,
And smote him such a blow upon his buckler
That he threw him, legs in air, into the press.[24]
Now he would have cut off his head, but he was too late; .
For Persians and ' Acopars ' came to the rescue,
And bore their lord away to his standard.[25]

The *Chanson d'Antioche* also narrates another spectacular exploit in which Robert overthrew and slew the great emir ' Red Lion ' during the same battle; [26] but this episode seems not to have been repeated in other compilations, and it occupies a far less important place in the *Chanson d'Antioche* than has been supposed by modern writers, who have sought to trace a connection between it and the Robert medallion in Suger's famous stained glass window at Saint-Denis.[27] The later compilation of the Godfrey matter, edited by Reiffenberg, contains no mention of Robert's combat either with Kerboga or with Red Lion; but it relates a very similar exploit in which he overcame a ' Saracen king of Tabarie.' With his lance at the thrust, and raising the triumphant war cry

[23] The reading and the meaning are here uncertain. I follow the conjecture of the editor.

[24] " Le trebuche el begart." According to *Godefroy* (*Dictionnaire de l'ancienne langue française*) the meaning of *begart* is undetermined. Again I follow the conjecture of the editor.

[25] *Chanson d'Antioche*, ii, pp. 245–246.

[26] *Ibid.*, p. 261. Red Lion is perhaps to be identified with Kilij Arslan, sultan of Iconium.

[27] Paul Riant and Ferdinand de Mély, in *Revue de l'art chrétien*, 1890, pp. 299–300. Their view has been rightly rejected by Gaston Paris in *Comptes rendus de l'Académie des Inscriptions et Belles-Lettres*, 1890, p. 208. See Appendix G. In *Le Chevalier au Cygne et Godefroid de Bouillon*, ed. F. A. F. T. le Baron de Reiffenburg (Brussels, 1846–59), ii, pp. 231–232, Red Lion is killed by Count Baldwin.

This version of the Godfrey matter has been assigned to the fourteenth century both by Paulin Paris (*Histoire littéraire*, xxv, p. 508) and by Célestin Hippeau (*La conquête de Jérusalem*, p. ix), but A.-G. Krüger, in a more recent discussion, has placed it as late as the first half of the fifteenth century. " Les manuscrits de la Chanson du Chevalier au Cygne et de Godéfroi de Bouillon," in *Romania*, xxviii (1899), p. 426.

"Normandy!", he bore down upon the Saracen with such force that he pierced his shield a full palm's breadth and a half, and wounded him deeply "between lungs and liver." [28]   Finally, mention must be made of Robert's prowess in the legendary battle on the plain of Ramleh before Jerusalem, as told in the fantastic account of the *Chanson de Jérusalem*. This time it was a Turkish King Atenas whom he slew, and many others besides, so that the ground was strewn with the enemy dead. But at last he was surrounded and all but overborne by numbers. His horse was struck down under him, and it was only after desperate fighting against almost hopeless odds that he was finally rescued, when bleeding from many wounds, by his fellow princes.[29]

Thus the Robert Curthose of the legends enjoyed a marvellous repute for warlike prowess; and when Jerusalem had at last been won, his valor was rewarded, we are told, with an offer of the crown of the Latin Kingdom, which he promptly rejected.[30]   Rest-

[28] *Le Chevalier au Cygne et Godefroid de Bouillon*, ii, p. 212-213.

[29] *La conquête de Jérusalem*, ed. Célestin Hippeau (Paris, 1868), pp. 308–311. There is as yet no edition of this poem worthy of the name. Much difference of opinion has been expressed as to the date of its composition. It has been ascribed by its editor to the thirteenth century. *Ibid.*, pp. xviii, xix, xxv. But Paulin Paris held it to be a part of the work of Grandor of Douai, compiler of the *Chanson d'Antioche*, and thought it, too, like the latter, was based upon the lost work of Richard le Pèlerin. *Histoire littéraire*, xxii, p. 370, and cf. p. 384. And Molinier has somewhat carelessly assigned it to *circa* 1130. *Sources de l'histoire de France*, no. 2154. On the other hand Henri Pigeonneau, while he would ascribe it to the late twelfth century, still holds that it certainly is not by the author of the *Chanson d'Antioche*, and that it is a later composition than the latter. *Le cycle de la croisade et de la famille de Bouillon* (Saint Cloud, 1877), pp. 42-55. Certainly one works over the poem with a growing conviction that it is late rather than early. It is almost wholly a work of imagination, in which traditions of events centring around Antioch are hopelessly mingled with others pertaining to the region of Jerusalem. One can hardly say whether the imaginary battle of Ramleh contains more of the battle of Ascalon or of the battle against Kerboga.

It may be noted in passing that in the battle of Ascalon Robert performed an actual feat of arms (cf. *supra*, pp. 115–116) which may perhaps form the basis of all the legendary exploits which we have been passing in review. The references to the enemy's 'standard' in Wace (*supra*, p. 190) and in the *Chanson d'Antioche* (*supra*, p. 195) would seem to lend some color to this view. But it should be borne in mind that such exploits of knightly valor are a commonplace of the *chansons de geste*, and are attributed to Godfrey and to other chiefs as well as to Robert.

[30] Gaimar is specific in his statement that the election of Robert was due to his reputation for valor (*supra*, p. 191), as is also the author of an anonymous Norman

ing upon no valid contemporary authority,[31] this tradition arose very early, and lent itself to strange distortions as it passed from author to author. It appears first in William of Malmesbury,[32] but it is also to be found before the middle of the twelfth century in Henry of Huntington [33] and in the *Historia Belli Sacri*.[34] In its simplest form it long continued to be repeated by both English and Norman writers.[35] But it also developed strange variations. As has elsewhere been explained, the position of ruler at Jerusalem was actually offered to Count Raymond of Toulouse and declined by him before the election of Godfrey.[36] Perhaps we have here the historical basis of the tradition that the crown was offered to Robert. It seems possible to trace the growth of the legend. By Albert of Aix it is said that when the honor had been declined by Raymond it was offered in turn to each of the other chiefs, and that the humble Godfrey was prevailed upon to accept it only when all the others had refused.[37] In the *Chanson de Jérusalem* the matter has gone much further. According to this version, Godfrey was first elected by general acclamation of the people, but modestly declined the honor and responsibility. Then the crown was offered to the count of Flanders, to Robert Curthose, to Bohemond, and so in turn to the other leaders, until all had declined; whereupon it was decided to seek divine guidance through the ancient miracle of the holy fire which was accustomed to descend at Jerusalem each year at Easter tide. Accordingly

chronicle of the thirteenth century, excerpted by Paul Meyer from a Cambridge manuscript in *Notices et extraits des manuscrits,* xxxii, 2, p. 65: " Li quens Rob., por les granz proesces que il feseit e qu'il avoit fetes, e por sa grant valor e son grant hardement, fu eslit a estre roi de Sulie."

[31] *Supra*, p. 114.
[32] *G. R.*, ii, p. 461.
[33] Pp. 229, 236.
[34] *H. C. Oc.*, iii, p. 225.
[35] *Chronique de Robert de Torigni*, i, p. 87; *Annales de Waverleia*, in *Annales Monastici*, ii, p. 207; *Gesta Henrici Secundi*, i, p. 329; Gervase of Tilbury, *Otia Imperialia*, in *H. F.*, xiv, p. 13; *Chronique de Normandie, ibid.*, xiii, p. 247; Matthew Paris, *Chronica Maiora*, v, p. 602; *Flores Historiarum*, ii, p. 32; Robert of Gloucester, ii, pp. 607–608; John Capgrave, *Chronicle of England*, ed. F. C. Hingeston (London, 1858), p. 133; idem, *Liber de Illustribus Henricis*, ed. F. C. Hingeston (London, 1858), p. 55.
[36] *Supra*, p. 114.   [37] *H. C. Oc.*, iv, p. 485.

the barons assembled in the church of the Holy Sepulchre, each with an unlighted taper. In the darkness of the night a single candle burned within the great basilica. At midnight a fierce storm arose with lightning, wind, and thunder. The sole light was extinguished. The whole edifice was plunged in darkness. The barons were filled with fear. Suddenly there was another flash from heaven, and it was observed that Godfrey's taper was burning brightly. The divine will had expressed itself, and the good duke of Bouillon bowed before it.[38] Clearly it was in Godfrey's honor that this legend of a miraculous designation first arose. Yet in the late twelfth or early thirteenth century it was said by Ralph Niger that it was Robert's candle which was lighted by the miraculous flame.[39] And once so told, the legend in this form was handed on from writer to writer to the close of the Middle Ages.[40] Langtoft, indeed, declares that Robert was thrice designated by the holy fire.[41]

The miracle as told in Robert's favor, however, involved a logical difficulty which met with a characteristically mediaeval solution. According to early tradition Robert had refused to accept the crown of Jerusalem. The explanation offered by the *Historia Belli Sacri* is natural and reasonable. Said Robert: " Although I have come hither in God's service, yet have I not abandoned my county altogether, in order to remain here. And now that I have fulfilled my vow, if God permits, I desire to return to my own dominions." [42] But if Robert had been chosen for the kingship of Jerusalem by divine will and favor, as was almost

[38] *La conquête de Jérusalem*, pp. 183–191. The legend is repeated in substantially the same form in *Le Chevalier au Cygne et Godefroid de Bouillon*, iii, pp. 81–88.

[39] *Chronica Universalis*, in *M. G. H.*, Scriptores, xxvii, p. 334.

[40] An inedited Flemish chronicle of uncertain date, cited by Pigeonneau, *Le cycle de la croisade*, p. 76; Roger of Wendover, ii, p. 146; Matthew Paris, *Historia Minor*, i, pp. 149–150; Ranulf Higden, *Polychronicon*, ed. J. R. Lumby (London, 1865–86), vii, p. 424; *Eulogium Historiarum*, ed. F. C. Haydon (London, 1858–63), iii, p. 64. Roger of Wendover and Matthew Paris make the explanation that when his candle had been lighted, Robert secretly extinguished it, meaning to refuse the crown.

[41] Peter Langtoft, *Chronicle*, ed. Thomas Wright (London, 1866–68), i, p. 460.

[42] *H. C. Oc.*, iii, p. 225. The account of the election given in *Li estoire de Jérusalem et d'Antioche* appears to have no connection with any of our other sources. *Ibid.*, v, p. 639.

universally believed, how was it possible that he should reject
such a token of heavenly grace without committing a sin and in-
curring divine displeasure ? Did not the disasters which so
quickly overtook him make it abundantly clear that the divine
favor had departed from him ? This, indeed, was the mediaeval
explanation. In refusing the Latin crown, Robert had contemned
and spurned the gift of God. Hence his defeat at Tinchebray and
wellnigh thirty years of incarceration. No feature of the Robert
legends was more persistent or more universally accepted than
this. Appearing first in Henry of Huntingdon, it is repeated
again and again to the close of the mediaeval period.[43]

It remains to notice the legends of pathetic interest which concern themselves not with Robert's prowess as a crusader but with
the tragedy of his long imprisonment. It seems clear that Henry
I began by keeping his fallen brother in free custody and treating
him with remarkable liberality.[44] Indeed, one tradition has preserved a not unattractive picture of the easy conditions under
which Robert was allowed to live, his food and clothing and daily
exercise and amusements all bounteously and richly provided for
him.[45] Yet, strange to say, the official historian of the reign of
Henry II makes the statement — if indeed it is to be found no
earlier than this — that the king had his brother blinded;[46]
and this ugly tale soon spread far and wide and came to be very
generally accepted.[47] But how account for such cruel and in-

[43] Henry of Huntingdon, pp. 229–230, 236; *Chronique de Robert de Torigni*, i,
pp. 87, 128–129; *Annales de Waverleia*, in *Annales Monastici*, ii, p. 207; *Gesta
Henrici Secundi*, i, pp. 329–330; Roger of Wendover, ii, p. 146; Matthew Paris,
Chronica Maiora, ii, pp. 106–107, 132; v, p. 602; idem, *Historia Minor*, i, p. 205;
Flores Historiarum, ii, p. 32; Robert of Gloucester, ii, pp. 607–608, 628–629; Cap-
grave, *Chronicle of England*, p. 133; idem, *De Illustribus Henricis*, pp. 55, 57.

[44] *Supra*, p. 179.

[45] " Rex autem, memor fraternitatis, eundem comitem Robertum in libera
carceris custodia, sine ciborum penuria vel luminis beneficio vel preciosarum vestium
ornatu, salvo tamen fecit reservari. Liceret etiam ei ad scaccos et aleas ludere.
Robas etiam regis, sicut ipse rex, accipiebat; pomeria vicina et saltus et loca de-
lectabilia perambulando, ex regis licentia, visitavit." *Flores Historiarum*, ii, p. 39.

[46] *Gesta Henrici Secundi*, i, p. 330.

[47] *Annales de Wintonia*, in *Annales Monastici*, ii, p. 50; *Chronicon Thomae
Wykes*, ibid., iv, p. 15; *Annales de Wigornia*, ibid., iv, p. 378; Matthew Paris,

human treatment from a king of such eminent justice and virtue as Henry I ? Another legend soon supplied the needed explanation. Geoffrey de Vigeois, writing before 1184, informs us that Henry had released Robert upon certain conditions, and that the latter, violating the agreement, had levied a force against the king and had been captured a second time; and he adds the significant statement that he did not need to be captured a third time (*et tertio opus non fuit*).[48] In the versions of Matthew Paris and in the related *Flores Historiarum* this legend has been elaborated into an episode which is not without its ludicrous as well as its tragic aspects. Friends of Robert, weighty men, had early protested to the king against the duke's imprisonment. It would disgrace the king and the realm of England throughout the world, they said, if a brother should hold a brother in long incarceration. And so they prevailed upon the king to grant Robert's release, upon condition that the latter renounce all claim to both Normandy and England and depart from the realm within a period of forty days. But instead of going, Robert took advantage of his liberty to conspire with the earl of Chester and others, with intent to raise an army and drive Henry from the throne. But the plot was discovered, and the king sent messengers to summon Robert before him. When the duke saw them approaching, he turned and fled, but his palfrey ran into the mire and stuck fast, and so the unfortunate fugitive was taken. And when the king learned what had happened, he ordered his brother to be placed in close and perpetual confinement without any hope of release, and had him deprived of his sight.[49]

Nevertheless, Henry continued to provide Robert with the best of daily food and with royal vestments.[50] And this brings us to the tale of the scarlet robe, with which our account of the Robert legends may fittingly end. " It so happened that on a

Chronica Maiora, ii, p. 133; idem, *Historia Minor*, i, pp. 30, 213; *Flores Historiarum*, ii, p. 39; Henry Knighton, *Chronicon*, ed. J. R. Lumby (London, 1889–95), i, p. 113; *Eulogium Historiarum*, iii, p. 58; Capgrave, *De Illustribus Henricis*, p. 65.

[48] *H. F.*, xii, p. 432.

[49] Matthew Paris, *Historia Minor*, i, pp. 212–213; idem, *Chronica Maiora*, ii, p. 133; *Flores Historiarum*, ii, p. 39.

[50] Matthew Paris, *Historia Minor*, i, p. 213.

feast day, when the king was getting himself a new scarlet robe, and according to his custom was sending one of the same stuff to his brother, he tried to put on the hood, and finding the neck so small that he ripped one of the seams, he said, ' Take this hood to my brother, for his head is smaller than mine.' And when it was brought to Robert, he put it on, and immediately discovered the rent, which the tailor had carelessly neglected to mend, for it was very small; and he said, ' Whence comes this rent which I feel ? ' And the king's messenger laughingly told him all that had happened. Then the duke cried aloud, as if he had been deeply wounded, and said, ' Alas! alas! now have I lived too long. Why do I still continue to draw out my unhappy days ? Behold my brother, even my betrayer and supplanter, now treats me with contempt, and holds me so cheap that he sends me for alms as his dependant his old and torn clothes.' And weeping bitterly he vowed thenceforth to take no more food, nor would he drink; but he raged against himself, and wasted away. And so he died, cursing the day of his birth." [51]

[51] Matthew Paris, *Historia Minor*, i, p. 248. The translation is a free and somewhat condensed rendering of the original. Cf. the same, *Chronica Maiora*, ii, pp. 160–161; Capgrave, *De Illustribus Henricis*, p. 65.

APPENDICES

APPENDIX A

NOTE ON THE SOURCES

In a field already so well explored as that of Normandy and England in the eleventh and twelfth centuries, there is little need to enter into a detailed discussion of primary materials. A brief review, however, of the sources upon which the present volume is based may be a convenience and serve a useful purpose.

Among the narrative sources for the life of Robert Curthose, the *Historia Ecclesiastica*[1] of Ordericus Vitalis is, of course, by far the most important. One of the greatest historical writers of the twelfth century, the monk of Saint-Évroul has treated of Robert's character and career at great length and with much vivacity and insight. And while one may admit with Gaston Le Hardy[2] that he was no friend of the duke, indeed, that as a churchman and as a lover of peace and of strong and orderly government he was strongly prejudiced against him and sometimes treated him unfairly, still it must be confessed that in the main his strictures are confirmed by other evidence and are presumably justified. Unfortunately, Ordericus Vitalis stands almost alone among early Norman writers in paying attention to the career of Robert Curthose. Some assistance, however, has been gained from William of Poitiers[3] and from the *Gesta Normannorum Ducum*, a composite work once solely attributed to William of Jumièges, but now at last made available in a critical edition which distinguishes the parts actually written by William of Jumièges, Ordericus Vitalis, Robert of Torigny, and others.[4] The *Roman de Rou* of Wace[5] has also been drawn upon, sometimes rather freely, but it is hoped always with due caution and discretion, for much picturesque detail concerning events in western Normandy, about which the author clearly possessed special information. For Robert's relations with Maine, the contemporary *Actus Pontificum Cenomannis in Urbe degentium*[6] have

[1] Ed. Auguste Le Prévost. 5 vols. Paris, 1838–55. The critical introduction (i, pp. i–cvi) by Léopold Delisle is definitive.

[2] Cf. *supra*, pp. vii–viii.

[3] *Gesta Willelmi Ducis Normannorum et Regis Anglorum*, in *H. F.*, xi, pp. 75–104.

[4] Ed. Jean Marx. Paris, 1914. Most of the material of value for the present study comes from the interpolations of Robert of Torigny.

[5] Ed. Hugo Andresen. 2 vols. Heilbronn, 1877–79.

[6] Ed. *G.* Busson and A. Ledru. Le Mans, 1901 (*Archives historiques du Maine*, ii).

been an almost constant guide, often confirming and even supplementing the more extensive but less precise narrative of Ordericus Vitalis.
Matter of much importance has also from time to time been gleaned
from the works of French and Flemish writers, such as the famous
Vie de Louis le Gros by Abbot Suger of Saint-Denis,[7] the anonymous
Chronique de Morigny,[8] and the *Histoire du Meurtre de Charles le Bon*
by Galbert of Bruges.[9]

The English writers of the period have naturally proved invaluable.
Of these, William of Malmesbury,[10] as we should expect, possesses the
keenest insight into Robert's character; but the *Anglo-Saxon Chronicle*
treats [11] of the events of Robert's life with greater fulness and in more
coherent and trustworthy chronological order. Florence of Worcester [12] is in general dependent upon the *Chronicle*, but occasionally
he presents a different view or supplementary matter of independent
value; and the same may be said of the *Historia Regum*, which is commonly attributed to Simeon of Durham,[13] in its relation to Florence of
Worcester. Henry of Huntingdon,[14] who is also largely dependent
upon the *Anglo-Saxon Chronicle*, professes himself a first-hand authority from the accession of Robert Curthose and William Rufus to the
ducal and royal thrones in 1087;[15] and his narrative becomes increasingly valuable as it advances, though he cannot be considered a
really independent writer before 1126, i.e., a score of years after the
close of Duke Robert's active career at the battle of Tinchebray. For
all the facts bearing upon Robert's life with which it deals, the *Historia Novorum in Anglia* of Eadmer,[16] the companion and confidential
adviser of Archbishop Anselm, is a strictly contemporary narrative of
the highest value, though its specialized character considerably re-

---

[7] Ed. Auguste Molinier. Paris, 1887.

[8] Ed. Léon Mirot. Paris, 1909.

[9] Ed. Henri Pirenne. Paris, 1891.

[10] *De Gestis Regum Anglorum*, ed. William Stubbs. 2 vols. London, 1889. *De
Gestis Pontificum Anglorum*, ed. N. E. S. A. Hamilton. London, 1870.

[11] *Two of the Saxon Chronicles Parallel*, ed. Charles Plummer. 2 vols. Oxford,
1892–99.

[12] *Chronicon ex Chronicis*, ed. Benjamin Thorpe. 2 vols. London, 1848–49.

[13] Simeon of Durham, *Opera Omnia*, ed. Thomas Arnold, ii. London, 1885. Cf.
infra, p. 216.

[14] *Historia Anglorum*, ed. Thomas Arnold. London, 1879.

[15] " Hactenus de his quae vel in libris veterum legendo repperimus, vel fama
vulgante percepimus, tractatum est. Nunc autem de his quae vel ipsi vidimus, vel
ab his qui viderant audivimus, pertractandum est." *Ibid.*, pp. 213–214.

[16] Ed. Martin Rule. London, 1884.

stricts its usefulness for the purposes of the present study. The brief chronicle of Hyde abbey,[17] which was compiled during the reign of Henry I, has often proved helpful, as have also other minor monastic narratives such as the chronicle of Abingdon [18] and the annals of Winchester,[19] of Waverley,[20] etc.

The documentary sources for the life of Robert Curthose are very meagre; but, such as they are, they are now all conveniently accessible. As a result of prolonged researches in the archives and libraries of Normandy and in the Bibliothèque Nationale, and after a careful sifting of all the printed materials, Professor Charles H. Haskins has been able to give us, in another volume of the *Harvard Historical Studies*, a definitive edition of seven hitherto unpublished ducal charters, together with a complete and annotated list of all the charters of the reign.[21] The best guides to the remainder of the documentary material bearing upon Robert's life are the *Regesta Regum Anglo-Normannorum* by H. W. C. Davis [22] and the *Calendar of Documents preserved in France illustrative of the History of Great Britain and Ireland* by J. H. Round.[23] While both these works leave something to be desired, they have proved invaluable in the preparation of the present study; and it is earnestly to be hoped that the publication of the second volume of Davis's work, containing the charters of Henry I, will not be long delayed.[24] For the full texts of documents, and for other scattered materials not calendared by either Round or Davis, it has been necessary to consult many special collections, e.g., the *Livre noir* of Bayeux cathedral,[25] the *Chartes de Saint-Julien de Tours*,[26] the

[17] *Chronicon Monasterii de Hyda*, in *Liber de Hyda*, ed. Edward Edwards, pp. 283–321. London, 1866.

[18] *Chronicon Monasterii de Abingdon*, ed. Joseph Stevenson. 2 vols. London, 1858.

[19] *Annales Monasterii de Wintonia*, in *Annales Monastici*, ed. H. R. Luard, ii, pp. 1–125. London, 1865.

[20] *Annales Monasterii de Waverleia*, *ibid.*, pp. 127–411.

[21] *Norman Institutions* (Cambridge, Massachusetts, 1918) pp. 285–292, 66–70.

[22] Vol. i. Oxford, 1913.

[23] Vol. i. London, 1899 (*Calendars of State Papers*).

[24] "An Outline Itinerary of King Henry the First," by W. Farrer, in *E. H. R.*, xxxiv, pp. 303–382, 505–579 (July, October, 1919), came to hand just as the present volume was going to press. I am indebted to it for the location of certain charters which until then had escaped my notice.

[25] *Antiquus Cartularius Ecclesiae Baiocensis*, ed. V. Bourrienne. 2 vols. Paris, 1902–03.

[26] Ed. L.-J. Denis. Le Mans, 1912 (*Archives historiques du Maine*, xii).

Cartulaire de l'abbaye de Saint-Vincent du Mans,[27] the letters of Pascal II,[28] of Ivo of Chartres,[29] and of St. Anselm,[30] which are too numerous to be listed here in detail, and which have been fully cited in their proper places in footnotes.

The Crusade forms a special chapter in the record of Robert's life for which it is necessary to draw upon a different group of sources. Of works by contemporary or early writers on the Crusade, the anonymous *Gesta Francorum*[31] is, of course, invaluable for all the facts with which it deals; but the *Historia Hierosolymitana* of Fulcher of Chartres[32] has proved of even greater service in the present study, because of the author's close association with Robert Curthose on the Crusade from the time when the expedition left Normandy until it reached Marash in Armenia; concerning later events also Fulcher was by no means ill informed. The *Historia Francorum qui ceperunt Iherusalem* of Raymond of Aguilers[33] is also a first-hand narrative by an eyewitness; and, while the author is at times rather hostile to Duke Robert and the Normans, he is nevertheless invaluable as representing the point of view of the Provençaux. Inferior to any of the foregoing, but still by a writer who was in the East and who was well informed, the *Gesta Tancredi* of Ralph of Caen[34] has proved of great assistance, as has also the voluminous, but less trustworthy, work of Albert of Aix,[35] which, when it has been possible to check it with other evidence, has contributed valuable information. Of western writers on the Crusade who did not actually make the pilgrimage to the Holy Land, apart from Ordericus Vitalis,[36] who has already been mentioned, Guibert of Nogent[37] and Baldric, archbishop of Dol,[38] have been most helpful. The English writers, except William of Malmesbury,[39] —

[27] Ed. R. Charles and S. Menjot d'Elbenne, i. Le Mans, 1886.
[28] Migne, clxiii.
[29] *H. F.*, xv.
[30] Migne, clix.
[31] Ed. Heinrich Hagemneyer. Heidelberg, 1890.
[32] Ed. idem. Heidelberg, 1913.
[33] *H. C. Oc.*, iii, pp. 235–309.
[34] *H. C. Oc.*, iii, pp. 587–601.
[35] *Liber Christianae Expeditionis pro Ereptione, Emundatione, Restitutione Sanctae Hierosolymitanae Ecclesiae, ibid.*, iv, pp. 265–713.
[36] Bk. ix of the *Historia Ecclesiastica* is devoted to the history of the First Crusade.
[37] *Gesta Dei per Francos*, in *H. C. Oc.*, iv, pp. 115–263.
[38] *Historia Hierosolymitana, ibid.*, pp. 1–111.
[39] *G. R.*, ii.

whose account is based almost wholly upon Fulcher of Chartres, and, apart from an occasional detail, is of little value — have not treated the Crusade with any fulness, and are of little service except for the beginnings of the movement. Of the Greek sources only the *Alexiad* of Anna Comnena [40] has been of much assistance. The Oriental writers are in general too late to be of great importance for the First Crusade, and they had, of course, no particular interest in Robert Curthose; but their writings have not been overlooked, and Matthew of Edessa,[41] Ibn el-Athir,[42] Kemal ed-Din,[43] and Usama ibn Munkidh [44] have been of service. The contemporary letters bearing upon the Crusade have been admirably edited, with exhaustive critical notes, by Heinrich Hagenmeyer.[45] Of charters, or documents in the strict sense of the word, there are almost none relating to the Crusade; but such as there are, they have been rendered easily accessible by the painstaking calendar of documents dealing with the history of the Latin Kingdom of Jerusalem by Reinhold Röhricht.[46] It would be going too far afield to describe at this point the scattered materials from which the attempt has been made to draw up a list of the known associates and followers of Robert on the Crusade. They are fully cited in Appendix D.

For the chapter on Robert Curthose in legend, with which the narrative part of the present volume ends, it has been necessary to depart from the narrow chronological limits within which the rest of our researches have been conducted, and to explore a wide range of literature extending to the close of the Middle Ages. Most of the Robert legends make their appearance early, and can be traced to a certain extent in William of Malmesbury and Henry of Huntingdon and in Robert the Monk and Ralph of Caen. But their elaboration was in the main the work of chroniclers and romancers of a later period. Among Norman and English sources, the works of Geoffrey Gaimar, Wace, William of Newburgh, Ralph de Diceto, and Ralph Niger have

---

[40] *H. C. G.*, i, 2, pp. 1–204.

[41] *Chronique*, in *H. C. A.*, i, pp. 1–150.

[42] *Histoire des Atabecs de Mosul*, in *H. C. Or.*, ii, 2, pp. 1–375; *Kamel-Altevarykh, ibid.*, i.

[43] *Chronique d'Alep, ibid.*, iii.

[44] *Autobiographie*, French translation by Hartwig Derenbourg. Paris, 1895.

[45] *Die Kreuzzugsbriefe aus den Jahren 1088–1100: eine Quellensammlung zur Geschichte des ersten Kreuzzuges.* Innsbruck, 1901.

[46] *Regesta Regni Hierosolymitani.* Innsbruck, 1893. *Additamentum.* Innsbruck, 1904.

proved most helpful for the twelfth century; of Roger of Wendover, Matthew Paris, and Robert of Gloucester, together with the anonymous *Flores Historiarum* and *Livere de reis de Engletere*, for the thirteenth; of Peter Langtoft, Ranulf Higden, and Henry Knighton, together with the anonymous *Eulogium Historiarum*, for the fourteenth; while Thomas Walsingham in the fifteenth century has occasionally been of service. Much material of a legendary character relating to Robert's exploits in the Holy War has also been gleaned from the various versions of the poetic cycle of the Crusade, the most notable of which are the *Chanson d'Antioche* of the late twelfth century, the *Chanson de Jérusalem*, which probably dates from the thirteenth century, and the *Chevalier au Cygne et Godefroid de Bouillon*, edited by the Baron de Reiffenberg, which belongs to the fourteenth or fifteenth century. Such detailed criticism as it has seemed necessary to make of these widely scattered materials bearing upon Robert Curthose in legend has been placed in the footnotes of Chapter VIII, where the editions used have also been fully cited.

APPENDIX B

DE INIUSTA VEXATIONE WILLELMI EPISCOPI PRIMI [1]

THE anonymous tract *De Iniusta Vexatione Willelmi Episcopi Primi* [2] is worthy of more attention and of a more critical study than it has yet received.[3] Since it gives the only detailed account which we possess of the dispute between William Rufus and William of Saint-Calais, bishop of Durham, and of the trial of the latter before the *curia regis* at Salisbury upon a charge of treason in connection with the rebellion of 1088, final judgment as to the bishop's guilt or innocence must in large measure depend upon a just estimate of its value. Freeman was very reluctant to recognize its high authority as compared with his favorite ' southern writers,' the Anglo-Saxon chronicler, Florence of Worcester, and William of Malmesbury; [4] but his distrust appears to be unwarranted.

The tract is manifestly made up of two distinct parts: (1) the main body of an original *libellus*, concerned exclusively with the bishop's ' vexation,' and beginning (p. 171), " Rex Willelmus iunior dissaisivit Dunelmensem episcopum,'" and ending (p. 194), " rex permisit episcopo transitum "; and (2) introductory and concluding chapters, which contain a brief sketch of the bishop's career before and after his unfortunate quarrel with the king and his expulsion from the realm. The joints at which the separate narratives are pieced together are apparent upon the most cursory examination. Not only is there a striking contrast between the detailed and documentary treatment found in the body of the *libellus* and the bare summaries which make up the introductory and concluding paragraphs, but the reader is actually warned of the transition in the last sentence of the introduc-

[1] Reprinted with slight revision from *E. H. R.*, xxxii (1917), pp. 382–387.

[2] Published in William Dugdale's *Monasticon Anglicanum*, new ed. (London, 1817–30), i, pp. 244–250, and in Simeon of Durham, *Opera Omnia*, ed. Thomas Arnold (London, 1882–85), i, pp. 170–195. References are to the latter edition.

[3] Professor *G.* B. Adams has recently made it the basis of an admirable article entitled " Procedure in the Feudal Curia Regis " (*Columbia Law Review*, xiii, pp. 277–293); but he has confined his attention in the main to forms of procedure, and has dealt only incidentally with the critical problems involved.

[4] *William Rufus*, i, pp. 28 ff.; ii, pp. 469–474.

tion by the phrase (p. 171), " quam rem *sequens libellus* manifestat ex ordine." The two parts of the tract are evidently derived from different sources and written at different times by different authors.

The *libellus* properly so called, i.e., the central portion of the tract, is a narrative well supplied with documents; it has all the appearance of being contemporary and by an eyewitness, and is manifestly a source of the greatest value for the facts with which it deals. Liebermann, with his unrivalled knowledge of mediaeval English legal materials, has declared that there is no ground for doubting its authenticity; [5] and Professor G. B. Adams, who also finds abundant internal evidence of its genuineness, points out, as an indication that it was written by an eyewitness in the company of Bishop William, the fact that no attempt is made to tell what went on within the *curia* while the bishop and his supporters were outside; and further, he considers it more " objective and impartial " than Eadmer's better known account of the trial of Anselm before the council of Rockingham. [6] The author, it may be conjectured, was a monk of Durham who stood in somewhat the same favored position among the intimates of Bishop William as that occupied by Eadmer with regard to Anselm; and while we know nothing of his personality, it is perhaps worth remarking in passing that he may very well be the ' certain monk ' (*quendam suum monachum*) who acts on at least two occasions as the bishop's messenger (pp. 172, 175). The account in the earlier instance is so intimate and personal as strongly to support this hypothesis: " Ipsum quoque monachum episcopi, qui de rege redibat, accepit et equum suum ei occidit; postea peditem abire permisit."

The introduction and the conclusion of the tract, on the other hand, are not a first-hand narrative; and fortunately we possess the source from which they are derived. The introduction (pp. 170 f.), dealing with the bishop's career prior to 1088, contains nothing which is not told with much greater fulness in the opening chapters of the fourth book of the *Historia Dunelmensis Ecclesiae* of Simeon of Durham. [7] It is in fact a mere summary of those chapters; and while the author is no servile copyist, he evidently had no other source of information. It seems safe to conclude, therefore, that he was not identical with the author of the original *libellus*. Judged by style and method, the

[5] *Historische Aufsätze dem Andenken an Georg Waitz gewidmet* (Hanover, 1886), p. 159, n. 10.

[6] *Columbia Law Review*, xiii, pp. 277 f., 287, 291.

[7] Simeon, *H. D. E.*, pp. 119–122, 127 f.

conclusion of the tract (pp. 194 f.) appears to be by the same author as the introduction. It, too, is clearly an abridgment of certain chapters of the *Historia Dunelmensis Ecclesiae*,[8] though with this notable difference from the introduction, that it contains some matter not to be found in the *Historia*, e.g., the statement that the exiled bishop was intrusted by the duke with the administration of all Normandy, and the notices of the expedition of William Rufus against King Malcolm in 1091, and of the presence of the Scottish king at the laying of the first stones in the foundation of the new cathedral at Durham in 1093. Apparently, for these more recent events, the writer was drawing upon his own first-hand knowledge. The date at which the introductory and concluding chapters were appended to the original Durham *libellus* cannot be fixed with exactness. The reference to Anselm as " sanctae memoriae " (p. 195) shows that they were written after his death in 1109;[9] and since, as will appear below, they in turn were used in the *Historia Regum,* which is commonly attributed to Simeon of Durham, the *terminus ad quem* cannot be placed much later than 1129.[10]

The relationship between the above mentioned additions to the Durham *libellus* and the *Historia Regum* may be displayed by the following quotations.

The introduction to the Durham tract closes with the following sentence (p. 171):

. . . sed orta inter regem et primates Angliae magna dissensione, episcopus [i.e., William of Durham] ab invidis circumventus usque ad expulsionem iram regis pertulit, *quam-rem sequens libellus manifestat ex ordine;*

and the conclusion opens as follows (pp. 194 f.):

Anno sui episcopatus octavo expulsus est ab Anglia, sed a Roberto fratre regis, comite Normannorum, honorifice susceptus, totius Normanniae curam suscepit. Tertio autem anno, repacificatus regi, recepit episcopatum suum, ipso rege cum fratre suo totoque Angliae exercitu, cum Scotiam contra Malcolmum tenderent, *eum in sedem suam restituentibus, ipsa videlicet die qua inde pulsus fuerat. Tertio Idus Septembris,* secundo anno suae reversionis, ecclesiam veterem, quam Aldunus quondam episcopus construxerat, a fundamentis destruxit.

---

[8] Simeon, *H. D. E.,* pp. 128 f., 133–135.

[9] Cf. Arnold's introduction, p. xxv. The *Historia Dunelmensis Ecclesiae* which they abridge was composed between 1104 and 1109. *Ibid.,* p. xix.

[10] On the date of the composition of the *Historia Regum* see Simeon, *H. R.,* pp. xx–xxi; cf. Simeon, *H. D. E.,* p. xv.

The account of the rebellion of 1088 in the *Historia Regum* — at this
point almost wholly independent of Florence of Worcester — ends
with the expulsion, not of Bishop William of Durham, but of Bishop
Odo of Bayeux:

. . . et ita episcopus [i.e., Odo] qui fere fuit secundus rex Angliae, honorem
amisit irrecuperabiliter. *Sed episcopus veniens Normanniam statim a Rodberto comite totius provinciae curam suscepit; cuius ordinem causae libellus
in hoc descriptus aperte ostendit. Etiam Dunholmensis episcopus Willelmus,
viii. anno episcopatus, et multi alii, de Anglia exierunt.*[11]

And in a later passage the king's restoration of Bishop William to his
see is thus recorded:

*Veniens Dunelmum, episcopum Willelmum restituit in sedem suam, ipso
post annos tres die quo eam reliquit, scilicet iii. idus Septembris.*[12]

Thomas Arnold, the editor of Simeon's *Opera*, remarks upon the
clause " cuius ordinem causae libellus in hoc descriptus aperte ostendit " of the *Historia Regum*, " This ' libellus,' describing Odo's administration in Normandy, appears to be lost." [13]   Taken by itself
the passage is obscure, and it is perhaps not surprising that the editor
wholly mistook its meaning.   But a comparison of it with the clause
" quam rem sequens libellus manifestat ex ordine " of the Durham
tract at once reveals dependence and resolves the difficulty.   The
verbal similarities are striking, and the author of course uses the puzzling " causae " because the source from which he drew was in fact the
account of a *causa*, viz., the trial of William of Saint-Calais before the
curia regis.   It is clear, therefore, that the *libellus* to which the author
of the *Historia Regum* refers his readers is not a lost treatise on the
administration of Bishop Odo in Normandy — as Arnold supposed —,
but in fact the Durham tract on the ' unjust vexation ' of Bishop William, which Arnold had himself already published in the first volume
of Simeon's works.   A further comparison of all the passages which
have been indicated by italics in the foregoing excerpts fully confirms
this conclusion and reveals the extent of the debt of the *Historia
Regum* to the Durham tract.   Not only the verbal agreements but the
close similarities in thought are so marked as to preclude every possibility of independence.

We are now in a position to see how the author of the *Historia
Regum* worked.   Having before him the chronicle of Florence of Worcester — which he regularly followed — with its dark picture of Bishop

---

[11] Simeon, *H. R.*, pp. 216–217.   [12] *Ibid.*, p. 218.   [13] *Ibid.*, p. 217, n. *a*.

William's treason, and the elaborate Durham tract in his defence, he chose to suppress all reference to the bishop of Durham in connection with the rebellion, and substituted for him Odo of Bayeux as a scapegoat. Then at the end of his chapter he added, apparently as an afterthought, and borrowing directly from the Durham tract, that Bishop William ' departed ' from England in the eighth year of his episcopate. The statement of the *Historia Regum*, therefore, that Odo of Bayeux upon his expulsion from England after the fall of Rochester went to Normandy and had the ' care ' of the whole duchy committed to his charge, is valueless. If that honor belongs to any one, it is to William of Saint-Calais, bishop of Durham, as set forth in the conclusion of the tract *De Iniusta Vexatione*.[14]

But the author of the *Historia Regum* was a clumsy borrower, and we have not yet reached the end of the confusion which has arisen as the result of his easy way of juggling with his sources. In a later passage in which he deals with the return of Bishop William to his see at the time of the expedition of William Rufus against King Malcolm in 1091, he explains that the restoration of the bishop took place on the third anniversary of his retirement, " that is, on the 3d before the Ides of September." Freeman, relying upon this text, but apparently mistaking Ides for Nones, states that the arrival of the king in Durham and the reinstatement of the bishop took place on 3 September.[15] Comparison with the parallel text of the Durham tract, however, makes it clear that the author of the *Historia Regum* has here again made an unintelligent and altogether misleading use of his source, copying almost verbatim, but detaching the phrase " iii. idus Septembris " from the next sentence, where it properly refers to an event of the year 1093. It is necessary, therefore, to get back to the evidence of the *De Iniusta Vexatione*, which not only says that Bishop William was reinstated on the third anniversary of his expulsion, but fixes that earlier date with exactness: " Acceperunt ergo Ivo Taillesboci et Ernesius de Burone castellum Dunelmense in manus regis, et dissaisiverunt episcopum de ecclesia et de castello, et de omni terra sua xviii. kal. Decembr." (p. 192). The bishop's restoration, accordingly, should be dated 14 November 1091. If it cause surprise that William

---

[14] Cf. Simeon, *H. D. E.*, p. 128: " quem comes Normannorum non ut exulem, sed ut patrem suscipiens, in magno honore per tres annos, quibus ibi moratus est, habuit." The charters also bear evidence of the honored position which he enjoyed in Normandy during his exile. See Haskins, p. 76.

[15] *William Rufus*, i, p. 300.

Rufus should have undertaken a campaign in the northern country so late in the season, it may be noted that he previously had his hands full with an expedition against the Welsh,[16] and that Florence of Worcester in describing the campaign makes the significant statement, " multique de equestri exercitus eius fame et frigore perierunt." [17]

It remains to raise a question as to the authorship of the *Historia Regum*. As is well known, the evidence on which both it and the *Historia Dunelmensis Ecclesiae* are attributed to Simeon of Durham is not contemporary and not conclusive,[18] though a better case can be made out for the latter than for the former. Without discussing this evidence anew, and without entering at this time upon the more extended inquiry as to whether it is credible that two works of such different character and of such unequal merit can be by a single author, it is still pertinent here to remark their striking difference in point of view with regard to the controversy between William Rufus and the bishop of Durham. The *Historia Dunelmensis Ecclesiae* speaks of the quarrel and of the bishop's expulsion and exile without any reserve; and, moreover, it contains remarkably full information concerning his fortunes while in exile.[19] In all this it is freely reproduced in the additions to the Durham *libellus* (pp. 171, 194 f.). And they in turn are used by the author of the *Historia Regum*.[20] Yet with these additions and the original *libellus* and Florence of Worcester all before him, he suppresses every reference to the alleged treason of Bishop William, persistently declines to use such words as expulsion and exile in connection with him, and steadily ignores the quarrel. For him the bishop ' went out ' of England, although he unconsciously slips into an inconsistency in a later passage when he notes that the bishop was ' restored ' to the see which he had ' left.' [21] If the *Historia Dunelmensis Ecclesiae* and the *Historia Regum* are by one and the same author, then assuredly he had a bad memory for what he had himself previously written, and his point of view had curiously shifted during the intervening years.

---

[16] William of Malmesbury, *G. R.*, ii, p. 365.

[17] Vol. ii, p. 28. It is also clear from Florence that the king did not arrive in Durham until after the destruction of the English fleet, which took place a few days before Michaelmas; cf. *A.-S. C.*, a. 1091. A reference to these events in the *miracula* of St. Cuthbert makes mention of the summer heat (*tempus aestatis fervidum*), but this evidently is to be connected with Malcolm's raid of the previous summer and not with the later expedition of William Rufus against him. Simeon, *H. R.*, p. 340.

[18] For the evidence see Arnold's introductions, i, pp. xv–xxiii; ii, pp. x–xi, xx–xxi.

[19] Simeon, *H. D. E.*, p. 128.

[20] Simeon, *H. R.*, pp. 216 f.   [21] *Ibid.*, pp. 217 f.

APPENDIX C

ARNULF OF CHOCQUES, CHAPLAIN OF ROBERT CURTHOSE

ARNULF OF CHOCQUES, who went on the First Crusade with Robert Curthose and ended his dramatic career in 1118 as patriarch of Jerusalem, is a character of more than ordinary interest, and his provenance and early career are worthy of more careful investigation than they have yet received.[1] The foundation for such a study was laid in 1904, when, by the publication in a new and scholarly edition of a little-known text of the early twelfth century, entitled *Versus de Viris Illustribus Diocesis Tarvanensis*, the Belgian scholar Charles Moeller identified Arnulf's birthplace as the village of Chocques in the diocese of Thérouanne on the river Clarence, an affluent of the Lys.[2] Thus Moeller returns to the view of the Flemish annalists Meyer and Malbrancq,[3] who manifestly knew and used this text; though modern writers upon the Crusades, overlooking it and relying mainly upon Albert of Aix,[4] have said that Arnulf was ' of Rohes, a castle of Flanders,' which no one has ever been able to identify.[5] If further evidence

---

[1] New light has been thrown upon Arnulf's career in Normandy by the publication of Professor Haskins's *Norman Institutions* (pp. 74–75) since this Appendix was originally written; but it seems worth while to let it stand with slight modifications, since it may still serve to bring together in convenient form all the known facts concerning Arnulf's early history. For the fullest treatment of Arnulf's career as a whole see Eduard Franz, *Das Patriarchat von Jerusalem im Jahre 1099* (Sagen, 1885), pp. 8–16. See also the critical and bibliographical notes in Ekkehard, *Hierosolymita*, ed. Heinrich Hagenmeyer (Tübingen, 1877), p. 264, n. 8; *G. F.*, p. 481, n. 14; *Kreuzzugsbriefe*, p. 409, n. 15; Fulcher of Chartres, *Historia Hierosolymitana (1095–1127)*, ed. Heinrich Hagenmeyer (Heidelberg, 1913), p. 590, n. 24.

[2] " Les Flamands du Ternois au royaume latin de Jérusalem," in *Mélanges Paul Fredericq* (Brussels, 1904), pp. 189–202. The decisive lines are (p. 191):

> Primus Evremarus sedit patriarcha Sepulchri;
> Post hunc Arnulfus: oriundus uterque Cyokes.

[3] Jacques de Meyer, *Commentarii sive Annales Rerum Flandricarum* (Antwerp, 1561), *a.* 1099, fol. 34 v; Jacques Malbrancq, *De Morinis et Morinorum Rebus* (Tournay, 1639–54), ii, p. 684.

[4] *H. C. Oc.*, iv, p. 470: " Arnolfus de Zokes castello Flandriae."

[5] E.g., Riant, Hagenmeyer, and Röhricht at various places in their well known works. Hagenmeyer in his recent edition (1913) of Fulcher of Chartres (p. 590, n. 24) accepts Moeller's conclusion; but Bréhier, writing in 1907 (*L'église et l'Orient au moyen âge*, p. 83), still says " Arnoul de Rohez."

were needed to establish the correctness of Moeller's conclusion, it is found in a charter of 15 August 1095 by Robert Curthose in favor of Rouen cathedral, among the witnesses to which appears "Ernulfo de Cioches capellano meo." [6] This document is also important as confirming and supplementing the meagre notices of the chroniclers, on which one is compelled to rely almost entirely for all that is known about Arnulf of Chocques before he went on the Crusade and came into prominence and controversy.

As to Arnulf's family, practically nothing is known; though one may safely infer that he was of lowly origin from the speech which his friend and former pupil, Ralph of Caen, puts into his mouth when he makes him say to the princely leaders of the Crusade, " You have promoted me from a humble station, and from one unknown you have made me famous, and, as it were, one of yourselves." [7] His enemies openly charged that he was the son of a priest; [8] and that their accusations were not without foundation is evidenced by a letter of Pope Pascal II, replying in 1116 to complaints which had been made against Arnulf, and reinstating him in the patriarchal office from which he had been suspended by the papal legate. While clearing him entirely from two of the charges which had been brought against him, the pope announced that the third complaint, viz., the general belief as to a stain upon his birth, was to be overlooked, ' by apostolic dispensation,' in view of Arnulf's great services and of the needs of the church. [9] The statement sometimes made that Arnulf had a niece named Emma, or Emelota, [10] who figures in the charters of the Latin Kingdom, [11] and who was the wife, first of Eustace Garnier, lord of Caesarea, and then of Hugh II, count of Jaffa, appears to rest upon the sole authority of William of Tyre. [12]

[6] Haskins, p. 70, no. 31; p. 74, n. 28. It is true that the text as printed from an original now lost has " Ernulpho de Croches," but this is probably a misreading for Cyoches or Cioches. G. A. de La Roque, *Histoire généalogique de la maison de Harcourt* (Paris, 1662), iii, preuves, p. 34.

[7] *H. C. Oc.*, iii, p. 699.

[8] Raymond of Aguilers, *ibid.*, iii, p. 302; Guibert of Nogent, *ibid.*, iv, p. 233; William of Tyre, *ibid.*, i, p. 365.

[9] *Cartulaire de l'église du Saint Sépulchre*, ed. Eugène de Rozière (Paris, 1849), no. 11.

[10] Du Cange, *Les familles d'outre-mer*, ed. E.-G. Rey (Paris, 1869), pp. 274–275, 339, 431; T. W. Archer and C. L. Kingsford, *The Crusades* (London, 1894), pp. 118, 193.

[11] Reinhold Röhricht, *Regesta Regni Hierosolymitani*, and *Additamentum* (Innsbruck, 1893 and 1904), nos. 104, 112, 147, 102 a, 114 b.

[12] *H. C. Oc.*, i, p. 628.

Considering the age in which he lived, Arnulf doubtless received an excellent education,[13] though where it is impossible to say; and while still a young man he appeared in Normandy as a teacher, presumably at Caen. Ralph of Caen, who later became the distinguished historian of the First Crusade, was among his pupils; and upon the completion of his great work, the *Gesta Tancredi*, dedicated it in grateful remembrance to his old master.[14]

Far more important for Arnulf's future, however, was the connection which he early established with the Anglo-Norman ruling family when he was made tutor in grammar and dialectic to the oldest daughter of William the Conqueror, Cecilia, the pious nun of La Trinité at Caen, who later became the second abbess of her mother's great foundation.[15] It was probably through the friendship thus established with the royal princess that the Flemish schoolmaster succeeded in rising to higher things; for Cecilia is said to have obtained from her indulgent brother, Duke Robert, the promise of episcopal honors for Arnulf, in case any of the Norman bishoprics should fall vacant;[16] and while he never gained that preferment, it can hardly be doubted that it was through her influence that he entered the service of the duke as chaplain. The charter to which attention has been called above furnishes proof that Arnulf already held that position in August 1096 (*supra*, n. 6). But his official connection with the ducal court undoubtedly began at least a year earlier, for the contemporary biographer of Abbot William of Bec states very specifically that on, or shortly after, 10 August 1094 he went on an important official errand for the duke in the capacity of ' chancellor.'[17]

[13] Guibert of Nogent, *H. C. Oc.*, iv, p. 232: "in dialecticae eruditione non hebes, quum minime haberetur ad grammaticae documenta rudis"; Ralph of Caen, *ibid.*, iii, p. 604: "nullius etenim liberalis scientiae te cognovimus exsortem"; cf. the interesting passage (*ibid.*, iii, p. 665) where Arnulf is represented while on the Crusade as learning astrology from a ' didascalus.' The other sources, while not particularizing, bear unanimous testimony to Arnulf's learning. Cf. *G. F.*, pp. 479–480; Raymond of Aguilers, in *H. C. Oc.*, iii, p. 281; Ekkehard, *Hierosolymita*, p. 264.

[14] *H. C. Oc.*, iii, p. 604: " Praesertim mellita mihi erit quaecumque erit correctio tua, si, quem sortitus sum praeceptorem puer iuvenem, nunc quoque correctorem te impetravero vir senem."

[15] Guibert of Nogent, *ibid.*, iv, p. 232: "regis Anglorum filiam monacham ea . . . diu disciplina docuerat." Ordericus Vitalis (ii, p. 303), without mentioning any particular teacher, remarks upon Cecilia's unusual education: "Quae cum grandi diligentia in coenobio Cadomensi educata est et multipliciter erudita."

[16] Guibert of Nogent, in *H. C. Oc.*, iv, p. 232.

[17] Milo Crispin, *Vita Venerabilis Willelmi Beccensis Tertii Abbatis*, in Migne, cl, col. 718.

One other fact remains to be noticed as indicating Arnulf's intimate relationship with another member of the Conqueror's family. Although he was chaplain of the duke before and during the Crusade, he is said to have set out for the Holy War in the company of Robert's uncle, Bishop Odo of Bayeux, who upon his death at Palermo, early in 1097, left him the greater part of his splendid outfit.[18]

[18] *Guibert of Nogent*, in *H. C. Oc.*, iv, p. 233: " Cuius comitatui idem Arnulfus sese indidit; et quum huic ipsi episcopo citra, nisi fallor, Romaniae fines finis obtigisset, ex illo maximo censu quem post se reliquerat, hunc legatarium, pene ante omnes, suppellectilis suae preciosae effecit."

APPENDIX D

ROBERT'S COMPANIONS ON THE CRUSADE

It cannot be said with certainty that every one who appears in the ensuing list actually went on the First Crusade with Robert Curthose. Since it was desired to make the list as complete as possible, doubtful names have been included and marked with an asterisk (*). The evidence is fully set forth in each case, so that no confusion can arise.

1. ALAN, " dapifer sacrae ecclesiae Dolensis archiepiscopi." Baldric of Dol, in *H. C. Oc.*, iv, p. 33; Ordericus, iii, p. 507.

2. ALAN FERGANT, duke of Brittany. His presence is recorded at the siege of Nicaea (Albert of Aix, in *H. C. Oc.*, iv, p. 316) and at the siege of Antioch (Baldric of Dol, *ibid.*, p. 50, n. 9, being the variant from MS. G). His absence from Brittany during the Crusade is indicated by his disappearance from the charters of the period. The latest document which I have noted in which he appears before his departure is dated 27 July 1096. *Cartulaire de l'abbaye de Sainte-Croix de Quimperlé*, ed. Léon Maitre and Paul de Berthou, 2d ed. (Paris, 1904), no. 82, pp. 234-235. He was back again in Brittany 9 October 1101, when he made grants in favor of the abbey of Marmoutier. P. H. Morice, *Mémoires pour servir de preuves à l'histoire ecclésiastique et civile de Bretagne* (Paris, 1742-46), i, cols. 505, 507; cf. col. 504.

3. ALAN, son of Ralph de Gael. He was present with Robert at Nicaea, and advanced with him from there. Baldric of Dol, in *H. C. Oc.*, iv, p. 33; Ordericus, iii, p. 507.

4. ALBERIC OF GRANDMESNIL. Ordericus, iii, p. 484; cf. *supra*, p. 107, n. 88.

5. ANONYMOUS, engineer of Robert of Bellême: " ingeniosissimum artificem, . . . cuius ingeniosa sagacitas ad capiendam Ierusalem Christianis profecit." Ordericus, iii, p. 415.

6. *ANONYMOUS, wife of Thurstin, *prévot* of Luc. See no. 44 *infra*.

7. *ANONYMOUS, son of Thurstin, *prévot* of Luc. See no. 44 *infra*.

8. ARNULF OF CHOCQUES, chaplain of Robert Curthose. Raymond of Aguilers, in *H. C. Oc.*, iii, pp. 281, 302. Cf. Appendix C.

9. ARNULF OF HESDIN: " Ernulfus de Hednith," who was accused of complicity in Robert Mowbray's conspiracy, and cleared himself by a judicial duel; but " tanto dolore et ira est commotus, ut abdicatis omnibus quae regis erant in Anglia, ipso rege invito et contradicente, discederet; associatus autem Christianorum exercitui, Antiochiam usque devenit, ibique extremum diem clausit. Cumque ei infirmanti principes medicorum curam adhibere vellent, respondisse fertur, ' Vincit Dominus quare medicus me non continget, nisi ille pro cuius amore hanc peregrinationem suscepi.' " *Chronicon*, in *Liber de Hyda*, pp. 301–302. Arnulf ceases to appear in charters from about the period of the First Crusade. Cf. Davis, *Regesta*, nos. 315, 319; Round, *C. D. F.*, no. 1326.

10. *AUBRÉE LA GROSSE. See no. 20 *infra*.

11. BERNARD OF SAINT-VALERY. Baldric of Dol, in *H. C. Oc.*, iv, p. 33; Ordericus, iii, p. 507. Ralph of Caen credits him with having been the first to scale the wall of Jerusalem. *H. C. Oc.*, iii, p. 693.

12. CONAN DE LAMBALLE, second son of Geoffrey I, called Boterel, count of Lamballe. He was present with Robert at Nicaea and advanced with him from there. Baldric of Dol, in *H. C. Oc.*, iv, pp. 28, 33; Albert of Aix, *ibid.*, p. 316; Ordericus, iii, pp. 503, 507. He was killed by the Turks at Antioch 9 February 1098. Ralph of Caen saw his tomb there years afterwards. *H. C. Oc.*, iii, p. 648.

13. EDITH, wife of Gerard of Gournay and sister of William of Warenne. Her husband died on the Crusade, and she returned and became the wife of Dreux de Monchy. *Interpolations de Robert de Torigny*, in William of Jumièges, pp. 277–278.

14. EMMA, wife of Ralph de Gael and daughter of William Fitz Osbern. She accompanied her husband on the Crusade. Ordericus, ii, p. 264; *Interpolations de Robert de Torigny*, in William of Jumièges, p. 287.

15. ENGUERRAND, son of Count Hugh of Saint-Pol. He died at Marra in Syria. Albert of Aix, in *H. C. Oc.*, iv, pp. 372, 451; Raymond of Aguilers, *ibid.*, iii, p. 276.

16. *EUSTACE III, count of Boulogne. It seems impossible to determine the route taken by Eustace of Boulogne on the First Crusade. According to the *Anglo-Saxon Chronicle* (a. 1096), Henry of Huntingdon (p. 219), and Albert of Aix (*H. C. Oc.*, iv, p. 314), he went with Robert Curthose; Baldric of Dol (*ibid.*, p. 20), Ordericus Vitalis (iii, pp. 484–485), and Robert the Monk (*H. C. Oc.*, iii, p. 732), on the

other hand, all say that he went with his brother Godfrey of Bouillon. Cf. *G. F.*, p. 465, n. 17.

17. FULCHER OF CHARTRES, historian of the Crusade. See the introduction to Hagenmeyer's edition of the *Historia Hierosolymitana*.

18. GEOFFREY CHOTARD, one of the barons (*proceres*) of Ancenis: " anno dedicationis Maioris Monast. ab Urbano papa facte statim post Pascha, cum dominus abbas noster tunc temporis Bernardus rediret a Nanneto civitate per Ligerim, anno scilicet ordinationis sue .xiii. venit ad portum Ancenisi," and Geoffrey Chotard, "post parum temporis iturus in Ierusalem cum exercitu Christianorum super paganos euntium," came to him and granted to Saint-Martin freedom from customs on the Loire. P. H. Morice, *Preuves*, i, col. 488.

19. GERARD OF GOURNAY. Ordericus, iii, pp. 484, 507; Albert of Aix, in *H. C. Oc.*, iv, p. 316; Baldric of Dol. *ibid.*, p. 33. He was accompanied by his wife Edith, and died on the Crusade. *Interpolations de Robert de Torigny*, in William of Jumièges, pp. 277–278. Cf. no. 13 *supra*.

20. *GILBERT, an architect (?). " Tunc Gislebertus, quidam laicus, de Ierusalem Rotomagum venit, et a praefato patre [i.e., Abbot Hilgot of Saint-Ouen, 1092–1112] ad monachatum susceptus, ecclesiae suae digniter profecit. Opus enim basilicae, quod iamdudum admiranda magnitudine intermissum fuerat, assumpsit; ibique pecuniam Alberadae Grossae, dominae suae, quae, in via Dei moriens, thesaurum ei suum commendaverat, largiter distraxit, et inde, aliorum quoque fidelium subsidiis adiutus, insigne opus perficere sategit." Ordericus, iii, pp. 432–433.

21. GILBERT, bishop of Évreux. He was present at the council of Clermont as *legatus* of his fellow bishops. Ordericus, iii, p. 470. He was with Bishop Odo of Bayeux at the time of the latter's death at Palermo early in 1097. *Ibid.*, iv, pp. 17–18; iii, p. 266. Cf. no. 29 *infra*. If Gilbert completed the Crusade, he must have returned from Jerusalem far more quickly than most of his comrades, for he was back in Normandy by the middle of November 1099. Ordericus, iv, p. 65; cf. v, pp. 159, 195–196.

22. *GUY, eldest son of Gerard le Duc. He received five *solidi* from Saint-Vincent of Le Mans " cum pergeret ad Ierusalem cum Pagano de Monte Dublelli." *Cartulaire de S.-Vincent*, no. 666. The editors, without good reason, date the document " circa 1096." Cf. no. 30 *infra*.

23. *Guy de Sarcé, a knight of Saint-Vincent of Le Mans. He surrendered his fief to the abbot and monks of Saint-Vincent, and received from them 20 *livres manceaux* and 300 *solidi*. This was done in the chapter on 22 June 1096, " eo videlicet anno quo Urbanus papa adventu suo occiduas illustravit partes, quoque etiam innumerabiles turbas populorum admonitione sua, immo vero Dei suffragante auxilio, Ierosolimitanum iter super paganos adire monuit." It is not improbable that Guy's brothers, Nicholas and Pain, accompanied him on the Crusade. *Cartulaire de S.-Vincent*, no. 317. This charter was witnessed, among others, by William de Braitel, who is no. 47 of our list *infra*.

24. *Hamo de Huna. He made a grant to Saint-Vincent of Le Mans on 29 July 1096; and " post non multum vero temporis . . . antequam Ierusalem iret quo tendere volebat," he added another gift, and received from the monks 20 *solidi*. " Hoc actum fuit in domo monachorum apud Bazogers, in adventu Domini iv die ante natale Domini." *Cartulaire de S.-Vincent*, no. 460. This was 22 December, presumably of the year 1096. Hamo, therefore, did not accompany the other crusaders in the autumn, but he may very well have overtaken them in Italy the following spring.

25. Hervé, son of Dodeman. He is named among those who advanced with Robert after the capture of Nicaea. Baldric of Dol, in *H. C. Oc.*, iv, p. 33; Ordericus, iii, p. 507; cf. n. 6, *ibid.*, where Le Prévost remarks that ' Breton chronicles' name Hervé, son of Guyomark, count of Léon, in place of Hervé, son of Dodeman.

26. Hugh II, count of Saint-Pol. He set out from Normandy with Robert in 1096. Ordericus, iii, p. 484. He was present at the siege of Nicaea, and advanced with Robert from there. *Ibid.*, pp. 502–503, 507; Baldric of Dol, in *H. C. Oc.*, iv, pp. 28, 33. He was present at the siege of Antioch. Albert of Aix, *ibid.*, p. 372.

27. *Ingelbaudus: " Ego Ingelbaudus illud Sepulchrum volo petere." In view of the proposed journey he made various grants to Saint-Vincent of Le Mans. *Cartulaire de S.-Vincent*. no. 101. The editors date the document " circa 1096," but there are no chronological data. Most of the documents among which this appears are of the late eleventh century.

28. Ivo of Grandmesnil. Ordericus, iii, p. 484. Cf. *supra*, p. 107, n. 88.

29. Odo, bishop of Bayeux. He was present at the council of Clermont as *legatus* of his fellow bishops. Ordericus, iii, p. 470. He .

was in touch with Abbot Gerento of Saint-Bénigne of Dijon, the Pope's special agent, who was promoting the Crusade in Normandy during the summer of 1096. Haskins, pp. 75–76. But it seems probable that he undertook the Crusade rather to escape the wrath of William Rufus than from any religious zeal. Ordericus, iv, pp. 16–17. He died at Palermo, in February 1097 according to Ordericus Vitalis (*ibid.*), though his obit was celebrated in Bayeux cathedral on Epiphany (6 January). Ulysse Chevalier, *Ordinaire et coutumier de l'église cathédrale de Bayeux* (Paris, 1902), p. 410. He was buried by his fellow bishop, Gilbert of Évreux, in the cathedral church of St. Mary at Palermo, and Count Roger reared a splendid monument over his grave. Ordericus, iv, pp. 17–18; iii, p. 266; cf. Guibert of Nogent, in *H. C. Oc.*, iv, p. 233. Odo's epitaph is published, from a late seventeenth century MS., by V. Bourrienne, in *Revue catholique de Normandie*, x, p. 276.

30. *PAIN DE MONDOUBLEAU. See the quotation from *Cartulaire de S.-Vincent*, no. 666, in no. *22 supra*. The editors accept this as convincing evidence that Pain de Mondoubleau went on the First Crusade, but in the absence of any definite date there is no proof. And indeed it seems hardly likely that we have to do here with the First Crusade, since in 1098, according to Ordericus Vitalis — who, however, is a very untrustworthy guide in matters of chronology — Pain was in Maine and handed over the castle of Ballon to William Rufus. Ordericus, iv, p. 47; cf. Latouche, *Maine*, p. 47; Auguste de Trémault, " Recherches sur les premiers seigneurs de Mondoubleau," in *Bulletin de la Société archéologique du Vendômois*, xxv (1886), pp. 301–302. The latter mentions no evidence of Pain's having gone on any crusade.

31. PAIN PEVEREL. The distinguished Norman knight who acted as Robert's standard-bearer on the Crusade, and who upon his return was granted a barony in England by Henry I, and became the patron of Barnwell priory. He is described as " egregio militi, armis insigni, milicia pollenti, viribus potenti, et super omnes regni proceres bellico usu laudabili." He endowed the church of Barnwell with notable relics which he brought back from the Holy Land: " reliquias verissimas super aurum et topazion preciosas, quas in expedicione Antiochena adquisierat cum Roberto Curthose, dum signiferi vicem gereret, necnon quas a patriarcha et rege et magnatibus illius terre impetraverat." *Liber Memorandorum Ecclesie de Barnewelle*, ed. J. W. Clark (Cambridge, 1907), pp. 54, 55, 41, 46. According to the editor this

anonymous work was written in its present form in 1295–96; the author had access to documents, and probably based his narrative on the work of an earlier writer (introduction, pp. ix–x, xiv). The part dealing with our period contains notable chronological inaccuracies, but for the fundamental facts of the life of Pain Peverel it may probably be relied upon.

32. PHILIP OF BELLÊME, called the Clerk, fifth son of Roger of Montgomery. He set out with Robert from Normandy in 1096, and died at Antioch. Ordericus, iii, pp. 483, 426.

33. *RAINERIUS DE POMERA. " Ista quae narravimus [i.e., the details of a miracle wrought by St. Nicholas of Bari] a quodam bono et fideli homine, nomine Rainerio, de villa quae dicitur Pomera, didicimus, qui haec vidit et audivit et iis omnibus praesens affuit, dum rediret de itinere Ierusalem." *Miracula S. Nicolai conscripta a Monacho Beccensi*, in *Catalogus Codicum Hagiographicorum Latinorum in Bibliotheca Nationali Parisiensi*, ed. the Bollandists (Brussels, 1889–93), ii, p. 427.

34. RALPH DE GAEL. Baldric of Dol. in *H. C. Oc.*, iv, pp. 28, 38; Ordericus, iii, pp. 484, 503, 507; *Interpolations de Robert de Torigny*, in William of Jumièges, p. 287. Emma, his wife, and Alan, his son, went with him. Cf. nos. 14 and 3 *supra*.

35. RICHARD, son of Fulk, of Aunou-le-Faucon: " quidam miles, genere Normannicus, vocabulo Ricardus, filius Fulconis senioris de Alnou." After the capture of Jerusalem he was saved from shipwreck off the Syrian coast through the miraculous interposition of St. Nicholas of Bari; and upon his return to Normandy he became a monk of Bec. *Miracula S. Nicolai conscripta a Monacho Beccensi*, in *Catalogus Codicum Hagiographicorum Latinorum in Bibliotheca Nationali Parisiensi*, ed. the Bollandists, ii, p. 429. On Fulk of Aunou, see Ordericus, ii, p. 75.

36. RIOU DE LOHÉAC. He died while on the Crusade, but sent back to Lohéac a casket of precious relics, among them a portion of the true Cross and a fragment of the Sepulchre: " Notum sit . . . quod Waulterius, Iudicaelis filius de Lohoac, quidam miles nobilissimus et illius castri princeps et dominus . . . Sancto Salvatori suisque monachis quoddam venerandum et honorabile sanctuarium, quod frater suus, videlicet Riocus, dum iret Hierosolyman, adquisierat, et post mortem suam, nam in itinere ipso obiit, per manum Simonis de Ludron sibi transmiserat, scilicet quandam particulam Dominicę Crucis et de Sepulchro Domini et de cęteris Domini sanctuariis, cum maximis

donariis quę subter scribentur, honorificę dedit et in perpetuum habere concessit." These relics were placed in the church of Saint-Sauveur at Lohéac in the presence of a great concourse of clergy and people, among them being the famous Robert of Arbrissel, " quidam sanctissimus homo." The document was attested, among others, by Walter and William, Riou's brothers, and by Geoffrey his son, Gonnor his wife, and Simon de Ludron. " Hoc factum est in castello de Lohoac, iuxta ipsam aecclesiam monachorum, .iii. kal. Iul., in natali apostolorum Petri et Pauli, anno ab incarnatione Domini millesimo centesimo .i., luna .xxix., epacte .xviii., Alano comite existente, Iudicahele episcopatum Sancti Maclovii obtinente, et hoc donum cum suo archidiacono Rivallono annuente, data .vi. non. Iulii." *Cartulaire de l'abbaye de Redon*, ed. Aurélien de Courson (Paris, 1863: *Documents inédits*), nos. 366, 367. Baldric of Dol names him among those who advanced with Robert from Nicaea. *H. C. Oc.*, iv, p. 33.

37. ROBERT OF JERUSALEM, count of Flanders. One of the well known leaders, who was closely associated with Robert Curthose during most of the Crusade and who returned with him at least as far as southern Italy. See Chapter IV, *passim*.

38. *ROBERT THE VICAR (*vicarius*). Before he went to Jerusalem (*priusquam Ierusalem pergeret*) he made donations to Saint-Vincent of Le Mans — his wife, son, and brothers consenting — and received from Abbot Ranulf and the monks four *livres manceaux*. *Cartulaire de S.-Vincent*, no. 522. The document is undated, but the mention of Abbot Ranulf places it between 1080 and 1106. The editors date it " circa 1096."

39. ROGER OF BARNEVILLE. *G. F.*, p. 185; Ordericus, iii, p. 503. He was captured and beheaded by the Turks at Antioch early in June 1098; and was buried amid great sorrow by his fellow crusaders in the church of St. Peter. *Kreuzzugsbriefe*, p. 159; Raymond of Aguilers, in *H. C. Oc.*, iii, p. 252; Ordericus, iii, pp. 549, 538; Robert the Monk, in *H. C. Oc.*, iii, pp. 808–809; Albert of Aix, *ibid.*, iv, pp. 407–408.

40. ROTROU OF MORTAGNE II, son of Geoffrey II, count of Perche. His father died during his absence, having made provision for Rotrou to succeed him in the countship upon his return from the Crusade. Ordericus, iii, p. 483; v, p. 1.

41. SIMON DE LUDRON. It was he who brought back the relics which had been obtained by Riou de Lohéac while on the Crusade. See the extract from the Redon cartulary quoted in no. 36 *supra*.

42. STEPHEN, count of Aumale. He was one of the Norman rebels who had previously sided with William Rufus against Robert Curthose. Ordericus, iii, p. 475. But he was on friendly terms with the duke by 14 July 1096 — doubtless as a result of the pacification which had been brought about by the Pope — since Robert attested a charter by Stephen on that date. *Gallia Christiana*, xi, instr., col. 20; cf. Haskins, p. 67, no. 5. Stephen also attested a charter by the duke in 1096. Archives de la Seine-Inférieure, G 4069 (*Inventaire sommaire*, iii, p. 255). Albert of Aix records his presence at Nicaea; and Ralph of Caen names him among those who at Antioch were obligated to Robert Curthose by gifts or homage. *H. C. Oc.*, iv, p. 316; iii, p. 642.

43. STEPHEN, count of Blois and Chartres. One of the well known leaders of the Crusade. He was closely associated with Robert Curthose at least as far as Nicaea. He became faint-hearted and turned back home after the expedition had reached Antioch. See Chapter IV, *passim*.

44. *THURSTIN, son of Turgis, *prévot* of Luc-sur-Mer. In 1096 he pledged his allod (*alodium*) of forty acres at Luc for four marks and a mount (*equitatura*): " si ipse Turstinus aut uxor eius vel filius post vi annos rediret, redderet Sancto Stephano ad finem vi annorum iiii^{or} argenti marcas." Probably the Crusade was in contemplation, though it is not specifically mentioned. R. Génestal, *Rôle des monastères comme établissements de crédit* (Paris, 1901), p. 215; cf. pp. 29–30.

45. WALTER OF SAINT-VALERY. Ordericus, iii, pp. 483, 507; Baldric of Dol, in *H. C. Oc.*, iv, p. 33.

46. WIGO DE MARRA, a crusader from Perche. " Rediens a Ierosolimitano itinere, tempore profectionis communis Aquilonensium et Occidentalium," he passed through Tours; and while he rested there with the monks of Saint-Julien, he gave them his church at Bellou-sur-Huîne, a gift which he afterwards confirmed upon reaching home. *Chartes de S.-Julien de Tours*, no. 51. The document is dated 1099, " regnante Willelmo rege Anglorum et duce Normannorum," and is of special interest as indicating the early date at which some of the crusaders got back to western Europe.

47. *WILLIAM DE BRAITEL (en Lombron), son of Geoffrey the *vicomte*. With the consent of his brothers he made a donation to Saint-Vincent of Le Mans in 1096, " eo videlicet anno quo papa Urbanus occidentales partes presentia sua illustravit." *Cartulaire de S.-Vincent*, no. 738. The similarity of dating between this charter and

no. 317 of the same cartulary (cf. no. 23 *supra*), as well as the fact that many of the witnesses are identical in both, makes it seem not im- probable that they were drawn up on the same occasion. If William actually went on the First Crusade, his return appears to have been delayed until 1116. In that year a precious relic which he brought back from Jerusalem for Adam, a Manceau who had become a canon of the church of the Holy Sepulchre, was presented to the cathedral church of Le Mans. *Actus Pontificum*, p. 407. Cf. Samuel Menjot d'Elbenne, *Les sires de Braitel au Maine du XIe au XIIIe siècle* (Mamers, 1876), p. 38.

48. WILLIAM, son of Ranulf de Briquessart, *vicomte* of Bayeux. He is named among those who advanced with Robert from Nicaea. Baldric of Dol, in *H. C. Oc.*, iv, p. 33; Ordericus, iii, p. 507.

49. *WILLIAM DE COLOMBIÈRES. On 7 June 1103 Henry de Colom- bières granted to Saint-Martin of Troarn " all that his father William had given and granted before he went on crusade (*Ierosolimam per- geret*)." Round, *C. D. F.*, no. 471.

50. WILLIAM DE FERRIÈRES. He is named among those who ad- vanced with Robert from Nicaea. Baldric of Dol, in *H. C. Oc.*, iv, p. 33; Ordericus, iii, p. 507.

51. WILLIAM DE PERCY, benefactor of Whitby abbey. He died while on the Crusade. " Denique nobilissimus Willielmus de Perci Ierosolimam petens, apud locum qui vocatur Mons Gaudii, qui est in provincia Ierosolimitana, migravit ad Dominum, ibique honorifice sepultus est." *Cartularium Abbathiae de Whiteby*, ed. J. C. Atkinson (Durham, 1879–81), i, p. 2. The quotation is from the " Memorial of Benefactions," which, according to the editor, was written in the second half of the twelfth century, certainly before 1180. It is probably only a legend that William's heart was brought back and buried at Whitby abbey. His son had evidently succeeded him by 6 January 1100. Davis, *Regesta*, no. 427.

52. WILLIAM DU VAST. On 9 September 1096, " vadens in Ieru- salem," he pledged his land to the abbey of Fécamp for a loan of three marks until his return. Léopold Delisle, *Littérature latine et histoire du moyen âge* (Paris, 1890), pp. 28–29.

APPENDIX E

LAODICEA AND THE FIRST CRUSADE

LAODICEA, as a commodious port on the Syrian coast directly opposite the fertile island of Cyprus, was a maritime base of the utmost importance to the crusaders, and it has a special interest for the life of Robert Curthose. Its history during the period of the First Crusade is obscure, and it may be admitted at the outset that it will not be possible to elucidate it entirely from such meagre and contradictory materials as have survived. Nevertheless, the problems are by no means hopeless; and the sources, such as they are, are worthy of a more careful and critical examination than they have yet received.[1]

From the oriental sources it seems reasonably certain that during the period immediately preceding the arrival of the crusaders in Syria Laodicea was in the hands of the Turks. Previous to 1086 it had belonged to the Munkidhites of Shaizar;[2] but it passed from their hands into the possession of Malik-Shah when in that year he established himself at Aleppo.[3] Malik-Shah granted it to Kasim ed-daula Aksonkor, who held it until his death in 1094.[4] There is no evidence that it passed out of Turkish control between this date and the arrival of the crusaders and their associates from the West in 1097; and, in view of the precarious situation of the Eastern Empire and the preoccupation of the Greek Emperor with other problems during this period, there seems to be no ground for such a supposition. According to Kemal ed-Din — who wrote towards the middle of the thirteenth century, and whose statement would perhaps deserve little consideration were it not so specific — a fleet of twenty-two ships came from Cyprus on the 8th of the month of Ramadan in the year 490 of the Hegira (19 August 1097), entered the port of Laodicea, pillaged the town, and carried off all the merchandise.[5]

---

[1] In general on Laodicea and the First Crusade see Riant, *Scandinaves en Terre Sainte*, pp. 132 ff.; Chalandon, *Alexis Ier*, pp. 210 ff.; Röhricht, *Geschichte des ersten Kreuzzuges*, pp. 205-207.

[2] Usama ibn Munkidh, *Autobiographie*, French translation by Hartwig Derenbourg (Paris, 1895), p. 107.

[3] Ibn el-Athir, *Histoire des Atabecs de Mosul*, in *H. C. Or.*, ii, 2, p. 17.

[4] *Ibid.*

[5] *Chronique d'Alep*, *ibid.*, iii, p. 578. There is possibly some confirmation of this in the following statement of Cafaro of Genoa: " In tempore enim

The western sources dealing with Laodicea in 1097–98 are numerous; but at some points they are contradictory, and at best they yield but scanty information. It will be well to analyze them separately with some care: —

(1) The letter of Anselm de Ribemont to Archbishop Manasses of Rheims, written from Antioch near the end of November 1097, states definitely that Laodicea had been taken — evidently by some one acting in the interest of the crusaders, and pretty clearly before the arrival of the land forces at Antioch on 21 October 1097.[6]

This statement is confirmed by the anonymous *Florinensis Brevis Narratio Belli Sacri*,[7] as it is also by the account of Raymond of Aguilers.

(2) Raymond of Aguilers, who, because of his actual presence in Syria and his close association with the count of Toulouse, is by all odds the best and most reliable chronicler dealing with the events now under consideration, seems to have received but little attention from modern scholars in this connection. According to his account, which is quite full, English mariners, who were fired with enthusiasm for the Crusade, sailed via Gibraltar to the eastern Mediterranean, and with much labor obtained possession of the port of Antioch (evidently Port St. Simeon is meant) and of Laodicea before the arrival of the land forces. And during the siege of Antioch, together with the Genoese, they rendered important services to the crusaders by means of their fleet, keeping open commercial intercourse with Cyprus and other islands, and in particular protecting the ships of the Greeks from attack by the Saracens. Finally, when the crusaders were about to advance from Syria upon Jerusalem, the English, finding that their ships had been reduced by wear and tear from thirty to nine or ten, abandoned them or burned them, and joined the land forces on the southward march.[8]

captionis Antiochiae arma manebat [Laodicea], nisi ecclesia episcopalis ubi clerici morabantur." *Annales Genuenses*, in *H. C. Oc.*, v, p. 66.

[6] " XII Kalendas Novembris Antiochiam obsedimus, iamque vicinas civitates Tharsum et Laodiciam multasque alias vi cepimus." *Kreuzzugsbriefe*, p. 145.

[7] *H. C. Oc.*, v, p. 371.

[8] " Sed antequam ad reliqua perveniamus, de his praetermittere non debemus qui, pro amore sanctissimae expeditionis, per ignota et longissima aequora Mediterranei et Oceani navigare non dubitaverunt. Etenim Angli, audito nomine ultionis Domini in eos qui terram Nativitatis Iesu Christi et apostolorum eius indigne occupaverant, ingressi mare Anglicum, et circinata Hispania, transfretantes per mare Oceanum, atque sic Mediterraneum mare sulcantes, portum Antiochiae atque civitatem Laodiciae, antequam exercitus noster per terram illuc veniret, laboriose

Now, of the actual presence of English mariners on the Syrian coast acting in coöperation with the crusaders, there can be no doubt. Apart from the foregoing narrative, the fact is proved beyond question (a) by the well known letter of the clergy and people of Lucca in which they state that their citizen Bruno had journeyed from Italy to Antioch " with English ships," had taken part in the siege, and had stayed on for three weeks after the victory;[9] and (b) by the letter of Patriarch Dagobert, written from Jerusalem in the spring of 1100, which mentions the presence of English ships, apparently at Jaffa.[10] While the English ships referred to in these letters are not necessarily, or even probably, identical with those mentioned by Raymond of Aguilers, the letters are still of great importance as demonstrating the general fact of the presence and activity of English mariners at this period in these distant waters.

As will appear below, Raymond's account receives some further confirmation from Ordericus Vitalis and from Ralph of Caen.

(3) The narrative of Ordericus differs widely from that of Raymond of Aguilers. According to him, at the time when the Christians were themselves being besieged at Antioch(6–28 June 1098), a great number of pilgrims from England and other islands of the ocean landed at Laodicea and were joyfully welcomed by the inhabitants, who accepted their protection against the Turks. The chief among these pilgrims was Edgar Atheling.[11] Taking Laodicea under his protection, Edgar afterwards handed it over to Robert Curthose, whom he loved as a brother. Thus Robert gained possession of Laodicea, and came

obtinuerunt. Profuerunt nobis eo tempore tam istorum naves, quam et Genuensium. Habebamus enim ad obsidionem, per istas naves et per securitatem eorum, commercia a Cypro insula et a reliquis insulis. Quippe hae naves quotidie discurrebant per mare, et ob ea Graecorum naves securae erant, quia Sarraceni eis incurrere formidabant. Quum vero Angli illi vidissent exercitum proficisci in Iherusalem, et robor suarum navium a longinquitate temporis imminutum, quippe quum usque ad triginta in principio naves habuissent, modo vix decem vel novem habere poterant, alii dimissis navibus suis et expositis, alii autem incensis, nobiscum iter acceleraverunt." *H. C. Oc.*, iii, pp. 290–291.

[9] " Civis quidam noster, Brunus nomine, . . . cum Anglorum navibus ad ipsam usque pervenit Antiochiam." *Kreuzzugsbriefe*, p. 165. The letter contains a number of chronological data, from which it is clear that Bruno set out from Italy in 1097 and that he arrived in Syria shortly before 5 March 1098. Hagenmeyer reasons plausibly that he landed at Port St. Simeon on 4 March 1098.

[10] *Kreuzzugsbriefe*, p. 177.

[11] Grandson of Edmund Ironside, and claimant to the English throne upon the death of Harold in 1066.

and dwelt there for some time with Normans, English, and Bretons. Then, leaving his own garrison in the fortresses, Robert pursued his way to Jerusalem. But meanwhile Ravendinos, protospatharius of Emperor Alexius, and other Greek officers came with an expedition by sea, and laid siege to Laodicea; and the citizens, sympathizing with the Greeks, their compatriots, expelled the men from beyond the Alps and admitted imperial governors.[12]

William of Malmesbury is the only other writer who mentions a journey of Edgar Atheling to the Holy Land, and his account is very different from that of Ordericus Vitalis. He makes no mention of English mariners, and he places Edgar's arrival in the East, in company with a certain Robert, son of Godwin, at the time of the siege of Ramleh by the Saracens (May 1102).[13]

(4) Raymond of Aguilers is authority for the statement that Robert was absent from Antioch in the third month of the siege, apparently about Christmas 1097.[14]

A fuller explanation of this absence seems to be supplied by Ralph of Caen, who says that Robert, disgusted with the tedium of the siege, withdrew to Laodicea in the hope of ruling there; for the English at that time were holding it for the Emperor, and being menaced by a wandering band, had called in Robert as their protector. Robert accordingly went to Laodicea and gave himself up to idleness and sleep. Yet he was not altogether useless, for, having come upon opulence, he shared it generously with his needy comrades at the siege. Laodicea was then the only city on the Syrian coast which was Christian and which obeyed the Emperor; and Cyprus had filled it with an abundance of wine, grain, and cattle. Robert was very loath to turn his back upon such ease and plenty; and it was only after he had been thrice summoned, and even threatened with excommunication, that he reluctantly yielded to the entreaties of his comrades and returned to the hardships of the siege.[15]

[12] Ordericus, iv, pp. 70–71.

[13] *G. R.*, ii, p. 310; cf. p. 449. Davis — who by a slip of the pen names him Baldwin — places this Robert among the native Englishmen who joined Robert Curthose at Laodicea. *Normans and Angevins*, p. 109. But William of Malmesbury, who is the sole authority, makes no mention of him before the siege of Ramleh. Freeman is more careful. *William Rufus*, ii, p. 122.

[14] " Normanniae comes ea tempore [i.e., in tertio mense obsidionis] aberat." *H. C. Oc.*, iii, p. 243.

[15] " Abscesserant interea ex castris, exosi taedia, comites, Blesensis in Cyliciam, Laodiciam Normannus; Blesensis Tharsum ob remedium egestatis, Normannus ad

From the place which this incident occupies in Ralph's general narrative one would judge that it belongs to the spring of 1098; but he does not date it exactly, and his chronology at best is confused and by no means trustworthy. It may be conjectured that this account is to be connected with the above mentioned briefer but more trustworthy statement of Raymond of Aguilers, thus placing the episode in the winter of 1097–98. Ralph's chronology is not to be regarded as impossible, however, since there is no record of Robert's presence at Antioch between 9 February and the end of May, or even the first of June, and he may very well have enjoyed more than one sojourn in Laodicea.

Further evidence of the duke's connection with Laodicea is found in a curious statement of Guibert of Nogent that Robert had once held it, but that when the citizens were unable to bear his excessive exactions, they drove his garrison from the fortresses and threw off his domination, and out of hatred abjured the use of the money of Rouen.[16]

Finally, the twelfth-century poet Gilo remarks that English victors gave Laodicea to the Norman count.[17]

(5) The problem of Laodicea in its relation to the First Crusade is still further complicated by a statement of Anna Comnena that the Emperor wrote — she gives no date — to Raymond of Toulouse, directing him to hand over the city to Andronicus Tzintzilucas, and that Raymond obeyed.[18] Both Riant[19] and Chalandon[20] accept this

Anglos spe dominationis. Angli ea tempestate Laodiciam tenebant, missi ab imperatore tutela; cuius fines vagus populabatur exercitus, ipsam quoque cum violentia irrumpere tentantes. In hac formidine Angli assertorem vocant praescriptum comitem, consilium fidele ac prudens. Fidei fuit fidelem domino suo virum, cui se manciparent, asciscere; iugo Normannico se subtraxerant, denuo subdunt, hoc prudentiae: gentis illius fidem experti et munera, facile redeunt unde exierant. Igitur Normannus comes, ingressus Laodiciam, somno vacabat et otio; nec inutilis tamen, dum opulentiam nactus, aliis indigentibus large erogabat: quoniam conserva Cyprus baccho, cerere, et multo pecore abundans Laodiciam repleverat, quippe indigentem, vicinam, Christicolam et quasi collacteam: ipsa namque una in littore Syro et Christum colebat, et Alexio serviebat. Sed nec sic excusato otio, praedictus comes frustra semel atque iterum ad castra revocatur; tertio, sub anathemate accitus, redit invitus: difficilem enim habebat transitum commeatio, quam comiti ministrare Laodicia veniens debebat." *H. C. Oc.*, iii, p. 649.

[16] *Ibid.*, iv, p. 254.

[17] *Ibid.*, v, p. 742.

[18] *H. C. G.*, i, p. 66.

[19] " Inventaire critique des lettres historiques des croisades," in *Archives de l'Orient latin*, i, pp. 189–191.

[20] *Alexis Ier*, pp. 208–212.

statement and assign the Emperor's letter to the first half of 1099. Their reason for so doing appears to be found in the strange narrative of Albert of Aix, which is unique among the sources.

(6) According to Albert of Aix, while Baldwin and Tancred were at Tarsus on the way to Antioch (*circa* September 1097) a strange fleet approached the Cilician coast. It proved to be made up of ' Christian pirates ' from " Flanders, Antwerp, Frisia, and other parts of Gaul [*sic*]," who under their commander, a certain Guinemer of Boulogne, had been pursuing their calling for the past eight years. But when they learned of the Crusade, they concluded a treaty with Baldwin, and, landing, joined forces with him and advanced as far as Mamistra. But here they turned back, and, reëmbarking, sailed away to Laodicea, which they besieged and took. Then resting there in the enjoyment of ease and plenty, they sent no aid to their Christian brothers at Antioch. But presently they were attacked and cut to pieces by 'Turcopoles'[21] and men of the Emperor, who recovered the citadel and threw Guinemer into prison, Godfrey and the other chiefs at Antioch being ignorant of the whole affair. Later Guinemer was released at the request of Godfrey.[22]

Elsewhere Albert sets forth another version of these curious events. Guinemer and his pirates, he tells us, had assembled their fleet in conjunction with the Provençaux of the land of Saint-Gilles under the dominion of Count Raymond.[23] Then, sailing to Laodicea, they had taken it and driven out the Turks and Saracens whom they found there. Then, after the siege of Antioch, they had handed their prize over to Count Raymond. Still later, Guinemer, the master of the pirates, had been captured by the Greeks, and after long imprisonment had been released through the intervention of Duke Godfrey. Then, when the advance to Jerusalem had been decided upon, Raymond had restored Laodicea to the Emperor, and so kept his faith inviolably.[24]

Thus, if we could rely upon Albert of Aix, Laodicea came into the hands of the count of Toulouse after the siege of Antioch, and

---

[21] Turcopoles are defined by Albert as " gens impia et dicta Christiana nomine, non opere, qui ex Turco patre et *G*raeca matre procreati [sunt]." *H. C. Oc.*, iv, p. 434.

[22] *Ibid.*, pp. 348–349, 380, 447.

[23] " Hi collectione navium a diversis terris et regnis contracta, videlicet ab Antwerpia, Tila, Fresia, Flandria, per mare Provincialibus in terra Sancti Aegidii, de potestate comitis Reimundo, associati."

[24] *H. C. Oc.*, iv, pp. 500–501.

Alexius might naturally be expected to write him demanding its restoration to the Empire, as Riant and Chalandon suppose in accepting the above mentioned statement of Anna Comnena regarding the Emperor's letter. It should be noted, however, that from Albert's statement that Raymond handed over Laodicea to Alexius when the advance to Jerusalem had been decided upon,[25] it follows that the transfer could not have taken place later than 16 January 1099, the date on which Raymond moved southward from Kafartab;[26] whereas Chalandon has shown that the letter of which Anna speaks cannot be earlier than March 1099.[27] Albert of Aix and Anna Comnena, therefore, are not mutually confirmatory.

(7) Finally, note should be taken of the statement of Cafaro of Genoa — who passed the winter of 1100–01 at Laodicea, but who wrote as an old man years afterwards — that, at the time of the capture of Antioch by the crusaders, Laodicea with its fortresses was held by the Emperor, and was under the immediate command of Eumathios Philocales, duke of Cyprus.[28]

So much for an analysis of the sources. It remains to consider what conclusions may reasonably be drawn from them. And since the efforts which have been made to accept them all as of equal validity and to bring them into reconciliation have plainly not been successful, it will be well to begin with a consideration of some things which must probably be eliminated.

And first, it seems clear that the account of Ordericus Vitalis, which represents Edgar Atheling as landing at Laodicea between 6 and 28 June 1098 at the head of a great body of English pilgrims, cannot be accepted without serious modification; for we know from reliable English sources that towards the end of 1097 Edgar was engaged in Scotland, assisting his kinsman, another Edgar,[29] to obtain the Scottish throne;[30] and it would, it seems, have been impossible for him to have made the necessary preparations for a crusade and to have journeyed from Scotland to Laodicea within the limitations of time

---

[25] " Post captionem Antiochiae, decreto itinere suo cum ceteris in Iherusalem." *H. C. Oc.*, iv, p. 501.

[26] Cf. Hagenmeyer, *Chronologie*, no. 341.

[27] *Alexis Ier*, p. 212.

[28] *Annales Genuenses*, in *H. C. Oc.*, v, p. 66.

[29] Son of Malcolm Canmore.

[30] *A.–S. C., a.* 1097; Henry of Huntingdon, p. 230. The former places Edgar's expedition to Scotland after Michaelmas (29 September), the latter after Martinmas (11 November). Cf. Florence of Worcester, ii, p. 41.

which our sources impose. It is perhaps conceivable that he should have made a hurried trip to Italy in the winter of 1097–98 with a small band of attendants, and sailing from there, have reached the Syrian coast by June. But according to Ordericus he arrived at the head of " almost 20,000 pilgrims . . . from England and other islands of the ocean." Further, if the account of Ordericus were to be brought into chronological accord with the other sources which deal with Robert's sojourn at Laodicea, the arrival of Edgar Atheling would probably have to be placed several months earlier, indeed, in the early winter of 1097–98, almost at the very time he is known to have been in Scotland. The chronology of Ordericus, therefore — which in general is notoriously unreliable — seems at this point unacceptable; and William of Malmesbury, who places Edgar's arrival in the East in May 1102, appears to give the necessary correction. In view of the testimony of both Ordericus Vitalis and William of Malmesbury, it can hardly be doubted that Edgar Atheling actually went to the Holy Land; but that he reached Laodicea in time to have anything to do with the calling in of Robert Curthose seems highly improbable, if not impossible.

The tale of Guinemer of Boulogne and his fleet of Christian pirates, as told by Albert of Aix, must also meet with rougher handling than it has yet received, and for the following reasons: (1) The description of this fleet with its " masts of wondrous height, covered with purest gold, and refulgent in the sunlight " [31] is not such as to inspire confidence, particularly in such a writer as Albert of Aix, where one expects at any time to meet with the use of untrustworthy poetical materials. (2) As the narrative proceeds it becomes self-contradictory. At one point we are told that Guinemer was captured by the Greeks during the siege of Antioch, whereas at another he seems to have held Laodicea throughout the siege — since he turned it over to Count Raymond after the siege —; and his capture and imprisonment by the Greeks are placed still later. (3) Albert of Aix is in direct contradiction with Raymond of Aguilers, the best of all our authorities, who tells us that the English held Laodicea during the whole of the siege of Antioch and rendered important services to the crusaders; whereas, according to Albert's account, Guinemer and his pirates held it and refused to aid the crusaders. (4) Not a scrap of evidence concerning Guinemer and his pirates has come to light in any source except Al-

---

[31] " Navium diversi generis et operis multitudinem . . . quarum mali mirae altitudinis, auro purissimo operti, in radiis solis refulgebant." *H. C. Oc.*, iv, p. 348.

bert of Aix — unless perchance their fleet is to be identified with the ships which, according to Kemal ed-Din, came from Cyprus 19 August 1097, pillagéd Laodicea, and sailed away;[32] and this seems unlikely. (5) In any case, outside the pages of Albert of Aix, evidence is lacking that such a piratical fleet held Laodicea for any considerable period; and apparently the only reason why Riant and Chalandon have accepted this fantastical tale of Guinemer and the Christian pirates is the fancied possibility of connecting it with the letter which, according to Anna Comnena, the Emperor wrote at an undertermined date to Raymond of Toulouse, directing him to hand over Laodicea to Andronicus Tzintzilucas. But Riant and Chalandon have somewhat arbitrarily assigned this letter to the first half of 1099.. If Raymond was directed to hand Laodicea over, he must have possessed it. Therefore, so the argument seems to run, the Guinemer episode should be accepted as explaining how Raymond came into possession of Laodicea. But, as has already been pointed out, this explanation involves a serious chronological inconsistency. Further, the evidence is not conclusive that the letter ever existed — it rests upon the sole statement of Anna Comnena — and, if it did exist, it may with more reason, and with less violence to Anna's chronology, be assigned to the period between September 1099 and June 1100, when Raymond is known to have been in possession of Laodicea and on terms of close understanding with the Emperor.[33]

The foregoing considerations are not, it may be conceded, sufficient to prove that there is no shadow of truth in the tale of Guinemer and the pirates; but they do constitute a strong case against the narrative as it stands, and suggest the probability that it is one of the strange pieces of fiction occasionally to be met with in the pages of Albert of Aix.

Having now somewhat cleared the ground, it is possible to set forth the probable course of events at Laodicea on the basis of the more reliable sources.

There can be little doubt that Laodicea had already been taken from the Turks when the crusaders arrived at Antioch, 21 October 1097;[34] and we may accept without question the statement of Raymond of Aguilers — which Riant and Chalandon appear to ignore without reason — that it was taken by the English, who had come by sea, and

---

[32] *Supra*, p. 230.
[33] Chalandon, *Alexis I*[er], pp. 212–214, 217.
[34] *Supra*, p. 231.

who held it during the siege of Antioch and assisted the land forces by protecting commerce and keeping communications open with Cyprus and the other islands. These English mariners were unquestionably acting in coöperation with the Emperor,[35] who at this time, as Chalandon has shown, was supporting the crusaders in accordance with his treaty obligations.[36]

At some time during the siege of Antioch by the Christians Robert Curthose was called to Laodicea by the English — probably because of dangers on the landward side which made their situation there precarious — and he remained there for a time, in the enjoyment of ease and plenty, until he was obliged by repeated summonses and by a threat of ecclesiastical censure to return to Antioch.[37] The date of Robert's sojourn at Laodicea cannot be determined with certainty, but it may probably be assigned to December–January 1097–98,[38] 8 February being the extreme limit for his return to the siege.[39] Yet there is no record of his presence at Antioch between 9 February and the beginning of June, or between the end of June and 11 September; and the possibility of his having paid more than one visit to Laodicea must be recognized. The accounts of Ralph of Caen and of Ordericus Vitalis, interpreted strictly, point to sojourns in the spring and in the summer of 1098; but the chronology of these authors is not trustworthy, and it is not unlikely that they have fallen into inaccuracies here, and that they really refer to Robert's earlier sojourn at Laodicea, for which we have the indirect but more reliable evidence of Raymond of Aguilers.

The arrangements which were made at Laodicea upon Robert's final departure before his advance to Jerusalem must remain a matter of doubt. According to Ordericus Vitalis and Guibert of Nogent he left a garrison, which was later driven out by the citizens. Guibert is curiously circumstantial. He says that the citizens, unable to bear the duke's excessive exactions, drove his men from the citadel, threw off his domination, and abjured the use of the money of Rouen. But this incident is confirmed by none of the early writers who were in the East; and in the absence of any other evidence of Robert's having

[35] This is clear from the accounts of both Raymond of Aguilers and Ralph of Caen. Cf. *supra*, pp. 231, 233.

[36] *Alexis I^(er)*, ch. vii.

[37] Ralph of Caen, *supra*, pp. 233–234.

[38] Raymond of Aguilers, *supra*, p. 233.

[39] Tudebode, in *H. C. Oc.*, iii, p. 43.

attempted to secure for himself a private possession in Syria, we may well wonder whether Guibert and Ordericus have not blundered through a misunderstanding of the actual situation in the East and of the spirit in which Robert undertook the Crusade.

Finally, what is to be said of the statement of Cafaro of Genoa that, at the time of the capture of Antioch by the crusaders, Laodicea was under the rule of Eumathios Philocales, duke of Cyprus? It would not be surprising if Cafaro, writing long after the event, should be mistaken on a point of this kind; yet he is by no means to be ignored, and on the whole his account does not seem inconsistent with established facts. The sojourn of Robert Curthose at Laodicea was apparently a passing episode rather than a lasting occupation. But throughout the period under consideration the Syrian port was clearly in the hands of crusaders, mainly English mariners, who were acting in coöperation with the Greeks. Under existing treaty obligations the place might fairly be regarded as a Greek possession from the moment the Turks were expelled [40] — unless there were a Bohemond or some other like-minded chief to seize and hold it in defiance of imperial rights. And the Emperor would most naturally delegate authority over Laodicea to the head of his administration in Cyprus. From the Greek standpoint, therefore, it might well be regarded as subject to Eumathios Philocales, though actually held by the Emperor's allies, the crusaders.

Between the departure of the crusaders from northern Syria early in 1099 and their return in September after the capture of Jerusalem, Laodicea seems to have become definitely a Greek possession; but whether there was any violent expulsion of the garrison of a crusading chief, as Ordericus and Guibert suppose, or any formal transfer,[41] must remain uncertain. When the crusaders moved southward from northern Syria to Jerusalem, their influence at Laodicea must, it seems, inevitably have declined, while that of the Greeks increased;

[40] On the treaty relations between Alexius and the crusaders see Chalandon, *Alexis I*[er], ch. vi.

[41] Albert of Aix says that it was handed over to the Emperor by Count Raymond, but, as has been pointed out above, his account is hardly trustworthy. There is a statement in Raymond of Aguilers to the effect that during the siege of Arka (spring of 1099) Count Raymond sent Hugh de Monteil to Laodicea to fetch the cross of the late Bishop Adhemar: " Misit itaque comes Guillelmum Ugonem de Montilio, fratrem episcopi Podiensis, Laodiciam, ubi crux dimissa fuerat cum capella ipsius episcopi." *H. C. Oc.*, iii, p. 287. It is possible that this indicates some closer Provençal connection with Laodicea at this period than I have allowed.

and without any formal transfer it is conceivable that the place might gradually and almost imperceptibly have passed under full Greek control.

But for this later period there are some further scattered notices in the chronicles of Albert of Aix and of Raymond of Aguilers and in the anonymous *Gesta Francorum*, which must now be considered, and which make it clear that at this time Laodicea was still in Christian hands and served as a most important base for the further prosecution of the Crusade.

Albert of Aix, who is the fullest and most specific, explains that the crusaders still remaining in Syria gathered in council at Antioch on 2 February 1099, and, determining upon an advance to Jerusalem, fixed 1 March as the date for a general rendezvous of all the forces at Laodicea, a city which was then under Christian dominion.[42] Pursuant to this decision, Godfrey, Robert of Flanders, and Bohemond assembled their forces at Laodicea on the appointed day. And from Laodicea Godfrey and Robert moved on southward to the siege of Jebeleh; but Bohemond, ever suspicious and anxious lest through some fraud he should lose a city which was 'impregnable by human strength,' returned to Antioch.[43] This very specific account of Albert of Aix is confirmed by the much briefer statements of the *Gesta Francorum*, which record the meeting of the leaders at Laodicea, the advance of Godfrey and the count of Flanders to the siege of Jebeleh, and the return of Bohemond to Antioch.[44] It is also clear from Raymond of Aguilers that in the spring and summer of 1099 — at least until June — the port of Laodicea was open to the ships of the Greeks, Venetians, and Genoese who were engaged in provisioning the crusaders at Arka and at Jerusalem.[45]

There can be little doubt, therefore, that until June 1099, Laodicea was held in the interest of the crusaders, and that its harbor was open

---

[42] "Quae Christianae erat potestatis." *H. C. Oc.*, iv, p. 450.

[43] *Ibid.*, p. 453.   [44] *G. F.*, pp. 428–429.

[45] *H. C. Oc.*, iii, pp. 276, 295. In the former passage Raymond, writing from the standpoint of Arka, mentions the arrival of Greek, Venetian, and Genoese (?) provision ships, which, in the absence of a port directly opposite Arka, were obliged to turn back northward and put in at Tortosa and Laodicea; in the latter, recording the disaster which overtook the Genoese ships at Jaffa in June, he notes that one escaped and returned to Laodicea, "ibique sociis et amicis nostris, de nobis qui eramus Iherosolymis, sicuti erat, denuntiavit.". For the date cf. Hagenmeyer, *Chronologie*, no. 394. For the identification of *naves nostrae* or *naves de nostris* with the ships of the Genoese, cf. *H. C. Oc.*, iii, pp. 294, 298.

to the ships of Greeks and Italians without distinction. Albert of Aix nowhere explains what he means when he says that Laodicea was " under Christian dominion "; but, in the absence of valid evidence of its retention by any of the crusading chiefs, or by the fleet of any Italian city, the most reasonable hypothesis appears to be that it was held by the Greeks in the interest of the common enterprise.

We get our next information concerning Laodicea when, in September 1099, Robert Curthose, Robert of Flanders, and Raymond of Toulouse, upon their return from Jerusalem, found the place undergoing a prolonged siege at the hands of Bohemond, who was assisted in his nefarious enterprise by a fleet of Pisans and Genoese.[46] Since the early summer, when ships of Genoese, Venetians, and Greeks had all enjoyed free entry to the port, a complete change had come over the situation at Laodicea.[47] What had happened to produce this ? As is well known, it was the fixed policy of the Emperor to turn the Crusade to his own advantage, and to utilize the efforts of the Franks for the recovery of the lost provinces which had formerly belonged to the Greek Empire in Asia. To this end, he had been on the whole successful in coöperating with the crusaders. But in Bohemond of Taranto he had encountered opposition from the beginning; and, since the capture of Antioch by the crusaders, it had been the little disguised policy of this crafty and ambitious leader to hold it for himself, and to make it the capital and centre around which he hoped to build up a Norman state in Syria. It was, of course, inevitable that the Emperor should set himself to thwart such plans by every means at his disposal; and when the departure of the main body of the crusaders for Jerusalem left Bohemond with a free hand in the north, open hostilities became imminent. Undoubtedly foreseeing what was to come, Bohemond had separated from Godfrey and Robert of Flanders at Laodicea in March, and had returned to Antioch to mature his plans.[48] A few weeks later, ambassadors from the Emperor arrived in the crusaders' camp at Arka and lodged a complaint against Bohemond.[49] But the Emperor was in no position to take vigorous measures at that time. Such a course might even have endangered his friendly relations with the other leaders. But neither was Bohemond in a position to resort to an overt act against Laodicea so long as he was

---

[46] Albert of Aix, in *H. C. Oc.*, iv, p. 500; Ordericus, iv, pp. 70, 71; letter of Dagobert, Godfrey, and Raymond, to the Pope, in *Kreuzzugsbriefe*, p. 173.

[47] Cf. Chalandon, *Alexis Ier*, chs. vi, vii.

[48] *Supra*, p. 241.   [49] Raymond of Aguilers, in *H. C. Oc.*, iii, p. 286.

powerless to meet the imperial fleet at sea. In the late summer of 1099, however, all this was changed by the arrival of a Pisan fleet under the command of Dagobert, archbishop of Pisa; for Bohemond, with true Norman adaptability and shrewdness, came to an understanding with the Pisans and secured their aid for an attack upon Laodicea.[50] And with this, the slight naval supremacy which the Greek Emperor had been vainly striving to maintain in the eastern Mediterranean came to an end.[51]

Such was the situation at Laodicea when in September 1099 Robert Curthose and the counts of Flanders and Toulouse arrived at Jebeleh on their way home from the Crusade. The siege had already been going on for some time and was making progress. The place seemed to be on the point of falling.[52] But never were the plans of Bohemond to end in more egregious failure. His unprovoked attack upon a friendly city which had rendered important services to the crusaders roused the indignation and jealousy of the returning leaders. The archbishop of Pisa suddenly discovered that he had been led into a false position by the crafty Norman, and, deserting Bohemond, he threw his powerful influence on the side of Raymond, Robert Curthose, and Robert of Flanders. The Greeks too, who, though hard pressed, were still holding out, well understood that Bohemond was their real enemy and that it behooved them to make terms quickly with the leaders who had kept faith with the Emperor. Accordingly, an agreement was promptly reached among the Pisans, the Laodiceans, and the returning leaders. An ultimatum was despatched to Bohemond demanding that he withdraw forthwith; and thus suddenly confronted with superior force, he had no choice but to yield. Wrathfully he retired under the cover of darkness; and next morning Robert Curthose and the counts of Flanders and Toulouse entered Laodicea with their forces, and were enthusiastically welcomed by the inhabitants.[53]

Count Raymond placed a strong garrison in the citadel, and raising his banner over the highest tower, took possession of the city [54] — in the Emperor's name, it may be supposed, since by this time he clearly

---

[50] *Gesta Triumphalia Pisanorum, H. C. Oc,* v, p. 368.

[51] On the decline of the Byzantine fleet in the eleventh century see Carl Neumann, " Die byzantinische Marine," in *Historische Zeitschrift,* lxxxi (1898), pp. 1–23.

[52] Albert of Aix, in *H. C. Oc.,* iv, p. 500.

[53] *Ibid.,* pp. 500–503; Ordericus, iv, pp. 70–72; *Kreuzzugsbriefe,* p. 173.

[54] Albert of Aix, in *H. C. Oc.,* iv, p. 503.

had an understanding with Alexius.[55] A few days later he met Bohemond outside the city and concluded peace.[56]

After a fortnight's sojourn at Laodicea the two Roberts and a large number of humbler crusaders took ship and proceeded on their homeward way. But Raymond, still suspicious of the prince of Antioch, remained to keep a close guard upon Laodicea and Tortosa until the following summer, when he went to Constantinople and entered the Emperor's service.[57]

[55] Chalandon, *Alexis I*^{er}, pp. 207 ff.

[56] Albert of Aix, in *H. C. Oc.*, iv, p. 504; cf. Ordericus, iv, p. 72.

[57] Albert of Aix, in *H. C. Oc.*, iv, p. 504; Ordericus, iv, pp. 72–75; Fulcher, pp. 320–321, 342–343; *Translatio S. Nicolai Venetiam*, in *H. C. Oc.*, v, p. 271.

APPENDIX F

THE BATTLE OF TINCHEBRAY[1]

THE tactics of the battle of Tinchebray have been the subject of much discussion among recent writers, including the specialists in military history. There is general agreement as to the strategical stroke by which the victory was won, viz., a surprise attack upon the flank of the ducal forces by a band of mounted knights from Maine and Brittany. But as to the disposition of the troops in the two main armies, widely different views are held upon two points.

(1) Oman thinks that the battle formation on each side was an extended line made up of a right, centre, and left.[2] Ramsay, on the other hand, holds that the opposing forces were " marshalled in column, in successive divisions ";[3] and this view is accepted by Drummond,[4] by Delbrück,[5] and by Davis,[6] the two latter conjecturing a formation in échelon. Ramsay's view is pretty clearly supported by the sources. Ordericus Vitalis (iv, p. 229) designates a first, second, and third *acies*, or division, on the side of the king, and a first and last (*extrema*) *acies* on the side of the duke; and, according to his account, only the first *acies*, i.e., the leading elements, of the two opposing forces engaged in the fighting. The contemporary letter of a priest of Fécamp, which is discussed below, is also specific with regard to the royal forces, describing a first and a second *acies*.[7]

---

[1] For the recent discussion see C. W. C. Oman, *History of the Art of War: the Middle Ages* (London, 1898), pp. 379–381; J. H. Ramsay, *Foundations of England* (London, 1898), ii, pp. 254–255; J. D. Drummond, *Studien zur Kriegsgeschichte Englands im 12. Jahrhundert* (Berlin, 1905), pp. 35–43; Hans Delbrück, *Geschichte der Kriegskunst* (Berlin, 1900–07), iii, pp. 411–412; H. W. C. Davis, " A Contemporary Account of the Battle of Tinchebrai," in *E. H. R.*, xxiv, pp. 728–732; " The Battle of Tinchebrai, a Correction," *ibid.*, xxv, pp. 295–296.

[2] *Art of War*, p. 379.

[3] *Foundations of England*, ii, p. 254.

[4] *Kriegsgeschichte Englands*, pp. 39–40.

[5] *Geschichte der Kriegskunst*, iii, p. 412.

[6] *E. H. R.*, xxiv, p. 732.

[7] See pp. 246–247 and n. 14 *infra*. It would doubtless be unwarrantable to put a strict technical interpretation upon the language of our sources, but the designation of numbered *acies* certainly suggests successive elements one behind another rather than any other arrangement.

(2) The larger question in debate between the specialists, however, turns upon the relative importance of cavalry and infantry in the battle of Tinchebray. Oman, relying upon a very specific passage in Henry of Huntingdon (p. 235), and placing a strained interpretation upon Ordericus Vitalis (iv, p. 229), holds that the battle was almost wholly an affair of infantry, and therefore almost without precedent in the tactics of the period.[8] For Ramsay, on the other hand, it was mainly an engagement of cavalry, the foot soldiers playing but a minor part.[9] Drummond has gone even further and taken great pains to demonstrate that it was a " ganze normale Schlacht des XII. Jahrhunderts," i.e., a battle between mounted knights, the foot soldiery that happened to be present being held entirely in reserve;[10] and Drummond's conclusions have been accepted without question by Delbrück.[11]

It is surprising that in none of the discussion above noted has any account been taken of the most important extant source for the tactics of Tinchebray, viz., a letter from a priest of Fécamp to a priest of Séez written a very few days after the engagement, and describing with exactness certain tactical features of the battle. If not actually by an eyewitness, the letter is still by one who was in touch with the king and who was well informed as to the disposition of the royal forces. It is, therefore, entitled to rank as an authority above any of the accounts in the chronicles. It was first discovered by Paul Meyer in an Oxford manuscript,[12] and published in 1872 by Léopold Delisle as a note in his great edition of the chronicle of Robert of Torigny (i, p. 129). But, strangely overlooked by all the military historians, it remained unused, and was rediscovered by H. W. C. Davis and published with extensive comment in 1909 in the *English Historical Review* (xxiv, pp. 728–732) as a " new source." As afterwards turned out, Davis's transcription of the letter had been exceedingly faulty — rendering, indeed, a part of the text which was fundamental for tactics quite unintelligible — and in a later number of the *Review* (xxv, p. 296) it was again published in a corrected text. By a comparison with the original edition of Delisle[13] it appears that, by an almost unbelievable

---

[8] *Art of War*, p. 379.
[9] *Foundations of England*, ii, pp. 254–255.
[10] *Kriegsgeschichte Englands*, pp. 35–43.
[11] *Geschichte der Kriegskunst*, iii, p. 411.
[12] Jesus College, MS. 51, fol. 104.
[13] *Chronique de Robert de Torigni*, i, p. 129, note.

coincidence, the same omission of an entire line of the manuscript was made there as in the edition of Davis. Yet all transcripts have been made from a single manuscript, viz., Jesus College, Oxford, no. 51, fol. 104. We have, then, at last, a correct edition of this important source in the *English Historical Review*, xxv, p. 296.[14]

Davis, in commenting on the tactics of the battle in the light of this letter, but from his own faulty transcript, maintains that neither of the extreme views is correct, and suggests " a third interpretation of the evidence, midway between the two existing theories."[15] He holds that infantry played an important part in the action, but still assigns much prominence to the cavalry. Apropos of the corrected text of the priest's letter, however, he remarks: " Taking the omitted words into consideration, it is clear that the foot soldiers played a larger part in the battle than I allowed in my article. The second of Henry's divisions, like the first, was composite, containing both infantry and cavalry." [16] This, indeed, is the correct view. Our conception of the battle of Tinchebray must be based upon the sources, and not upon a preconceived theory of the all-importance of the mounted knight in twelfth-century warfare. Drummond and Delbrück have quite unjustifiably ignored Henry of Huntingdon in favor of Ordericus Vitalis. Whatever the theorists may hold, foot soldiers did play an unusually large part in the battle of Tinchebray. In view of the explicit statement of Henry of Huntingdon (p. 235) and of the priest of Fécamp [17] it cannot be denied that, on the king's side at least, some knights were dismounted and fought on foot, in order that they might stand more firmly (*ut constantius pugnarent*). On the other hand,

---

[14] That part of the letter which is descriptive of tactics reads as follows, the italics indicating the line omitted from the editions of Davis and Delisle: " In prima acie fuerunt Baiocenses, Abrincatini, et Constantinienses, omnes pedites; *in secunda vero rex cum innumeris baronibus suis, omnes similiter pedites.* Ad hec septingenti equites utrique aciei ordinati; preterea comes Cenomannis et comes Britonum Alanus Fergandus circumcingentes exercitum, usque ad mille equites, remotis omnibus gildonibus et servis, nam totus exercitus regis prope modum ad xl milia hominum estimabatur. Comes vero ad vi milia habuit, equites septingentos, et vix una hora prelium stetit, Roberto de Belismo statim terga vertente, ex cuius fuga dispersi sunt omnes." Evidently the error in transcription was due to the fact that the omitted clause ended in the same word as that immediately preceding it. Davis also wrote *horum* for *hominum* in the last word but one of the following sentence. Delisle's edition has this correctly.

[15] *E. H. R.*, xxiv, p. 728.

[16] *Ibid.*, xxv, p. 296.

[17] See the excerpt in n. 14, *supra*.

Oman, while perfectly justified in pointing out the unusual prominence given to foot soldiers, certainly exaggerates in representing the battle as almost wholly an affair of infantry. The large part played by cavalry is clear both from the explicit statement of the priest of Fécamp and from the account of Ordericus Vitalis. The battle of Tinchebray may, therefore, still claim to stand as an important precedent in the development of mediaeval tactics because of the unusual combination of infantry and cavalry in the fighting line.

APPENDIX G

THE ROBERT MEDALLION IN SUGER'S STAINED GLASS
WINDOW AT SAINT-DENIS

A RECENT writer has described Suger's reconstruction of the abbey church of Saint-Denis as " le fait capital de l'histoire artistique du XIIe siècle ";[1] and certainly among the most remarkable features of that great achievement were the stained glass windows, which were the abbot's pride, and which he caused to be wrought " by the skilful hands of many masters from divers nations."[2] The oldest painted windows of known date which survived from the Middle Ages,[3] most of them were destroyed during the French Revolution; and there would be no occasion to mention them in connection with the life of Robert Curthose, were it not that a series of ten medallions from one window, representing scenes from the First Crusade, has been preserved for us by the venerable Benedictine, Bernard de Montfaucon, in copperplate engravings of the early eighteenth century.[4] The

---

[1] Émile Mâle, in André Michel, *Histoire de l'art* (Paris, 1905–), i, p. 786. On the rebuilding of the church see Otto Cartellieri, *Abt Suger von Saint-Denis, 1081–1151* (Berlin, 1898), p. 105, and the references there given; Michel Félibien, *Histoire de l'abbaye royale de Saint-Denis en France* (Paris, 1706), pp. 170–176; Paul Vitry and Gaston Brière, *L'église abbatiale de Saint-Denis et ses tombeaux* (Paris, 1908), pp. 9–10; and above all Anthyme Saint-Paul, " Suger, l'église de Saint-Denis, et Saint Bernard," in *Bulletin archéologique du Comité des Travaux historiques et scientifiques*, 1890, pp. 258–275.

[2] " Vitrearum etiam novarum praeclaram varietatem, ab ea prima quae incipit a *Stirps Iesse* in capite ecclesiae, usque ad eam quae superest principali portae in introitu ecclesiae, tam superius quam inferius, magistrorum multorum de diversis nationibus manu exquisita, depingi fecimus." *Oeuvres complètes de Suger*, ed. A. Lecoy de la Marche (Paris, 1867), p. 204.

[3] " Les plus anciens vitraux à date certaine qui subsistent encore. . . . [Ils] furent mis en place de 1140 à 1144." Michel, *Histoire de l'art*, i, p. 784. Nevertheless it may be doubted whether all the windows were actually completed at the time of the consecration of the choir and the translation of the relics, 11 June 1144. The windows, only fragments of which have escaped destruction, are most fully described by Ferdinand de Lasteyrie, *Histoire de la peinture sur verre d'après ses monuments en France* (Paris, 1853–57), i, pp. 27–37; ii, planches iii–vii.

[4] *Les monumens de la monarchie françoise* (Paris, 1729–33), i, planches l–liv, between pages 390 and 397. Montfaucon says (p. 384): " Cette première croisade est representée en dix tableaux sur les vitres de l'église de S. Denis, à l'extrêmité du

eighth scene in the series has given rise to much discussion. It portrays a Christian knight in the act of unhorsing a pagan warrior with a mighty thrust of his lance, and bears the inscription: R DVX NORMANNORVM PARTVM PROSTERNIT.[5] Clearly we have here some spectacular victory of Robert Curthose over a Saracen; and it is the oldest graphic representation of the duke now extant. The only problem is to identify it either with a historic or with a legendary exploit of Robert on the Crusade. Ferdinand de Mély, assuming that it had nothing to do with veritable history, has supposed that it represented Robert's legendary combat with the emir ' Red Lion ' during the great battle of the Franks against Kerboga, as related in the *Chanson d'Antioche*;[6] and at Riant's suggestion he has gone further and proposed that it may offer a *terminus ad quem* for determining the date of composition of that poem.[7] Gaston Paris has very properly rejected both these hypotheses. But he still holds that the Robert medallion can only be explained by reference to the *Chanson d'Antioche*, and he identifies the scene portrayed with Robert's legendary victory over Kerboga himself rather than with that over Red Lion.[8] On the other hand, Hagenmeyer, who is better qualified to speak upon such matters, sees not legend at all but sober history in the scene in question. Indeed, upon comparison of the whole series of Montfaucon's engravings with the original narratives of the First Crusade, he finds all the scenes portrayed to be in remarkably close agreement with historic facts. " L'artiste qui a fait ces peintures," he says, " a été,

rond-pont derrière le grand autel, dans cette partie qu'on appelle le chevet. Ces tableaux qu'on voit tous sur une même vitre, furent faits par ordre de l'abbé Suger, qui s'est fait peindre plusieurs fois dans ces vitres du chevet avec son nom *Sugerius Abbas*." There seems no reason to doubt Montfaucon's identification of this window with one of those executed at Suger's order, and modern writers have accepted it without question. It ought to be noted, however, that no fragment of this particular window appears to have escaped destruction, and that Suger, although he describes two of the windows in detail and names a third, makes no specific mention whatever of this one. And, moreover, it is the very windows which he does describe which have in part been preserved. But on the other hand, Suger makes no pretence at a complete list or description of the windows; and he himself indicates that there were many. *Oeuvres de Suger*, pp. 204-206; Lasteyrie, *Histoire de la peinture sur verre*, i, pp. 27-37; ii, planches iii-vii.

[5] Montfaucon, *Monumens*, i, planche liii, opposite p. 396.

[6] Vol. ii, p. 261.

[7] " La croix des premiers croisés," in *Revue de l'art chrétien*, 1890, pp. 298-300.

[8] " Robert Courte-Heuse à la première croisade," in *Comptes rendus de l'Académie des Inscriptions et Belles-Lettres*, 1890, pp. 207-208.

sans aucun doute, très au courant des événements marquants de la première croisade. . . . A proprement parler, aucune de ces peintures ne contient d'épisode légendaire." And the scene in the Robert medallion he considers to be no more than a pictorial rendering of a text from the *Gesta Francorum* describing the battle of Ascalon: " Comes autem de Nortmannia cernens ammiravisi stantarum . . . ruit vehementer super illum, eumque vulneravit usque ad mortem." [9]

Although Mély in quoting Hagenmeyer's opinion does not accept it,[10] there can be little doubt of its correctness. The scenes from the Crusade in Suger's window do not, it is true, agree in every minute detail with the primary literary sources, but the deviations are certainly not greater than should be expected from a mediaeval painter striving to produce an artistic result within the limitations of his craft. The arrangement and numbering of Montfaucon's engravings leave some doubt as to the original sequence of the medallions, but so far as it is possible to determine, the outstanding events of the Crusade from the siege of Nicaea to the battle of Ascalon appear to have been portrayed in chronological order. About the first six scenes, as arranged by Montfaucon, there can be practically no doubt. And the great battle against Kerboga is set in its proper place between the capture of Antioch and the storming of Jerusalem; and there is no indication that Robert played a special part in it, any more than there is in the strictly historical literary sources.

The last four medallions as given by Montfaucon present peculiar difficulties; and it will be well to describe them briefly, preserving his numbering.

No. 7. The flight of defeated horsemen through a gate into a walled city. Inscription: ARABES VICTI IN ASCALON FVGIVNT.

No. 8. The Robert medallion which has been described above.

No. 9. A single combat between a Christian and a pagan horseman, each supported by a band of warriors who fill the background. Inscription: DVELLVM PARTI ET ROTBERTI FLANDRENSIS COMITIS.

No. 10. A general combat between Christian and pagan warriors fighting on horseback. Inscription: BELLVM AMITE ASCALONIA IV;

[9] Letter to Riant, printed in *Revue de l'art chrétien*, 1890, pp. 300–301; G. F., pp. 494–495.

[10] " M. Hagenmeyer . . . me semble être allé beaucoup trop loin, dans le cas qu'il fait de nos cartons pour l'explication des textes qu'ils représentent. Je ne saurais le suivre sur ce terrain, persuadé que les détails de faits qui se sont passés en Orient ont incontestablement été modifiés par des artistes qui n'avaient jamais quitté la France." *Revue de l'art chrétien*, 1890, p. 300.

and an unfilled space at the end seems to indicate that it is incomplete. Evidently this inscription has become corrupt in transmission, and as it stands it is not wholly intelligible. It seems clear enough, however, that we have here a representation of the great battle of the Franks against the Egyptian emir Malik el-Afdhal near Ascalon.

Now if the four medallions in question be taken in the order in which they have just been described, it is difficult, if not impossible, to reconcile them with the literary sources as a representation of actual events in chronological order. But it is very doubtful whether Montfaucon has placed them in their proper sequence. We have no way of checking him as to the arrangement of nos. 8 and 9; but a glance at his engravings reveals the fact that nos. 7 and 10 are not perfectly circular like the rest, but are considerably cut away, the former in the upper right hand sector and the latter in the upper left hand sector.[11] Clearly they were placed side by side at the top of the window in the restricted space beneath the pointed arch, no. 10 being on the left and no. 7 on the right. Now the general sequence of the medallions in the window appears to have been from the bottom to the top; and in that case nos. 10 and 7 must have been the last two of the series. If this arrangement be accepted the interpretation of the last four medallions does not seem to offer greater difficulties than that of the first six. All four have to do with events centring around Ascalon and the great contest of the Franks with the Egyptian emir. Nos. 8 and 9 portray the individual feats of arms of Robert Curthose and Robert of Flanders as set forth in the literary sources.[12] No. 10 (with the corrupt inscription) probably represents the general engagement in which the exploits of the two Roberts were such notable features. And no. 7, properly belonging at the end, represents the flight of the vanquished pagans through the gate within the protecting walls of Ascalon. It is true that our best literary sources in describing the pursuit which followed the battle make no mention of this particular feature. But we know that the inhabitants of Ascalon closed their gates and successfully bid defiance to the crusaders;[13] and it certainly does not seem improbable that some of the fugitive Saracens should have escaped thither. At any rate, the artist might very well have assumed that they so escaped.

---

[11] Montfaucon, *Monumens*, i, planches liii, liv, opposite p. 396.
[12] See *supra*, p. 116; cf. *Revue de l'art chrétien*, 1890, p. 300.
[13] *Supra*, p. 116.

INDEX

INDEX

Mediaeval names of persons are arranged alphabetically under the English form of the Christian name.